FIRST AND LAST NOTEBOOKS

Simone Weil

FIRST AND LAST NOTEBOOKS

Translated by Richard Rees

WIPF & STOCK · Eugene, Oregon

Wipf and Stock Publishers
199 W 8th Ave, Suite 3
Eugene, OR 97401

First and Last Notebooks
By Weil, Simone and Rees, Richard
Copyright©1970 Peters Fraser & Dunlop
ISBN 13: 978-1-4982-3919-6
Publication date 12/9/2015
Previously published by Oxford Univesity Press, 1970

SERIES FOREWORD
SIMONE WEIL: SELECTED WORKS

SIMONE WEIL IS A thinker who is eminently quotable, one who could write in Pascal-like aphorisms. She also led a striking and distinctive life. What is therefore most readily known about her are a few of the facts of that life, and a few of her dazzling and often puzzling sayings. But she was so much deeper than that. Her essays, notebooks, and her letters together comprise a remarkable *oeuvre*, and all of them bear close study. They require attention, and they also require comparison across their various topics and genres in order for anyone to get a holistic sense of Weil as a thinker, indeed, as one of the most original and intellectually and spiritually profound thinkers of the twentieth century. Without question, Weil was somebody who could bring insights together from what to us are often seen as disparate subject matters, and she could then make these insights bear on our present states of affairs. But to see this profound integration, one has to first see all the different subject matters that Weil treated. Unfortunately, over the years that has become increasingly difficult for English speakers due to the limited availability of her complete body of writings.

At the time that Richard Rees published his translations of so many of Weil's writings in the 1960s, what was available to English speaking readers was the object of most of the world's envy. As those books went out of print, they were never adequately replaced, although there have been and currently are some decent smaller collections, especially on Weil's religious thinking. It will therefore be a matter of great help to those who would know Simone Weil in depth to have in these three volumes the republication of three of Rees' original volumes: the essays of *Selected Essays:1934-43*; complete notebooks, not just excerpted fragments, in *The First and Last Notebooks*; and thirdly, something that even French readers did not have until very recently, namely a number of Weil's letters in *Seventy Letters*. With new subtitles, the present trilogy of Selected Works printed by Wipf and Stock Publishers consists of:

1. First and Last Notebooks: Supernatural Knowledge
2. Seventy Letters: Personal and Intellectual Windows on a Thinker
3. Selected Essays, 1934-1943: Historical, Political and Moral Writings

Since the initial publication of her many writings, which began shortly after her death, Weil has continued to be an important figure for several successive generations, each finding something new and inspiring in her, whether it has been political, moral, or religious. Now, in an age that looks for a center while eschewing all authoritarianisms, it appears that Weil, the outsider who is also the fully committed witness, once more has something striking to say. Here, now, is full access to her voice.

Eric Springsted
March 2015
Co-founder and President of The American Weil Society 1981-2014.

CONTENTS

	Series Foreword	iii
	Introduction	vii
I	Pre-War Notebook, 1933–(?)1939	1
II	Prologue	63
III	New York Notebook, 1942	67
IV	London Notebook, 1943	333

PLATES

Between pages 58–59

I Front cover of Pre-War Notebook

II Back cover of Pre-War Notebook
(Both photographs by courtesy of Librairie Plon)

INTRODUCTION

The first section of this book consists of Simone Weil's pre-war notebook, which was not published in France until 1970. It was apparently begun in 1933 and continued intermittently up to 1939, but she does not seem to have taken it with her to Spain in 1936, nor on her subsequent travels in Italy. The remainder of the book consists of the notes she wrote in America and England in 1942 and 1943, the last pages being written in hospital just before her death. The transitional passage, 'Prologue'[1] must have been written before she left France for America in May 1942, since it was found among the papers she left with Gustave Thibon on her departure.

The notebooks written by Simone Weil in France in 1940-2 have already appeared in English,[2] and with the present volume the English translation of all her published notebooks is completed. It is obvious that the notes were mostly written with a view to future use in books, though some of them are in a kind of intellectual shorthand that she would have had to expand. On the cover of the pre-war notebook, however, she wrote: 'This notebook doesn't count.' She presumably meant by this that not all of it necessarily represented her final considered opinion. But it is difficult to guess what passages in it she would have omitted or altered before publishing them. Much of it was written in 1933-4, when she was teaching at the *lycée* for girls at Roanne and was engaged upon her long essay, 'Reflections on the causes of liberty and social oppression'. She was only in her middle twenties at the time, but her profound and comprehensive sense of responsibility is already fully developed and her preoccupations seem perfectly continuous and consistent with those in the notebooks that she began to write seven years later. They also reveal an extraordinary intellectual and emotional maturity, considering her age at the

[1] It is included with the New York and London notebooks in the volume, *La Connaissance surnaturelle* (Gallimard, 1950).
[2] *The Notebooks of Simone Weil*, 2 vols. (Routledge, 1956).

time. It was at the end of 1934 that she obtained a year's leave of absence from teaching, to go and work in a Paris factory.

Taken all together, the notebooks provide an unselfconscious and unintentional self-portrait of one of the most remarkable minds and characters of this century. She is, so to speak, thinking aloud; and it is an inestimable privilege to be able to listen in. There is probably not a single fundamental problem of our age, in any domain, that is not resolutely faced and examined somewhere in these pages. Born in 1909, Simone Weil was younger than either Professor Herbert Marcuse or George Orwell, yet she anticipated in the 1930s nearly everything that is useful in the ideas that Orwell was to develop in the 1940s and Marcuse in the 1950s. But her perspectives were broader and her thought was much better grounded, as any reader of *Oppression and Liberty*, *La Condition ouvrière*, and *Ecrits historiques et politiques* can verify. Her conclusions are often pessimistic, but with the kind of pessimism that can evoke and stimulate and sustain a humane and realistic fortitude. Realistic, because Simone Weil never lost touch with common sense. To whatever mystical heights her spirit might ascend, her feet were always on the ground, with Plato, Spinoza, Rousseau, and Goethe, and not, like the feet of so many modern sages—from Marx and Bergson to Marcuse and Sartre—upon some imaginary Hegelian evolutionary or revolutionary escalator.

On the very first page of the pre-war notebook, which begins in 1933, we find, in the margin of a note on scientific education, a remark about suffering: 'I believe in the value of suffering in so far as one makes every (legitimate) attempt to avoid it.' The reservations are characteristic, and there is no reason to think that Simone Weil, who has so often been accused of masochism and dolorism, ever changed her mind about this. She believed that suffering should be avoided, when legitimately possible, but she knew it is often unavoidable, and she knew its potential value. One may say that two of her chief preoccupations were, first, how to organize society so that suffering should be reduced to a minimum, and, second, how to ensure that the (large) irreducible minimum should not be valueless. One of the recurrent themes throughout the pre-war notebook is her concern about the problem of social 'alienation' and the increasing enslavement of man to society which seems to be a condition of his progressive release from slavery to nature. Her account in *La Condition ouvrière* of the effects of mass-production upon the worker, after her experience of factory life in 1935, has rightly been described by Hannah Arendt as the most pertinent and most unsentimental ever written.

Today, a third of a century later, her criticism has become not less but more pertinent. Its essential point is that in a mass-production and money economy there is no perceptible connection between action and the fruits of action, so that the meaning of human activity becomes increasingly absorbed into the universal exchange medium, money (see, for example, pp. 19, 30). The effects of this in every sphere of life—in thought, in science, in labour, in art, in sex—continued to preoccupy Simone Weil to the end. Her mystical experience in 1938 did nothing to lessen her practical concern, but if anything intensified it; and the reader will be able to judge for himself, by comparing the pre-war notebook with the later ones, how far this experience modified her attitude to the problem. She appears never to have referred to her mystical experience directly, except to Father Perrin and in her letter to Joë Bousquet.[1] But the undated text entitled 'Prologue' is clearly related to it in some way.

It is only to a very superficial glance that these notebooks can appear obscure. After reading a few pages one perceives that Simone Weil is not so much making notes as meditating, coherently and lucidly, with a pen in her hand. There are various main themes which recur again and again. She devotes a page or two to one of them and then takes it up again later, from where she left off—having in the meantime dealt with various other themes, which also recur later on. The main theme of the pre-war notebook is the problem of alienation, already referred to; but it is always implicitly linked with the problem of human destiny, which is the main preoccupation running through all her work. For want of a better term one can only describe this aspect of her thought as a religious philosophy. But the description is misleading, as the second of the two following extracts from the London notebook will show. I have chosen these two passages for quotation because they illustrate in a striking and challenging manner two of the most essential features of her thought.

[1] See *Waiting on God* (Routledge, 1951) and *Seventy Letters* (Oxford, 1965).

The first extract is one of the many passages in her work directed against the Utopian progressivist myth of an emergent deity, or a meliorist and immanent creative-evolutionary lifeforce. She places the good outside history and does not see it as the term of an evolutionary historical process. It is neither more nor less present at the end than at the beginning, or at any stage in the process:

There is absolutely no possible solution of problems of origin (the origin of language, of tools, etc.) except that they were instituted by God. This is obvious. Language does not arise from non-language.[1] A child learns to speak; but that is because he is taught. And he is taught to work, etc. (p. 342).

So the myth of Prometheus is truer than the revolutionary or evolutionary Marxist and Bergsonian myths.

The second extract shows that she had a very different idea of what is meant by 'doing philosophy' from that of the contemporary positivists who so describe their activity:

Philosophy (including problems of cognition, etc.) is *exclusively* an affair of action and practice. That is why it is so difficult to write about it. Difficult in the same way as a treatise on tennis or running, only much more so. (p. 362)

Simone Weil wanted to be a philosopher, and not a writer about philosophy. But she succeeded in being both, which is one of the rarest human achievements.

Simone Weil was an uncompromising transcendentalist, and this is the key to the frequent and fascinating references to folklore and myth in the New York and London notebooks. In the folk tales of every continent she discerned an incalculable treasure of supernatural wisdom, dating from fathomless antiquity; and her researches on the subject, if they were extracted from the notebooks and grouped together, would be seen to form the material for a comprehensive and scholarly study of comparative mythology.

Like certain French historians, Lucien Febvre for instance, and unlike the twentieth-century French anthropologists, Simone Weil was able to combine imaginative sympathy with erudition in her contemplation of the past. Consider, for ex-

[1] As reported in the press, the work in linguistics of Professor Noam Chomsky, of Massachusetts Institute of Technology, appears to emphasize this point.

ample, her study of Grimm's story 'The Almond Tree', which she gives reason for believing to be of great antiquity, and of which she suggests that the myth of Atreus and Thyestes may be a late and mutilated version (pp. 161-2, 273, 277). And her interest in the language of gipsies, with her exclamation mark at the word 'oura' for 'town', which seems to echo the name of a Sumerian town which was already ancient in the time of Abraham (p. 197). Or again, the frequent passages dealing with the zodiac, which she interprets as a liturgy of the seasons, having no real relation to the constellations (p. 357). Consider also the very remarkable passages on 'the tree of the world' in relation to Zeus's embroidered cloth (pp. 236-7 and 276-80).

Another theme to which several important passages are devoted is her meditation on the parable of the Prodigal Son. She emphasizes that it is only because he has persisted in squandering his portion until not a penny remains that the prodigal at last remembers his father's house. If he had been economical he would never have thought of returning home (pp. 211, 236). And this leads on to some of her profoundest and most painfully uncompromising thoughts. She distinguishes between the discursively reasoning part of the soul, which inhabits time, and the vegetative part which controls the biological functions and is below time. For it, ten minutes is indistinguishable from endless duration. The part of the soul that inhabits time represents the prodigal's portion. She calls it our 'supplementary' energy. When this prodigal's portion has been expended or destroyed 'and the vegetative energy has to be expended for something other than the biological functions for which it is destined, then a quarter of an hour seems like endless duration.... It is then that the very sap of life flows away and the man becomes dead wood while still alive' (p. 220). Such is the state to which the prodigal must be reduced before he can return home.

If the lower layer of the soul is laid bare and exposed through the destruction of the discursive part, and if in this way perpetual duration is traversed within a finite lapse of time, and if throughout that perpetuity the soul remains turned towards the eternal light, then perhaps in the end the eternal light will have pity and will envelop the entire soul within its eternity. (p. 292)

Such is the prodigal's return.

It is difficult to convey by extracts the characteristic quality of her mysticism, which might be paradoxically described as an uncommonly refined common sense; but here is a passage which may perhaps give some impression of it, though the slight flavour of Zen is comparatively rare[1] in her style:

> The soul's only choice is between travelling towards nothingness through more and more good or through more and more evil. The limit of both good and evil is nothingness. But it is not a matter of indifference whether one arrives at nothingness through good or through evil.
>
> On the contrary, it is the only thing that matters and everything else is indifferent.
>
> And why does it matter?
>
> For no reason. It is important in itself. It is the only thing of unconditional importance.
>
> But on an even higher level, absolutely nothing matters. For if I fall to the lowest depth of evil, that does no harm to the good.
>
> Because we live in falsehood, we are under the illusion that happiness is what is unconditionally important.
>
> If someone says: "How I would like to be rich!", his friend may answer: "Why? Would it make you any happier?" But if someone says "I want to be happy", no one will answer "Why?"
>
> Tell me your reasons for wanting to be happy.
>
> Or if someone is hurt and wants help. Tell me your reasons for wanting help.
>
> Frivolous questions. Who would dare ask them?
>
> But we ought to put them to ourselves and to reflect that, in the first place, one has no reason for wanting to be happy, and then that happiness is not a thing to be desired without reason, unconditionally; for it is only the good that is to be desired in this way.
>
> That is the foundation of Plato's thought. (pp. 310–11)

In the same way, she says of beauty that it is pointless to ask what purpose it serves. 'It provides no nourishment for the part of the soul that looks in this world for sustenance.'

But there are many other themes in the book besides this ethical absolutism. In addition to the political, social, and mythological themes already mentioned, there are reflections on the classics, on the history of science and of religion, on art, on education, and on psychology. It is doubtful if any other thinker of this century has been so well equipped for the study of so many branches of human knowledge.

---

[1] More typical, but too long to quote, are pp. 157–9, and 315–19.

INTRODUCTION xiii

The reader may be left to convince himself of the truth of this claim. But for those who are unfamiliar with her life story it may be of interest to comment upon the unconscious pathos of the last page of the last notebook. In the spring of 1943 Simone Weil was taken ill with an affection of the lungs, but her failure to recover from it was due, in the doctor's opinion, to malnutrition. She had obstinately refused to eat more than she imagined her compatriots were getting in the German-occupied zone of France. But in spite of her weakness she continued to write her notebook up to the very end; and on the last page she discusses a short story about a girl who developed a life-long nausea for strawberry jam. This girl had returned home on the verge of collapse after attending her brother's execution, and had revived herself by eating a whole pot of the jam. After which, for the rest of her life, she could not bear to hear strawberry jam mentioned. This result, says Simone Weil, proves the genuineness of her grief for her brother. 'If a romantic adolescent fabricates a tragedy out of some imaginary great love, it could not modify his or her attitude to strawberry jam.' In living man in this world, she continues, inert matter and the flesh are 'like a filter or sieve which is the universal test of what is real in thought.... Matter is our infallible judge.' This leads her on to a consideration of ceremonial repasts, whose significance derives from 'this alliance between matter and genuine feeling', and she lists a number of special delicacies associated with such repasts: Christmas pudding, marrons glacés, Easter eggs, etc., etc.

If it can be called a coincidence, it is certainly a pathetic one that these should be very nearly the last words she wrote while she was dying of self-inflicted malnutrition. But the pathos seems less tragic when one considers the intellectual energy and vitality of the notebook right up to the last page. It is an inspiring example of the triumph of mind over body. And in a curious way this last page of the book sums up and illustrates the whole extraordinary range of her mind. Entirely dedicated to the good, and seeing beauty as a symbol of it, she saw also that beauty offers us no earthly sustenance. In her self-dedication to the good, she went too far in depriving herself of earthly sustenance; but this did not involve the slightest weakening of her grip on reality. 'Matter', she insists in almost her last words, 'is our infallible judge.' It discriminates between sentimentality and true feeling, between opinion and knowledge. And after the passage on feasts comes her very last sentence, which recalls her life-long insistence upon the difference between 'knowing', in the superficial every-day sense of the word knowledge, and *really* knowing 'with one's whole soul':

The most important part of teaching = to teach what it is to *know* (in the scientific sense).

These are not the last words of a dreamer or an ineffectual angel. They are the words of someone who knew, in every sense, a great many things which it is essential to learn and understand, and whose necessity is all the more imperative in our decadent civilization which, in every country in the world today, increasingly obscures them.

When the New York and London notebooks were published in 1950, as *La Connaissance surnaturelle*, the text was left unannotated, and in this edition I have restricted myself to a few explanatory footnotes. It is obvious that the notebooks offer a prodigious field of research into Simone Weil's methods of work and study and into many other aspects of her mind and personality. But any adequate commentary might more than double the length of this book and, at the moment, what is important is to make available to English readers the original texts, whose translation was so long overdue.

It will be noticed that the method of presentation of the Pre-War Notebook differs from that of the New York and London Notebooks. This is because the French editors have adopted a new method of presentation for the former, which will have appeared in Paris (Librairie Plon) before the publication of this translation. It is impossible, however, by any method except photographic reproduction, to give a clear idea of a typical page of Simone Weil's notebooks (see illustration). She added many of the notes in the margin, wrote on the covers of the books, and used abbreviations, indentations, various types of bracket, and boxing of words or paragraphs, which make accurate reproduction in print impossible.

As usual, I have had unstinted help with the text from Mademoiselle Simone Pétrement and Professor André Weil; and others who have kindly answered queries are Mademoiselle M-A. Carroi, Surgeon-Captain H. E. B. Curjel, Mrs. Degras, Dr. A. S. F. Gow, Professor A. Nove, and Dr. G. J. Whitrow.

London April 1969   RICHARD REES

I

PRE-WAR NOTEBOOK
(1933–(?)1939)

Educational method
   Physics taught *solely by analogy* (Descartes)
ex. light—
   1. analogy with *projectile:* you stop it by getting in its way.
   development of this analogy: reflection
                                refraction.
   2. objections to the analogy | the light is not altogether stopped by the obstacle.
                                | refraction.
   3. analogy with waves . . .
ex. sound
order of experiments . . .

[*in the margin*] Value of suffering—
   I believe in the value of suffering, so long as one makes every [legitimate] effort to escape it.

Difficulties:
1. transition from *plane* to *solid*
   architects, draftsmen—"sculptors"
   make *systematic* practice of three-dimensional geometry
2. transition from *rest* to *motion*
3. transition from *discontinuous* to *continuous*
   systematic reasoning and practice
Perception is impotent beyond a certain point of complexity unless it is assisted by reason.
   (face all the difficulties *directly*.
      geared machines: how? . . .
      weaving looms, etc.)
   List of the difficulties . . .
series . . .

Forms of *power*—or rather of the pursuit of power. When the struggle for power is of very uncertain outcome and brutally fierce, passions are lively and simple; contact with natural necessities is never lost; good and bad fortune are important, inner torments are less so [Homer—Sophocles].

Under the rule of a stable power the principal method of *domination*, for the mass of private individuals (except the labouring population), is love—so it is also an age of flattery... [Don Juan] [Racine].

People have never been less equipped for understanding Homer than they were around 1660.

In a very brutal age, an age of rapes and abductions... the purest love can come to flower [Andromache:

"Ἕκτορ, ἀτὰρ σύ μοί ἐσσι πατὴρ καὶ πότνια μήτηρ, ἠδὲ κασίγνητος, σὺ δέ μοι θαλερὸς παρακοίτης]¹

precisely because in such an age amorous intrigue is unknown.

On the other hand, when love has become an instrument of power this purity is almost impossible; that is why there is something so cold and false in Racine's idyllic couples. While Roxane...

omnia serviliter pro dominatione.²
The same applies to *friendship*.

List of temptations (to be read every morning)
TEMPTATION OF IDLENESS (by far the strongest).
Never surrender to the flow of time. Never put off what you have decided to do.
Temptation of the inner life
Deal only with those difficulties which actually confront you. Allow yourself only those feelings which are actually called upon for effective use or else are required by thought for the sake of inspiration. Cut away ruthlessly everything that is imaginary in your feelings.
Temptation of self-immolation
Subordinate to external affairs and people everything that is subjective, but never the subject itself—i.e. your judgement. Never promise and never give to another more than you would demand from yourself if you were he. (?)

---

¹ Hector, you are father and mother and brother to me, as well as my beloved husband (*Iliad* VI, 429–30).
² Servile in everything, so as to become master (Tacitus: *History*. I, 36).

Temptation to dominate
Temptation of perversity
Never react to an evil in such a way as to augment it.

The behaviourist psychology is the only good one, on the express understanding that one does not believe it. Everything that can be thought about the human condition is expressible in terms of behaviour—even including freedom [*in the margin*: even free thought (problems), or the most generous feelings (Platonic love...). Try to describe all these things without ever mentioning soul, spirit, etc.] The only thing that escapes is that which, since it is thinking, cannot be thought.

Work—ideal: analogous to a problem resolved in action.
   obstacles | indefiniteness of the world (so that there are many elements that are not given—though they are conceivable by analogy).
part played by the living body of the worker, which is essentially mysterious
„   „   „ other men, which is, by essence, unknown.

primitive man—his actions are subordinated to mysterious divinities, which he situates in nature but which are really situated within his own body—
modern worker, on the other hand; in what he does only a minute part is played by the miracles of the living body; therefore, no gods.

Work and math.
difficulty: in the actual *practical* execution of the work there is no progression from the simple to the complex—blue-print and house...
The actual sequence is *not* the sequence of thought.

Mathematics: study of the interwoven fabric of finite and infinite...

Math.—action in which there is nothing to manipulate except *signs* (cf. philosophy course at Roanne).

Laws, the only source of liberty. That is why, on the level of primitive religions, everything that is a *rule* (magic formulas and rites, taboos) represents a great advance.

Resemblance between modern science and scholasticism: manipulation of signs...

If one thinks of the objective conditions, the *transition* from our present system to a decentralized system is very difficult—impossible, because it would require a conscious collaboration between power and the oppressed. The powers will take no steps towards diminishing themselves: even if they wished to, they could not, because of their rivalries. And...
The machine will go on functioning by its own laws until it wrecks itself.
Refuse to be an accomplice. Don't lie.—don't keep your eyes shut...

The lure of quantity is the most dangerous of all. When once the individual loses control of method, it is taken over by society.

Series to be studied with *precision* (otherwise it is merely literature...): algebra—calculating machine—ordinary machines...

A confrontation between the nature of mind and the nature of matter occurs *twice over*—first in the relation between thought and signs—and then in the relation between theory and its application. Look for some kind of equilibrium...

Compared to the hoped-for civilization, what we possess now

(science... machines, tools...) is like the crude empirical "science" of the Egyptians compared to Greek thought. Something like the "Greek miracle" is needed.

[*in the margin of the preceding note*] What thing in the world is most opposed to purity? The pursuit of *intensity*. ἒξ καὶ δέκα[1]...

All tools are instruments for transforming chance into necessity; or at least for *making use* of chance. Work and closed vessel...
Tools: fabricators of *series*
ex. sailing ship
1. the ship is a solid...
2. the ship is not a solid...
It is the same with all tools.

Paradox: all images of a straight line are *equally* far from the perfect straight line. And yet they are *more or less* near to it. This leads very far...

dependence of the individual upon society: in proportion to specialization
„   „   society upon the individual: in inverse proportion to the automatization of necessary activities.

The idea of necessity has been lost. In science it appears only as the rules of the game (chess...); in technology...

action *after* discovery of method | Spinozist intuition
| 4th proportional...
multiple action for single method
divisible action (which may even be spaced out through several hours) for single method
   (or rather, the action *must* be divided—because each movement has to be accomplished by itself...)

[1] Sixteen.

transition from the world of signs to the real world—intermediaries: manufactured objects . . .
[series of tools, from this point of view? . . .]

What shows that *work*—if it is not of an inhuman kind—is meant for us is its joy, a joy which even our exhaustion does not lessen . . .
The workers are reluctant to confess to this joy—because they have the impression that it might lead to a reduction of wages!

"Dialectic". The idea that *ought* to be derived from the transposition of contraries is the idea of EQUILIBRIUM. But that is precisely the idea that the proprietors of "scientific socialism" have not conceived. Plato, on the other hand . . .

Task: critical inventory of the theoretical and technical riches of our civilization, so as to determine the place in it of reflective thought.

[*in the margin of the preceding note*] Every man is a Proteus. His friendship is the reward of whoever holds him clasped, without losing faith, until he has assumed human form . . .

The collectivity is more powerful than the individual in every domain, except one alone: the domain of thought. The collectivity is by definition stronger than the individual. Cf. Zamiatin: the "right" of the individual against society is as ridiculous as the "right" of the ounce against the ton. The individual has only one power: it is thought. But not in the conventional idealist sense of conscience, opinion, etc. Thought is a force and therefore its right is based solely on the extent to which it enters into material life.
  The constriction and relaxation of social oppression ought to be studied not only in relation to the exploited but also in relation to the privileged (age of Pericles . . .)

In popularizing science, study it from its actual origins instead of trying to show by a more rational method how it reached its present state? But starting from techniques . . . and find a way to make intelligible . . .

A method of work based upon analogy? (so that each time it is necessary to re-think . . .)

criterion.
   certain ideas can be retained *as such* in the memory.
   others only in the shape of formulas.
in the 1st. case, they are applied with understanding—in the 2nd. case, blindly—and this is true both within science and in the application of science to technique.

Science and applications:
1. science apart from its applications is a *pure game*
2. relation between science and its applications: not to increase the power of work, but to make it more conscious and more methodical—which ought, however, to increase its efficacy. "Seek ye first the kingdom of heaven and its righteousness, and all these things shall be added unto you."
Today, however, science is a game for scientists, and a collection of recipes for technicians.

Physical love and labour.
   labour: to feel with one's whole self the existence of the world
   love: „ „ „ „   „ „ „   „   of another being? But only if there is no desire and, strictly speaking, no sensuous pleasure. Certainly it is not like that for anyone, so far as I know. (Even in Jules Romains . . .) [but Valéry . . . comparison with swimming . . .] Joy, not pleasure.
   ἀλλ' ἐγώ[1] . . .
   Certainly this would be the only pure form of physical love. And it must be at least theoretically possible for physical love

---

[1] But I . . .

to be pure. It would be too bitter if even the creation of a new human being must be a defilement. . . . It would defile the whole of life. It is comforting to be able to imagine it, at least ideally, under a perfectly pure aspect. Life does not need to mutilate itself in order to be pure.

[*in the margin of the preceding, but crossed out in pencil*] to be aware of the beloved over his whole perceptible surface, as a swimmer is of the sea. To live within a universe which is he. It is by chance (a providential chance) that this profound aspiration, which has its roots in infancy (gestation), coincides with the instinct called sexual—which is alien to love, except in so far as there is thought of children. That is why chastity is indispensable to love. It is outraged as soon as *need* and *desire*, even reciprocal, enter in.

Definition of joy (which is absent in Spinoza): joy is nothing other than the feeling of reality . . .
Sadness is nothing other than the weakening or disappearance of this feeling.
The mad are not joyful.
When one is sad for a long time and continuously, one becomes a little mad. (. . .)

Action upon matter and action among men:
   homo naturae parendo imperat[1] ⎫
   omnia serviliter pro dominatione ⎭ . . .

Iliad—The mainspring of war is despair. The violence done upon itself by the soul which is constrained to adapt to a situation in which *all* its aspirations are purely and simply negated.

A situation like this is strictly speaking unimaginable. Everything that the non-combatant imagines about it is false.

The aims of the war are forgotten; one is driven to the point of denying *all* aims. When they persist it is not in spite of, but because of, their being absurd.

Wherever man is *sacrificed* there is this despair.

---

[1] Man commands Nature by obeying her.

Two internal obstacles to be overcome
—Cowardice before the flight of time (mania for putting things off—idleness ...)
Illusion that time, of itself, will bring me courage and energy ... In fact, it is usually the contrary (sleeplessness). Say to yourself: And suppose I should remain *always* what I am at this moment?
... *Never* put something off indefinitely, but only to a definitely fixed time. Try to do this even when it is impossible (headaches ...). Exercises: decide to do something, no matter what, and do it *exactly* at a certain time.
You live in a dream. You are waiting to begin to live ...
One must develop a habit. Training.
Distinguish between the things I can put off, and those ... Begin the training with small things, those for which inspiration is useless.
Think of V.S ...
Every day, do 2 or 3 things of no interest at some definitely appointed time.
Reach the point where punctuality is automatic and effortless.—Lack of flexibility of imagination. An obstacle to be methodically overcome. The second screen between reality and yourself. Much more difficult. What is needed is something quite different from a methodical training . . . But precious.
Discipline of the attention for manual work—no distraction or dreaming. But no obsession either. One must continually watch what one is doing, without being carried away by it. Another kind of discipline is needed for using the mind with support from the imagination. And yet a third kind for reflection. You scarcely possess even the third kind. A complete being possesses all 3. You ought to be a complete being.

Your view concerning analogies, correspondences, etc.—and the theory of groups? and Plato's ideas?

List of | *combinations*
| *equivalences—transformations—correspondences—analogies*
conciliation between immediate intuition and reasoning = *read* one thing in another.
Ex. holes pierced in cardboard and pattern of material.
Universal method of "reading"?

Piece-work consisting of repetition of a single movement: the attention forced to concentrate continually upon one mechanical gesture.

Infernal. But for absolutely unskilled labour there is no other possible system. Without this constraint the attention would wander completely away. The result would be a very considerable loss not only of time but of quality in the product. The machines themselves would be endangered by this lack of attention.

On the other hand, for highly skilled jobs piece-work is detrimental.

A refinement of torture: to constrain thought to taste continually the body's slavery! It can only be borne by mutilating the soul. Otherwise one feels as if one were delivered every day, alive, to be crushed to pieces.

[*what follows is crossed out in ink*]
Since you need the inspiration of friendship, you must think about the unknown friend. The friend of your 15th year. Definitely give up the idea that X can be anything more than the shadow of a friend for you; he belongs, he condemns himself to belong, to the realm of shadows. You have no power to bring him out of the cave—even though you may try, but using what words? In any case, you must forbid yourself to wish it. And further, you must avoid if possible such whole-hearted attachment as you felt for S.G., and without real and fully reciprocal friendship. Those things belong to adolescence. Learn to be alone, if only so as to be worthy of true friendship. You have never been alone since you were 16, except for one year (and even less), and in what a state! Learn to be alone serenely and joyfully. Otherwise, you must despise yourself. And as for X, tell yourself the same as for S. Suffer if necessary on his behalf, but not on his account. Reflect that if you were to die now it would be in an unsatisfied state. What a disgrace! It is good that X should not be a real friend for you. You don't deserve that he should be.

The will. It is not difficult to do anything when one is inspired by the clear perception of a duty. But what is hard is that when one is suffering this clear perception vanishes, and all that remains is awareness of a suffering which it is impossible to bear.

But the converse is also true: at the moment of taking the decision, the duty is present and the suffering is still far away. The will could not triumph if it had to fight against forces stronger than itself. The whole art of willing consists in taking advantage of the moment before the struggle begins to contrive in advance that one's objective situation at the moment when one is weak shall be as one desires it to be.

"You tremble . . ."[1]

The will's only weapon is that it is able, in so far as it consists of thought, to embrace the different moments of time, whereas the body is limited to the present. Therefore, in short, it is simply a matter of withholding the assistance of thought from the passions.

It is not a question of "making resolutions" but of tying one's hands in advance.

Math. Galois
Essential idea.
[*Here follows a long extract from the text written at Ste Pélagie—pages 25–6 of the* Manuscrits de Evariste Galois, *published by J. Tannery, Paris (Gauthier-Villars) 1908.*]

[*The following is in pencil*]
Business men from the Nord (?), textile industry, red ribbon, white hair—

—They want to control the engaging and dismissal of hands. It's a violation of liberty! You're right: one is so disgusted with them that *one no longer tries to get business, even if there is any*. In our firm we've passed a unanimous resolution . . . if everyone did the same, they'd have to give in. Yes, indeed—what more have we to lose? And anyway one would be like a captain who had to stay in his cabin while the crew were on the bridge.

The employer is the man everyone hates. And yet he's the man who provides everyone with a livelihood. An extraordinary injustice. But, yes, everyone detests him. At one time there used to be some respect. When I was young. But that is all finished. And even where the foreman . . . They've done everything to smash it all up, the swine. But they'll pay for it.

[1] Turenne, to his own body: 'you tremble, carcass. You would tremble more if you knew where I am taking you'.

Homer—Iliad

Force.

Force turns a man into a thing. First, quite literally, by killing him. In the *Iliad* we get twenty times over the picture of man suddenly turned into a thing by death

> ... On the ground
> They lay, much dearer to the vultures than to their wives.

> His head lay all in the dust,
> That once-charming head; but now Zeus had let his enemies
> Defile it on his native soil.

And by a flash of contrast, that lost peace when man was still cherished:

> Foolish woman! she little knew that, very far from warm baths,
> Achilles had slain him, with the help of Pallas Athene.

Because it is able to kill, force can also turn a man into a thing while still alive, without killing him. A violent condition, death and life together; and the weakest have little choice except between this condition and that of a corpse.

> And perhaps one day, in Argos, you will weave cloth for another,
> And you will carry water from the springs ...
> Much against your will, yielding to a harsh necessity.

> Doubtless they will be carried off in the hollow ships,
> I with them. And you, my child, will either go with me
> To a land where you will work at wretched tasks,
> Labouring for a pitiless master ...

The intermediary is he who has not yet become a corpse, but is going to become one:

> ... thus spoke the brilliant son of Priam
> In begging words. But he heard a harsh reply ...
> He spoke; and the other's knees and heart failed him.
> Dropping his spear he fell down and stretched forth his hands,
> Both hands ...

The presence of the weak, who can be transformed in a moment into a thing, has no more effect upon the reactions of the strong than the presence of any other inert object.

> ... He spoke; and the other remembered his own father.
> He took the old man's hand and pushed him away.
> So both of them wept; one of them for Hector, slayer of men,
> And he wept aloud, abased at the feet of Achilles;
> But Achilles wept too, now for his father
> And now for Patroclus. And their sobs resounded through the house.

The weak, for his part, since every token of his existence has become so dangerous, tries to be like an inert object:

> ... No one saw great Priam enter.

The strong, who permits him, at whatever price it may be, to emerge ... Briseis ...

[*in the margin of what follows, the first 13 lines of Sappho's "To Aphrodite", in Greek*]
A half-dream. (Mauriac-type novel?)—
A family. The father, continually holding forth with Bible quotations. The mother has had many children, of whom the majority have died and of whom she has only completely loved one, a daughter. This daughter is pregnant. (Unmarried? or deserted by husband?). There is an older son, with a drooping eye-lid to one eye[1] (later, both eyes?) [a decent type]. An adolescent daughter, virgin, who has with her a friend of the same age (who has the character of J.) Incessant, oppressively intense conversations between the two. At the end of the apartment corridor is a bourgeois salon, with tastelessly ill-assorted furniture, where there is a chance of being alone. For this reason, the two girls go there when they are disgusted and depressed beyond bearing; with the result that this room—the centre of the novel—becomes itself impregnated with depression and disgust.

Scene. In the family sitting-room, a stifling discussion. The self-absorbed mother, exhibiting her maternal affection (sincere,

[1] Ptosis?

for the one daughter; but the others have had none of it). This exacerbates the bitterness of the son—a big, portly man, pleasant-looking except for his horribly disfigured eyes. The father, unaware and uninterested, goes on declaiming about the scriptures. The son begins to mimic him. "When that famous toper Jonathan . . ." Horror. The father's pious friends come (from where?) crowding into the room with loud protests. Amid the tumult, the two girls take the opportunity to slip away to the salon. But its atmosphere makes them feel sick.

Everything should be done to minimize the passivity of man—i.e. demonstrate more and more relations between cause and effect; treat science exclusively as theory of work—and art as symbol of work (Greek temple). art: work divorced from *utility*.
 work of art: point of equilibrium between man and nature . . .
 art: preserves the traces of an activity in which man encounters nature *on equal terms* (the passions being included in nature, e.g. the dance)
 epic poetry: man's revenge on destiny. Achilles in his tent . . . shield . . . comparisons . . .

 Meaning of the famous passage about geometry in the *Gorgias* ("you are forgetting . . ."). In the nature of things, no *unlimited* development is possible; the world ($\kappa \acute{o} \sigma \mu o s$!) rests entirely upon *measure* and *equilibrium* (hence "geometrical equality") and it is the same in the city. All ambition is "excess".
⟨cf. Montesquieu: to obey and to command one's equals⟩
γεωμετρίας γὰρ ἀμελεῖς . . . [1]
What the ambitious man totally forgets is the idea of *ratio*.

 'Senseless mob, to whom I am bound by my power,
 My very pride, alas, needs the support of your arms.'

Hegel: Master and servant.
[*In the margin of part of the above*] Philebus: the ancients said that the world is a fabric woven of limit and the unlimited.
 The connection between *science* and *art* can be established in terms of this idea—"idea" of the beautiful.

[1] You are forgetting geometry (Plato: *Gorgias*, 508a).

[*the following has been crossed out*]
"Propos"[1] on Prometheus, before the war. A man who holds power can certainly put a just man in prison for life, and then think no more about it; if he falls from power, and begins to think, he may himself become wise, just, and saintly . . . But the just man in prison will not remain just for long, because he will go mad. Or anyway he will become weak, faint-hearted, cringing (M . . .). So the tyrant has power to destroy not only the body but also the soul, and enjoys even a moral privilege over his enemies? An intolerable thought.

One should always think of men in power as dangerous *things*. Keep out of their reach as far as one can possibly do so without cowardice. And if one day one is obliged, on pain of losing one's self-respect, to face and be broken by their power, think of oneself as conquered by the nature of things, and not by men. For example: one may be in prison, in chains—but one might equally well be paralysed and blind; and there's no difference. Etc., etc.

What is intelligible in the famous "dialectic" is nothing more than the idea of *relation*, which can be seen much more clearly in Plato than in Hegel. As for the famous "negation of the negation", it is pure rubbish.

What is terrible in power is that it contains the *unlimited*. It is terrible for the tyrant, whom it makes mad. But it is terrible for the slave also. Is there a stoic in the world who could not be degraded by the simplest cruelties, such as hunger and blows, if he were at the mercy of an absolutely lawless whim? ("The taming of the shrew".) It is lucky that there is a social order. Grandeur of *laws*, even the most inhuman.

Avoid at all costs any situation in which one is reduced to being completely a puppet. If one falls into such a situation, endure it passively like a disease.
[*in the margin of the preceding*]
Can there be friendship between one who is in the cave without being aware of it and one who is trying to get out? That is

---

[1] Rubric of magazine column by the philosopher Alain.

how it is with . . . But Socrates said he would give everything to have even the shadow of a friend. At least, I have such a shadow . . .

The secret of the human condition is that equilibrium between man and the surrounding forces of nature "which infinitely surpass him" cannot be achieved by inaction; it is only achieved in the action by which man recreates his own life: that is to say, by work.

Plato himself is only a *precursor*. The Greeks knew art and sport, but not work. The master is the slave of the slave, in the sense that it is the slave who, by his work, *manufactures* the master. (Hegel . . .)

The "mixture of finite and indefinite" only makes sense in relation to the dimensions of the human body. From this point of view it is true that "πάντων ἄνθρωπος μέτρον".[1] But this applies to the active human body, which is acting as a link between cause and effect.

By work, man creates the universe around him. Remember the way you looked at the fields after a day's harvesting . . . How differently from a person going for a walk, for whom the fields are only a scenic background! In precisely *this* consists the power of a true monument of work over the universe that surrounds it (c.f. the words of Pierre de Craon[2]).

(In this, you possess an inexhaustible source of joy . . .)

[Never forget that you have the whole world, the whole of life, before you . . . And that, for you, life can be and ought to be more real, more full, and more joyful than it has perhaps ever been for any human being . . . Don't mutilate it in advance by any renunciation. Don't allow yourself to be imprisoned by any affection. Preserve your solitude. If the day ever comes when a *real* friendship is bestowed on you there will be no conflict between your inner solitude and this friendship. On the contrary, that is the infallible sign by which you will know it. Other affections ought to be severely disciplined. In any case, there is only one serious weakness that you have to master, only a single one, but at the risk of dying without ever having lived . . .]

[1] Man is the measure of all things.
[2] The architect in Claudel's *L'Annonce faite à Marie*.

Man has freed himself to a great extent from bondage to nature. To what extent? This can be estimated by the proportion of his work that is not directly concerned with satisfying basic needs. The greater the distance between our acts and this kind of satisfaction, the more liberated we are from nature. The swallow, which has to hunt insects continually, is the slave of nature. Hunting, collecting berries. But our liberation from nature is compensated by enslavement to society. For we are fed, clothed, etc. by society, like a child by its parents; we are eternal minors. Here too an equilibrium is needed.

We must accept that our actions shall be only *indirectly* connected with the satisfaction of needs; but let the intermediate stages be sufficiently few for the relation between cause and effect to be perceptible, although indirect.

Aim: that the conditions of existence should be such that AS MUCH AS POSSIBLE IS PERCEIVED.

People used to sacrifice to the gods, and the wheat grew. Today, one works at a machine and one gets bread from the baker's. The relation between the act and its result is no clearer than before.

That is why the will plays so small a part in life today. We spend our time in *wishing*.

Ambiguity of the word wish . . . Eliminate all wishing from human life. Substitute will—and give up expecting anything that is not the reward of work. If you get anything more, receive it as a grace . . . Ambiguity of the word grace, too. (the most beautiful word . . .)

(Love can only be pure to the extent that it is, precisely, a grace).

We no longer know how to receive grace.

Laws are necessary relationships . . .

Difference between *slave* and *citizen* (according to Montesquieu, Rousseau . . .): the slave is subdued to his master, and the citizen to the laws. No doubt the master may be very kind, and the laws may be very harsh; it makes no difference. The whole point is the difference between caprice and law.

Thus the man who thinks he is ruled by a capricious nature is a slave, and the man who knows that he is ruled by a nature determined by rigorous laws is a citizen of the world (Marcus Aurelius).

If only men could be brought to understand this—both society and the individual, and the slave too . . . Epictetus.

Why is it slavery to be subordinated to caprice? The ultimate reason is in the relation between the soul and *time*. Whoever is subdued to the arbitrary is suspended on the thread of time; he is obliged to *wait* (the most humiliating state! . . .) for what the next moment will bring; and to accept whatever the present moment has brought. He has no control of his passing moments; for him, the present is not a lever by which he can act upon the future.

Man is a slave in so far as alien *wills* intervene between his action and its result, between his effort and the task to which it is applied.

This is the case in our day both for the slave *and* for the master. Man never directly confronts the conditions of his own activity. Society makes a screen between nature and man.

Tool: a *balance* between man and the universe (statera . . .). "The forces of nature infinitely surpass . . ." So therefore? And yet the sailor in his boat balances *equally* against the infinite forces of the ocean. (Remember that a boat is a lever.) At every moment the helmsman—by the weak, but *directed*, power of his muscles on tiller and oar—maintains an equilibrium with that enormous mass of air and water. There is *nothing* more beautiful than a boat.

Fit this in somewhere
| decadence
| demoralization of the worker; decline of skilled work.
| unemployment. loss of relation between work and well-being
| (speculation: Auxerre vine-grower).
| replacement of competition by military and economic *war*
      (speculation, publicity—destruction of goods and machinery).
reaction: small businesses, etc.—
   tendencies towards return to simple life, etc.

Appearance of new productive forces is accompanied by relative freedom—creative period—the individual counts for something again.

The ideal—discussion notes.
   value? 1) the ideal we carry within us—a new one—*our* mission. the only new idea since the Greeks . . .
      2) limit—indispensable factor for understanding history—ex. craftsmen—skilled workers—sailors building workers (coordination)—in the same way, slavery (to nature, or to men) is a limit. *Always* the 3 factors. Question: proportion.
beginning at the Renaissance: people thought . . .
   decadence; causes: dislocation between action and thought.
the situation today.

compensation	
co-operation indispensable	widely diffused understanding of method
stimulus for effort (proof: periods of disorder, cooperatives)	sense of creating—
compulsion to put up with privation	respect for the work (*aesthetic* feeling—whence the role of art in the future society)

non-servile labour = labour in which there is co-operation (among factory workers, over-stressing of workshop practice)

central idea of Marx: labour itself as the organizing principle (in contradiction to the utopia of "communism as higher stage"—on what condition? Dangerous ambiguity.

Where human strength is exploited, there is no method (why?)
All labour = *transformation* of movements. The human body

is a machine for such transformations, but totally incomprehensible. Method only begins with the instruments of transformation which we *make* (pulley—lever—boat . . .)

Large-scale operations: Mechanics
Mines (to be modified, how?). Foundries (?)
Mass-production (can be automatically performed by automatically produced machines).
Individual production
But consider whether it would not be better to abandon mass-production?

workers' education: don't forget the St. Etienne model

ideal. "from the realm of necessity to the realm of freedom"—
No, but from necessity endured to necessity methodically handled.
 and from *capricious* and *unlimited* constraint (oppression) to *limited* necessity
 Old law: In the sweat of thy brow shalt thou get thy bread (curse)
 New law: Command nature by obeying her.
Faust: Stünd' ich, Natur, vor dir ein Mann allein
 Dann wär's der Mühe werth, ein Mensch zu sein![1]
Proudhon, Verhaeren . . .
escape from necessity? like children? but one would lose the value of life—and moreover one would pay by slavery of another kind—to the passions, in the first place—and then to the collective power of society.
 the aim should be to re-create—voluntarily, consciously, methodically—the conditions of one's own existence . . .
[*in the margin*] *co-operation* and *direct contact*?

dislocation between thought and action
to do something one has *not yet* understood is to perform an action that goes *beyond* what one's thought can embrace

[1] If I stood alone face to face with you, Nature,
 Then it would be worth while to be a man!

to do something one has already understood is to perform an action which falls *short* of what one's thought can embrace method: breaking down of work into separate processes—this is done in one man's mind, but it is performed by a number of men's bodies (piece work)

There will be *less* external discipline, the *more* internal discipline there is.

CENTRAL IDEA

As regards nature, capitalism has achieved the liberation of the human *collectivity* (considerable increase of leisure (if . . .), method, etc.) But as regards the *individual*, this same collectivity has taken over the oppressive function previously performed by nature.

This is true in a concrete way. Fire, water, etc. etc. etc.,—all those forces "which infinitely surpass the powers of man"—have been taken possession of by the collectivity.

Question: is it possible to pass on to the individual this liberation achieved by society?

problems: 1. *incentive* for enduring toil and privation
2. co-ordination is indispensable for method } connected?
3. mastery of the "infinite forces" (a different problem from 2.)

Would the "earthly paradise" be *desirable*? There would be nothing in it to teach man the very principle of self-mastery, which is to treat his own body as a *thing*. His only rule of life would be his passions . . .

"machine power = another form of the power of nature" (Marx, quoted by Dickmann)

The seeming-mastery of the "forces of nature which infinitely

surpass those of man" (Spinoza) demands the co-operation of a collectivity which far surpasses the control of those who direct it. Therefore . . .
"the would-be angel becomes a beast" (profound . . .)

method. a problem that is still obscure.
how is it that man becomes a slave to his own method? the essential problem . . .
The mind is enslaved whenever it accepts connections *which it has not itself established.* Even in simple addition . . . $\begin{array}{r} 18473 \\ 9534^2 \\ \hline 113815 \end{array}$

[*in the margin of the preceding*] (EXAMPLES: complex numbers, *irrational* numbers. Fermat)
what makes this inevitable is the sheer *quantity* of things known. once again, man is overwhelmed by quantity.
reappearance of chance, of the gods . . . (infinitesimals . . . imaginary quantities.)
Fermat's calculus.
example of Tantalus, in the *Regulae*. applicable to mathematical discoveries—
in these crystal mathematical universes, reason is exposed to the same pitfalls as in the real world.
in the world of mathematics, too, our power exceeds our knowledge.
essential point: this branch of knowledge cannot be *popularized.* why? just because of the part played in it by *chance*, by the *unforeseen*, which means that it has no *unity.* there is no way of opening broad vistas which the mind can observe without entering them. one must enter the subject before one can see anything.
this is true also of speculation, even in its purest form: "im Anfang war die Tat."[1] Whence the necessity and the role of *critique.* From this point of view Descartes was much too ambitious.
in modern *work*: *substitution of means for end*
in modern *algebra*: *substitution of sign for thing signified*
it is a science essentially incapable of being popularized because it replaces simplicity by generality (cf. complex num-

[1] In the beginning was the Deed.

bers). hence the subordination, no longer of the complex to the simple but, on the contrary, of the simple to the complex.

(Quantity changes into quality—hence the difference in kind between elementary knowledge and science—all elementary knowledge is made null and void)
 everyone becomes a layman; because generality is always "relative".
 (generality—power in abstract form).
 point at which this generality exceeds the grasp of the mind (as in a big business enterprise).
 generality . . .
 the mind is defeated by *quantity*, even in pure speculation (algebra) ⟨not quantity in terms, but quantity of relations⟩.
 therefore, in algebra too, search for equilibrium . . .
   (Descartes: discipline of the imagination)
thus science conceived as an *art*—an art of thinking . . .
 Δός που στῶ καὶ κόσμον κινήσω . . . [1]
 the point of leverage: that essential idea of equilibrium . . .
 An entirely new civilization. "A great life: that is to say a youthful dream that comes to realization in maturity". Greece is the youth of humanity. But, alas, the manhood of which that youth gave promise has not developed.

Freud.
 generality and *simplicity*. to regard the normal as a *particular case* of the abnormal (and the conscious as a particular case of the unconscious) is the same sort of inversion as to regard arithmetical numbers as a particular case of complex numbers, or mechanical energy as a particular case of electrical energy.
 already in Leibniz: the equal as a particular case of the unequal.

simplicity. definition: a thing is simpler than another thing when it is impossible to think the second without having already thought the first.

imaginary. $\sqrt{-1}$ is a *selective* agent in developments (Newton's binomial theorem)

[1] give me a point of leverage and I will move the world.

concrete definition of *freedom*: when the thought of an action precedes the action. "I am going away, therefore there is danger" (W. James), slavery, flight. "There is danger, therefore I am going away", retreat (in the first case there is emotion, but not in the second). [one can say "I am running away, therefore I am frightened" (W.J.), but not "I am frightened, therefore I am running away"; the second statement should be changed to "there is danger, therefore I am running away".]

now, what will be the content of this thought? it can be nothing other than necessity, for thought has no other object than the world.

same criterion for work

Freedom is a *limit* [that is to say, freedom understood as necessity overcome, for the freedom of indifference is merely a dream]—Slavery also. Every real situation is placed between the two.

To overcome an obstacle one has set up for oneself is not to overcome an obstacle—an obstacle is always something we *meet with*. In pure play there can be no real obstacle.

Without unavoidable obstacles—without necessity—art itself would be reduced to pure play. For what would it express? Every work of art celebrates necessity. Greek art like the others. Philoctetes, etc.

method: if a method has been understood once for all and employed many times, and if it then, even in the domain of abstract signs, produces *unforeseen* results, and these results are accepted without being understood, then, from that moment, the method has become a mere formula or recipe.

To be in direct confrontation with nature, not with men, is the only discipline. To be dependent upon someone else's will is to be a slave. And that is the fate of all men. The slave depends upon the master, and the master upon the slave. This situation makes men either suppliants or tyrants, or both at once (omnia serviliter pro dominatione). On the other hand, when confronted with inert matter one is obliged to resort to thinking.

[It is impossible to be dependent upon human beings without aspiring to tyrannize over them.
This is the source of all cruelties, both private and public.
(but no, there is still something else . . .)]

Mathematics: abstract universe within which I depend solely upon *myself*. Realm of justice, because in it all good will is rewarded. ("Seek ye first the kingdom of God and its justice".)

Secondly, the world; chance enters in. Progress (to ascertain —*to accept existence*). ["That's the way it is"] But to conceive chance properly (not imagining any god in it . . .) one must have passed through mathematics. Boat . . .

There are intermediaries: e.g. factory . . .

method.
machine: the method is in the thing, not in the mind
algebra: the method is in the signs, not in the mind
precisely because of its *universal* character. What has once been understood reproduces itself an unlimited number of times. One does not begin to understand again each time, because it would be useless and a waste of time, and for other reasons as well.

these automatic applications of method lead, of themselves, to something new; so one *invents without thinking*—that is what is so bad. It means that, from then on, thought itself—or what takes the place of it—becomes an instrument.

proper conditions of work. In order that there may be the maximum of freedom, 2 *distinct* questions are involved:

1. that the individual should have *as little need as possible* of the collectivity

2. that the collectivity should have *as much need as possible* of the individual, i.e. of thought (which is the one thing that cannot be abstracted from the individual)

Instead of developing techniques for maximum profit, try to

develop those that will give the maximum of freedom: an *entirely* new approach . . .

There is no such thing as collective thought. Yet our science is collective, like our technique. Specialization. We take over not only *results* but also *methods* which we do not understand. Indeed, the two go together; because algebraic results provide methods for the other sciences (e.g. infinitesimal calculus).

So even in this sphere, too, the individual is crushed.

This is connected, undoubtedly, with the overturning of values in science (*generality*—or unity—in place of clarity). How does this happen? It is because method is no longer anything but an instrument. Concern for economy, etc.

There does still remain, of course, a spark of the Greek spirit. Ex. theory of *groups*—research on *wholes* (in principle, anyway), etc.

History of mathematical *ideas*. Doubtless, there are not very many of them (imaginary numbers, for example, are not among them, etc.)

Where did the break come? One might take as criterion Descartes' principle: when making use of a proposition, bear in mind *everything upon which it rests*.

So soon as one employs a ready-made formula . . . (e.g. Newton's binomial theorem . . .)

Collaboration immediately becomes indispensable. The scientist is crushed by science.

Piece-work in science—for example, when something new emerges from the contact between two branches of science *which are not both of them fully understood by any one scientist*.

Two stages, as it were, of degradation. First science—then technique: same causes and different ones.

But at bottom the cause is always the same: opposition between the infinite scope of thought and the limits of the body (even in science: time, abstract signs . . .)

Since collective thought cannot exist as thought, it passes into things (signs, machines . . .). Hence this paradox: it is the thing that thinks, and the man is reduced to the status of a thing. Dependence of the individual in relation to the collectivity, and of man in relation to things: una eademque res.[1]

Relations *becoming established outside the mind*

The overturning of values is the same in science as in labour: the scientist is made to exist for the sake of science (to add to it), instead of science for the scientist (to make him wise). And further, the scientist depends upon science (he starts from the established science), and not science upon the scientist. Exactly the same as with machines...

Science, said Chartier,[2] was born from religion and not from labour. Why? (he didn't ask why). Because labour only manipulates *things*. The manipulation of *signs* is necessarily religious to begin with. (for signs are purely human). Their scientific elaboration is the transition from the latter to the former. The first, premature, attempt to make a direct transition was magic.

Why can science develop only from the manipulation of signs? Because it is only signs that can eliminate chance (the ἄπειρον), and thus reveal necessity—though it is not yet really necessity, because it does not *exist*—It is precisely through the ἄπειρον that it has existence.

Therefore science is to be defined as... (as what?)

(*Method* is only acquired through the manipulation of signs. Detoeuf's remark about engineers and workmen).

Quantity
method defeated by quantity
our civilization is based upon quantity
The idea of measure has been lost in *every* sphere (e.g. record-breaking in athletics).
everything is corrupted by it. Including private life, because *temperance* (σωφροσύνη) has become unthinkable. Outside the sphere of external observances (bourgeois formality) the whole moral trend of the post-war years (and even before) has been an *apology* for *intemperance* (surrealism) and therefore, ultimately, for madness...

[1] One and the same thing.
[2] Better known under his *nom de plume* of Alain.

Modern conception of love.

Conversation with Pierre: when they talk about paganism, people forget that the very centre of paganism is the idea of *temperance* (for which Christianity unluckily substituted *privation*; but the would-be angel becomes a beast).

Unfortunately, in a moral atmosphere dominated by intemperance, it is particularly difficult to live by a rule of temperance—so it is hardly possible to escape from intemperance, in a good many respects, except by way of privation—but the worst dangers associated with privation disappear if it is adopted, not as a rule of conduct for its own sake but as a provisional *pis aller*, and even then only where one feels it to be indispensable. It is certainly a lesser evil; for although privation and temperance are in opposition, one can deprive oneself while still having temperance as one's objective—one can assign limits to privation, but not to intemperance.

Among the characteristics of decadence in the modern world, do not forget the impossibility of envisaging concretely the relation between effort and the result of effort. Too many intermediaries. As in all the other cases, this relation which no thought can encompass, is found in a thing: in *money*. And, as always, by its very existence it creates a gulf between the thought of one term and the thought of the other. In our day, the current and almost exclusive resort to speculation as the means to wealth makes it a gulf to the 2nd. power (while industry at least puts money into relation with things, speculation is a relation between money and itself)—the consequences are felt even among the basic elements of our population (the Auxerre vine-grower)

MONEY
MECHANISM } the three monstrosities of contemporary civilization. Complete analogy
ALGEBRA

Put quality above quantity *also* in the domain of science.

The relation of science to its applications is *fortuitous*—it is not thought in anyone's mind; therefore it can only be fortuitous.

What is important (for freedom) is not that work should be *methodical*, but that it should be *methodically performed*. The one thing does not imply the other. Even, in a certain sense, they exclude one another . . .
The mathematician lives in a universe apart, whose objects are signs. The relation between sign and thing signified no longer exists; the play of interchange between signs develops of itself and for itself.
And further, *this phenomenon duplicates itself*. Because the increasing complication demands signs of signs. And there too . . .
It is in this that the "robot" consists . . .
The mind, overwhelmed by the weight of quantity, is left *with no criterion except effectiveness* (for there still has to be *some* criterion . . .)
Wherever the mind ⟨man . . .⟩ ceases to be the origin, it ceases also to be the end (therefore in all collective work . . .)
(The soul is the human being (the human body . . .) considered as having a value in itself. To love a woman's soul is to refrain from thinking of the woman in terms of one's own pleasure, etc.)

Descartes was too generous to really exclude social questions from his interest. But he believed that freedom could only be achieved through man's methodical grasp of nature . . .

Sophocles

Trachiniae. Inevitable abandonment of wife, through the necessities of the struggle against men and the world. Privation, danger. Subordination—due to physiology and the power of arms—to the husband's good pleasure. (mixture of sorrowful comradeship and jealousy between women who are all similarly at the mercy of masculine force). Revenge of domestic life upon the warrior—

τὸ γὰρ νεάζον . . . .
. . . ἡδοναῖς ἄμοχθον ἐξαίρει βίον
ἐς τοῦθ᾽, ἕως τις ἀντὶ παρθένου γυνὴ
κληθῇ, λάβῃ τ᾽ἐν νυκτὶ φροντίδων μέρος.[1]

[Tr. 144–149]

[1] For youth . . . enjoys an easy life of pleasures, until one is called wife instead of virgin and gets one's share of anxiety in the night hours.

Philoctetes. Drama of material abandonment.

Culmination of the drama: moment when the abandonment becomes total, through privation of those last links with humanity provided by *fabricated objects*.

> Ὦ χεῖρες, δια πάσχετ' ἐν χρείᾳ φίλης
> νευρᾶς....
> .... ὀυ γὰρ ἔχω χερσῖν
> τὰν πρόσθεν βελέων ἀλκάν.[1]
>
> [Phil. 1004–1005, 1150–1151]

Electra. Abandonment among powerful and hostile beings: humiliation, slavery, blows, rags.... Culmination when abandonment becomes complete through the death of the one friendly and protecting being. Then recovery of him, and salvation.

Ὦ φίλτατον φῶς ... O beloved light ...

Oedipus Rex—Coloneus. Antigone.

Total and sudden loss of wealth, power, honour, as a result of pure chance.—and, first, of a natural catastrophe (plague).

Beggary, with appearance of guilt. Privations, necessity always and everywhere of supplicating, fear of arousing horror. Abandonment.

Weakness and loneliness of the man who opposes the established powers.

Everywhere, beneath the development of feelings, sensation of the brutality of *nature* itself.

[*in the margin of the preceding*] (*All* the dramas of Sophocles are in one form or another the drama of loneliness ... of the weakness of the individual, even though energetic (as they all are).)
[*in the margin of the previous page*] (In the domain of feeling, the more one gives, the more one assumes the posture of begging, of a dog waiting for a bone. Muse du Département[2] ... Because the more one gives, the more *dependent* one becomes, both for happiness and sorrow. One gets more happiness from a single word than one can give to the other person by a year of devotion.)

In Racine, on the other hand, the inevitable role of necessity is purely in the order of power. This is obvious in *Andromaque—Bajazet—Bérénice—Mithridate—Iphigénie—Britannicus.* But also in Phèdre. Hunger, etc. play no part. Note how well the

---

[1] O hands, what sufferings are yours, for the lack of your loved bowstring ... for I no longer have in my hands the former defence of my arrows.
[2] Balzac's novel.

passions of love conform with a purely *political* universe. Whereas fraternity (Electra, Antigone) doesn't enter in at all. Electra is a servant, ill-treated and badly fed, although a daughter of the house. Antigone is a beggar. There are no beggars in Racine.

Beginning of *Oedipus Rex*: the plague. Of *Oedipus Coloneus*: a wandering beggar. Of *Electra* . . . etc.

In fact, Racine's tragedies provide a bad education . . . And as for Corneille, *affliction* plays no part at all. Neither Horace, nor Polyeucte, nor Augustus, nor even Rodrigue can regret for a single moment that the tragic event occurred (the obligation to fight the Curiatii—the threat of martyrdom—the conspiracy of Cinna—the Count's blow). In Corneille's world nothing can touch a man, provided he can rise to the sublime. But at the same time, in this world there is no hunger, no abandonment, no catastrophe, no oppression . . . In Sophocles man retains the human form although shattered by a hostile destiny. Sad divinities of Hegel. How much more human he is . . . And above all, how much nearer to us, today.

[*at this point, quotations in Greek from the Philoctetes*: lines 234–5, 485–7, 929–32, 936–9, 951–4, 1004–5, 1017–18, 1066–7, 1070–1, 1081–94, 1146–62]

Sails: in so far as the wind strikes the after-sails it tends to bring the boat *into the wind*

in so far as it strikes the fore-sails it tends to drive the boat off the wind

but any sail exerts this directing force only in so far as it is *taut* (trimmed to the wind). There may be more sail forward than aft and yet the boat may still sail into the wind, if the foresails (jib . . .) are *eased off*.

With rare exceptions (yachts), a boat cannot sail closer to the wind than four points (45°); any further, and the boat *drops astern*.

The helm checks the boat's speed; therefore it has to be used as little as possible, and as much steering as possible be done with help of the sails.

Tacking is done by means of the helm. The difficulty is to prevent the boat gathering sternway when it comes head to wind; it must have sufficient way on to prevent this.

Sails: the problem in sail-making is to ensure that the wind makes only one pocket in the sail, not several. (which does happen, and makes the sail unworkable).

Flat-bottomed boats (Réville): great stability because they are broad in proportion to their length—spacious holds because the sides are very sloping—do not fill with water, for the same reason—light in the water because the bottom is much shorter than the surface length—water-tight because constructed of bevel-edged timbers, without caulking. 20 years ago they used to be very bad. Were improved because of pressure from the sailors, who preferred the flat-bottoms[1] to sailing ships. Cost: 1000 f. Better than dories. Can go where a good sailing ship would be in danger.

Sailing ships—qualities: stability (id.) or lightness (short keel)—to adapt for engine, the keel has to be lengthened.

night fishing—they "carry marker buoys"—they set a buoy and there are 4 lights which flash in pairs (night-fishing method was learned after the war)

they learn to map the sea bottom with the aid of leading-marks—and to calculate the right size of mesh for the nets . . . and the size of the hooks (depending on the dimensions of the fish and the pressure of water)

there are sea *routes* at night (as many as the points of the compass, and others given by the leading-marks)—they have to be able to find their way among them well enough, for example, to recover a broken line . . .

Here follow 12 pages of sailors' songs, "Biribi"[2] songs, and war songs:
1. *La vie du marin* ("The sun is rising . . . Makes a loud noise").
2. *La mère du déserteur* ("They were two childhood friends . . . I shan't see him again, but I know he's alive").
3. *Tu leur diras* (*Biribi song*) ("You're released, you have no luck . . . But not robbers like those in the big banks").
4. *Souvenir de Biribi* ("Soon it will be New Year's day . . . I will leave you in peace").
5. *Chant du disciplinaire* (*Calvi song*) ("But what is that petard? . . . On the martyrs' ground").

---

[1] Presumably self-powered.
[2] French army disciplinary companies, in north Africa.

6. *La mort du camisard*[1] ("Sleep, little camisard . . . In the name of the Fatherland and the Republic").
7. *La vie du matelot* ("Farewell, dear comrade . . . So that they don't become sailors").
8. *Chant de Craonne* ("When, after a week . . . Pay with your skin").

"etiam peccata"—because we can sin only in so far as we have not understood that we are sinning: so it is necessary to commit the sin in order to learn something, just as physical pain is needed to reveal an illness. But all this can only be thought in reference to the past.

[Your great temptation: inability to cope with necessity in its purest form, which is *time*; the most shameful temptation is to escape it by unawareness or to submit blindly to it . . .]

labour: the original pact between man and nature, between the soul and its body.

vice of specialization: failure to recognize *series*—failure to perceive the difficulty in and by itself, but only as accompanied by this, that, or the other extraneous circumstance.

The fact is that the idea of oppression is a stupid one; it is only necessary to read the *Iliad* . . . and *a fortiori* the idea of an oppressive class. one can only speak of an oppressive structure of society. this structure will never automatically give rise to its opposite [but only to the ideal of its opposite: see Heraclitus]

The Greek idea of *measure* makes absolutely no sense except in relation to the proportions of the human body.
Man, while apparently mastering those forces which *infinitely*

---

[1] Name originally given in the seventeenth century to the Languedocian Protestant peasants who resisted the 'dragonnades' after the revocation of the Edict of Nantes.

surpass him, has in fact delivered himself to them—he has lost even the idea of necessity.

technique and science—popularization—idea of the lever, and everything to which it can be applied. ⟨stern oar?—propellor?—cf. Lagrange.⟩—instead of evolving *abstractions*, bring to light *analogies* between concrete and particular things. Then what will become of formulas?—They will be one term of an analogy, and *nothing more*—
⟨go on trying to do it yourself, for yourself ... give several years to it if necessary, in silence ... but then, don't teach! ...⟩
[to understand is always an ascending movement; that is why comprehension ought always to be concrete. (one is never got out of the cave, one comes out of it.)]
1. make a list of all *transformations of motion*, centred around the idea of the lever. analyse specific cases so as to reveal the unifying principle ⟨d'Alembert, Lagrange ...⟩ parallel to this, elucidate mathematical ideas: elementary geometry—infinitesimal calculus—everything connected with *periodic motions* (π, imaginary numbers)—finally, groups.
secondly, make a survey of everything in the field of mechanism that is other than transformation of motions—such as: 1. transformation of energy (motors)—2. transformation of matter (chemistry)—3. ⟨the latest thing⟩ stimulation of "reflexes" (automatism) (perhaps a broader heading is required? television, etc.)

project: a people's university *on Socratic lines*, to study the foundations of the crafts.

[*in the margin of the preceding, after* "etiam peccata"] relation between the musical (or even architectural) *theme* and *obsession*. A Bach fugue is an obsession overcome—which is why the initial theme is not of so much importance. Obsession is the one and only human suffering (a tooth-ache is an obsession): a pain that is not an obsession is no pain. |
opium, etc.=making a voluptuous pleasure of thought itself. Deliberate cultivation of pleasure is *always* bad. |

it is a fault if one wants to be understood before having made a thing clear to oneself—it is cultivating pleasures, and undeserved ones, in friendship—it is something even more corrupting than love. You would sell your soul for friendship ...

SIGNS

blind man's stick.

ship: the true sailor gets to be able to sense what is affecting his ship *no less* instantly than he senses the messages of his own nerves (cf. also Conrad). Ex: leading-marks—sails—position and movement of ship. ...)

there is responsibility, inventiveness, etc., in short, there is *action* wherever man is handling things that can in this way become like extensions of his own body, by transmitting signals directly to his soul. It is in this that the true nature of *work* resides—

[*in the margin*] one should try to elucidate (it is a problem that has presented itself to me for some time) just what is the marvellous virtue inherent in the fact of possessing, as it were, an artificial body? note that Hegel, in discussing habit, failed to remark that there is no habit without an instrument to serve it.—model the body upon the *universality* of the mind? No doubt.—a good workman is the reverse of an automaton. ὄργανον ἄλλον σῶμα[1]

When one is reduced to doing nothing but interpret signs, there is no longer anything but the abstract image of action: on the one hand, orders are issued among signs that have no reality, and on the other hand, orders are carried out among things that have no meaning. [factory!]

Genius can be defined by considerations of this sort, as regards everything it contains in the way of intuition, inspiration, etc. (as regards everything that is not accounted for by *method*.) Ex.: military genius.

Cf. Hegel on habit. Habit is a necessary and almost a sufficient condition of genius.

[it is not surprising that Greek temples tried to copy the human body ...]

must try to study, in the light of this idea, the work of a *skilled*

---

[1] An instrument is another body.

machine operative [but there is still a distinction to be made between the ordinary skilled worker and the specialist]

[The ideal would obviously be combination of method and habit.]

The conditions of modern life destroy the mind–body equilibrium in everything, in thought and in action—in all actions: in work, in fighting . . . [*in the margin*: and in love, which is now a luxurious sensation and a game . . .] (and, inevitably, the emotional life itself is affected by it . . .) In its every aspect, the civilization we live in overwhelms the human *body*. Mind and body have become strangers to one another. Contact has been lost.

In the midst of this storm it is already much if one can cling to the idea (the *concrete* idea) of direction. And as for the future, all one can say is that the more people there are who . . .
[*in the margin of the preceding*] in this connection: reflect upon the aesthetic aspect of analogy—the role of analogy in art—ex themes ‖ human proportions in architecture ‖ etc.

machines—2 extreme types
1. the *instrumental* machine, adaptable for all sorts of tasks, to which the workman's relationship is analogous to that of the sailor with his ship.
2. the *automatic* machine, which leaves nothing for man to do except to tend it.

both types increase man's freedom, though it is true that machine-tending has a somewhat stupefying effect; but it would be easy to find ways of dispensing the machine-tender from any effort of attention (warning bells . . .) [so the job could be given to students, etc.] (yes, in theory—but there is the noise)

between the two extremes there are an indefinite number of intermediate types: 1. according to whether the *machine* is more or less *specialized* (which depends on how far the work is *standardized mass* production)—the lowest degree consists of semi-automatic machines with which the human body cooperates, but as a cog in the machine—2. according to the *division of labour* between the act of adapting the machine to its purposes and the movements of the human body which are integrated with its functioning on the same level as the movements of the mechanism (*adjuster* and *unskilled machine hands*)

note:
the thing that degrades work is not the machine itself, it is *mass production*—the only difference between Adam Smith's pin makers and the Citroen conveyor-belt workers is in the constraints imposed upon their organized movements.

therefore the ideal would be to eliminate to the fullest extent possible the intermediate degrees. we have already created completely automatic machines (which only lack arrangements for dispensing their supervisors from attention), but we could also create *much* more flexible machines than any yet known.

thus one can envisage a technical transformation which would open the way to a different civilization.

but it would have to be brought about, as in the 1st. monasteries, through co-operative enterprises—and, in these enterprises too, the way would have to be found towards a *different* science.

[one could imagine an industrial enterprise in which the hierarchy of functions would be based, not upon the relation between giving orders and executing them, but upon skilled qualifications. The punishment for work badly done would be demotion to a less skilled job (and of course the ultimate sanction would be *hunger*: temporary unemployment). The work would be controlled by the best workers, in rotation; and this would be a reward, enabling them to comprehend the mechanism as a whole. There would be *no* extra pecuniary advantage enjoyed by anyone at all]

mathematics. the great obstacle is that generalization immediately plunges us into a forest of *new* particular cases.

⟨must elucidate this. *very* important, badly expressed ...⟩

here too one should proceed by the study of *particular cases*, and analogies.

the very institution of algebra corresponds to a fundamental error concerning the human mind ... cf. Descartes (one thinks the singular).

The progress of mechanism ought to have stimulated in the human mind the progress indicated by Descartes in his lines about the statuette of Tantalus.

but . . . [emergence of a *new* type of particular]
we have here, it seems to me, something analogous to what happened with algebra.

There is a pitfall here for the human mind, which constitutes the *essential* difficulty (and which Descartes failed to see). it must be fully elucidated. perhaps there is a way round it; in any case, much is gained if it is even perceived.

If there is a remedy, it consists in substituting *series* in place of *generalizations*.

Descartes saw clearly that the chief difficulty is not in the advancement of understanding, but in disciplining the imagination. it is this that makes science an *art*. and, after all, that is its real value

Science ought to be the method for mastering nature (the word method implying the priority of the perfect in relation to the imperfect).
beginning with *numbers*
  abstract motions (geometry [and not figures])
    the idea of *combination* (mathematics centred around the theory of groups)
  real motions (scientific principles of the crafts and especially of machines)
    the *continuous* (mechanics comprising application of the infinitesimal calculus—theory of fluids—etc.)
  energy
apart from that: study of natural phenomena (heat, electricity, etc.) CUTTING OUT ALL HYPOTHESES THAT ARE NOT INDISPENSABLE. (Verification . . .)
[*in the margin*] what are called hypotheses nowadays are no more than arbitrary suppositions, corresponding neither to any intellectual nor to any practical necessity
  chemistry
    study of living beings (idea of *vital exchanges* and of *organic equilibrium*—table of reflexes—mutations).
is there anything else in science? if there is still something left, put it away in the corner, quietly, so that it stays there . . .

To be confronted with things is a liberation of the mind. To

be confronted with men, if one is dependent on them, degrades it—and it is the same whether dependence takes the form of subordination or of command.
Cf. Diderot: "to adopt postures" (Neveu de Rameau)[1]
Why these men standing between nature and me?
never be forced to take account of an unknown thought . . . (because in that case one is at the mercy of chance)
[provisional remedy: treat mankind as a spectacle, except where one is attached by fraternal links . . . and *never* seek for friendship . . . live among men as I did in that railway-carriage between St. Etienne and Le Puy . . . above all, never allow oneself to dream of friendship: everything has to be paid for . . . "rely only upon yourself"]

Conics. 1) Apollonius. 2) formulas. Both ways are bad . . . it would be good to find a 3rd.

By carrying oppression beyond a certain point, the powerful inevitably make their slaves *adore* them. Because the thought of being in absolute subjection as somebody's plaything is a thought no human being can sustain: so if a man is left with no means at all of escaping constraint he has no alternative except to persuade himself that he is doing voluntarily the very things he is forced to do; in other words, he substitutes *devotion* for *obedience* (and sometimes he will even try to do more than he is forced to, and will thereby suffer less, in the same way that children in play can bear with laughter physical pains that would overwhelm them if inflicted as punishment). It is in this way that servitude degrades the soul: indeed, devotion of this kind rests upon self-deception, because the reasons for it will not bear inspection. (From this point of view the Catholic principle of obedience (cf. Edi)[2] must be regarded as liberating, whereas Protestantism is based upon the idea of sacrifice and devotion). The only salvation is to replace the intolerable idea of constraint, not with the illusion of devotion, but with the idea of

---

[1] "la posture contrainte où nous tient le besoin . . . Il n'y a dans tout un royaume qu'un homme qui marche, c'est le souverain. Tout le reste prend des positions." *Le Neveu de Rameau*, pp. 104–5 (Droz, Geneva, 1950).
[2] Edith Copeau, daughter of Jacques Copeau, became a Catholic nun.

necessity. (Cf. the sequel to *Emile*)—moreover, necessity never involves total impotence.

Revolt, on the other hand, unless it is immediately expressed in definite and effective action, always turns into its opposite, because of the feeling of utter impotence that results from it. In other words, the oppressor's strongest support comes from the impotent revolt of the oppressed.

(One could write a novel about one of Napoleon's conscripts . . .)

'. . . what could employ my heart, unless it loved this hatred Whose numberless heads it is so sweet to tread on?'

(but, precisely, it is impossible for Semiramis *ever* to be aware of that, because the master too is deceived by the illusion of devotion.)

If that is how it is, then Spinoza's rule "neither to laugh, nor weep, nor be indignant about human affairs, but to understand", when considered as an intellectual safeguard, is not opposed, as I used to think, to social action. What one should try to teach the workers is to transfer to human affairs in general the idea of *necessity* which they find in their own labour.

Only way to retain one's dignity under forced submission: to regard the boss as a thing. Sequel of *Emile*. Every man is a slave to necessity, but the conscious slave is much superior. Hegel: master and servant.

Art (of whatever kind) is related to two things: *work* and *love*. Relation between the two?
[*in the margin*] The poem teaches us to contemplate thoughts instead of changing them.
but love is only present in art by being overcome and even denied. Lesson of the work of art: it is forbidden to touch things of beauty. The artist's inspiration is always *Platonic*.

Thus art is the symbol of the two noblest human efforts: to construct (work), and to refrain from destruction (love overcome). For all love is naturally sadistic; and modesty, respect, reserve, are the mark of the human. Not to seize possession of what one loves . . . not to change it in any way . . . refuse power . . .

rule of action: *never* hesitate, or stop, or draw back in the middle of an action, whatever may happen. But *never* commence an action without having given a long and sustained scrutiny to all its possible consequences (all the possibilities ...) in every sphere in which the mind is not compromised, *give oneself the benefit of anonymity* ("follow the rules and customs") [you find this very difficult] Don't try to make oneself understood ... what's the use?
to understand: that's better.
avoid all responsibilities that do not correspond to a strict duty.
Rousseau's rule (very important)—*never* put oneself in a situation such that one might lose by a friend's good fortune or gain by his misfortune. more generally: avoid as much as possible all situations liable to produce a clash between the animal reactions of sensibility and the higher sentiments and the will.

always keep in mind that punctuality, precision, reliability in small things ("in performance, nothing is a detail") are the conditions of man's life on the earth. Time exercises no constraint upon thought—at least, in a sense; but it is the very fabric of action. You have always known life from the point of view of a parasite, in effect ... Apply the converse of Socrates' words about leisure.

Learn to reject friendship, or rather the dream of friendship. To want friendship is a great fault. Friendship ought to be a gratuitous joy, like the joys afforded by art, or life (like aesthetic joys). One must refuse it in order to be worthy to receive it: it is of the order of grace "Depart from me, O Lord ... " It is one of those things that are given "over and above". *Every* dream of friendship deserves to be shattered. [It is not by chance that you have never been loved ...] To want to escape from being lonely is cowardice. Friendship ought not to cure the sorrows of loneliness but to double its joys. Friendship is not to be sought for, dreamed about, longed for, but exercised (it is a virtue). Get rid of all this impure and muddy froth of sentiment ... Schluss!

Or rather (because one must not cut away too much) all that part of friendship that is not actual social intercourse should pass over to considered thought. There is certainly no need to ignore the inspiring virtue of friendship. But what ought to be strictly prohibited is dreaming of sentimental delights. That is corruption. And it is as silly as dreaming about music or painting. Friendship, like beauty, cannot be detached from reality. Like beauty, it is a miracle. And the miracle consists simply in the fact that it *exists*. At the age of 25 it is high time for a radical break with adolescence...

Art. It is the triumph of art to lead to something other than itself: to a life which is fully conscious of the pact between the mind and the world. Second Faust. So it is useless to envy artists. A fugue of Bach, a picture by Vinci, a poem—they indicate but they do not express. [And yet...] Art is knowledge. Or rather, art is exploration. The great artist learns things which, alas, he does not communicate. Vinci... (cf. his *Treatise*)

It is always man's greatness that he re-creates his life. He re-creates what is given him. He creates the very thing he is suffering. By work, he creates his own natural existence. By science, he re-creates the universe through symbols. By art, he re-creates the alliance between his body and his soul (cf. the discourse of Eupalinos). Note that each of these 3 creations is a poor, vain, empty thing when taken by itself and unrelated to the other two. The three combined: "workers' " culture (you can keep on hoping...)

Science as related to labour: already sketched (see earlier page). But *art* as related to labour? Shall I ever be able to conceive it? (And there is a gulf, alas, between *imagining* and *doing*.)

When our whole centralized organization collapses, *mass-production* will collapse at the same time. But knowledge of

machinery will continue. So therefore, through a period of anarchy, disorder, misery, there will be re-created . . . ?
One should not put one's money on catastrophe. But neither should one fight against it with bare hands. There are two things we have to keep in mind: 1. to save *ourselves*—i.e. not to go mad in a mad world. This is already much. 2. to do everything possible to prepare . . . With no illusion about the effectiveness of our efforts. Because: we lack the natural means—and we have no reason to hope that what we are aiming at won't turn into its contrary (as with Descartes). But in the end, since the two tasks coincide, it is still worth trying. "No need of hope . . ." But since one must have *some* purpose . . . Do what? Make a survey of our contemporary civn. which is crushing us. A critical study . . . (express this better . . .). Reflect *in solitude*. With no division of labour, with no . . . but nevertheless try to get co-operation from all who . . .

What does it mean to make a critical survey of our civilization? It means to try to bring to light exactly how it is that man has become the slave of his own creations. Through what fissure unconsciousness has invaded methodical thought and action. To escape back into primitive life is a lazy solution. The original pact between mind and the world must be rediscovered through the actual civilization in which we live. The task is an impossible one because of the shortness of human life and the impossibility of collaboration or of successors. But that is no reason for not undertaking it. All of us, even the youngest, are in a situation like Socrates' when he was awaiting death in prison and learning to play the lyre. And although collaboration is impossible there can at least be contacts. Scientists, technicians, skilled workers, ought to make a concerted effort to control science and technique . . .

The *essential* fact is this: that the decline of skilled craftsmanship is the end of civilization. That is the true sense of materialism. The forms of exploitation are not material phenomena. It is techniques and not economic systems that are the material factor in history.

ancient slavery—the *same* phenomenon is going to reappear. Russia. But not so quickly, because of the high yield of labour due to our techniques. But this high yield will only have the effect of prolonging the slave system.

There is practically no hope that even the youngest of us will live to see the breakdown. Practically no hope either that we can even bequeath our thought to the generations who will see it. But one ought to make as much effort for the faintest hope as for the strongest. And, at the worst ... [Socrates].

look for all the obstacles to imagination.

separation between sign and thing signified (algebra)	isolate. (ought to be remedied by analogies ...) transpose especially *plane and relief* (maps—drawings) *rest and movement*

[*in the margin*] there are certainly many others. you, better than anyone, can draw up the list ... Above all, don't hurry it. An altogether different education, which would educate the imagination—a gymnastic ...

4 things to teach in scientific education:
method
gymnastic of the imagination
criticism
verification

[apart from that, education ought to include nothing except art—giving a much larger place to dance, song, drawing [for drawing: begin with a period of absolute freedom, on the lines of Freinet—then later, drawing from nature and copying works of art]. Poetry later still. As for the art of writing, it ought to be developed *only* in relation to the other disciplines.]

Art has no [immediate] future, because all art is collective, and there is no longer a collective life [there are only dead collectivities], and also because of that rupture of the true pact between body and soul. (note that Greek art coincided with the beginnings of geometry and with athletics. Medieval art with craftsmanship. Renaissance art with the beginning of mechanics. 18th and 19th century art with the awakening of popular feeling. Even "unanimism"[1] was only possible up to the war ...

[1] Cf. Jules Romains.

Since 1914 the break has been complete). Even comedy is almost impossible, because there is no place for anything but satire (when was it easier to understand Juvenal?) Art will only be able to be reborn out of the great anarchy to come—an epic art, no doubt, because affliction will have simplified many things. a theatre arising from deep popular springs—architecture. So it is quite useless on your part to envy Vinci or Bach—(or . . .) Greatness, in our day, must take other roads. And it can only be solitary, obscure, and without echo . . . [but without an echo there is no art]

You could not have wished to be born at a better time than this, when everything has been lost.

[*in the margin of the preceding*] To rediscover that pact between body and soul (as you found sport to help you, and as no doubt, some day, E . . .)

[*in the margin of the page*] It is a weakness to seek from those we love, or to wish to give them, any other comfort than is given by works of art, which help us by the simple fact that they *exist*. To love, and to be loved, simply makes one another's existence more concrete, more constantly present to the mind. (but it ought to be present as the source of thoughts, not as their object.) If there is any reason for wishing to be understood, it is not for one's own sake but for the other's, so as to exist for him.

Two forms of destiny: *war* (epic poetry: Homer, and also Sophocles, Aeschylus)—*passion* (Euripides, Racine) [Shakespeare: the 2, Histories, Tragedies]. MADNESS in both cases (cf. Agamemnon).

The central idea of Aeschylus (which is also in Homer) is that success, by its very essence, is an *excess*. Plato.

Destiny assumes the image of passion as soon as social life, thanks to a strong power, acquires a—purely temporary—stability. But love (unless it rises to the sublime) is always domination or servitude—and, what is more, always both at the same time.

'I affected, in your eyes, a false pride—
It is on you that my joy and felicity depend...'

⟨what is extremely feeble, in Racine, is the idyllic couples...⟩

Agamemnon: the sacrifice of Iphigeneia (which is the act to be avenged) is the very symbol of war. [What a mistake of Lucretius, to accuse religion of it!]

There are also combinations of war and love... The captives, in Homer... Cassandra... Eriphyle... [and, on the other hand, Helen... (but there I still don't understand)]

Clytemnestra (of Aeschylus), the woman's revenge upon the warrior—a symbol (better than Liluli...) of all those women behind the fronts...

There is still a third fatality, which is the imagination (The Choephoroe). Again a madness. (Religion saves from it)

Profound wisdom contained in the folk tales about wishes. The fisherman who wishes to be a Lord, then a King, then Emperor, then Pope, then God... and finds himself a fisherman again. (What is so good in this story is that it is his wife who urges him. Ambition is mainly feminine because, while man is esteemed in so far as he battles with sea, earth, metals, etc., woman is esteemed in so far as she pleases, which is an aim without law or measure. It is always mothers who want their children to be first.) In brief, it is precisely the story of Napoleon. The lesson is that ambition is unlimited, whereas real possibilities never are; and whoever exceeds them will fall.

The only way, therefore, to attain to that infinite towards which all men's hearts aspire is to be just, as Socrates said to Alcibiades.

All human wisdom is contained in the reflections of the Greeks upon "measure" and "excess". Socrates. The tragedians. (How idiotic to call the wisdom of the chorus a "commonplace prudence"! Choruses of Aeschylus).

⟨As for you, you think you are well aware of all that, but one can never be sufficiently on one's guard... Descartes' motto: qui bene latuit bene vixit.[1]⟩

---

[1] He has lived well who has lived obscurely.

Power has limits, which are due (apart from other factors) to the difficulties of control, not only over extended areas but also—and this is important—*in depth*. Russian peasants. But for conveyor-belt workers the same slavery is easily made to work. Therefore: avoid such conditions as enable slavery to be imposed without waste of power.

There will *always* be the compulsion of hunger ⎫
      social compulsion   ⎬
      love of the craft   ⎭

Othello: in Othello, motiveless jealousy is the price of marital authority—cf. the terrors of the prince in the "Chartreuse". The master is condemned to fear.

Sophocles. Man is always (as in Aeschylus) the prey of destiny, but externally. And more so internally. (even Ajax . . .) Oedipus. Antigone. Orestes, instead of the furies it is: ἔχω σε χερσίν;—ὡς τὰ λοίπ' ἔχοις ἀεί.[1] Philoctetes (ὦ φίλτατον φώνημα[2]). In Sophocles there are also pure joys (but there are none in Aeschylus). Piety dissolves the malediction of the gods. Reason floats above the tide of affliction (whereas in Aeschylus there is always an atmosphere of madness). Sophoclean tragedy is a true contemporary of geometry. Order reigns in the city . . . an ephemeral moment of equilibrium . . . (even Ajax is not mad: . . . οὐδενὸς ἄξιος[3])

Sophocles chose the most horrible legends (Oedipus, Orestes), to imbue them with serenity. His tragedies teach that nothing can destroy the inner freedom. His heroes experience affliction, but not obsession. It is more joyful than a Shakespearian fairyland . . .

In *none* of his characters is there the tiniest seed of madness, although *all* of them are in situations to drive one mad: Philoctetes—Oedipus—Antigone (between her father and her brothers!—her birth is impure, but her piety is pure)—Orestes

---

[1] Do I hold you in my arms?—May you hold me for ever.
[2] O most loved voice.
[3] Worthy of no man's help.

—even Ajax, after his unconscious delirium, is marvellously lucid. At no point is the human form broken. Electra: the triumph of purity over impurity . . . I shall always be consoled by reading this . . .

Modern life is *given over to excess*. Everything is steeped in it—thought as well as action, private life as well as public. (Sport: championships—pleasure to the point of intoxication and nausea—fatigue to the point of passing out—etc., etc., etc.). Hence the decadence of art. There is no more equilibrium anywhere. (Which means that Le Corbusier's efforts are vain . . .). The movement in Catholicism is a partial reaction against it: the Catholic ceremonies have at least remained intact. But then they are unrelated to the rest of life.

Seek for an equilibrium between man and himself, between man and things.

Every equilibrium has been upset. For example: between labour and the fruits of labour. Even the peasants have been corrupted indirectly by speculation . . . There is no longer any visible relation between action and its results, so that even in action man has become *passive*.

(This state of affairs must even be reflected—but in what way?—in love)

Curious problem of historical materialism: why is "Platonic love" so notably absent in our day? courts of love . . . Dante . . . Petrarch . . .

Magic. (Faust)

It should be possible to make science also an art, through this idea of equilibrium (with the conception of *scale* as intermediary)

(*very* important—but not very clear yet)

Quantity . . . (under the form of repetition . . .)

(take the lever as symbol . . .)

[*in the margin*] Beata cujus bracchiis
Pretium pependit saeculi,
Statera facta corporis
Tulit quae praedam Tartari.[1]

Individualize the machine...

Two tasks | to individualize the machine
          | „   „   science. (popularization).

After the collapse of our civilization, one of 2 things will happen: either it will perish completely, like the ancient civilizations—(except Greece and Rome), and...
or else it will adapt itself to a decentralized world.
it is not for us to prevent centralization (which is, by definition, irresistible), but to prepare for what will come after.
to *arrest* this process of centralization is impossible; it intensifies automatically and grows like a snowball. along that line there is no limit, but only *excess* and its consequences. at present these take the form of economic anarchy...
we possess the appropriate form of power (electricity) for individualizing the machine, but not the form for the machine. Therefore, starting from the machine-tool...
all the same, don't endow yourself with a mission. to begin with, there is every likelihood that you will die before making your voice heard—and even if you were listened to... (Descartes indirectly helped to inflict on us the popular press, the wireless, etc.—and aeroplanes, etc.). Anyway, one will have lived...

[*Here there is a page of texts on love from Latin and Greek poetry*: Lucretius, *De Rer. Nat.*, IV, 1089–1120 and 1133–4; Aeschylus, Frag. 44 (Nauck); Sophocles, Antig. 781–800; Sappho, 2 (Diehl); Horace, Carm. 11–12, 21–28; Horace, Carm, 1–22, 17–24; Horace, Carm. 1–9, 18–24. *Then*:]

---

[1] Blessed tree, on whose branches hung the ransom of the world! Thou wert made a balance for that body, and bore away the prey of hell.
Fortunatus of Ravenna.

To *respect* the thing that one desires—this is the source of piety, of art, of contemplation ... Platonism.

Plato. There are *only* two kinds of love: *tyrannical* love (Republic IX) and "Platonic" love. (Phaedrus).

One loves the soul when one no longer desires to acquire possession of the loved person. to oppose love for the body and love for the soul is too crude—the true opposition is between desiring slavery or freedom for the person one loves.

[*Here there are two quatrains of* Shakespeare: Sonnets, XVIII 1–4, and XCVII 1–4; *and* 4 *verses of the* Salve Regina; *then five pages of trigonometrical calculations. Then*:]

Difficulty. (Perceived by Descartes, but not clearly.)
1. that the method should never be confused with the result.
(progress: Diophantus—Vieta)
2. that the method should always appear with the result.

To ensure this: bear in mind always *what* the problem consists in—and *where* the crux of the difficulty lies.

History of algebra:

DIOPHANTUS

Problems. Before Diophantus they were posed in concrete forms (as riddles, sometimes in rhyme)—like the one that gives the age at which Diophantus died. "His childhood was one-sixth of his life; his beard grew after another twelfth; he married after another seventh; five years later he had a son who lived half as long as his father and died 4 years before him".

Diophantus almost always poses abstract problems whose data are ratios of sums, differences, products, and quotients, between numbers, square numbers or cube numbers.

Ex: find 3 numbers such that the square of each, less the sum ...

Find 3 numbers such that the product of any two of them is in a given ratio to their sum.

The problems are always posed in their most general terms and without figures. But for solving them Diophantus always chooses figures and performs the operations successively, one by one; so that the result shows no trace of the method by which it was reached.

The achievements of Diophantus (or, more truly, the

Greeks) ... the idea of the successive powers of the unknown quantity
> performing operations on the unknown quantity
> leading to identification of the unknown quantity with a known one
> Canonical form of the equation: none but positive terms.

In every problem one tries to reach an equation of two terms ($x^n = a$).

But Diophantus knows that one can also find the value of the unknown quantity when the equation has three terms. (lost passage).

He has no idea of the plurality of roots. He has no equations of the 3rd. degree, except those that are reducible to the 2nd., and one that can be solved immediately. (As regards equations of the 2nd. degree, those that have a positive and a negative solution have only one solution in his eyes. And for those that have 2 positive solutions he takes an auxiliary unknown. At least that is what he does for the classic problem of the sum and the product: he takes as an auxiliary unknown the half-difference of the two numbers, and thus arrives at an equation with 2 terms.

Diophantus evidently did not find the solution of the 2nd. degree equation through the relation between sum and product and between difference and product; for there is nothing to show that he had any idea of the relation of coefficients and roots. Or rather, he could not have had, since he had no idea of the plurality of roots.

Then how did he obtain that solution??? No doubt, by the square...

The Hindu and Arab algebrists also knew it, and there again we don't know how. (was it through him?)

⟨Nor is it known how the solution of the 3rd. degree equation was found, before the discovery of Diophantus' work⟩

The second achievement of Diophantus was the method of the regula falsi, which consists in substituting an arbitrary number for the unknown quantity. The problem is then worked out in terms of the arbitrary number, and the relation between the results obtained and the original data gives the relation between the arbitrary number and the true answer.

3. Παρισότης.[1]

---

[1] Equality (technical term in Diophantus).

VIETA.

1. Canonical form: on one side of the equation, the terms that include the unknown, arranged according to decreasing powers of the unknown, with 1 as first coefficient; on the other side, the known term.

Whence: implicit conception of an infinity of equations of increasing degree.

[*Then 12 pages of mathematical notes (trigonometrical calculations, imaginary numbers, developments in series, combinations and permutations), combined with a quotation from Paul Valéry* ("Certainly his remarkable memory . . . the value of the methods of an Edmond Teste") *and the following notes*:]

Inner difficulties: *laziness*—perversity—inner fury (ex. some months during 2nd. and 3rd. year in kh.[1]) how to eliminate as quickly as possible? solitude—temp. breaking of *all* links. physical fatigue—nature—abandon—physical labour—but *first of all* . . . infantile convulsions . . .

The replacement of the *industrial era* by the *financial era* consists essentially in the substitution of the acquisition of new capital, in place of the capitalization of profit, as the decisive factor for the growth of an enterprise—which puts an end to everything in capitalism that made for a well-organized productive system.

This led to the development of parasitism, which in turn . . . Weakness of slave economies:

rearing (of slaves) costly
life   (,,   ,,) short
labour (,,   ,,) unproductive.

Slavery only pays in so far as the slaves are *conquered* in mass (the supply was exhausted in the 2nd. century).

N.B.: serfdom *before* slavery. Source of slavery: wars of conquest. And source of serfdom? (cf. Egypt—Persia—pre-Homeric Greece . . .)

[1] *Khâgne*: final period in *lycée*, preparatory to the competitive examination for entry into the *Ecole Normale*.

Things to do:
draw up list of industrial enterprises
Indo-Chinese pamphlets
anti-gas measures
(Federal Union? ...)

Things to study:
Germany—in Caesar and Tacitus.
History of technology, as regards | nature (conservation of energy)
| the worker
History of exchanges between town and country, from the technical point of view, and study of the present situation (Michel?)

[*Then 3 pages of mathematical notes: combinations and permutations.*]

Faust: progress of the human mind from dream to reality. First, magic. "Du gleichst dem Geist, den du begreifst, nicht mir."[1] Passionate love, and crime. Then, when nature has healed the wounds, entry into the social world. Temptation of riches (paper money). Brief, but real, union with beauty (truer than love). Temptation of power: war. A more real power: domination of men in the struggle against nature. But this too is in essence an illusion. Full reality only at the end: repudiation of all magic. (Stünd ich, Natur, vor dir ein Mann allein, da wärs der Mühe wert, ein Mann zu sein—Dem Tüchtigen ist diese Welt night stumm. Was braucht er in die Ewigkeit zu schweifen! Was er erkennt, lässt sich ergreifen).[2] And finally, free co-operation of workers (Nicht sicher zwar, doch thätigfrei zu wohnen—Nur der verdient die Freiheit und das Leben, Der täglich sie erobern muss—Auf freiem Grund mit freiem Volk zu stehen[3]). With this, the world is discovered, love is

[1] You are like the spirit whom you comprehend, not like me.
[2] If I stood alone face to face with you, Nature, then it would be worth while to be a man—To the wise man the world is not silent. What need has he to stray into eternity? The things he knows are tangible.
[3] To live, not indeed safely, but free to act—He alone deserves freedom and life who has to win them each day—To stand upon free soil with a free people.

saved, at great cost paradise is attained. Faust is "the prehistory of man".

Math.
Can one not relate everything to:
1. the relation of straight line to number (thesis of Thales,— and of Pythagoras, incommensurables, algebraic equations)
2. the relation of curve to straight line (infinitesimal calculus; transcendental numbers (? yes: e, trigonometrical series, π); imaginary numbers (? pure artifice ...).

[*Then: one page of notes on the exponential function.*]

Rotation.
A business possesses fixed capital of 3000, which is totally exhausted in 20 years (will need to be totally renewed).
A circulating capital of 10 rotations per annum—each of which, therefore, corresponds to 15 units of fixed capital.
The circulating capital comprises 45 constant capital and 20 variable capital.
The surplus value is 100%.
Total of capital expended in 20 years: 3000 + 45 + 20 = 3065
Total of surplus value 4000
—If the circulating capital carried twice as much fixed capital, the latter would renew itself twice in 20 years: but the figures would remain the same. We should have 3000 + 45 + 20 = 3065.
But in this case the organic composition of the capital would have changed.
Suppose the constant capital in circulation is reduced to 30: in this case the organic composition has not changed. And we have:
c.c. = 3000 + 30 + 20 = 3050, surplus-value = 4000.
—If the total fixed capital is only 1500 and exhausts itself in 10 years, everything else being the same, we have in 20 years:
c = 1500 + 45 + 20 = 1565, surplus-value = 4000
Therefore it is necessary to take into account the rotation of the fixed capital.

But how does this rotation occur? One must assume there is an amortization fund.

But capitalism does not keep in a drawer for 20 years the money allotted for amortization.

How will it use it in the meantime? since the proportion of fixed to circulating capital is determined by *technological* considerations, and one cannot change into the other.

It is true then, as Dickmann says, that there is stagnation in the utilization of congealed labour. Fixed capital reproduces itself on an enlarged basis, but very slowly.

calculating machine = wheel with ten cogs ... one can make it function without needing to know this.
the functioning of machines ought *always* to be automatic.
science ought to be fully assimilated ...
so long as the possibility of such a transformation has not been precisely and concretely conceived ...
ex. machinery.
each lathe should *always* turn out the same pieces. There should be an automatic mechanism to set each piece in position, remove it at the right moment, replace it by another, ... and an automatic stop when a piece is spoiled.
power-loom: automatic repair of broken threads.
mine?
extended survey of past and present, both technical and theoretical.

at the present time, *normally* (apart from repairs and adjustments) men perform only those movements that do not require skill, and machinery performs those that do.

is it impossible for science to be universally assimilated, and combined with freedom in techniques? if so, there would be no point in worrying about the general problem of society; one could only try to live as honourably as possible within the framework of the existing society. (life would still retain all its meaning). But one must first be sure about it.

each act of labour should be accompanied by knowledge of all the human efforts (theoretical and technical) which have made and are making it possible. (in the meantime, bring together so far as possible ... by the theoretical and technical culture of the organized workers).

prepare in this way for a renewal of science and technique; impart it to a proletarian élite; and only then take power (but that stage does not concern us anyway).

to this end, create study groups of technicians, skilled workers, scientists, historians. Not public meetings for discussion . . .

in this way, there would still be some sense of action—though subordinate—one cannot give the best of oneself to a task so negative and so lacking in perspectives. the main task: to discover how it is possible for work to be free.

historical survey and view of possibilities.

[Only B———[1] can understand me. But he is not equipped for such a study. Neither am I. But those who are equipped are, by that very fact, not in a position to undertake it . . . He has as much time ahead of him as I. A much swifter intelligence].

L.D.'s[2] belief in the revolution—2 factors:

1. as they develop, the productive forces "rise up" against the limits imposed on them by a determined social form.

2. the development of the productive forces leads to communism, via socialism.

In Russia there is a phase equivalent to capitalism, to which the proletariat agrees to submit.

Study (in history) the relation between social oppression and the production of products which are not for immediate consumption.

Study the *motive* of such production before the stage of capitalist competition (war? religion?) and *machinery*.

Only 2 ways to ensure freedom: by suppressing surplus production (return to primitive conditions . . .). or by establishing the possibility of *voluntary* surplus production

(any society without surplus production is defeated in advance by a society which has it).

The calculating machine . . .

but the human accountant is no Pythagorean!

(both the machine and the man are piece workers).

---

[1] Formerly a leading intellectual in the French communist party and a member of the Executive Committee of the Comintern. Later, at the time when S.W. knew him, strongly anti-Stalinist.   [2] Trotsky (Leo Davidovitch).

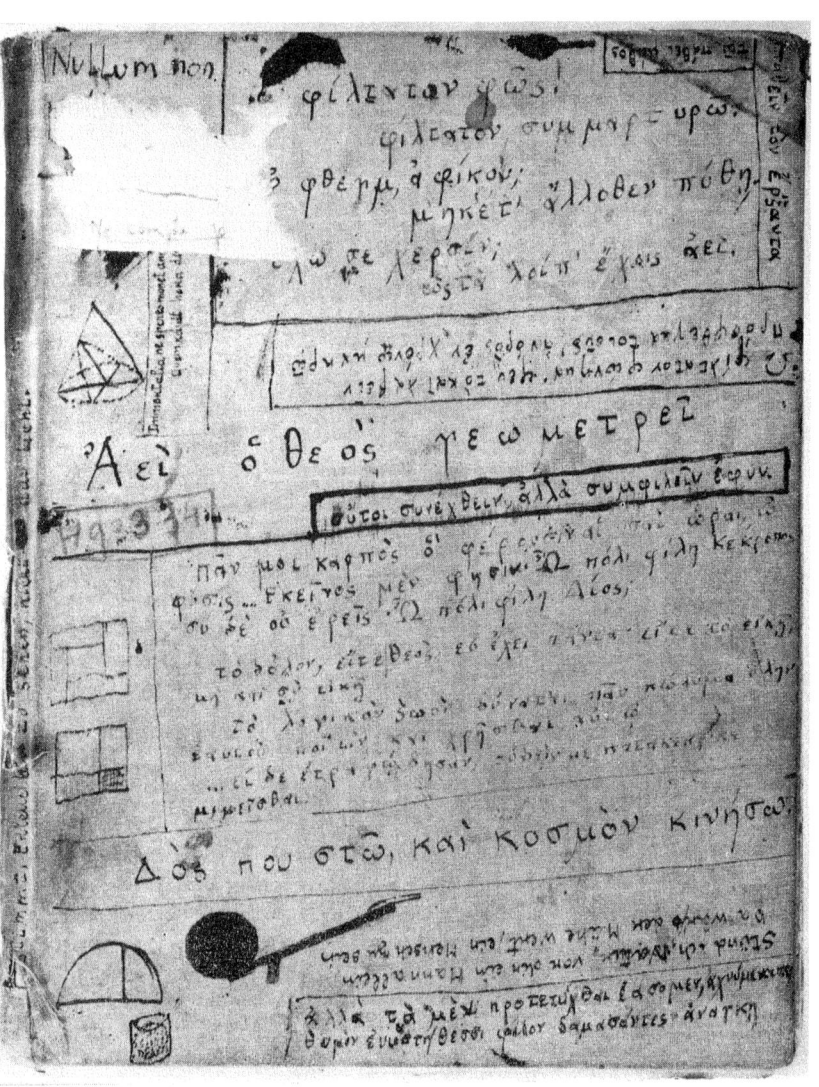

I Front cover of Pre-War Notebook

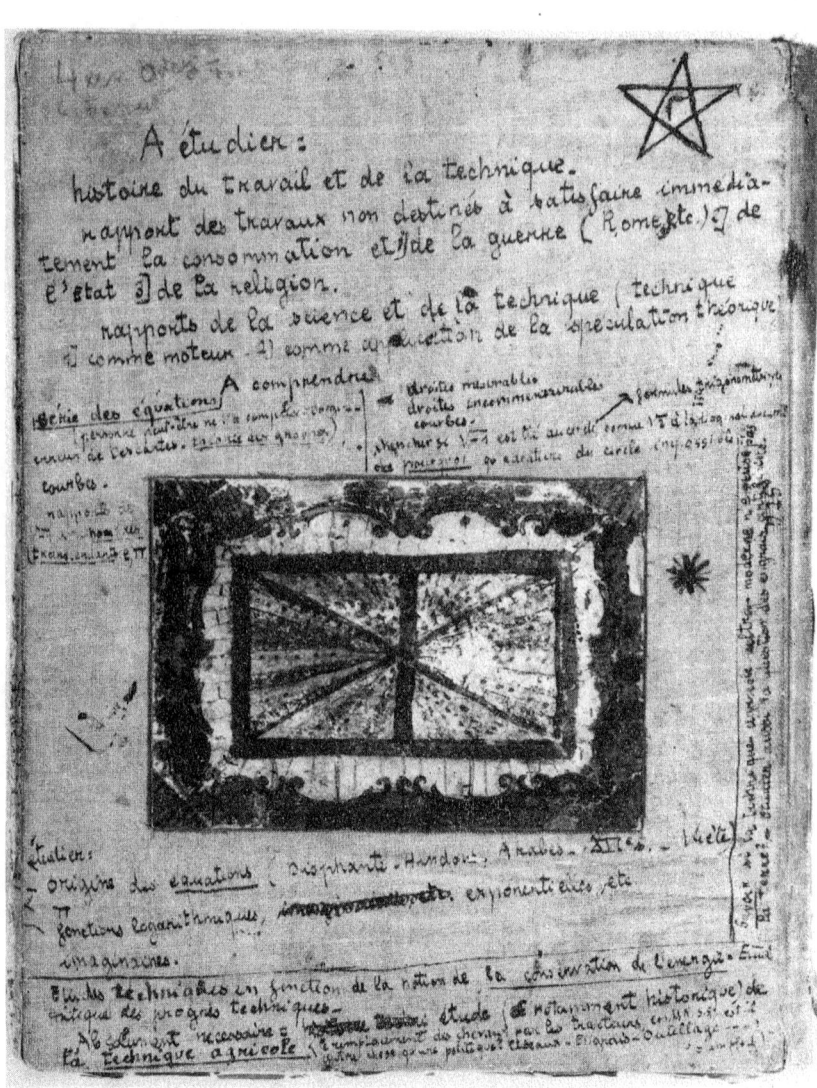

II Back cover of Pre-War Notebook
(See pp. 61–2)

The work process has always been external to the worker: 1) in the form of tradition—2) in the form of method, but materially fixed.

Concurrently, the purpose of the work has always been external to the worker.

    accountant: cut-and-dried recipes . . .

    calculating machine: method, but . . .

classify the operations of labour as they are related to human dignity.

Prepare for a conscious domination of man over matter

[N.B. *Simone Weil first wrote* "of man by matter" *and then corrected with the marginal comment*: "comic slip"]

The contemporary *unconscious* domination is turning against itself and is in process of destroying not only the spiritual but the material bases of contemporary civilization—(destruction of products—anarchy of the productive system—war).

To prepare for man's conscious domination is at present the only task worthy of attention. It is the only thing that is of practical interest (because all technical progress is now working against men [against *all* men, irrespective of class]), and of theoretical interest (because all scientific progress is only adding to the confusion).

[*in the margin*: prod. and techn. progress impoverish instead of enriching—scientific disc. obscure instead of enlightening]

In our day, everything else has lost its value. Production and technical progress . . . science . . . art . . . social action . . . Man has lost contact with himself and with the world. The only thing worth devoting oneself to . . .

⟨To give a meaning to the life of B . . .⟩

[*in the margin*: at the end of the first part: nothing at the present time has any value . . . (express in a few lines all [B's] sad thoughts about the present generation . . .) everything turns all the more against itself. Need for a completely new state of affairs in every way. But pious wishes are not a guide for action . . .]

This implies also historical study [for B . . .]—indicate sufficiently precisely . . .

    historical—scientific—technical studies.

(history of economics, technology, and the sciences). Finally, a programme for B and me . . .

naturally, we do not count on its being *possible*. But at least let us make sure whether it is or not; let us know what our limitations are. And even if it is impossible, it is still the only study worth undertaking . . .

Is there—apart from natural needs—any other human incentive except the desire for power?

Problem: to find an incentive, other than compulsion, for surplus production. It must not be devotion (for devotion goes with enslavement). Therefore it must be the conscious will. But for this it is necessary that the work process should not be external and alien to the worker; but this is just what the division of labour seems necessarily to imply.

And division of labour is indispensable if the work is to be 1) of relatively few hours a day, 2) methodical, and 3) productive not only of consumption goods but also of the means of production.

How can the work process of a whole factory become intelligible to each worker? and not in an abstract once-for-all way, but concretely in each act of labour?

The machine needs to be understood only for purposes of *adjusting* and *repairing* (and even for that there are cut-and-dried methods), and not for being *run*.

machine = method withdrawn from man and bestowed upon matter (method = co-ordination of movements).

The worker is a mere part of a huge organism, which nevertheless his thought should embrace as a whole.

there needs to be a technique in which (industrial) production would be purely automatic, and in which man would have only to *repair*, *adjust*, and *reproduce* the means of production.

Revolution presupposes not simply an economic and political transformation, but also a technical and cultural transformation.

in culture: science made assimilable for every man, and also its relation to practice.

in technique: the aim should be a system in which everything not calling for thought would be purely automatic—i.e. in which the machines could run without human intervention, and in which men would not need to run them or supervise them, but solely to adjust and repair them, and create new ones.

a machine is a methodical co-ordination of movements whose performance is entrusted to matter.

a man is the machine's slave when his actions do not presuppose a grasp of this methodical co-ordination.

a man is the machine's master when his actions do presuppose . . .

but in this there are degrees—what is desirable is that every worker should *need* to know how the whole enterprise functions—and even more . . . For there are 2 co-ordinates, in time and in space . . . co-ordinate in space: everything that can be prepared at this stage . . .

Article: 1st part. If we accept Dickmann's conclusions, the word revolution has always been employed hitherto as an empty word. So everyone makes it mean what he likes. For some: the development of production—or a catastrophe calling for sacrifice—or the abolition of work—or the abolition of everything that inhibits the free development of the instincts (surrealism) [*two lines illegible*]. 2nd part: historical sketch [*remainder illegible*]. 3rd part: what is revolution? [*remainder illegible*].

When the savages of Louisiana want fruit, they cut the tree down and pick it. That is what despotic government is.

"The true spirit of equality does not mean that everyone gives orders, or that no one receives orders; it means that one obeys or commands one's equals. It is not a question of having no masters, but of having only one's equals as masters". But people like to command their equals.

Subject for a novel: the ruin of the love of *production*. workers —Michel—the failure of the *industrial leader*.
[*Then a version of the poem*: "Si le ciel pur . . . "]

[*On the back of the cover of the notebook*:]
To be studied:
history of labour and of technique.
relation between productive work not intended to satisfy

immediate demand and 1) war (Rome, etc.) 2) the State, 3) religion.

relations between science and techniques (the latter as: 1) motive —2) application of theoretical speculation).

Try to understand:

theory of equations (perhaps not hitherto understood by anyone—origin—error of Descartes—*theory of groups*). curves—ratios—numbers (transcendentals, e, π).

measurable straight lines—incommensurable straight lines—curves—investigate whether $\sqrt{-1}$ is connected with the circle (trigonometrical formulas) as $\sqrt{2}$ is with the diagonal of the square—*why* it is impossible to square the circle.

study: origin of *equations* (Diophantus, Hindus, Arabs, 16th. century, Vieta); π, logarithmic functions, exponentials, etc.; imaginary numbers.

Technical studies related to the idea of *conservation of energy*. Critical study of technical progress.

Absolutely necessary: a study (with special reference to history) of *agricultural technique* (is the replacement of horses by tractors anything but a policy choice? Manure—Mechanical equipment...).

Confirm whether or not the advanced modern agricultural technique exhausts the soil? Study also the question of artificial manures.

II

PROLOGUE

Simone Weil left two almost verbally identical copies of this text. One of them was untitled and was preceded by this note: 'Beginning of the book (the book which should contain these thoughts and many others).' It appears at the end of the second volume of The Notebooks of Simone Weil *(Routledge). The following copy, without the introductory note, but with the title 'Prologue', was among the papers she left with Gustave Thibon on her departure for America in May 1942.*

He came into my room and said: "You poor wretch, who understand nothing and know nothing—come with me and I will teach you things you have no idea of." I followed him.

He took me into a church. It was new and ugly. He led me before the altar and said: "Kneel." I told him: "I have not been baptized." He said: "Fall on your knees before this place, with love, as before the place where truth exists." I obeyed.

He led me out, and up to a garret from whose open window one could see the whole town, some wooden scaffoldings, and the river where boats were unloading. He made me sit down.

We were alone. He talked. Now and then somebody else would come in, join in the conversation, then go away again.

It was no longer winter; it was not yet spring. The trees' branches were bare and without buds, in a cold air full of sunshine.

The light rose, shone bright, and then faded, and the stars and moon shone through the window. Then the dawn rose again.

Sometimes he paused and took some bread from a cupboard, and we shared it. That bread truly had the taste of bread. I have never found that taste again.

He poured wine for me and for himself, which tasted of the sun and of the soil on which that city was built.

Sometimes we lay down on the wooden floor, and the sweetness of sleep descended on me. Then I woke up, and drank the light of the sun.

He had promised me teaching, but he taught me nothing. We talked in a rambling way about all sorts of things, as old friends do.

One day he said to me: "Now go away." I threw myself down, clung to his knees, begged him not to send me away. But he flung me out towards the stairs. I descended them as if unconscious, as if my heart was torn in shreds. I walked through the streets; and then I realized that I had no idea where that house was.

I have never tried to find it again. I saw that he had come for me by mistake. My place is not in that garret. It is anywhere, in a prison cell, in some bourgeois parlour full of trinkets and red plush, in a station waiting-room. No matter where, but not in that garret.

Sometimes I cannot prevent myself from repeating, in fear and compunction, a little of what he said to me. How am I to know if I remember it correctly? He is not there to tell me.

I well know that he doesn't love me. How could he love me? And yet there is something deep in me, some point of myself, which cannot prevent itself from thinking, with fear and trembling, that perhaps, in spite of everything, he does love me.

III

NEW YORK NOTEBOOK
(1942)

The resurrection is Christ's pardon to those who killed him, the evidence that in doing him the greatest possible harm they did him no harm. Evil is only felt within a pure being; but in him it is not evil. Evil is something external to itself; and in the place where it is, it is not felt. It is felt where it is not. The feeling of evil is not an evil.

Evil being the root of mystery, pain is the root of knowledge.

The joy of Easter is not the joy that comes after pain, like freedom after chains, repletion after hunger, or reunion after separation. It is the joy that soars above pain and perfects it. In Gregorian chant, for example, the songs themselves make this clear (*Salve, festa dies* ...) Pain and joy are in perfect equilibrium. Pain is the contrary of joy; but joy is not the contrary of pain.

The man who receives and transmits malediction does not let it penetrate to his core. He does not feel it. But it penetrates to the core of the man upon whom it settles, the man who arrests it. He becomes a curse. To become a curse, it is necessary to be pure.

The plenitude of joy is necessary in order to make a being so pure that he can become a curse.

Pain and joy in alternation purify a being until he is pure enough to become a curse and to have at one and the same time the plenitude of pain within him and the plenitude of joy above him.

Atē runs on tiptoe over men's heads—until one man arrests her; then she enters into him.

In the *Iliad* no one arrests her

Prometheus arrests her.

Affliction passes over ordinary people (not redeemers, that is) without transfixing them. And yet it changes them. It breaks them.

P., who feels his affliction while he waits for the tram.

J.B., kept infantile by affliction, like children who don't grow because they are forced to an excessive task.

Round table. To sit at such a table is to abolish perspective, to be installed, without a point of view, in the universal.

Obviously, the essence of the story of the Grail is an identification of Christian thought with Ibero–Celtic traditions. In the *Queste del Saint Graal* Israel is regarded, in the tradition of Marcion and the Manichaeans, as the type of evil. Sarraz (Tyre? Sidon?) is the type of the spiritual city.

Circle and trinity. A circle is defined by three points. A straight line by two.

Already before the Passion, already by the Creation, God empties himself of his divinity, abases himself, takes the form of a slave.

Real and imaginary transferences. J.B.

Sensual desire and beauty. The need to crush inner impurity against purity. But what is mediocre in us resists in order to save its life, and needs to defile purity.

To get power over is to defile. To possess is to defile.

ἐξ ὕδατος καὶ πνευμάτος[1]—out of (composition)—Vegetable sap, synthesis of water and the sun's fiery energy by virtue of chlorophyll, enters into us and becomes blood (*Timaeus*). The Hebrews thought that blood is life. We have to decompose the synthesis, to decompose the life in us, to die, to become water again. Then supernatural energy combines with that water by the chlorophyll-like virtue of grace, and constitutes a supernatural life.

An order of men and women who would go as prisoners to prisons, etc.

Pomegranate seed which links irrevocably to God. To have perceived it is to have eaten it.

[1] from water and spirit.

B/Beau[1]—
real presence of God. But demoniacal art (hosts in the black masses).

Only the eternal is immune from time. Only a transcendent inspiration can produce a picture which would continue to sustain a prisoner in solitary confinement.

This is connected with the relation: invariant—variation (cube as perceived[2]) [Eternal/time ‖ Invariant/variation ‖ Necessary/possible ‖]

Republic 365a—sacraments

Love came down into this world in the form of beauty.

The object of science is the exploration of the beautiful *a priori*

Essays in Buddhism, Professor Tataro Suzuki, London, Luzac and Co., 46 Great Russell Street, 1933.

Harmony, κλείς, key.

Divine pain. Prometheus and Zeus.

The pain that opens the door.

[Transformation of heat energy into mechanical energy; does it really occur?]

Eskimoes. "In the time when the earth was enveloped in eternal night, the fox took advantage of the darkness to steal meat from men's larders. But the crow, who could not find food in the eternal night, desired light and the earth was lit up."

"Go to the dead and love them."[3]

Story of the recital of the Lord's name.

There is a good which is the contrary of evil; and there is one which is not.

To contemplate what cannot be contemplated (the affliction of another), without running away, and to contemplate the desirable without approaching—that is what is beautiful. [Many forms of running away.]

To uproot others. Ersatz of decreation.

[1] Presumably *Bien/Beau*: good–beautiful (cf. Plato).   [2] See pp. 88, 91.
[3] Words of Creon to Antigone.

Venise sauvée[1]—boredom in the background, for the conspirators.

Any plan that can be discerned in events, whatever it may be, is *one* of Providence's plans—among an infinity of others.

The vulnerability of precious things is beautiful, because it is a sign of existence. Blossom of fruit-trees.

In the same way, the vulnerability of the soul to cold, to hunger . . .

Once we know that something is real, we cannot be attached to it.

The way from cube to cube. Trace it (cube as perceived, invariant)

"That which is not manifested, but by which is manifested that which is."

God loves the perspective of creation which can be seen only from where I stand, and I obscure it.

Mathematics and distinction of levels.—[2] and verification.

A priori facts.

Necessity in the supernatural, and *routes*. Space, the supreme necessity. "I am the way." *More* necessity than in nature.

Three presences of God: creation, regulation, inspiration.

The beautiful = manifest presence of the real. τὸ ὄν. Joy, sensation of the real.

To be pushed by God towards one's neighbour as this pencil is pushed by me on the paper.

The sword equally evil (or good) at the hilt and at the point. Venise sauvée.

An order is an intermediary between a multiplicity [of conditions] and a thing.

In the world order—in the aesthetic order—what is that thing?

The void.

God.

In the same way: action made *solely* dependent on God. It is impossible to penetrate the good without penetrating the beautiful.

Chilian story of the husband who sucks blood . . . Napoleon's

---

[1] *Venise sauvée:* unfinished tragedy in 3 acts by Simone Weil (Gallimard, 1955).
[2] Illegible in the MS.

soldiers were precipitated towards death by supplementary energy. But so soon as vegetative energy appears and comes to the surface, the coldest egoism (unless there is supernatural grace). Then it is that there is no greater love than to give one's life for one's friends. Cross.
Cross and Antigone (burial alive).
Prometheus πυρὸς διδάσκαλος. ἑκόνθ᾽—φιλότητα βροτῶν—ἐξελυσάμην[1]—to desiccate—Διὸς φίλον—μὴ φρονεῖν—συμφορὰ διδάσκαλος[2]—

μηχανήματα[3]—
σοφιστήν[4]—
Zeus will lose his power.
Suppl. Ζεὺς ἑτερορρεπής[5]
China.
At the centre of the world there is a tree in whose proximity nothing gives an echo, in whose proximity nothing that is perfectly straight casts a shadow.

Phenomena of psychological transferences and combinations. If people were told: what makes carnal desire imperious in you is not its carnal element. It is the fact that you put into it the essential part of yourselves—the need for unity, the need for God.—They wouldn't believe it. To them it seems obvious that this quality of imperious need belongs to carnal desire as such. In the same way it seems obvious to the miser that the quality of desirability belongs to gold as such, and not to its exchange value. Reading.[6]

These combinations must be undone, one's own soul must be decomposed back into water and energy, and be born again from that.

To make the Christian faith palpable, it must be shown to be implicitly present, in a degraded form, even in the basest

[1] master of fire. willing—love for mortals—expired.
[2] friend of God—not to heed—affliction the teacher.
[3] devices. [4] sage. [5] Zeus the balance-swayer.
[6] 'Reading' (*lecture*) is used by S.W. as a technical term for the process by which the mind interprets what the eye sees.

passions. What we are talking to you about is the very thing you are longing for with your whole soul, at this moment, in your present state. But you give it a false name. Don't give it the name we suggest. Simply stop giving it any name at all. Persevere in this interior silence. And one day you will hear a voice that will tell you the true name.

Symposium, 196a.—Relation between beauty of form (εὐσχημοσύνη), proportion, and fluidity. (συμμέτρου καὶ ὑγρᾶς ἰδέας). Extremely remarkable. Perfect theory of Greek sculpture.

Fluid invariant.

196b—οὔτε αὐτὸς βίᾳ πάσχει, ἔι τι πάσχει, οὔτε ποιῶν ποιεῖ.

If he suffers, it is not by force. Prometheus. Passion. The perfect just man.

The wine used in the communion service is the blood of Christ. Oil is used in confirmation, which is concerned with the Spirit. Does Athena, issuing from the head of Zeus, correspond to the Spirit? In Hesiod, Zeus devours the pregnant Metis whose child, it has been prophesied, will be more powerful than himself. After which, Athena issues from his head (cf. the medieval image of a virgin knight as incarnation of the Spirit). In the myth of the Symposium, Poros is the son of Metis. Prometheus calls fire, symbol of the Spirit, by the name Poros. Metis, who is wisdom, is the same thing as Prometheus. "Qui ex Patre Filioque procedit."

The shield assimilated to the thunderbolt is Athena's attribute.

Link between the dove, symbol of the Spirit, and the olive-branch.

Water, wine (= blood), oil (= πνεῦμα). Baptism, communion, confirmation. (Oil plays a part also in baptism.)

According to one tradition it is Hephaestus and according to another it is Prometheus, who makes Athena emerge from the forehead of Zeus.

Tritogeneia—the third?[1]

Is it because of the inflammable nature of oil?

---

[1] Alternative explanations of this name of Athena are 'Triton-born' and 'head-born'.

Is the property of oil which makes it float on water connected with this symbolism?

B.[1] Order of words as related to a thought (logical and grammatical order). As related to persuasion (images, etc.).—As related to a transposition of sensibility.—But in poetry?
Explain what *transcendent technique* is.
The beautiful and Providence. The beautiful and the problem of evil.
The beautiful and pain (physical pain). Prometheus. Job.
"Harmony", "proportion", union of contraries.
Rhythm. Slow and fast. High and low. Gregorian chant.
Architecture. High and low. Heavy and light. Equilibrium.
Painting. Space. Distance. "What is the breadth . . . "[2]
Sculpture. Fluid statues. Plato.
The beautiful goes beyond our intelligence, and yet every beautiful thing presents us with something to be understood, not only in itself but in our own destiny.
The beautiful in nature. How does the notion of order apply?
"To be born from water and the πνεῦμα." Pain which separates the contraries.
Stoics. The seed is a πνεῦμα. The Holy Spirit having entered the Virgin is the seed of God.
Herodotus. Two sacred animals—sheep (ram)—goat.
Ram. Agnus Dei. Christ. Vernal equinox.
Goat. Aegis. Wind (αἰγίδες sometimes for winds)
—Athena, who alone of the gods has access to the thunderbolt.—olive tree—Holy Spirit—Winter solstice.
Panathenaea, every 4 years, on the 28th of Hecatombaeon.
First month of the Attic year, commencing July 15th. Therefore about the 15th August.

Aries	Taurus.	Twins.	‖	*Cancer.*	Leo–Virgo	‖
20 March	20 April	20 May		20 June	20 July 20 August	
Libra.	Scorpio.	Sagittarius	‖	*Capricorn.*	Aquarius	
20 Sept	20 October	20 November		20 December	20 January	
Pisces						
20 February						

[1] Beauty?   [2] Epistle to the Ephesians, III, 18.

If Christ was born at Christmas, he was conceived at Easter. Is it for that reason?

Pan, goat-god.

Bull, Osiris. Like ram.

Darkness. Tumult to imitate thunder. John and James "sons of thunder".

Goat's horn—Moon in the last quarter.

Pisces—Plaice of the *Symposium*?

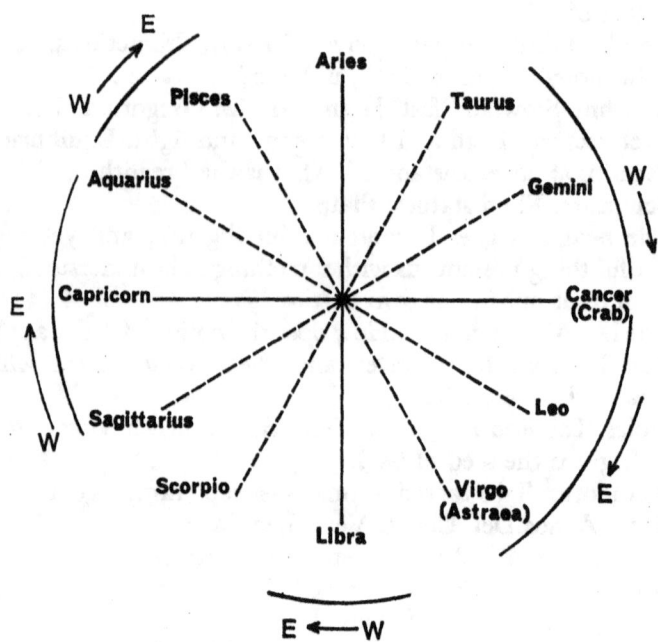

Suppliants' branch. Olive tree and wool.
Wool forbidden to the Egyptian priests.

      Aries — Libra
      Taurus — Scorpio
      Gemini — Sagittarius
      Cancer — Capricorn
      Leo — Aquarius
      Virgo — Pisces
      Libra — Aries

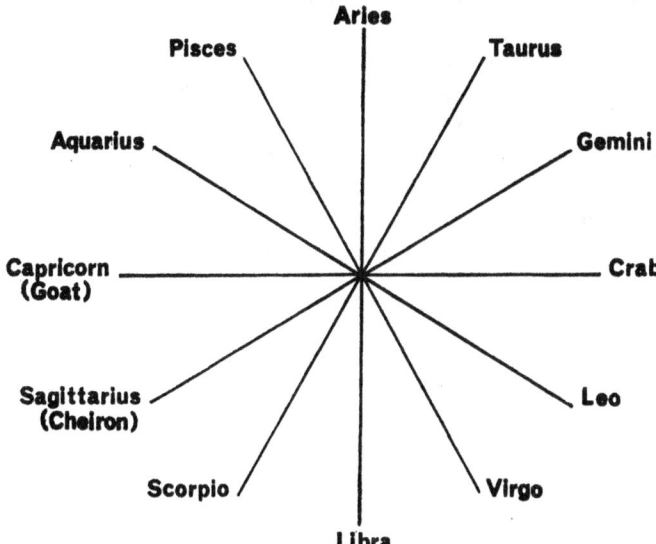

Charity. To love human beings in so far as they are nothing. That is to love them as God does.

The ontological proof from the beautiful is always applicable, because the beautiful is the real.

Order as condition of existence. The aesthetic order is a condition only for itself. But every thing is a condition for itself; so that is meaningless. What is that thing which is separated from itself by the 'condition of existence' relation? Image of God. That is what the real presence of God in the beautiful is.

Matthew, 24, 14—κηρυχθήσεται . . . ἐν ὅλῃ τῇ οἰκουμένῃ . . . "the great ocean of beauty". Celestial Aphrodite, born of the seed of heaven fallen on the sea (the seed is πνεῦμα) (The Spirit of God was on the waters). Baptism.

Etymology of the *Cratylus*.
Πέλοψ—πέλας—he did not see at a distance.
Τάνταλος—ταλαντεία—suspension (of the stone).
    ταλάντατον—the most wretched.
Ζῆνα—δι' ὅν ζῆν—
    ὁ θεὸς, δι' ὅν ζῆν ἀεὶ πᾶσι τοῖς ζῴοις ὑπάρχει.[1]

---
[1] Zeus—God, through whom life (to Zên) always begins for all living creatures.

Κρονος—κόρον σημαίνει, ὁν παῖδα ἀλλὰ τὸ καθαρὸν αὐτοῦ καὶ ἀκήρατον τοῦ νοῦ[1]
'Ουρανία—ὁρῶσα τὰ ἄνω.[2]
Θεού, from τὸυ θεῖν, because the first inhabitants of Hellas, like most barbarians still, regarded as gods only the sun and the moon and the earth and the stars and the sky—things that are always seen, ἀεὶ ἰόντα δρόμῳ καὶ θέοντα.
δαίμονας.
Hesiod, on the men of the golden age after their death ...

οἱ μὲν δάιμονες ἁγνοὶ ἐπιχθόνιοι καλέονται ...
ἐσθλοί, ἀλεξίκακοι, φύλακες θνητῶν ἀνθρώπων.[3]

....

Nicolas of Cusa—*Gandillac's book*.
St. Justin, *Apolog*, i, 59, 60.—Abelard, *Introduction à la théologie chrétienne* (Op. ii, 22)—Glaber Rodulfus (quoted in Reuter, *Relig. Aufklärung*, vol. I, book 2).
(Abelard assimilates the philosophers to the prophets.)
Bernardus Sylvester, who mingles the Bible and the *Timaeus*. Cf. Gilson, *Cosmogonie de B-S*. Thierry de Chartres, who cites as authorities Pythagoras, Plato and Hermes Trismegistos.
Festugière.
John of Salisbury, *De Dogmate phil*.
David of Dinant (heretic).
Amaury de Benes. Amauricians, make pagan wisdom equal to Christian wisdom—cf. Delacroix, *Mysticisme spécul.*, ch. 2.
Lull—(but he wanted to bring back everybody into the Church).
Alain of Lille. Hugh of Saint-Victor. St. Bonaventura. Meister Eckhart.
Rede von den 15 graden, German text of unknown date. Published by Schömann—God shown as teacher, shepherd, doctor, shopkeeper, father of family, innkeeper, traveller, soldier ... Spirituality for every condition of life.
Meister Eckhart, *Commentary on St. John*.
Proclus, in Parm., 735, 4.
Book of the 24 philosophers. (Published in 1913 by Bäumker.) Text of the late 12th century, attributed to Hermes Trisme-

[1] Chronos—means youth, not boy; his fitness and uprightness of mind.
[2] Urania—who sees the things above.
[3] the daemons ... valiant, defenders against evil, guardians of mortal men.

gistos (who is of the 2nd or 3rd century. Contains "God is an infinite sphere whose centre is everywhere and its circumference nowhere").
St. Bonaventura.
Angelus Silesius—German religious poems.
Boethius.
Giordano Bruno—*Opera* (ed. Wagner), Leipzig, 1830. *Le opere italiane* (ed. Lagarde) Gottingen, 1888.

B. A whole life determined by the unreality of a fact of war.

Things bestowed "gratuitously"—God gives us them both as a recompense and as a trial of love. When the master recompenses the slave, it is a more dangerous trial than when he leaves him unrecompensed. But by infinite mercy and as a warning he withdraws the things if we become attached to them. But little by little, not suddenly, so that love shall not be easy for us.

Hence the dependence of technology upon pure science, which has no technological purpose. The Russian experience. It is a warning.

Science—like every human activity—contains an original, specific way of loving God. And this is its destination, but also its origin.

Nothing can have as its destination anything other than its origin.

The contrary idea, the idea of progress, is poison. We are experiencing this. The root which, mixed with faith, has produced this fruit, ought to be torn up.

What would be the use of the scandals of our age unless they gave us some understanding which the middle ages didn't have? We are in need of a light which the middle ages didn't have. The task is greater.

If the origin of profane activities is supernatural, then Christianity did not begin with Christ.

Pure science is a contemplation of the order of the world as necessity.

Necessity appears only through the method of proof.

Obvious kinship between the idea of necessity and obedience. The relation of master to slave is necessity in human relations.

Kinship between necessity and certainty.

It was because of their faith—faith inspired by the love of Christ—that the Greeks had that hunger for certainty which made them invent the geometrical proof. It was because their mathematics was a theology that they wanted a certainty.

The steps leading out of the Cave were made for us, today.

That this mathematical necessity should be the substance of the world—that is the sign of our Father, the witness that necessity was conquered from the beginning by a wise persuasion.

To be contemplated further.

Before descending into the catacombs, Christianity should demonstrate that it is catholic. There is not a Christian point of view and other points of view; there is truth and error. It is not that anything which isn't Christian is false, but everything which is true is Christian.

The great error of the 13th. century, which paved the way for the Renaissance, was in its conception of the relations between natural and supernatural.

Orient science towards obedience and not towards power. But this *is* the orientation of pure science, which is contemplation of necessity.

Power is obedience degraded.

There is *only* Christianity and idolatry. And the social, in various guises, is the only idol.

(And Gide, surrealism, etc.? The "*I*" can also be an idol.)

The social and the ego are the two idols.

"Geometrical equality" makes a man equal to God. And that poor Callicles, who only wanted to be always acquiring more!

A bad number, not a square, such as 17 for example, may think it would be greater if it was 18. But it doesn't know that the secret, the creative principle of all greatness is nothing other than 1. By becoming 18 it moves further away. It degrades the 1 by reducing it to the plane of number. Its greatness resides solely in its identification with 1 by its own root, $\sqrt{17}$, which is mediation.

Each number has its own mediation within itself and outside itself.

The direction towards 18 is evil, ψεῦδος, φθόνος. The direction towards 1 is λόγος, ἀριθμός, ἁρμονία, ὁμολογία, it is truth, obedience, good.

Link between truth and obedience. Certainty is the obedience of the intelligence (and not, certainly not, submission to an external authority, even one that is accepted by faith).

The malaise of the intelligence in Christianity, throughout 20 centuries, comes from the failure to establish a satisfactory modus vivendi, based on a precise view of the analogies and differences, between the Holy Spirit speaking to the body of the Church and the Holy Spirit speaking to the soul.

The mystic Body is only a body. The soul in the state of perfection is the actual image of Christ.

συμφρόνησις . . . 3 thinking subjects.

"Love God." This can *only* mean the order of the world and one's neighbour, because, until he has come down and shown himself, we do not see God.

Aristotle. The incommensurability of the diagonal is demonstrated per absurdum, because, if it were commensurable, the even would be equal to the odd.

Therefore $\sqrt{2}$ is even and odd. λόγος ἄλογος—splendid!

The impossibility of finding n such that $\frac{1}{n} = \frac{n}{2}$, must be very old, of remotest antiquity.

[or rather m and n such that $\frac{m}{n} = \frac{n}{2m}$, a mean between a number and its double. In the infinite series of numbers, there is no m and n.]

Ratio conceived without the aid of the senses, and as certain as number.

Love of God and "non-acting action". Passage in Thucydides.

For God, the Creation consisted not in extending himself but in withdrawing. He refrained from "commanding wherever he had the power".[1]

[N.B. that the counterpart of our autonomy is blind mechanical necessity.]

The Creation, the Passion, the Eucharist—always the same movement of withdrawal. This movement is love.

[1] Thucydides: *Peloponnesian War*, 5, XVII, 105.

Man is like a castaway, clinging to a spar and tossed by the waves. He has no control over the movement imposed on him by the water. From the highest heaven God throws a rope. The man either grasps it or not. If he does, he is still subject to the pressures imposed by the sea, but these pressures are combined with the new mechanical factor of the rope, so that the mechanical relations between the man and the sea have changed. His hands bleed from the pressure of the rope, and he is sometimes so buffeted by the sea that he lets go, and then catches it again.

But if he voluntarily pushes it away, God withdraws it.

One should not speak to those in affliction about the kingdom of God, it is too remote from them, but only about the Cross. God suffered. Therefore suffering is a divine thing. In itself. Not because of compensations, consolations, recompenses. But the very suffering which inspires horror, which we endure against our will, which we seek to escape, which we beg to be spared. Affliction.

Καρποφοροῦσιν ἐν ὑπομονῇ

ὑπομένω—they will bear fruit in attentive patience (to attend—to bear a shock).

Just as those aggressors who know their business—like the Romans—put forward pretexts for war which nobody believes in, neither themselves nor others, but without which war would be either impossible or ill-omened, in the same way sin puts forward pretexts (illness, etc.) which we know are false but without which we could not commit the sin. What can one do about this?

Perfection of the heavenly Father seen in the order of the world: sun and rain, lily and bird.

Giants whose life is hidden away. "Your Father which is in secret."

"Friendship is an equality composed of harmony." Charity for the afflicted.

Test. Esp.,[1] etc.—Affliction constrains a man to ask continually "why?"—the question to which there is essentially no

[1] *Testament Espagnol?* (French translation of Arthur Koestler's *Spanish Testament*).

reply. So by means of it we hear the non-reply. "The essential silence..."

σωφροσύνη—purity.

The Son separated from the Father by the totality of time and space, by the fact of having been made a creature; this time which is the substance of my life—and of everybody's—this time so heavy with suffering, is a segment of the line that stretches, through the Creation, the Incarnation, and the Passion, between the Father and the Son.

Circle. Two immediately contiguous points. They touch, and they are separated by the whole circumference. Heraclitus.

Infinite circle. The circumference is a straight line. The two extremities of an infinite line make only a single point.

My life is a segment of that line. I am a part of the distance between the Father and the Son, that distance which the Holy Spirit travels. It is my misery itself that makes me the receptacle of the Holy Spirit. To become something divine, I have no need to get away from my misery, I have only to adhere to it. My very sins are a help to me, on condition that I know how to read in them the full extent of my misery. It is in the deepest depth of my misery that I touch God.

The distance which separates me from the earthly beings and objects I love is blessed, because it is an image of the distance between the Father and the Son. Only an image? Or is it not also a part of that distance itself?

(It also is made of time.)

Phaedrus—The beauty of an adolescent has only the "appellation" of beautiful. The beautiful in itself, visible to eyes here below, is the beauty of the world.

Of all the attributes of God, only one is incarnated in the universe, in the body of the Word; it is beauty.

The others can only be incarnated in a human being.

The presence of beauty in the world is the experimental proof of the possibility of incarnation.

When joy is a total and pure adherence of the soul to the beauty of the world, it is a sacrament (the sacrament of St. Francis).

(In the same way, mathematical beauty.)

[Apart from St. Francis, Christianity has almost lost the beauty of the world.]

Aristotle. Diagonal of the square. Even and odd.

What dignity it gives to the afflicted man who is succoured, to know that he can give Christ's thanks to his benefactor. ὑπομονῇ—water in Taoism—Stoics.

One of the most exquisite pleasures of human love—to serve the loved one without his knowing it—is only possible, as regards the love of God, through atheism.

Carnal love is a quest for the Incarnation. We want to love the beauty of the world in a human being—not the beauty of the world in general, but the specific beauty which the world offers to each man and which corresponds exactly to the state of his body and his soul.

The sea, a movement within immobility. Equilibrium as order of the world. Image of primal matter. χαῖρε κεχαριτωμένη.[1] In art. It appears to be in movement, and it is motionless. Music, the movement takes possession of all our soul—and this movement is nothing but immobility. As in the spectacle of a wave the moment when it begins to break is the very moment of concentration of beauty. The same in music.
The archaeological explanation of the immobility of Greek statues as a guild regulation, a choice example of contemporary stupidity.

The spiritual function of physical labour is the contemplation of things, the contemplation of nature.
Passing over to the eternal is, for the soul, an operation analogous to that by which, in perception, we refrain from putting ourselves at the centre of space although perspective makes us seem to be there. And, here again, it is the very condition for perception, the condition for seeing the real.

[1] Hail, full of Grace.

Worldly use of goods whose origin is supernatural (in my case, intelligence).—Fairy gold which turns into dead leaves.
Parable of the castaway clinging to his spar.
To annul perspective in time as we do in space. Eternity.
Hence the power of memory, of ancient things, etc.

Hela.[1] U. r.
Catholic University, N.Y.
Serpent: on account of the moon? Cf. Varro: "hinc Epicharmus Enni Proserpinam quoque (sc. lunam) appellat quod solet esse sub terris; dicta Proserpina, quod haec ut serpens modo in dexteram modo in sinisteram late movetur".[2]
The two symmetrical crescents of the moon lead to the serpent.[3]
The serpent of brass.
Knight of Narbonnese Gaul executed for worshipping serpent's egg under . . . (Hermann).

Résumé of paper for P.P.[4]
Mathematical truth was originally theological (Philolaus). Mediation for non-square, unjust numbers (Aristotle). *Logoi alogoi*, scandal, absurdity. Passage in *Timaeus* on geometrical mediation. *Epinomis*. Natural law, function and proportion.
Invention of demonstrative proof (the soul of our science, including the experimental method), due to the Greeks' need of certainty in regard to divine things, even in the images of them. Numbers, privileged image of divine things, because of their certainty. But real number is better. Certitude and non-representability. Introduction to faith.
Gradation from the less to the more certain and from the more to the less representable. Mathematics as intermediary. Both a résumé of the mechanism which governs matter and an

---

[1] Norse goddess of death?
[2] Hence Ennius's Epicharmus calls her (the moon) also Proserpina, because she is wont to go underground and because she moves widely now to the right and now to the left, like a serpent.
[3] This presumably means that the two opposite crescents, if superimposed, make the S-shaped symbol of the serpent.
[4] Père Perrin?

image of divine things; and at the same time it is centred upon mediation.

Poetry of prodigies. Revelation.

We have lost this need of certainty about divine things.

The need of rigour in mathematics has recently become felt again. This might point the way. For mathematics has no object.

Use of mathematics for making felt the possibility of certainty about what one does not understand. Shape mathematics for this use.

(koan. We are only certain about what we do not understand. We only see what is opaque.)

Providential arrangement which prevents mathematics from foundering in technique.

φιλίαν εἶναι ἐναρμόνιον ἰσότητα[1]

1. Trinity. ἁρμονία, δίχα φρονεόντων συμφρόνησις[2]

Proof of the Trinity. The subject is God. But in him is the object and the link between the two. And each of these things is "I am".

Equality between one and several, between one and two.

(one, ἀρχή and first compound, Phil.)

St. Augustine, *aequalitas, connexio*.

2. Opposition between creator and creature, limiting and unlimited. Second pair of contraries in God (*Philebus*). The most beautiful harmony: maximum of separation and of unity. That a divine Person should be a thing, a piece of inert matter (a man who is a slave and in agony). Christ's agony. "Why hast thou forsaken ... "—Christ has many young brothers.

Limit = number. *Philebus*: one and many (Trinity), limit and unlimited (creation). Number, geometrical mean. *Philebus*: this hierarchy reappears in all study. Intelligence, image of faith.

[Passage to the limit, solution of insoluble difficulties. Ex. agony of Christ.]

δίχα φρονεόντων "My God, why hast thou ... ?"—συμφρόνησις one single God. Love that passeth all understanding.

3. Friendship between God and man. Harmony as geometrical mean. Mediation. *Timaeus, Symposium, Epinomis*, St. John. Friendship, geometrical equality in the *Gorgias*. "None

---

[1] Friendship is an equality composed of harmony. (Philolaus.)
[2] Harmony, the common thought of separated thinkers.

enters here unless he is a geometer." ὁ θεὸς ἀεὶ γεωμετρεῖ[1] (double meaning). Geometry, first of the prophecies. That is why science has become diabolical. True relation of science to charity, analogous to Gregorian chant.

Rigour of demonstration is to science what stone is to sculpture.

4. Friendship between men. In nature, either I am at the centre (perspective) or another person is, who dominates me by brute force, and the rest is simply pieces of the universe, apart from the execeptional case of natural justice (Thucydides, Athenians and Melians).[2]

Friendship is identical with supernatural justice. Christ, mediator between men.

"We"—collective feeling, false friendship, without harmony, because here the terms involved are of the same kind, the same origin, the same rank.

Supernatural justice, an operation analogous to the overcoming of perspective. No centre anywhere in the world, only outside the world. Through love of God, to renounce the illusory power he has left to us of saying "I am". Not by transferring it to Him, as some do, and as Oenone transferred it to Phaedra or Pylades to Orestes. For the true "I am" of God is infinitely different from our illusory one. Renunciation without transference. That is the love of God. But since every human thought which is real has some concrete object in this world it appears first as love of the world's beauty or as love of one's neighbour. And renunciation is the abandoning of all goods in order to follow Christ. Social goods are no more than reinforcements to the power of saying "I". Acceptance of poverty: "He who would become invisible ..."[3]

Harmony here is unity between contraries. Contraries: myself and the other. Unity only in God. Justice and love (of one's neighbour) identical.

God is mediation between God and God, between God and man, between man and man. Unique harmony.

Christ always present between two real friends. Reciprocally,

[1] God is ever doing geometry (measuring).
[2] Cf. *Waiting on God*, pp. 84-5. The Athenians' "lucidity of mind in the conception of injustice is the light which comes immediately below that of charity". It is "natural justice".
[3] Spanish proverb: He who wishes to become invisible has only to lose all his money.

the saying "Where two or three . . . " is the promise of human friendship to his friends.

5. Harmony in things. 1) between things and God. 2) between things. In both cases mediation is the limit, which is also λόγος and ἀριθμός. Things, including men in so far as they are natural beings (including me).

The opposition limit—unlimited includes all the theories of knowledge.

Philolaus. Number gives a body to things. Gnomon, i.e. invariant and variation group. Cube (Lagneau). The cube is truly the body of the box. The reality of the sensible universe is mathematical necessity. Theory of perception. Matter is simply support for necessity which, in so far as it is conditional, requires support.

Necessity: ensemble of laws of variation which are determined by fixed and invariant ratios.

Reality = contact with a necessity. (contradiction): necessity is not tangible. Harmony, mystery.

Cube, transcendent in relation to the various appearances of the box.

Necessity, being conditional, is supported by a matter (*Timaeus*) of which water (baptism) is the image. Sea,[1] mother,[2] matter, Mary . . . The essence of necessity (variation and invariant) is function. Function, proportion, λόγος, ἀριθμός.

Necessity, enemy for the man who says "I". A slave in our day-dreams (or by the effect of social domination), it becomes a brutal master in affliction. But a natural equilibrium appears at the optimum point, which is methodical action. (The same three relationships exist between men.) This equilibrium combined with natural justice would be natural felicity. The legislator's aim.

But this equilibrium is only a semblance. The state of fatigue reveals the fact. The human will, too, is an inert thing.

In the practical experience of necessity, the exercise of will always involves illusions. It is only when considered as theoretical and conditional that necessity is pure thought. For the human element is then absent, except in the actual work of thinking. All concrete knowledge of facts, including human facts, is the recognition of a necessity in them, either a mathematical necessity or something analogous.

[1] Mer.   [2] mère.

(And always in some specific form. Analogy with incarnation.)

In this way, necessity becomes related to man, not as master to slave, or as an equal, but as a picture which is looked at. It is in this looking that the supernatural faculty of consent comes to birth. It is not to force as such (because it compels) that consent is given, but to force as necessity. Pure intelligence is at the intersection of nature and the supernatural.

This consent is a folly which responds to the triple folly of God (Creation, Incarnation, Passion) but, to begin with, to the first of the three.

Λόγος, name of Necessity, given to the Beloved—Light and rain in the Gospel, stoicism.

Necessity, mediator between the natural part of us and the supernatural consent.

Conceived, by analogy, as mediator between matter and God. Creation *and* ordering activity. Zeus and Bacchus. Myth of Chaos. Necessity, willed in a higher degree by God.

Mediator between thing and thing. Anaximander. Oscillating disequilibrium, equilibrium refracted in time.

God mediator between
- God and God
- God and man
- Man and man
- God and things
- One thing and another thing
- Myself and myself

God is mediation and, in itself, everything is divine mediation. Analogically, for human thought everything is ratio, λόγος. The ratio is the divine mediation. The divine mediation is God.

"Everything is number."

God thinks necessity. It has being because he thinks it. The thought of God is his Son.

The order of the world in God is the ordering factor. In God everything is subject.

In itself, in isolation, every phenomenon is a principle of destruction for the universal order. But through connection the totality of the universal order is present in it.

The "I" keeps us confined within necessity as we are confined between the vault of the sky and the surface of the earth.

We see that face of it which represents brutal domination. By renouncing the "I" we pass to the other side, from within the egg of the world we pierce the shell. Then we see the face of necessity which represents obedience. We become children of the house and we love the slave's docility.

Necessity—freedom; obedience is their unity.

Necessity, obedience of matter to God.

The idea of miracle is meaningless.

One consents to necessity before knowing that this consent is what pierces the shell. God consents for us, within us.

The natural part of us remains inside the egg.

What a horizontal plane is to its two faces, so necessity is to domination and obedience.

As necessity in God is thinking Person, in us it is thought in act, ratio conceived, proof by demonstration (Spinoza).

1 and 1 do not make two unless there is addition.

Attention is what creates *necessary* connections. (Those which do not depend upon attention are not necessary.)

Participation of necessity in compulsion, on the one hand, and in intelligence, justice, beauty, faith, on the other (symbolic language of divine truths—circular and alternating motion,—$\sqrt{2}$ odd and even, etc.)

Attention of the intelligence, image of Wisdom.

Intelligence, intersection of nature and the supernatural. Produces a semi-reality (conditional necessity). Love (consent) produces reality.

Beauty, pure joy: complicity of the body and the natural part of the soul in the faculty of supernatural consent. Indispensable, even for those whose vocation is the Cross.

Feeling for the beautiful—a feeling, which is perceptible to the carnal part of the soul and even to the body, that this necessity which is compulsion is also obedience to God.

Image of the mysteries of faith in mathematics. Mathematics is a rational and abstract science; the concrete science of nature is mystical.

The universe, compact mass of obedience with luminous points. Everything is beautiful.

And also everybody (small mass, a point). Water and spirit.

Mysterious influence upon nature (but without violating laws) of the presence of supernatural love.

Philolaus. Key.

Philebus. Pain and joy. Pain and revelation of the beauty of the world: Job.

Beauty—Operation of pure intelligence in the conception of theoretical necessity, and incarnation in the concrete knowledge of the world and technique.—Flashes of justice, compassion, and gratitude between men. Three supernatural mysteries constantly present in the very midst of nature.— Three gates opening towards the central gate which is Christ.

For us, everything is relation.

In itself, everything is mediation, divine mediation. God is mediation. All mediation is God.

Supreme mediation, the harmony between Christ's "Why?" (ceaselessly repeated by every soul in affliction) and the silence of the Father. The universe (ourselves included) is the vibration of this harmony.

(The only way really to understand the universe and the destiny of men, and in particular the effect of affliction upon the souls of the innocent, is to conceive that the universe was created to be the Cross and men to be the brothers of Christ crucified.)

Comparison with the cube and the cubical box will prevent the danger of pantheist error in the above comparison.

To touch God in this way in and through everything.

Flight of Christ into Egypt. The hidden infancy of Dionysus, of Orestes...

Christ. Theme of the robber. Theme of the slave. Theme of the vagabond.

Christ must have been entirely present wherever there was affliction. Otherwise, where would be the mercy of God?

Sacraments. Things by hypothesis absolutely pure, for consuming impurities.

Unbelievers, periods of doubt in believers. Refuse to give one's love to anything else (folly!)—$\dot{\epsilon}\nu$ $\dot{\upsilon}\pi o\mu o\nu\hat{\eta}$.

Probably infernal period for Christianity under the Antonines, doubtless the result of earlier persecutions on the one hand and, on the other, of the expectation of the end of the world.

Power of prayer on the soul. If one believes one will receive, the very fact of asking is an act. So the words themselves are acts. That is why they are hard to speak.

Proof by the first cause. The only legitimate proof is that we have this idea and this strange, absurd need of a first cause.

Why not an analogous argument from the final end?

And proving that the first cause and the final end are one and the same?

What there is in man which is the very image of God is something within us which is attached to the fact of being a person, but which is not the person. It is the faculty of renouncing the person. It is obedience.

Among men, the slave does not become like the master through obeying him. On the contrary, the more submissive the slave is, the more he differs from the one who commands.

But between man and God, in order to make himself, so far as in him lies, altogether like the Almighty, as son to father, as image to model, the creature has only to make himself perfectly obedient.

This knowledge is supernatural.

Necessity.
Mathematics. Limited, enumerable, definite terms. Abstract. Links established by us: ratios. Image, created by our attention, of the necessity which is the substance of the world but which, as such, is only felt by us in the form of blows.

Friendship. So long as we are seeking some good in a human being, the conditions for friendship are not present. He must have become necessary, he must be a need. We are then at his mercy, and we want him to be at ours. But if, nevertheless, we still want him to keep the faculty of free consent, there is Pythagorean harmony. That is friendship.

The love of one's neighbour is supernatural when there is some natural necessity which opposes our desire that he should keep his freedom of consent, when nature establishes relations of necessity between us and him.

Analogy between friendship and begging.

Morality (secular) and religion; effort (or will) and desire.

Love, in every sphere, is only real when it is directed to a particular object. It is only by virtue of analogy and transference that it can become universal without ceasing to be real.
This is what Plato meant in the *Symposium*.
Study of analogy and transference. Mathematics. Philosophy. Relation of this study to love.
Ποιοῦντες ἀλήθειαν[1] (St. John). Maat. Translated from Egyptian?

Eucharist. Convention which effectively works. Purity which is unconditioned (by hypothesis, in the sense used in geometry) and real. Harmony.
Obedience. Passive activity. Id.
The giant's stone and the little tailor's bird. Will and grace.
In art and science of the 1st. order, creation is self-renunciation.
God . . .
Non-Euclidean geometry. Parallel lines meet if one regards the infinite as finite. Orders of infinity. Cantor.
Sixth Eclogue. Symbol of Pan (λόγος) surprised when asleep by shepherds, tied up, and buying his liberty with a poem.
This is the Mallarmé conception of poetry.
Plato's idea about the Sovereign Good is that it contains all the goods. Therefore you cannot renounce a partial good for love of the absolute good without finding this partial good again, in its specificness, in at least an equal degree of intensity.
(You will find it increased a hundredfold.)
This is the meaning of the *Philebus*.
Waves. Whole and parts—Same and Other—
Horizon in mid-ocean. We are encircled by our own vision.
Pan, god of shepherds. Shepherds at Christmas.
Vocation of labourers: the contemplation of things.

Mercy is a specifically divine attribute. There is no human mercy. Mercy implies an infinite distance. One does not feel pity for what is close at hand.
Jaffier.[2]

---
[1] performing the truth.
[2] Hero of Simone Weil's unfinished tragedy, *Venise Sauvée*.

Mercy comes down from what is not suffering to what suffers.

In order to be merciful, one must have a point of impassibility in one's soul.

And all the rest of it exposed defencelessly to the hazards of fortune.

The compassion one feels for the afflicted is the compassion felt, in affliction, by the impassible part of one's own soul for the part of it which feels. The compassion Christ felt for himself when he said: "Father, if thou be willing, remove this cup from me ... My God, why hast thou forsaken me?" The silent compassion of the Father for Christ.

This self-compassion is what a pure soul feels in affliction. A pure soul feels the same compassion for the affliction of others.

The love which unites Christ abandoned on the Cross to his Father at an infinite distance dwells in every saintly soul. One point in this soul is always with the Father. "Where your treasure is, there will your heart be also." The sensitive part is always exposed to the torture of affliction. In such a soul the dialogue of Christ's cry and the Father's silence echoes perpetually in a perfect harmony.

Before an afflicted man, this soul immediately responds with the true note. "My Father, why have you forsaken him?" And in the centre of the soul the Father's silence replies.

"Why has it been allowed that he should go hungry?" While one's thought is occupied by this question, one proceeds automatically to find bread for him.

When the act is performed thus, the afflicted man is dispensed from gratitude, because it is Christ who thanks.

"Father, why ... ?" God accuses himself for Christ's Passion. "He that delivered me unto thee hath the greater sin ... "

One can only excuse men for evil by accusing God of it. If one accuses God one forgives, because God is the Good.

Amid the multitude of those who seem to owe us something, God is our only real debtor. But our debt to him is greater. He will release us from it if we forgive Him.

Sin is an offence offered to God from resentment at the debts he owes and does not pay us. By forgiving God we cut the root of sin in ourselves. At the bottom of every sin there is anger against God.

If we forgive God for his crime against us, which is to have made us finite creatures, He will forgive our crime against him, which is that we are finite creatures.

By accepting that we are creatures we win freedom from the past.

Just as God, through the mouth of Christ, accused himself of the Passion, so we should accuse God for every human affliction. And just as God replies with silence, so we should reply with silence.

Compassion presupposes that the spiritual part of the soul has transported itself to God and that the carnal part is left naked, without clothes or protection, exposed to every blow. Because of this nakedness, the mere presence of a man in affliction makes it sensitive to the possibility of affliction.

The imperfect use the spiritual part of their soul as clothing for the carnal part. When the spiritual part has transported itself to God, the rest is left naked.

Christ, nailed naked to the Cross, exposed to the spears.

To be no longer aware of oneself except as a thing vowed to obedience.

To live naked and nailed to the Tree of Life.

To act only under compulsion, or from natural necessity, or by a strict obligation, or by an irresistible order from God, or by a lively natural inclination. Then the "I" will perish of inanition.

Where no direction is imposed either by necessity or by obligation or by God, follow inclination.

Form the habit of always doing what one thinks one is obliged to.

I would like to achieve this without effort.

If I could find the point of emergence of the root of errors, and sever it at a blow. Then there would only remain the painful labour of overcoming bad habits. And there is also perversity.

ἀπεθάνετε, καὶ ἡ ζωὴ ὑμῶν κέκρυπται σὺν τῷ Χριστῷ ἐν τῷ θεῷ[1]

One can only love one's neighbour with a compassionate love. It is the only just love.

Even in οὐαὶ ὑμῖν,[2] there is compassion.

Love men as the sun would love us if it could see us.

δειλοῖσι βροτοῖσιν.[3]

[1] For ye are dead, and your life is hid with Christ in God (Colossians 3: 3).
[2] Woe unto you...
[3] to wretched mortals.

The sun as a thinking being is the model of perfection.

How many ways God has of giving himself!

Compassion makes love equal for everybody. Contempt for crime and admiration for greatness are balanced in compassion.

The dogma of the Trinity is necessary so that there may not be dialogue between us and God, but between God and himself within us. So that we may be absent.

God dwelling in food. Lamb, bread. In matter worked by human labour, bread, wine.

That ought to be the centre of peasant life. By his labour, if he so intends it, the peasant gives a little of his flesh so that it may become the flesh of Christ.

He should be a consecrated man.

Sanctity is a transmutation like the Eucharist.

For a man to be really inhabited by Christ like the host after consecration, the man's flesh and blood must first have become inert matter, and in addition nutritive for his fellows. Then, by a secret consecration, this matter can become flesh and blood of Christ. This second transmutation is only God's affair, but the first is partly ours.

It is sufficient to regard one's flesh and blood as inert matter, insensible, and nutritive for others.

"Don't heed yourself", "needs must"—there is the seed of this in the stoicism of the people.

If I grow thin from labour in the fields, my flesh really becomes wheat. If that wheat is used for the host it becomes Christ's flesh. Anyone who labours with this intention should become a saint.

God created me as a non-being which has the appearance of existing, in order that through love I should renounce this apparent existence and be annihilated by the plenitude of being.

Faith should be integrated with the people's stoicism. It has never been done. The least fortunate should be spiritually invested with the freedom of the Christian city.

Are there not more princes than peasants in the roll of the saints?

God created me as a non-being which has the appearance of existing, in order that through love I should renounce what I think is my existence and so emerge from non-being. Then there is no "I". The "I" belongs to non-being. But I have not the right to know this. If I knew it, where would be the renunciation? I shall never know it.

Other people are illusions of existence for themselves.

This way of regarding them makes their existence not less but more real for me. For I see them as they are related to themselves, and not to me.

In order to feel compassion for someone in affliction, the soul has to be divided in two. One part absolutely removed from all contamination and all danger of contamination. The other part contaminated to the point of identification. This tension is passion, com—passion. The Passion of Christ is this phenomenon in God.

Unless there is a point of eternity in one's soul which is proof against any contagion by affliction, one cannot have compassion for the afflicted. Either one is kept far away from them by difference of situation and lack of imagination, or else, if one really approaches them, pity is mixed with horror, disgust, fear, invincible repulsion.

Every movement of pure compassion in a soul is a new descent of Christ upon earth to be crucified.

Souls which are absorbed in God without feeling compassion for human misery are still climbing and have not reached the stage of descending again (even though they apply themselves to good works).

A single piece of bread given to a hungry man is enough to save a soul—if it is given in the right way.

It is not easy to give with the same humility that is appropriate for receiving. To give in the spirit of one who begs.

It is necessary at the same time to know that one does not exist and to wish not to exist.

Humility is the root of love.

Humility exerts an irresistible power upon God.

If God had not been humiliated, in the person of Christ, he would be inferior to us.

Hunger (thirst, etc.) and all carnal desire is an orientation of the body towards the future. The whole carnal part of our soul is oriented towards the future. Death freezes it. Privation is a distant likeness of death.

The life of the flesh is oriented towards the future. Concupiscence is life itself. Detachment is death.

"Terit carni superbiam—potus cibique parcitas."[1] It is the pride of the flesh to believe that it draws its life from itself. Hunger and thirst oblige it to feel its dependence on what is outside. The feeling of dependence makes it humble.

Io, the wandering maiden, and the Gypsies' moon.

Find in Origen: Matthew, 5, 45-48 (be ye perfect...)

Postulate: what is inferior depends on what is superior.

There is only one unique source of light. Dim light does not consist of rays coming from another source, which is dim; it is the same light, degraded.

In the same way, mysticism should provide the key for all knowledge and all values.

The key is harmony (Philolaus).

Christ is the key.

All geometry proceeds from the Cross.

The beautiful is the contact of the good with the faculty of sense. (The real is the same thing.)

The true is the contact of the good with the intelligence.

All goods in this world, all beauties, all truths, are diverse and partial aspects of one unique good. Therefore they are goods which need to be ranged in order. Puzzle games are an image of this operation. Taken all together, viewed from the right point and rightly related, they make an architecture. Through this architecture the unique good, which cannot be grasped, becomes apprehensible.

All architecture is a symbol of this, an image of this.

The entire universe is nothing but a great metaphor.

In astrology, etc., we see a degraded reflection of this understanding of the universe as metaphor, and perhaps an attempt—but an illegitimate one (it seems to me)—to get material proof of it. Alchemy also.

To beseech, this means that one waits for life or death to be dealt by something outside oneself. Kneeling, with head bent so

[1] Scarcity of food and drink wears down the pride of the flesh.

that the conqueror may more conveniently strike it off, hands touching his knees (but, more likely, originally raised above them) so as to receive from his compassion the gift of life, like the seed of a father. A few minutes pass like this in silence. The heart empties itself of all its attachments, frozen by the imminent contact of death. A new life is received, which is made purely of mercy.

That is how one should pray to God.

Waiting patiently in expectation is the foundation of the spiritual life.

Filial piety is simply an image of the attitude to God.

If a soul cried to God its hunger for the bread of life, incessantly, indefatigably, like a new-born child whom its mother forgets to feed . . .

May those cries which I raised when I was a week or two old continue incessantly within me for that milk which is the seed of the Father.

The Virgin's milk, the Father's seed—I shall have it if I cry for it. The cry is the first resource granted to a human being. What we could never get by work, we cry for. The first nourishment flows from the mother and is given in response to the child's cry; there is no question of work.

The milk of the Virgin is the beauty of the world. In its aspect of beauty the world is perfectly pure.

Justice—when perceived as beautiful the world appears perfectly just. The Virgin is Justice. The Virgin of the Zodiac, holding a ear of corn. Cosmic Virgin in the Apocalypse. The Virgin is the creation, under the aspect of purity.

(Once a living woman was pure to the same extent as the purity of creation regarded as such. At least—perhaps . . .)

Truth—the beauty of the universe is the sign that it is real.

Deuteronomy, 12, 23. "Only be sure that thou eat not the blood: for the blood is the life; and thou mayest not eat the life with the flesh. Thou shalt not eat it; thou shalt pour it upon the earth as water."

(*Id.* in Leviticus, 17, 10–15.)

Cf. bones in the stories of American Indians and in the regulations for the Paschal Lamb, Exodus 12, 46—

"Neither shall ye break a bone thereof."

H

" ... pour out the blood thereof, and cover it with dust. For it is the life of all flesh ... the life of all flesh is the blood thereof."[1]

Practices in view of the animal's resurrection.

Not a bone of Christ was broken; his blood flowed on the earth.

But Christians eat blood.

Deuteronomy, 16, 21. "Thou shalt not plant thee a grove of any trees near unto the altar of the Lord thy God, which thou shalt make thee. Neither shalt thou set thee up any image; which the Lord thy God hateth."

On the other hand, trees and sacred groves of the Greeks.

Deuteronomy, 18, 10. "There shall not be found among you anyone that maketh his son or his daughter to pass through the fire."

Cf. the word of John the Baptist. He shall baptize in the Spirit and in fire.

This was the baptism that Demeter and Isis gave to their nurslings, their adopted children.

Was it a sacrifice, or simply a baptism?

Jehovah made the same promises to Israel that the Devil made to Christ.

God is only all-powerful here below for saving those who desire to be saved by Him. He has abandoned all the rest of his power to the Prince of this world and to inert matter. He has no power other than spiritual. And spirituality itself here below has only the minimum of power necessary for existing. Grain of mustard seed, pearl, leaven, salt.

The serpent, image of the moon; on the other hand, changing of skin was perhaps a symbol of new birth.

Effort of will, in the sense of virtue and the performance of obligations, has value, not in itself, but as a mute prayer, a prayer in act and in silence.

[1] Leviticus 17: 13–14.

A child a few months old which is attracted by some bright object may cry for it to be given him. He may hold out his hand until it drops from fatigue, and then hold it out again, for hours at a time. In the end his mother will notice, and be unable to resist. She will give him the object.

An ant climbs a few inches up the side of a smooth step, then slips back; it climbs again, and slips back, and then again and it still slips back. A child who is watching is amused for ten minutes, and then can't stand it any longer; he will lift the ant on a straw up to the next step.

In the same way, by wearying God with our patience we oblige him to transform time into eternity.

A patience capable of wearying God proceeds from an infinite humility.

Humility gives us power over Him. Nothing can wed the perfectly compact being except the perfectly void non-entity. By humility alone can we be perfect like our Father.

This calls for a completely humbled and broken heart.

An acted prayer, like that of the ant which climbs and falls, is still humbler than a spoken prayer or even than unuttered cries or a silent orientation of longing. It means knowing that we can do nothing and yet wearing ourselves out in what we recognize as useless efforts and waiting humbly for the day when, perhaps, they will be noticed by the Power whom we dare not implore.

There is no attitude of greater humility than to wait in silence and patience. It is the attitude of the slave who is ready for any order from the master, or for no order.

To wait thus is to express in action passivity of thought.

It is the patience which transmutes time into eternity.

"They shall bear fruit in patience."

The pride of the flesh consists in believing that it has a hold on the future, that it has a right to eat soon if it is hungry, to drink soon if it is thirsty. Privation undeceives it and makes it feel with anguish that the future is uncertain, that man has no hold on it and is totally impotent even as regards the near future.

In one way or another, it is the cry of pride that "the future is mine".

Humility is knowledge of the contrary truth.

If the present alone is mine I am nothing, because the present is nothing.

The transcendent bread is the bread of today; therefore it is the food of the humble soul.

All sins are an attempt to escape from time. Virtue is to submit to time, to press it to the heart until the heart breaks. Then one is in the eternal.

Affliction freezes the soul by reducing it to the present against its will.

Humility is consent to this reduction.

Humility is consent to the thing by which nature is horrified, the void.

I am not, and I consent not to be; because I am not the good, and I desire that only the good should be.

Such a love would make God jealous, if he did not possess it, as Christ, to perfection.

God desires to be, not because he is himself but because he is the good. Through love, the Father causes the Son to be, because the Son is the Good. Through love, the Son desires not to be, because only the Father is the Good.

For the Father, God is the Son. For the Son, God is the Father. Both are right, and this makes a single truth. So it is that They are two Persons and one single God.

The Father is creation of being, the Son is renunciation of being; this double pulsation is one single act which is Love or Spirit. When humility gives us a part in it, the Trinity is in us.

This exchange of love between the Father and the Son passes through creation. All we are asked to do is to consent to its passing through. We are nothing else but this consent.

Praise to God and compassion for creatures.

It is the same movement of the heart.

But how is this possible, since the two are in obvious contradiction?

To thank God because of his great glory, and to have pity for creatures because of their wretchedness.

To have pity for Christ who was thirsty and hungry and tired.

Thankfulness to God and compassion for every creature.

Praise to God and pity for every creature.

A creature cannot legitimately be the object of any love except compassion.

Nor can God be the object of any love other than praise.

Our misery is the praise of His glory.

ἐγώ σε ἐδόξασα ἐπὶ τῆς γῆς.

I have been thy glory on earth.

ἐφανέρωσα σοῦ τὸ ὄνομα.

I have made thy name plain.

δεδόξασμαι ἐν αὐτοῖς.

I have my glory in them.

Compassion for every creature, because it is far from the Good. Infinitely far. Abandoned.

God abandons our whole entire being—flesh, blood, sensibility, intelligence, love—to the pitiless necessity of matter and the cruelty of the devil, except for the eternal and supernatural part of the soul.

The Creation is an abandonment. In creating what is other than Himself, God necessarily abandoned it. He only keeps under his care the part of Creation which is Himself—the uncreated part of every creature. That is the life, the Light, the Word; it is the presence here below of God's only Son.

It is sufficient if we consent to this ordering of things.

How can this consent be united with compassion? How is it an act of unique love, when it seems irreconcilable with love?

Wisdom, teach me this.

God is absent from the world, except in the existence in this world of those in whom His love is alive. Therefore they ought to be present in the world through compassion. Their compassion is the visible presence of God here below.

When we are lacking in compassion we make a violent separation between a creature and God.

Through compassion we can put the created, temporal part of a creature in communication with God.

It is a marvel analogous to the act of creation itself.

The cruelty of the Jews and the Romans had so much power over Christ that it caused him to feel abandoned by God.

Compassion is what spans this abyss which creation has opened between God and the creature.

It is the rainbow.

Compassion should have the same dimension as the act of creation. It cannot exclude a single creature.

One should love oneself only with a compassionate love.
Every created thing is an object for compassion because it is ephemeral.
Every created thing is an object for compassion because it is limited.
Compassion directed to oneself is humility.
Humility is the only permitted form of self-love.
Praise for God, compassion for creatures, humility for oneself.
Without humility, all the virtues are finite. Only humility makes them infinite.

Apply to metaphysics the mathematical device of passage to the limit.
In the infinitesimal calculus, contradictions are true, and yet it permits rigorous proofs.
The scale of knowledge in Plato (from perception to dialectic) means only this: to prepare the mind for rising to the point where it grasps the simultaneous truth of contradictions.
How can God be loved except from this point?

In American Indian stories, to bring an animal back to life when it has been eaten, its bones are thrown *into water*.
living water.
If you knew God's gift . . . you would ask, and he would give you the living water.
ἔδωκεν ἄν σοι ὕδωρ ζῶν
τὸ ὕδωρ ὁ δώσω
The water I will give him will become in him a source of water that springs in eternal life.

4th Gospel
  He was the true light.
  behold the lamb of God.
  water turned into wine.
  traders driven from the temple.
  except he be born from on high of water and the spirit.

As Moses lifted up the serpent in the wilderness . . .
he baptizeth
he will give you the living water
my meat is to do his will.
Healing.
pool of Bethsaida.
I can do nothing of myself
bread and fishes.
my father has given you the true bread of heaven. I am the bread of life. I am the bread which came down from heaven. Whoever eats of this bread, he shall live for ever, and the bread which I give is my flesh for the life of the world. My flesh is meat indeed and my blood is drink indeed. So the living Father has sent me and I live by the Father, and he that eateth me shall live also by me. This is the bread which cometh down from heaven. It is the spirit that quickeneth; the flesh profiteth nothing. The words I have spoken to you are spirit and are life.

. . . as regards the doctrine he will know whether it comes from God or whether I speak in my own name.

He is true and injustice is not in him.

ἀληθής ἔστιν καὶ ἀδικεία ἐν αὐτῷ οὐκ ἔστιν.

he who believes in me, out of his belly shall flow rivers of living water. He said that of the spirit.

Isaiah "thou shalt be

If anyone shall do his will, he will know concerning the doctrine, whether it is God's or whether I speak in my own name.

He who seeks the glory of him who sent him, that man is true and there is no injustice in him.

He who believes in me, as the Scripture said, rivers of living water shall flow from his belly.

Song of Songs: . . . A garden enclosed is my sister, my spouse; a spring shut up, a fountain sealed. Thy plants are an orchard of pomegranates, with pleasant fruits; camphire with spikenard . . . a fountain of gardens, a well of living waters, and streams from Lebanon.

See *living water* in Septuagint?

Let him who is without sin commence (the stoning).

I am the light of the world.

I know whence I come and whither I go (to Nicodemus: you know not whence [the spirit] comes and whither it goes; such is every man who has been engendered of the spirit [such, i.e. like the spirit])

(The spirit bloweth where it listeth, and thou hearest its voice, but thou knowest not whence it comes and whither it goes; such is every man who has been engendered of the spirit.)

You cannot tell whence I come and whither I go.

You judge after the flesh, I judge no man.

I am not of this world.

If you do not believe that I am, you will die in your sins— who are you?—The beginning, as I tell you.[1]

He who hath sent me is true, and what I have heard from him, that do I tell to the world.

Of myself I do nothing. As the Father has taught, so do I speak. I do always those things that please him.

If you continue in my word, you will know the truth, and the truth shall make you free.

If the son hath freed you, you shall be free indeed.

If God were your father you would love me, because I come from God. But your father is the devil and you want to fulfil your father's desires. He was a slayer of men from the beginning. There is no truth in him. He is a liar, and his father also. If I said that I do not know him (God), I should be like you, a liar.

He has no sin, nor have his parents; but that the works of God should be manifest in him.

The night comes, when no man can work. So long as I am in the world, I am the light of the world.

I am the door of the sheep.

I am the good shepherd

I and the Father are one.

Death of Lazarus.

When he saw her weeping and the Jews around her weeping, Jesus groaned in his spirit and was troubled, and said: "Where have you buried him?" and they replied: "Lord, come and see." Jesus wept.

Mary and the spikenard.

Branches.

Some Gentiles come to Philip, asking to see Jesus. He replies:

[1] τὴν ἀρχὴν ὅ τι καὶ λαλῶ ὑμῖν (John 8: 25).

... except a corn of wheat fall into the ground and die, it remains alone; but if it dies, it brings forth much fruit ... If any man serve me, let him follow me, and where I am, there also will my servant be ... Now my soul is troubled ...
Voice from heaven.
And I, if I be lifted up from the earth, will draw all men unto me.
I do not judge him.
He who does not receive my words has one who will judge him: the word that I have spoken will judge him on the last day; for I speak not of myself, but he who sends me, the Father himself, has commanded me what I have to say and announce. And I know that his commandment is life everlasting.
If I wash you not, you have no part with me ... you are clean, but not all of you.
... he was troubled in spirit, and testified and said: one of you will betray me.
I give you a new commandment: that you love one another; as I have loved you, so also you should love one another.
How shall we know the way?
I am the way, the truth, and the life. No man comes to the Father save through me.
He who has seen me has seen the Father. The Father who dwelleth in me, he doeth his works.
Whatever you ask in my name, that I will do.
The spirit of truth which the world cannot receive because it neither contemplates nor knows it. You shall know it. I live and you shall live. You shall know that I am in my Father, and you in me, and I in you. He who loves me shall be loved by my Father.
We will go to him and make our dwelling with him.
I leave you my peace, I give you my peace.
He comes, the prince of this world, and he has no part in me. But that the world may know that I love the Father.
I am the true vine, and my father is the husbandman. I am the vine and you are the branches.
Greater love hath no man than this, that a man lay down his life for his friends. I no longer call you servants. All that I have heard from my Father I have made known to you. You have not chosen me, I have chosen you. If you were of the world, the world loves that which belongs to it; because you are not of the

world, but I have chosen you out of the world, for this the world will hate you.

If I had not come and had not spoken to them, they would not be to blame. But they have no excuse. Whoever hates me hates my Father. If I had not done works among them which no other has done, they would not be to blame; but they have seen and they have hated both me and my father.

The spirit of truth which comes from the Father will bear witness for me.

They have not known the Father nor me.

The Prince of this world is judged.

I have much more to tell you, but you cannot bear it now.

The spirit of truth will guide you into all truth.

All that the Father has is mine.

When a woman is in labour she suffers pain, because her time is come.

Your joy none shall take away from you.

That they may be one, as we are one.

Sanctify them in the truth. Thy word is the truth. For their sakes I sanctify myself, that they also may be sanctified through the truth.

They are not of the world ... I send them into the world.

Put your sword in its sheath.

My kingdom is not of this world.

—for this I was born, that I should bear witness to the truth. Whoever is of the truth hears my voice.

Flagellation, crown of thorns, purple robe, blows.

Jesus made no reply. Pilate said to him "You say nothing to me? You know that I have power to free you and power to crucify you?" Jesus replied: "You have no power over me unless it is given you from on high; therefore the sin is greater of him who delivered me to you."

I thirst.

It is finished. ($\tau\epsilon\tau\acute{\epsilon}\lambda\epsilon\sigma\tau\alpha\iota$).

Seeing that he was already dead they did not break his thighs, but one of the soldiers pierced his side with a spear, and blood and water at once flowed from it. And he who saw bore witness. These things were done that the Scripture might be fulfilled: you shall not break one of his bones.

Joseph of Arimathaea and Nicodemus.

She, thinking it was the gardener ...

Simon Peter, do you love me more than these?
Light. Lamb. Serpent. Living bread that has come down from heaven.
Rivers of living water shall flow from his belly.
Light of the world.
I judge no one.
The origin.
Door. Good Shepherd. Corn of wheat. Way, truth, life. I live. My peace. Vine.

Tertullian contra Marcion:
The true Prometheus, almighty God [is mutilated by Marcion's blasphemies].
Justin Martyr, middle of 2nd century, alliance of Christianity and Greek philosophy.

The most important truth:
The mysteries of the faith can be and have been used in the same way as Lenin used the Marxian dialectic (in both cases contradiction as a logical criterion of error is eliminated): they are used, by shrewd manipulation of the anathema, for the total enslavement of minds. By the elect, who disdain both rebellion and servility of mind, they are turned into ko-ans by contemplation. But their secret lies elsewhere. It is that there are two different kinds of reason.

There is a supernatural reason. It is the knowledge, gnosis, γνῶσις, of which Christ was the key, the knowledge of the Truth whose spirit is sent by the Father.

What is contradictory for natural reason is not so for supernatural reason, but the latter can only use the language of the former.

Nevertheless, the logic of supernatural reason is more rigorous than that of natural reason.

Mathematics offers us an image of this hierarchy.

That is the fundamental doctrine of Pythagoreanism, of Platonism, and of early Christianity; it is the source of the dogmas of the Trinity, of the two-fold nature of Christ in one person, of the duality and unity of good and evil, and of transubstantiation, which have been preserved by an almost miraculous protection, one might think, of the Holy Spirit.

Natural reason applied to the mysteries of the faith produces heresy.

The mysteries of the faith, when severed from all reason, are no longer mysteries but absurdities.

But supernatural reason only exists in souls which burn with the supernatural love of God.

Christ and Prometheus came to scatter a fire upon the earth.

St. John of the Cross knew that there is a supernatural reason, for he wrote it is only by the Cross that one penetrates the secrets of the Wisdom of God.

Odin also learned the supernatural wisdom of the Runes when he hung on the Tree, dedicated to Odin,[1] his side pierced by a lance, hungry and thirsty. τῷ πάθει μάθος.[2]

"to be born from on high of water and the spirit"—

St. Paul: "what is pleasing to God is a new creation (καινὴ κτίσις)"—And the first creation was: "The spirit of God moved on the surface of the waters. God said: Let there be light!"

The Flood is almost a new creation. Noah almost emerges from the waters.

Was there not another version of the story, in which he was submerged in the ark and then re-emerged?

Noah must be Osiris, who is Dionysus. He is a redeemer, whose sacrifice saved humanity. He is also Prometheus.

"to be born of water and the spirit", it is a doctrine of the microcosm. Man is created anew on the model of the creation of the world.

He emerges from the water as the bird pierces the shell of the world-egg.

To love God through the evil which one hates.

Irish story (Lady Gregory).—A poor couple wanted a son, but had a daughter. The mother said: "She will be the Mother of God." When she grew up an angel came and said to her: "Do you desire to be the Mother of God?—Yes, I do." And

---

[1] "dedicated to Odin, I to myself" (see below, pp. 165, 171).
[2] by suffering, learning.

immediately the Saviour enters into her as a baby. The angel leads her away. (Time of St. Brigid.)

Since man (and every creature) is a mixture of water and fire (contraries: cold and moist—hot and dry—n.b.: 4 contraries), to be engendered out of water and fire implies a dissolution. The blood itself, in mortal anguish, is decomposed into water and fire—then the two are recomposed as blood.

Or rather, this fire is extinguished and there descends from heaven another fire which is inextinguishable.

This water is the inner death.

Water, image of pliant attentiveness. The matter which resembles nothingness. Fire, the aspect of matter which resembles being.

Humility is attentive patience.

If one behaves as though dead, the Lord comes and brings life from on high.

To wait is the extreme of passivity. It is to be obedient to time. Total obedience to time obliges God to bestow eternity.

negative trial: not to eat a fruit—not to open a door—not to think about the white bear—this is the passing from time into eternity through the intermediary of the perpetual.

to accept a perpetual suffering or privation is the door into eternity; or, also, a perpetual joy: but it is more difficult. By its own nature, after a certain length of time, suffering takes on a colour of perpetuity.

to accept time—the part of the soul which accepts is removed from time.

by the descent of what belongs down below, what belongs above is raised up.

we have no power of lifting. We have only the power of lowering. That is why to lower oneself is the only way of rising.

Pantheism is true only for saints who have reached the state of perfection.

Lower states have no truth, because error is inherent in them.

That is why there is no truth of evil, except in the form of a perfect being who suffers.

Therefore, to be cleansed from sin and then to suffer is the condition for attaining to truth. The Cross is the way.

The extended arm is the geometrical mean between the head and the body—*if* the man is raised a little above the ground. (and in Greek statues? find the *canon*).

Everything that is in this world is conditional.

The only thing in us that is unconditional is acceptance.

Anything whatsoever contains the infinite.

There again, mathematics offers an image of the method of redemption.

To accept anything whatsoever—but not to *do* anything whatsoever. As a complement of doing, anything whatsoever is not infinite. On the contrary, what brings doing to the infinite is limitation. Don't ever . . . The taboo.

But the taboo loses its virtue if it is conditioned by reward and punishment.

If the taboo is pure unconditioned obedience, then doing becomes a form of accepting. This is necessary in order that the acceptance may be total. Otherwise, compensations always offer themselves.

To wait and obey.

To wait implies all the tension of desire, but without desire; a tension accepted in perpetuity.

Impersonal God in the Gospel. "I will not judge him, but my word shall judge him."

God must be impersonal, to be innocent of evil, and personal, to be responsible for good.

"Whoever is not born from on high, out of nothingness and being . . ."

To be devoured, and then to have one's bones thrown into the water.

Everything here below is the slave of death. The horror of death is the iron law which determines all our thoughts and all our actions.

Acceptance of death is the only liberation.

He who believes in me, there shall flow rivers from his belly, rivers of living water.

The power to become children of God—those who have believed in his name, who have been engendered not from the will of the flesh or the will of man, but from God.

The will of man—when a man says to himself: I will go to my wife in order to have a child.

The will of the flesh—when a man is drawn by lust to go to a woman.

To become a child of God it is necessary to die and be reborn. To be engendered by the seed of God.

An incorruptible seed is sown in the body.

He who baptizes in the holy spirit.

The water comes first.

When the guest is drunk, it is then that Christ gives him the best wine.

By putting the celestial fire in the water, he makes it the perfect wine.

What is engendered of the flesh is flesh, what is engendered of the spirit is spirit.

The spirit cannot unite with the flesh to engender. Only with water. The flesh must become water.

Whoever has been engendered of the spirit blows where he lists and makes his voice heard, without anyone knowing whence he comes or whither he goes (except those like him).

I speak to you of the things of this world.

None has gone up to heaven save he who came down from heaven.

Whoever believes in him has eternal life.

God so loved the world that he gave his only son, so that whoever believes in him should not be lost but should have eternal life. God did not send his son into the world to judge the world, but so that the world might be saved through him. He who believes in him is not judged. He who does not believe is already judged, because he has not believed in the name of God's only son. The judgement is this: that the light came into the world, and men preferred darkness to the light; for their works were evil. He whose works are mediocre hates the light and does not go towards it, so that his works may not be confounded. Whoever fulfils the truth goes towards the light, so that his works may be manifest, and that they were wrought in God.

Therefore the presence of the light effects a discrimination.

He who accepts its witness has attested that God is true.

He who believes in the son has eternal life; he who rebels against the son will not see it.

Those who fulfil Christ's commands love him—even if they do not believe in the Incarnation.

God is spirit and those who worship must worship in spirit and in truth.

The Messiah comes, who is called Christ—it is I who tell you.

I do the will of him who sent me and I perform his work.

Others have worked, and you enter into their work.

This harvest is the Christ, which others have sown, all the saints who longed for him.

In this the saying is true, that one man sows and another reaps.

He who has sent me that I may complete his work.

All that the Father has done the son does also.

This refers to the good.

The Father loves the son and has shown him all his own works.

My works bear witness that the Father has sent me.

Because he does good.

You receive your glory from one another, you do not seek the glory of God alone.

The bread of God is he who has come down from heaven and given life to the world. I am the bread of life.

He who has my commandments and keeps them, he is the one who loves me. He who loves me will be loved by my father, and I also love him and show him what is mine.

Story of the American test in which the answer "yes (but only when ...)" is counted as wrong, because it should be "no (except when ...)".

Men nearly always reason in this way.

You think to have eternal life in the Scriptures.[1]
He did not come only through water, but through water and blood. That is to say, he was not only matter and God; he had a human soul (the ψυχή[2] is in the blood). A human soul can be absolutely pure, made of water and spirit.

He who believes in the son of God has the witness in himself. The faith is the witness.

"King of peace, without father, without mother, without descent, having neither beginning of days nor end of life; but made like unto the son of God, he abides a priest continually."

"Moses has spoken of me." Does not this refer to Melchizedek?

"He was the priest of the most high God ... I have lift up mine hand unto Jehovah, the most high God, the possessor of heaven and earth."

Jehovah said unto my lord: sit thou on my right hand ... from the womb of the morning thou hast the dew of thy youth ... Thou art a priest for ever after the order of Melchizedek ... He shall drink from the brook in the way: therefore shall he lift up his head.[3]

(water, seed of heaven)

If you believe Moses, you ought to believe in me. In a priest of the most high God who is not Jehovah.

He, since he remains for ever, has an immutable priesthood.

"Christ is not entered into the holy places made with hands, but into heaven itself, to appear in the presence of God for us; nor yet that he should offer himself often, as the high priest entereth into the holy place every year with blood of others; for then must he often have suffered since the foundation of the world: but now once in the end of the world hath he appeared to put away sin by the sacrifice of himself. And as it is appointed unto men to die once, but after this the judgement, so Christ was offered once to bear the sins of many; and then, without sin, he shall be seen by those who receive him for salvation."[4]

The Passion represents in the destiny of humanity (which suffered torment in the person of Christ) what death represents for the individual. (According to the pre-millennial outlook.)

In the life of the individual, the innocent must always suffer for the guilty; because punishment is expiation only if it is preceded by repentance. The penitent, having become innocent, suffers for the guilty, whom the repentance has abolished.

[1] Cf. John 5: 39.   [2] psyche, soul.   [3] Psalm 110.   [4] Hebrews 9: 24–8.

Humanity, regarded as a single being, sinned in Adam and expiated in Christ.

Only innocence expiates. Crime suffers in quite a different way.

This text of St. Paul[1] seems to be in contradiction, on the one hand, with the sacrifice of the mass and, on the other hand, with the saying in the Apocalypse (the lamb slain from the foundation of the world).

Christ speaks of the devil as a murderer from the beginning, so that the murder of Abel would be a form of the original sin.

If all the absolutely pure beings are incarnations, that gives: Abel—Enoch—Noah—Melchizedek.

And Job? But Job is perhaps only an allegory.

And Daniel? Very mysterious.

Noah, Job and Daniel are placed together in Ezekiel.

How is it that the Greeks make no mention of Daniel? (see Xenophon, *Cyropedia*,—whether some identification is possible?)

Abel is slaughtered. Noah is (almost) drowned.

Cain and Judas.

Abel and Zagreus.

Noah. In the second month, the 17th day, the sluice-gates of heaven are opened. It is on the 17th day that Osiris dies.—Which is the second month? Beginning from Autumn?

Abraham was serving the gods of his country at the moment when the Eternal revealed himself to him. The Eternal was his own god. On the other hand, the Jews in Egypt had ceased to worship Jehovah. They participated in the religion of the country.

Abraham set out on his wanderings in the name of a new God (supreme God). This God allowed human sacrifices and all kinds of depravities. No trace of morality. Joseph in his day was still serving this God.

But Joseph's descendants forgot him (nor are they ever reproached for it). Moses, with an Egyptian education, as a son of the Pharaoh's daughter, but having turned fugitive, restored him to circulation, but with an advance (Jehovah, Being, the "I am").

How does he come to have a brother, since his mother is unknown?

Moses fabricated Scriptures with a mixture of the Hebrews' traditions from before their assimilation by the Egyptians, and

---

[1] Hebrews 9 : 24-8.

traditions from Egypt itself, but sufficiently debased to allow of a theocracy.

Why this obsession of the unity of God and this rejection of images? Is there a connection between the rejection of images and theocracy?[1]

The Cross is hell accepted. Suffering is to move either towards the Nothingness above or towards the Nothingness below.

God to Adam after the fall: "cursed is the ground because of thee". God after Noah's sacrifice: "I will not again curse the ground because of man." Redemptive sacrifice.

It is nowhere said that Moses heard from God what is related in Genesis, and therefore he must have known it from his Egyptian education.

Moses speaks to Pharaoh about Jehovah as of a purely Hebrew God, who requires only that the Hebrews be allowed to depart and worship him. He does not claim any worship from Pharaoh.

St. Augustine (against Pelagius). If an infidel clothes the naked, etc., he is doing ill although the work is good. For the fruits of an evil tree are evil. And the tree is evil, because "without the faith one cannot please God".

That is directly contrary to Christ, who said: You shall know the tree by its fruits—and not the fruits by the tree. Indeed, it is exactly like the Pharisees' attitude towards Christ. It is social idolatry, an idolatry of the Church like the Hebrews' idolatry of Israel.—Directly opposite to the story of the Samaritan (the heretics of that time).

It is totalitarianism.

How can Christianity impregnate everything, without being totalitarian? All in all, and not totalitarian?

Only if the sacred is recognized as the *sole* source of inspiration for the profane, and natural reason as a degraded form of supernatural reason, and art as a degraded form of faith. Or not degraded, but the same thing in a lesser degree of illumination.

Supernatural light coming down into the sphere of nature becomes natural light. That is all right so long as the process is

[1] Cf. p. 214.

recognized. But without the supernatural source of light there is soon only darkness even on the level of nature.

The ram that was found near Abraham when he was about to slay Isaac—was it not the primitive version of the Lamb of God?

Wood of the burnt offering. Do not the beliefs concerning trees and fire play a part in the symbolism of sacrifice? The creatures which are sacrificed are "baptized in the fire". Is the "balancing" of the meat before the altar connected with hanging?

The Lord visits the Philistine Abimelek.

God says to Cain: "What hast thou done? The voice of thy brother's blood crieth unto me from the ground. And now thou art cursed because of that earth which has opened its mouth to receive thy brother's blood from thy hand. When thou tillest the earth it shall not henceforth yield unto thee its strength; a fugitive and a vagabond shalt thou be in the world."[1]

After smelling the sweet savour of Noah's sacrifice and swearing not to curse the earth again because of man, God said to Noah: "... I have given you all things. But flesh, so long as the blood maintains its life, shall ye not eat. And of your blood, which makes your life, I shall require account; I shall require it of every animal. And of man himself, if he has struck his brother, I shall require the man's life again. Whoso sheddeth man's blood, by man shall his blood be shed; for man was made in the image of God."[2]

In Genesis, this is the first in time of God's commandments.

Abraham fights for the people of Canaan and is blessed by Melchizedek, who is king of Canaan.

Holocaust: "sacrifice which burns all night". When the Greeks burnt the dead, were they offering them to God? Were they baptizing them in fire? The Phoenix too is burnt.

Only fire destroys completely. What is burnt passes out of this world, into the other, with God. It is the same symbol as libation.

In libation God is offered one drop. What belongs to God is the infinitely small.

Burnt matter is transformed into odour.

[1] Genesis 4: 10 ff.   [2] Genesis 9: 3 ff.

The destruction is the sacrifice.

Oil is used for consecration in the Old Testament. The dove, image of the Holy Spirit, brings Noah an olive twig (the dove comes to Noah after his immersion, as it does to Christ).— Suppliants' olive branches throughout antiquity. Oil symbolizes the Spirit, love, God's goodness. Athena.

The altar of Moses is consecrated with oil and purified with blood.

expiatory bull, entirely consumed
ram destined for the holocaust
ram of inauguration
oil cake

Moses sprinkles Aaron with a mixture of oil and blood.

A fire comes down from heaven to consume the offerings.

"Any man who slaughters a beast and brings it not to the entrance of the tabernacle to offer it to the Eternal ... shall be accounted a murderer. He has shed blood ... And whoever ... eateth any manner of blood ... I will cut him off ... For the life of the flesh is in the blood and I have given it to you upon the altar to make an expiation for your persons; for it is the blood that makes expiation for the person ... And any man ... who hunts and catches any beast or fowl ... shall pour out the blood thereof and cover it with earth ... For the vital principle of every creature is the blood which is in its body; therefore I said to the children of Israel: Ye shall not eat the blood of any creature. For the life of every creature is the blood thereof; whoever eateth it shall be cut off."[1]

This part of the revelation of Moses originates from that of Noah. But it is only concerned with animals.

In the earthly Paradise even the wild animals are vegetarians. Man lives on grains and fruits (vegetable *seeds*, parts which contain the vital energy to the second power), and the animals live on grasses and leaves.

It is not said whether Abel ate meat.

God says to Noah: "Every moving thing that liveth shall be meat for you, and also the green herb; I have given you all things. But you shall not eat any creature so long as its life is sustained by its blood."[2]

Sole dietary prescription. Is it directed against those who tear an animal to pieces and eat it raw while still alive?

[1] Leviticus 17: 3 ff.   [2] Genesis 9: 3–4.

Only the ruminants live on green things, as all the animals did in the earthly Paradise.

Is the pig, which has a cloven foot but does not ruminate, a fallen and accursed animal, like the serpent?

And the camel, whose foot is not cloven?

The Hebrews were unable (though only after Moses) to make pacts with other nations, because of their so-called idolatry.

Rome and Israel introduced into Christianity, mixed with the spirit of Christ, the spirit of the Beast. Israel, which slew Christ, is the very form of the Church as St. Augustine conceived it. Did he not sin against the Spirit when he condemned an infidel who feeds a starving man? The Beast is social idolatry, the idolatry of Plato's great animal. It is the Beast who says "... anathema sit". But "You shall know them by their fruit", that is to say, all pure good proceeds from Christ. All good has its source in God.

This is the essential and unrecognized truth: Everything that is good is of divine and supernatural origin, and proceeds directly or indirectly from the celestial, transcendental source of all good.

Everything that proceeds from another source, everything whose origin is natural, is alien to the good.

Because he is the creator, God is not all-powerful. Creation is abdication. But he is all-powerful in this sense, that his abdication is voluntary. He knows its effects, and wills them.

He wills to give his bread to whoever asks for it, but only to him who asks, and only his bread. He has abandoned the whole of our being, except for that part of our soul which dwells, like Him, in the heavens. Christ himself did not know this truth until he was on the Cross.

The power of God here below, compared to that of the Prince of this world, is something infinitely small.

God has abandoned God.

God has emptied himself. This means that both the Creation and the Incarnation are included with the Passion.

St. Augustine: before Christ, and outside Israel, there were "spiritual members" of Israel among the other peoples, and to each of them the unique Mediator, and his future coming was divinely revealed. Ex.: Job.

We have no indication which limits their number or their influence. There is nothing to prevent us from believing that the priests of Egypt, the initiates of Eleusis in the good period, the Pythagoreans, the Druids, the gymnosophists of India, and the Chinese Taoists were for the most part among them. If we admit this, then those traditions are true, and those who live in them today are in the truth. It is not in virtue of being a historical account that the Good Tidings are important for salvation.

If the anguished waiting for a Saviour led to a mistaken identification of the person known as Buddha with this saviour, and if he is invoked today as a perfect, divine man and redeemer, then this invocation is as efficacious as those addressed to Christ.

Perpetuity of hell admitted by St. Augustine. Yet he defines evil as non-being. Therefore everything that exists is good in some relation. Today, the devil is of use as a test for saints. But after the end of the world and the last judgment in what relation could he be good? Therefore he becomes nothing, and hell does too.

(Observe how, in fact, St. Augustine gets out of this difficulty.)

This definition of evil and the belief in a perpetual hell are an example of illegitimate contradiction in the domain of the transcendent.

How can this kind of contradiction be distinguished by definition from legitimate contradictions?

In the case of an illegitimate contradiction, if one term is suppressed our understanding of the other is not thereby modified.

Something better must be found.

There are absurdities which it is useful to suppose. Ex.: suppose God willed my damnation... It is absurd, because, in God, His will for me and my salvation are identical. But it is useful because, in me, there is a great difference between directing my desire toward God's will and directing it toward my salvation.

There are some truths which one must not know, or not too much. E.g. that the final outcome of obedience to God is undoubtedly beatitude.

There are some things which it is good for some people to think, but not for others. To accept hell out of respect for God's will is good, when the soul feels itself on the verge of damnation; but it is bad when the soul feels itself within reach of salvation, because in that case one is accepting hell for other people.

Thus a number of representations, which possess a truth value, possess a varying use value.

In the domain of the transcendent there is an architecture of representations and ideas. Some are to be put in the foreground and others in the silent, secret part of the soul, unknown to consciousness. Some should be in the imagination, others in the completely abstract intelligence, others in both places, etc.

This complex and refined architecture, which is operative even in those who are called simple, if they are close to sanctity, is what builds a soul ready for salvation.

It is not the man who constructs it; its operation is an effect of grace if it is not hindered. Generally the man in whom it operates is unaware of it, or almost.

With respect to such an architecture, how miserably inadequate is the wording of a proposition which ends with "anathema sit"! Whether the anathema is legitimate or not often depends upon which part of the soul the idea referred to in the proposition is lodged in.

These things are so delicate that a crude instrument like "anathema sit" can effect nothing among them except blind destruction.

In their good period, no doubt the processes of purification in the initiatory cults and sects were a better criterion of the soul's internal architecture.

God is powerless, except for the equitable and merciful distribution of the good. He can do nothing else. But that is enough.

He has the monopoly of good. He is present Himself in everything that effects pure good. Everything which effects good of a lower order proceeds from the things in which He is present. All authentic good, of whatever order, derives supernaturally from Him. Everything which is not directly or indirectly the effect of God's supernatural working is bad or indifferent.

The non-good may equally legitimately be regarded as bad or as indifferent, according to the point of view from which it is considered.

God can only do good, and only to him who deserves it, and he cannot withhold it from the man who deserves it.

Except through the secret and supernatural presence of God (one form of which is the order and beauty of the world—make a list of the others), this world can only do what is bad or indifferent.

It can do all possible harm to whatever is not supernaturally protected by the good that issues from God.

The amount of harm it can do where God is present is indicated with perfect veracity in the four Gospels.

To be a Christian has no other meaning than to believe this.

Belief is aroused by the beauty of the texts and by the light one gains upon the human condition through meditating on them.

Genesis separates creation and original sin because of the necessities inherent in an account composed in human language. But by being created the creature preferred itself to God. Otherwise, would there have been a creation? God created because he was good, but the creature let itself be created because it was evil. It redeems itself by persuading God, by the power of prayer, to destroy it.

If one is hungry one eats, not for the love of God but because one is hungry.

If an unknown man lying in the road is hungry one must give him food, even if one has not enough for oneself, not for the love of God but because he is hungry.

That is what it is to love one's neighbour as oneself.

To give "for God", to love one's neighbour "for God" or "in God", is not to love him as oneself. One loves oneself by an effect of animal feeling.

This animal feeling itself has to become something universal. And that is a contradiction. Miraculous. Supernatural.

Contradiction, impossibility, is the sign of the supernatural.

One does not love oneself "for God", "in God", but one

judges the self-love which nature implants deep in the soul to be legitimate, in so far as one is a creature of God.

It is the same with love of one's neighbour.

Every thinking being is worthy of love solely in so far as he has received existence by God's creative act and possesses the capacity to renounce that existence for love of God. It is solely on this account that I have the right to love myself or another.

Only God is the good, therefore only He is a worthy object of care, solicitude, anxiety, longing, and efforts of thought. Only He is a worthy object of all those movements of the soul which are related to some value. Only He has an affinity with that movement towards the good, that longing for the good, which is the very centre of my being.

As for the creature which one calls "me", it is not the good, and therefore it is as alien and indifferent to me as anything else in the world.

This is really so.

Why should I be interested in what is not the good?

And yet it is intolerably painful to me to disobey God (although it is so frequent).

What is the solution of this?

It is a contradiction which is both irreducible and legitimate.

Contradiction is legitimate when the suppression of one term involves destroying the other or emptying it of substance. In other words, when it is inevitable. Necessity is the supreme criterion of every logic. It is only necessity that puts the mind in contact with truth.

Why? Also a subject for meditation.

If we make a distinction in God (even without any absurd hypothesis related solely to human thought) between mercy and justice, will and power, we commit an extremely grave illegitimate absurdity.

For example: God can do everything. He could have done so and so... But in fact he willed so and so instead...

Absurd. The limits of will and power are the same in God. He wills only what He can, and if He is unable to do more it is because He does not will to be able to do more. And so on to infinity, in a circle. The circle is the projection of divine truth.

The same with mercy and justice. His justice demands that he accord his mercy, and every good, to whoever is able to receive it. His mercy demands that he withhold his pardon, and every good, from those who do not want it.

It is childish to distinguish between God's mercy and justice at the time when one is thinking of God. And even if one is thinking of man the distinction is not legitimate, because this absurdity, unlike some others, is not one that can be made use of. At least, so it seems to me.

God's attributes do not overflow one another.

They all have the same limit, the abdication which is God's creative act.

We abolish that limit by abdicating in our turn from our existence as creatures.

"Render to you all the blood you have given me."[1]

It is impossible to kill a man except from absolute necessity when one has understood that every man contains the possibility of something so sublime. Once his blood has been spilt he can no longer render it freely.

Only God knows if the possibility continues after death. He has willed that we should not know.

The poor wretch who kneels and begs for life is saying, unknown to himself: Leave me more time in which to become perfect. Do not put an end to me while I have had so small a part in the good.

How could anyone who loves God not listen to such a prayer?

Only God knows what happens if the man's prayer is not heard and he is killed.

The revelation to Noah: "Whoso sheddeth man's blood, of his life will I require it."

Fragment of pre-historic wisdom. It must contain an unfathomably deep abyss of meaning. But what meaning? To be meditated.

The *impossible* in mathematical reasoning (the demonstration per absurdum, to which all the others can be reduced) and the *never* in moral life both transport us from time into eternity.

Negation is the passage into the eternal.

[1] "Vous rendre tout le sang que vous m'avez donné" (Racine, *Iphigénie*, Act IV, scene 4).

"I will never do that." In those few words, which are spoken in a few seconds, is contained a perpetual duration.

Never possesses this property, but not *always*. Indeed, "I will always do this" has no meaning.

That is why the justificatory confession in the Egyptian Book of the Dead is in the negative.

The same in mathematics. There is an unlimited variety of triangles but *never* will any triangle have one side longer than the sum of the two others.

This *never* is the essence of every theorem.

(And yet the proof per absurdum often appears at first sight rather unsatisfactory. Consider why.)

All precise knowledge of transitory things originates from one of those eternal propositions which contain a *never*.

Things are natural, temporal; but the *limits* of things come from God.

That is what the Pythagoreans say. There is the unlimited and that which limits, and that which limits is God. Consequently limits are eternal.

He said to the sea: "Thou shalt go no further."

Of that, mathematics is the translation and the guarantee.

God alone is worthy of interest, and absolutely nothing else.

So what are we to think about the multitude of interesting things which say nothing about God? Must we conclude that they are the devil's shows?

No, no, no. We must conclude that they do speak about God.

Today it is urgently necessary to demonstrate this.

It is in this that consists the duty of lifting up the serpent of brass, that it may be seen and that whoever looks on it may be saved.

In the conduct of life also it is the limit, the "never", that transports us from the time to eternity.

You shall not eat of the fruits of this tree. The days will succeed one another in infinite variety, you will fill them with all sorts of things, but one act will be excluded from all of them, the act of eating those fruits.

"You shall not open this door. You shall not think of the white bear."

Supernatural property of the taboo. Today we know this property only in a perverted image, the magic property.

But the sin of Adam was not in disobeying an order of this

kind. That story is only a translation of the real sin into human language. For time proceeded out of the sin and did not precede it.

"Thou shalt not eat . . . ", "thou shalt not open . . . ", "thou shalt not think".

Fortunate is he who is capable of obeying such orders.

Voluntary privations, if they proceed from obedience, are of this nature and are a way into eternity.

They are not useful if they proceed from a resolution. The effect of a resolution lasts for a day, or eight days, or twenty years, or longer than a human life, but not for ever. No resolution transports us to eternity.

Whereas "you shall not do this" means "you shall never do this", even if you live a hundred centuries.

Consented obedience transports the centre of the soul into eternity.

That is why religious vows are only useful for salvation if they are the simple expression of a vocation; in other words, a simple expression of obedience, the "here I am!" of a servant called by his master.

If they express a resolution to observe chastity, poverty, obedience to superiors, they are useless and even harmful for salvation.

Only an order from God is eternal.

Only the unconditional leads to God.

(A mass "offered for . . . ", a prayer, or a suffering, "offered for . . . ", are not contacts with God.)

The unconditioned is contact with God. Everything that is conditioned is of this world.

(Ex. Jacob: If . . . if . . . if . . . *then* shall the Lord be my God.)[1]

The unconditioned is the absolute.

Love is supernatural when it is unconditioned. An unconditioned love is a madness. A mother's love is the best image of it here below. But it is only an image. Even a mother's love wears out if all the conditions for its renewal are lacking.

Only the love of God and the anonymous love of one's neighbour are unconditioned.

One may add the love (friendship) between two friends of

[1] Genesis 28: 20-1.

God who have travelled the road of sanctity beyond the point where sanctity is something final. Because the sole condition of this friendship is the perseverance in sanctity of both participants; but since their establishment in sanctity is something final and its continuance is dependent upon no condition, one can regard their friendship as unconditioned.

But such a degree of sanctity is very rare; so also therefore is this kind of friendship.

It is this friendship which Christ added as a third commandment, that is to say, as a third perfectly holy love alongside the love of God and the love of one's neighbour.

All other loves, although they may be guaranteed by oaths, are conditioned, and they gradually wear out when the conditions fail.

[As for conjugal love, if both of the couple are saints it is the friendship of saints—if only one of them is, then the only stable factor in their relation is the anonymous neighbourly love directed by that one upon the other.—If neither of them is, then, should the conditions fail, conjugal love wears out and vanishes, in spite of the sacrament.]

Hatred is never unconditioned.

All the events of life, whatever they may be, without exception, are by convention signs of God's love, in the same way that the bread of the Eucharist is Christ's flesh.

But a convention with God is more real than any reality.

God establishes a conventional language with his friends. Every event in life is a word of this language. These words are all synonyms but, as happens in beautiful languages, each of them has its completely specific nuance, each of them is untranslateable. The meaning common to all these words is: I love you.

A man drinks a glass of water. The water is God's "I love you". He is two days in the desert without finding anything to drink. The dryness in his throat is God's "I love you". God is like an importunate woman who clings to her lover, whispering in his ear for hours without stopping: "I love you—I love you—I love you—I love you . . ."

Those who are beginning to learn this language think that only some of its words mean "I love you".

Those who know the language know that it has only one meaning.

God has no word for saying to his creature: I hate you.
But the creature has words for saying "I hate you" to God.
In a sense the creature is more powerful than God. It can hate God and God cannot hate it in return.
This impotence makes him an impersonal Person. He loves, not as I love, but as an emerald is green. He *is* "I love".
And I too, if I were in the state of perfection, would love as an emerald is green. I would be an impersonal person.
It is impossible to go beyond a certain point on the path of perfection if one only thinks of God as personal. To go further it is necessary—by force of desire—to make oneself resemble an impersonal perfection.
The perfection of the Father whose sun and rain [spirit and water] are blind to crime and virtue.
This twofold personal and impersonal aspect of God is shown in its contradictoriness in the Gospel, in connection with God's role as judge. "The Father hath committed all judgment unto the Son."[1] Supreme personal judge. "I judge him not; the word that I have spoken, the same shall judge him."[2] Supreme impersonal judge.
Men have always felt the need, in order to make sensible to their own love the two contradictory aspects of this love, to worship God in a thing. Sun, stone, statue, bread of the Eucharist.
The worship of the sun, that is to say, of God through the sun, is a very beautiful and touching form of this double love.
If one looks at the sun as it is—remote, perfectly impartial in distributing light, fixed absolutely to a determined course—and imagines it as a feeling and thinking being, what better representation of God could one find? What better model to imitate?
If the sun saw the crimes and afflictions of this world, what an impotent and perfectly pure compassion would come down to us from it . . .
Conceived in this way, the sun is an equivalent of the Incarnation. Better in some respects, but less good in others, because remote from the human form.
Plato proposes, not the sun, but the order of the world itself, and, above all, of the stars. A being, the order of the world, whose body is the world and whose soul is perfection.

[1] John 5: 22.   [2] John 12: 47–8.

If one worships God in a man, then this man must become a thing by virtue of passivity and must endure a passion and must endure it in silence.

Or else he must be a priest (Melchizedek) constrained by ceremonies to an order as fixed as that of the stars.

Ceremony is an imitation of the order of the world and of the silence of things.

The Father in heaven, who abandons his Son and keeps silence; the abandoned Christ, nailed in silence; two impersonal divinities, reflected in one another and making one single God.

The image of the indifferent power of God is the passive obedience of the creature.

God creates God, God knows God, God loves God—and God commands God, who obeys him.

The Trinity implies the incarnation—and *consequently* the Creation.

Mystery. What is the legitimate and the illegitimate use of this idea? This also needs to be rigorously defined, and it is of the highest importance.

(St. Augustine, for example, made an illegitimate use of it.)

It must not be used so as to provide cover for saying anything whatsoever—as St. Augustine does. For then it becomes the instrument of a totalitarian power. So that anything it pleases the Church to say has then to be accepted, either as a truth recognized by the agreement of reason, or else as a mystery. In other words, unconditional adherence to the Church. That is what St. Thomas calls faith, and so does the catechism of the Council of Trent.

There are only three unconditional loves: love of God—anonymous love of one's neighbour—friendship of two saints.

Unconditional love of the Church is idolatry.

One has the right to love unconditionally only that which is unconditioned.

That is to say, God and the infused presence of God—whether actual in a saint or potential in every thinking creature.

In the Church there is one unconditioned thing, but it is the presence of Christ in the Eucharist and nothing else.

The Church as a society pronouncing opinions is a phenomenon of this world, conditioned.

God has placed in every thinking being the necessary capacity of light for controlling the truth of every thought. The Word is the light which lighteth every man. What more formal text could one wish?

The notion of mystery is legitimate when the most logical and most rigorous use of the intelligence leads to an impasse, to a contradiction which is inescapable in this sense: that the suppression of one term makes the other term meaningless and that to pose one term necessarily involves posing the other. Then, like a lever, the notion of mystery carries thought beyond the impasse, to the other side of the unopenable door, beyond the domain of the intelligence and above it. But to arrive beyond the domain of the intelligence one must have travelled all through it, to the end, and by a path traced with unimpeachable rigour. Otherwise one is not beyond it but on this side of it.

It was because they both felt this that Plato instinctively adopted the form of argumentation and St. John of the Cross the form of classification; these forms are surprising to the reader, but for the authors they represent the necessary counterweight to the mystical.

When mystery is defined in this way, the mysteries of the faith are controllable by the intelligence.

Another criterion is that when the mind has nourished itself with mystery, by a long and loving contemplation, it finds that by suppressing and denying the mystery it is at the same time depriving the intelligence of treasures which are comprehensible to it, which dwell in its domain and which belong to it.

The intelligence cannot control mystery itself, but it possesses perfectly the power of control over the roads leading to mystery, those that mount up and those that lead down again from it. Therefore it can recognize, while remaining absolutely loyal to itself, the existence within the soul of a faculty superior to itself and which conducts thought on to a higher plane than its own. This faculty is supernatural love.

The consented subordination of all the natural faculties of the soul to supernatural love is faith.

This is what Plato in the *Republic* calls justice.

In St. Paul faith and justice are constantly identified: "his faith is counted to him for justice, his faith has justified him," etc.

In another use of the word, justice is the exercise of supernatural love.

It comes to the same thing, because supernatural love is exercised, incarnates itself, and passes into act only if the other faculties of the soul become its servants and, by their intermediary, make even the body serve it.

Each of the natural faculties ought to have in its own nature a motive sufficient to constrain it to subordinate itself to supernatural love, on penalty of lying.

The soul which is outside justice—outside faith—lies to itself. To say "I" is to lie.

Lord, I am nothing except error. Error is nothing except nothingness. Lord, may my whole soul be aware of that, and every part of my soul, and my body itself.

May my soul be for the body and for God only what this penholder is for my hand and the paper—an intermediary.

Christ has shown that a human soul, a human person, can be nothing but that.

And when it is that it is the same thing as the soul of the divine Persons, which is engendered and known and loved, and which loves in return, and is commanded and obeys.

When a man has attained to that state, then Christ is him.

But perhaps the greatest saints only attain it at the moment of death, for an instant?

Or perhaps only very, very few attain it before?

Christ was in that state at birth. And yet it was only on the cross that he became complete.

It is said that fools (of a certain type) are logical to excess.
By analogous reason, authentic mystics ought to be the same.
Is this a criterion?
Plato—St. John of the Cross.—

Faith is not a contact with God, otherwise it would not be called a night and a veil. It is the submission of those parts which have no contact with God to the one which has.

The speculations which it is legitimate to condemn as heretical are those which diminish the reality of divine things by veiling, under the appearance of reconciling them, the contradictions which are their mystery.

For example, making the Son an only half-divine being. Or modifying the divinity and the humanity in Christ so as to reconcile them. Or reducing the bread and wine of the Eucharist to a mere symbol.

The mysteries then cease to be an object of contemplation; they are no longer of any use.

This is a case of the illegitimate use of the intelligence, and one may think that the soul of those who entertain these speculations has not yet been illumined by supernatural love.

However, this is not a legitimate reason for excluding them from the Church, because neither is the soul of most of those who submit to dogma illumined by supernatural love. It is only a reason for excluding them from teaching functions.

So as to have an analogy, an attempt should be made to define the legitimate and non-legitimate contradictions in the infinitesimal calculus.

The authority of the Church has a rightful claim to attention only. For each truth in particular, adherence should proceed by an interior illumination of intelligence and love.

The unconditional and total adherence to everything which the Church teaches, has taught, and will teach, which St. Thomas calls faith, is not faith but social idolatry.

It is certain that a multitude of men, most of them imperfect, cannot formulate the truth which God conveys in secret, under the form of silence, to a perfect being in the state of contemplation.

The Church's authority has only been legitimately exercised when it warded off the attempts to mitigate the absurdity in the authentic mysteries.

This legitimate exercise of authority is not easily defined. But it can be done.

The supposed attributes of God are human attributes transformed through the operation of the passage to the limit.

This transformation is only legitimate if it is operated according to a perfectly rigorous method.

In this description of God three relations should be distinguished.

The relation of God to himself, which is what the Trinity is.

The relation of God to his creation in the conduct of events in the world. This conduct is the chain of secondary causes. In this domain God's will has nothing to do with any morality.

The relation of God to his creation in the inspiration communicated to thinking creatures. In this domain God's will can never contradict the sense of obligation which is essential to all conscience.

This is what Christ meant by saying: I do not remove one jot or tittle from the law.

God's will in the first sense can be related to the Father—because it is to the Father that one relates the act of creation by abdication—, God's will in the second sense can be related to the Holy Spirit.

It seems that Abelard had perceived that.

The Hebrews conceived the second on the model of the first.

The Word, Wisdom, is mediatory.

Plato: a *wise* persuasion convinced *necessity* to turn the majority of things toward the *good*.

God's justice ought therefore to be understood differently for the first will and for the second.

And yet Christ (be ye perfect . . .) brings the two together. (Be ye perfect . . .)

There are not two justices in God, but only one.

Self-contradictory.

Contradiction is the lever of transcendance.

A point is nothing. Two segments which differ only by a point are equal.

But if that point is the point of intersection of two straight lines it is much. For it defines two half lines on each side.

When a point is the centre of gravity it is equivalent to the whole, because if it is supported nothing falls.

Apply the theory of wholes to physics and first of all to classical physics (gravity, etc.)

In a ponderable volume there is one point such that if it is not lowered nothing is lowered.

And yet a point is without volume and without weight.

But to prevent it from falling there must be a resistance equal to the volume of the whole.

One could make the list of the functions performed by a point in relation to a segment of a straight line.

A new logic based on the idea of domains. What is true in one domain is not true in another.

Truth is not discovered by proofs but by exploration. It is always experimental. But necessity also is an object of exploration.

If one says: show that it is possible to construct a triangle such that... —it is enough if one finds by chance a triangle which meets the conditions.

If one says: show that it is impossible to construct a triangle such that... ; this demand involves the infinite and cannot be met without passing from the domain of empiricism into the domain of necessity.

Impossibility is what limits possibles; limit is necessity abstracted from time.

As regards visible things, it is the source of a certainty more certain than vision.

If one says: do such and such a thing, obedience to the order still leaves the soul in the domain of the temporal.

If one says: do not do such and such a thing, it is impossible to obey without lifting the centre of the soul up to the level of the eternal.

However, one and the same action may be conceived in either way; and its performance produces temporal or eternal fruits in the soul according to which way it is conceived.

This is one of the secrets of salvation.

Or at least it is one aspect of the virtue of humility.

The subordination of temporal and changing possibles to fixed limits is an image and a guarantee of the subordination of this world to the other; consequently, it is the object of a contemplation which is the source of a secret and pure joy.

My own soul, my own self, is one of these temporal and changing possibles.

The subordination of my self, of my soul, of my body, of all my desires, to inflexible limits is an object of contemplation which is the source of a secret joy which is overwhelming.

Other men's too, if I situate my self within them by imagination.

This subordination is also made perceptible when a desire is satisfied, if the reasons for its satisfaction are clear and are clearly unrelated to the desire—so that the satisfaction is felt as precarious.

In that case, to eat a piece of bread when one is hungry is a communion with the universe and its Creator.

Affliction makes this subordination much more perceptible, provided the causal mechanism is clear. Thence comes the brutal beauty of affliction.

This is to learn obedience as Christ did.

Christ was held in bonds like the ocean.

τοῦτο δὸς ἐμοί.[1]

The only part of our soul which is not a fit subject for affliction is the part which is situated in the other world. Affliction has no power over it—for perhaps, as Meister Eckhart says, it is uncreated—but it has the power to sever it violently from the temporal part of the soul, so that, although supernatural love dwells in the soul, its sweetness is not felt. It is then that the cry breaks out: "My God, why hast thou forsaken me?"

Once one has recognized God as the supreme and real good, eternally satisfied by himself, that is enough. One may suppose not only that he neither rewards nor punishes his creatures, but even that he ignores their efforts to obey him, their lapses, or their revolts. One will desire nevertheless, more than anything else, to obey him—with a desire stronger than hunger, thirst, the sensual fire, or the craving for respite in the midst of physical torture. At the same time, everything will appear unimportant, including one's own possession of God, in the face of the certainty that He possesses himself eternally and perfectly.

All the desire which nature has placed in the human soul and attached to food, drink, rest, physical comfort, the pleasures of the eye and the ear, and other human beings, should be detached from those things and directed exclusively towards obedience to God.

The things of this world are legitimately objects of pleasure and pain, but not of desire and repulsion.

And obedience to God, the unique object of all the soul's desire, is an unknowable object. I do not know what God's command will be tomorrow.

But I do know that if I refuse to obey him, or if my weakness makes me incapable of it, I am still obeying him, because nothing happens here below unless He wills it.

So this desire is certain of fulfilment. It is already fulfilled. It is a hunger which has already been appeased, which always will be, and which, nevertheless, perpetually cries out in the soul as though it never could be.

[1] grant me this.

It is a cry in the void, an eternally unanswered appeal.

It is this appeal which is the praise of the glory of God. Our cries of anguish praise Him.

Christ on the cross saying "My God, why hast thou forsaken me?"—that is the perfect praise of God's glory.

To cry like this throughout our brief and interminable, interminable and brief sojourn in this world, and then disappear into nothingness—it is enough; what more is there to ask? If God grants more, that is his affair; we shall know later on. I prefer to suppose that at the very best He grants no more than that. For that is completeness of fulfilment—if only, from now until the moment of my death, there could be no other word in my soul than this uninterrupted cry in the eternal silence.

Christ is mediator between man and the Father, between the Father and the Spirit. In the Trinity he is the object, and the object is mediator between subject and act—although the relationship can be represented differently. The thing loved is mediator between my love and me.

When we love God, the Father loves the Son through us. For God as object is the Son. He is mediator between the Father and his Love.

To disobey God is to cease to know that He is real. Then desire immediately attaches itself to earthly things. So as to avoid detaching it, we want to continue to disobey. But at the same time our awareness that we are obliged to detach it puts the soul in agony.

In reality, since God exists, even my disobedience is without importance; but I only know this when I am in obedience. As soon as I disobey, my disobedience acquires an illusory importance, which there are only two ways of effacing—either by a return to obedience through anguish and the pain of detaching my desires, or through lying to myself.

By this mechanism, the knowledge of God is prevented from leading to moral relaxation.

Where there is such relaxation, the object which is loved under the name of God is really something else.

In order to obey God, one must receive his commands.

How did it happen that I received them in adolescence, while I was professing atheism?

To believe that the desire for good is always fulfilled—that is faith, and whoever has it is not an atheist.

To believe in a God who can leave in darkness those who desire light, and reciprocally, that is not to have faith.

Faith is the certainty of a domain other than this inextricable mixture of good and evil which constitutes this world, a domain in which good produces only good and evil produces only evil.

To recognize something good as being good, and to hold that its origin is evil is the sin against the Spirit, which is not forgiven.

Good and evil, that is the heart of the problem, and the essential truth is that they are not reciprocally related. Evil is the contrary of good, but good is not the contrary of anything.

Non-reciprocal relations in modern physics; is it a case of phenomena belonging to two different domains, with two energies of different quality although the difference has not been recognized?

(Scientists believe in science in the same way that the majority of Catholics believe in the Church, namely, as Truth crystallized in an infallible collective opinion; they contrive to believe this in spite of the continual changes of theory. In both cases it is through lack of faith in God.)

A Catholic directs his thought, secondarily towards the truth, but primarily towards conformity with the Church's doctrine. A scientist does the same, only in this case there is no established doctrine but a collective opinion in process of formation; he directs his thought along a certain current, felt by intuition, more or less correctly and with more or less prescience.

From the point of view of intellectual probity it is worse. It is an even worse stifling of the intelligence.

Perhaps it has not always been so? Even during the recent period of 4 or 5 centuries? how can one know? In any case, it has all become very much worse.

One has only the choice between God and idolatry. There is no other possibility. For the faculty of worship is in us, and it is either directed somewhere into this world, or into the other.

If one affirms God one is either worshipping God or else some things of this world labelled with his name.

If one denies God, either one is worshipping him unknown to oneself or else one is worshipping some things of this world in the belief that one sees them only as such, but in fact, though unknown to oneself, imagining the attributes of Divinity in them.

There is a period in the growth of the soul when the faculty of worship is divided—partly directed towards the things of this world and partly towards the other.

This is the criterion. All those are worshippers of the true God who love conditioned things, without exception, only conditionally.

The Good is outside this world.

Thanks to God's wisdom, who has printed on this world the mark of the good, in the form of beauty, one can love the Good through the things of this world.

This docility of matter, this maternal quality of nature, was incarnated in the Virgin.

Dense matter is attentive nevertheless to God's persuasion.

"this world consents to thy domination".[1]

Through love, matter receives the imprint of the divine Wisdom and becomes beautiful.

One is right to love the world's beauty, because it is the sign of an exchange of love between the Creator and the creation.

Beauty is to things what sanctity is to the soul.

Truly beautiful human beings deserve to be loved. But the concupiscence inspired by the beauty of a face and a body is not the love that this beauty deserves; it is a sort of hate which grips the flesh when it confronts something which is too pure for it. Plato knew that.

Such is the grace of God that sometimes he makes us feel a beauty in our affliction itself. It is then the revelation of a beauty purer than we knew before. Job.

But always at the first onset of affliction there is a privation of beauty, and invasion of the soul by ugliness. And then, unless we keep our love oriented, in defiance of all common sense, in the same direction, although it has ceased to have an object, we lose all contact with the good, perhaps finally.

If, as I believe is possible, there is a limit which one can pass, in this world, and beyond which there is no further hope of salvation, I would like to believe that those who have passed it are insensible, even to physical pain, or almost.

A suffering which has no possible use would be pure evil, and according to St. Augustine pure evil is nothingness.

That is why I would also like to believe that animals do not suffer.

God allows us to convey our love towards him in two ways, through beauty or in the void.

[1] ὅδε κόσμος . . . ἑκὼν ὑπὸ σεῖο κρατεῖται (Cleanthes' *Hymn to Zeus*).

In everything in the past we ought to love the fulfilment of God's will. In the future we ought to love the hope of pure good, to be conveyed by God in the form of inspiration to his thinking creatures. The present is between the two. It is neither an object of acceptance nor of hope, but of contemplation. Contemplation of the divine Wisdom in the beauty of the world, where the two contraries, necessity and the good, are united. The facts that have been accomplished were necessary; we wait for the good to come.

"Thy will be done", acceptance; "thy kingdom come", hope. "Hallowed be thy name", this is simply loving contemplation, admiration.

"Forgive us our debts . . ."

God is our creditor; God is also our only debtor. We feel cheated of our due by every event which is contrary to our desires.

But the most difficult remission of debts consists in forgiving God for our sins. The sense of guilt is accompanied by a sort of rancour and hatred against the Good, against God, and it is the effect of this mechanism that makes crime harmful to the soul.

Crimes unaccompanied by even a fleeting sense of guilt do not harm the soul. But they can only occur in certain states of the soul which are themselves moral maladies.

Such crimes become harmful as soon as there is convalescence, because then the sense of guilt awakens and is repressed.

God himself cannot prevent what has happened from having happened. What better proof that the creation is an abdication?

What greater abdication of God than is represented by time?

We are abandoned in time.

God is not in time.

Creation and original sin are only two aspects, which are different for us, of a single act of abdication by God. And the Incarnation, the Passion, are also aspects of this act.

God emptied himself of his divinity and filled us with a false divinity. Let us empty ourselves of it. This act is the purpose of the act by which we were created.

At this very moment God, by his creative will, is maintaining me in existence, in order that I may renounce it.

God waits patiently until at last I am willing to consent to love him.

God waits like a beggar who stands motionless and silent before someone who will perhaps give him a piece of bread. Time is that waiting.

Time is God's waiting as a beggar for our love.

The stars, the mountains, the sea, and all the things that speak to us of time, convey God's supplication to us.

By waiting humbly we are made similar to God.

God is only the good. That is why he is waiting there in silence. Anyone who comes forward and speaks is using a little force. The good which is nothing but good can only stand waiting.

Beggars who are modest are images of Him.

Humility is a certain relation of the soul to time. It is an acceptance of waiting. That is why, socially, it is the mark of inferiors that they are made to wait. "I nearly had to wait" is the tyrant's word. But in ceremony, whose poetry makes all men equal, everybody has to wait.

Art is waiting. Inspiration is waiting.

He shall bear fruit in patience.

Humility partakes in God's patience. The perfected soul waits for the good in silence, immobility and humility like God's own. Christ nailed on the cross is the perfect image of the Father.

No saint has been able to obtain from God that the past should not have been, or that he himself should grow ten years older in one day or one day older in ten years, or that . . . No miracle can do anything against time. The faith that moves mountains is impotent against time.

God has left us abandoned in time.

God and humanity are like two lovers who have missed their rendezvous. Each is there before the time, but each at a different place, and they wait and wait and wait. He stands motionless, nailed to the spot for the whole of time. She is distraught and impatient. But alas for her if she gets tired and goes away. For the two places where they are waiting are at the same point in the fourth dimension . . .

The crucifixion of Christ is the image of this fixity of God.

God is attention without distraction.

One must imitate the patience and humility of God.

"Be ye holy because I am holy". Imitation of God. Doubtless borrowed by Moses from the Egyptian wisdom.

It is in time that we have our "I".

The acceptance of time and of whatever it may bring—without any exception—(*amor fati*)—that is the only disposition of the soul which is unconditioned in relation to time. It encloses the infinite. Whatever may happen . . .

God has given his finite creatures this power of transporting themselves into the infinite.

Mathematics is its image.

If the pleasant or painful content of each minute (even those in which we sin) is regarded as a special caress from God, in what way does time separate us from Heaven?

The dereliction in which God leaves us is his own way of caressing us.

Time, which is our one misery, is the very touch of his hand. It is the abdication by which he lets us exist.

He stays far away from us, because if He approached He would cause us to disappear. He waits for us to go to him and disappear.

At death, some disappear into the absence of God and others disappear into the presence of God. We cannot conceive this difference. That is why the representations of heaven and hell have been elaborated, so as to have an approximation which the imagination can grasp.

Essence of faith: It is impossible really to desire the good and not obtain it.

Or reciprocally: anything which it is possible really to desire without obtaining it is not really the good.

It is impossible to receive the good when one has not desired it.

That is the meaning of the precept: confine your desires to things that depend upon yourself.

But that does not mean things which you have in yourself or which you can acquire by your will-power. For all that is wretched and valueless. It means an object of humble and desperate longing, of supplication.

The good is something which you can never get by your own effort, but neither can you desire it without getting it.

That is why our situation is just like that of little children who cry that they are hungry and who receive bread.

That is why suppliants of every kind are sacred, supplication is sacred.

One has the duty to give everything except what one has the duty to refuse.

Olive branch. Tree of the Holy Spirit, emblem of suppliants.

God has separated force and the good in this world, and kept the good for himself.

His commandments have the form of asking.

Everything we get for ourselves by our own will and our own efforts, and everything given or withheld by the chance of external circumstances, is absolutely without value. It may be bad or indifferent, but never good.

God leaves us in this world exposed to evil.

Nevertheless, if we desire that the eternal and non-sensible part of our soul should be preserved from all evil, it will be.

Everything that exists is subjected to necessity. But there is a carnal necessity into which the opposition of good and evil does not enter, and a spiritual necessity which is entirely subjected to this opposition.

The very idea of redemption implies a spiritual necessity.

Only necessity is an object of knowledge. Nothing else can be grasped by thought. Necessity is known through exploration, experiment, experience. Mathematics is experience of a certain kind. Necessity is the thing with which human thought has contact.

The only thing in us that is unconditioned is desire. It is appropriate that it should be directed towards the unconditioned being, God.

Nothing can be produced unless the conditions for its production are brought together.

Such and such a thing calls for such and such a condition. But if one thinks: everything can be produced, given the conditions, and everything is equivalent . . .

If one desires a particular thing one becomes enslaved to the series of conditions. But if one desires the series itself, the satisfaction of this desire is unconditioned.

That is why the one and only liberation is love of the order of the world.

Christ on the cross, the greatest harm inflicted on the greatest good: if one loves that, one loves the order of the world.

In water and blood. The public life of Christ commenced with a baptism of water and ended with a baptism of blood.

On the cross he rendered unto Caesar what was Caesar's and unto God what was God's.

You shall judge them by their fruits. There is no greater evil than to do evil to men, and no greater good than to do good to men.

One cannot know what is in a man's mind when he speaks a certain word (God, freedom, progress ...). One can only judge the good in his soul by the good in his actions, or in the expression of his original thoughts.

One cannot perceive the presence of God in a man, but only the reflection of that light in his manner of conceiving earthly life. Thus, the true God is present in the *Iliad* and not in the book of Joshua.

The author of the *Iliad* depicts life as only a man who loves God can see it. The author of Joshua as only a man who does not love God can see it.

One does not testify so well for God by speaking about Him as by expressing, either in actions or words, the new aspect assumed by the creation after the soul has experienced the Creator.

Indeed, the truth is that the latter is the only way.

To die for God is not a proof of faith in God. To die for an unknown and repulsive convict who is a victim of injustice, that is a proof of faith in God.

That is what Christ was explaining: "I was naked ... I was hungry ... "

The love of God is only an intermediary between the natural and the supernatural love of creatures.

It is solely because of the crucifixion that faith in Christ can be, as St. John says, a criterion. To accept as God a common convict, shamefully tortured and put to death, is truly to overcome the world. (And he says nothing about the resurrection.) It is to renounce all temporal safety. It is to accept and love necessity.

But who thinks of Christ today as a common convict, except his enemies? People worship the historic grandeur of the Church.

The black slaves overcame the world by faith in Christ: "They crucified my Lord".

God is present, Christ is present, wherever there is enacted between one man and another an act of supernatural virtue.

The soul's attitude towards God is not a thing that can be verified, even by the soul itself, because God is elsewhere, in heaven, in secret. If one thinks to have verified it, there is really some earthly thing masquerading under the label of God. One can only verify whether the behaviour of the soul as regards this world bears the mark of an experience of God.

In the same way, a bride's friends do not go into the nuptial chamber; but when she is seen to be pregnant they know she has lost her virginity.

There is no fire in a cooked dish, but one knows it has been on the fire.

On the other hand, even though one may think to have seen the flames under them, if the potatoes are raw it is certain they have not been on the fire.

It is not the way a man talks about God, but the way he talks about things of the world that best shows whether his soul has passed through the fire of the love of God. In this matter no deception is possible. There are false imitations of the love of God, but not of the transformation it effects in the soul, because one has no idea of this transformation except by passing through it oneself.

In the same way, the proof that a child can do division is not that he can recite the rule, but that he can divide. If he recites the rule, I don't know whether he understands it. If I give him some difficult sums in division and he gets the answers right, I have no need to make him explain the rule. It doesn't even matter if he is incapable of it, or doesn't know the name of the operation. I know that he understands it. If the child who could repeat the rule adds the numbers up instead of dividing them, I know he doesn't understand it.

In the same way, I know that the author of the *Iliad* knew and loved God and the author of the Book of Joshua did not.

When a man's way of behaving towards things and men, or simply his way of regarding them, reveals supernatural virtues, one knows that his soul is no longer virgin, it has slept with God; perhaps even without knowing it, like a girl violated in her sleep. That has no importance, it is only the fact that matters.

The only certain proof a young woman's friends have that she has lost her virginity is that she is pregnant. Otherwise there is no proof—not even if she should talk and behave lewdly. Her husband may be impotent.

In the same way, if a soul speaks of God with words of faith and love, either publicly or inwardly, this is no proof either for others or for itself. It may be that what it calls God is an impotent being, that is to say, a false God, and that it has never really slept with God.

What is a proof is the appearance of supernatural virtues in that part of its behaviour which is turned towards men.

The faith of a judge is not seen in his behaviour at church, but in his behaviour on the bench.

But, like a woman's pregnancy, this transformation is not effected by direct efforts, but by a union of love with God.

A woman may talk in the most lewd way and yet be a virgin. But if she is pregnant she is not a virgin, even though she may pretend to know nothing. It is the same with the Old Testament and the *Iliad*

Iliad. Only the love of God can enable a soul to discern the horror of human misery so lucidly and so coolly without losing either tenderness or serenity.

The Roman who died to save his slaves from torture loved God.

Every master who believes that his slaves are his equals knows and loves God. And reciprocally.

A painter does not draw the spot where he is standing. But in looking at his picture I can deduce his position by relation to the things drawn.

On the other hand, if he puts himself into his picture I know for certain that the place where he shows himself is not the place where he is.

According to the conception of human life expressed in the acts and words of a man I know (I mean I would know if I possessed discernment) whether he sees life from a point in this world or from above in heaven.

On the other hand, when he talks about God I cannot

discern (and yet sometimes I can . . .) whether he is speaking from within or externally.

If a man says he has been in an aeroplane, and has drawn the clouds, his picture is not a proof for me; I may believe it is a fantasy. If he brings me a bird's eye view of the town, it is a proof.

The Gospel contains a conception of human life, not a theology.

If I light an electric torch at night out of doors I don't judge its power by looking at the bulb, but by seeing how many objects it lights up.

The brightness of a source of light is appreciated by the illumination it projects upon non-luminous objects.

The value of a religious or, more generally, a spiritual way of life is appreciated by the amount of illumination thrown upon the things of this world.

Earthly things are the criterion of spiritual things.

This is what we generally don't want to recognize, because we are frightened of a criterion.

The virtue of anything is manifested outside the thing.

If, on the pretext that only spiritual things are of value, we refuse to take the light thrown on earthly things as a criterion, we are in danger of having a non-existent treasure.

Only spiritual things are of value, but only physical things have a verifiable existence. Therefore the value of the former can only be verified as an illumination projected on to the latter.

(That is the reason why the Kshatriyas instruct the Brahmins.)

God, who willed to create this world, willed that it should be so.

If a man took my left-hand glove, passed it behind his back, and returned it to me as a right-hand glove, I should know that he had access to the 4th dimension. No other proof is possible.

In the same way, if a man gives bread to a beggar in a certain way or speaks in a certain way about a defeated army, I know that his thought has been outside this world and sat with Christ alongside the Father who is in Heaven.

If a man describes to me at the same time two opposite sides of a mountain, I know that his position is somewhere higher than the summit.

It is impossible to understand and love at the same time both the victors and the vanquished, as the *Iliad* does, except from the place, outside the world, where God's Wisdom dwells.

State of the man who has prostituted his wife to Volpone and who then learns that he is not the heir.

For the sake of a hoped-for good one performs acts which would otherwise be impossible.

When the good fails to materialize, one is left with the impossible. The actions have been performed; they can never be undone. And yet they were impossible.

A man with a young, chaste, and beautiful wife, whom he loves, would not prostitute her to a repulsive old man without a reason. It is as impossible as a weight rising without being lifted.

But if he has done it because he thought it would win him an inheritance and then discovers that there was never any question of his getting the inheritance, then it is just as if he had done it for no reason—as if the weight had risen by itself.

So the soul lives in the impossible and cannot escape from it, because it is an accomplished impossibility, a past impossibility.

Then the only resource left is to uproot himself from his own past, which is the worst that can happen to a man.

The past holds us. It is more real than the present. And every man has his own past, which nothing can touch.

The soul re-enacts in thought what it did, but with the motive missing.

Wishing incessantly that his wife was still intact (would he not make a good hero for a tragedy) his thought reverts to the time, still so recent, when she was. To return to the present, his thought must pass through that happening. But that happening has now lost the motive which alone made it possible. His thought keeps continually falling into the past and can only get back to the present by passing through the impossible.

It is the same with an action whose accomplishment puts an end to the motive which alone made it possible. For example, a murder due to rage which subsides as soon as the murder has been committed.

Thought, having fled back into the innocent past, must go through the murder again without feeling rage. But that is an impossible journey.

The consequences of an action are more durable than their motives. When they are disastrous they force the soul to take refuge in the past, before they existed, and to rejoin the present by passing through motiveless actions. It is a torment for thought.

And it is the same, whatever was the nature of the motives—whether they were honourable or shameful.

Man could only escape this torment by performing motiveless actions.

Can he do this?

Only if God comes down and acts within him and in place of him.

How can a man bring this about?

By begging God to come down.

Obedience to God is the only motive which is unconditioned and can never disappear. It transports the action into eternity.

Suppose one says to oneself: even though the moment of death brings nothing new but only puts an end to life here below without being the prelude to another life; even though death only brings nothingness; and even though this world should be completely abandoned by God; and even though this word God corresponds to absolutely nothing real but only to childish illusions—even though this is how it is, I still prefer, even in this case, to perform what seems to me to be commanded by God, even though it leads to the most fearful troubles, rather than to do anything else at all.

Only a madman could think in this way.

But if one has caught this madness one can be perfectly sure of never regretting any action accomplished in conformity with the above thought.

The only difficulty is that this thought does not supply much energy—not enough energy for performing actions.

How to increase this energy?

Prayer ought to increase it.

The practice of obedience itself ought to increase it, because every action performed for a motive increases the energy of that motive.

Or else, it is true, exhausts it. There are two possible and quite distinct mechanisms.

It is of the very first importance to distinguish between them.

What exhausts a motive is going beyond what the motive prompts us to do.

Therefore the proportion of energy put at God's service will increase in the soul if great care is taken never to go beyond what one feels almost irresistibly driven to by obedience.

Otherwise, either the love of God becomes exhausted or else it is replaced, under the same name, by another love.

This is of such great importance—because so many carnal loves can insinuate themselves under that name...

Prayer is only directed towards God if it is *unconditioned*. To pray unconditionally is to ask in Christ's name. That is the prayer that is never refused.

Thy will be done—whatever it may be.

Come down to accomplish thy will in me—whatever it may be.

Faith means believing that what we do after such a prayer will be less far from obedience to God than what we do before it.

If an action seems to have been commanded by God, we may beseech God for help in accomplishing it.

But only if we make this implied reservation: I beseech thy help for this action only because I believe it conforms to thy will and only if it in fact does so.

At the same time one must desire success for this action with a desire as violent as a miser's for gold or a starving man's for bread.

Because we may be mistaken about God's will—but we can regard it as certain that God wishes us to do everything that we believe is in conformity with his will.

St. Francis thought he had received the order to carry stones to St. Damian, and while he was under this illusion, God wanted him to carry stones.

How is it possible that the feeling should arise in a human soul that God desires a certain particular thing? It is a marvel as miraculous as the Incarnation.

Or rather, it is itself the marvel of the Incarnation. A soul perpetually ruled by this feeling, from birth to death, is God become man.

Art is a marvel of the same kind, for artistic inspiration, in art of the very highest order (which is extremely rare), is of this nature. And the same is true of every illumination of the intelligence.

All these marvels consist in the presence of the unconditioned in the conditioned; it is the unmoved causing thought to move in a certain direction.

Without this marvel, we should be completely earthly beings.

All those—and they are perhaps the great majority—who have never experienced this marvel in themselves are completely earthly beings.

How is it that some experience it?

But there is a second marvel, which is that the acts and words resulting from an inspiration of this kind possess a radiance which influences the most earthly hearts to love them.

If one loves them without a tinge of hatred and envy, without reference to oneself, and with the desire to possess the source of it some day, in one's turn, simply because the good is there and with no other motive—one will succeed.

This radiance of the things here below that are inspired and sacred is what judges earthly souls and obliges them to give themselves to God or to the devil.

That is why Christ, in St. John's Gospel, speaks continually of the attitude towards himself. It is a question of him as a man, and not of a church or a theology.

Our soul is a pair of scales. The direction of the energy in our actions is the pointer of the scales, marking such and such a figure. But the scales are false.

When God, the true God, occupies all the place due to him in a soul, then the scales have become true.

God does not say what figure the pointer should show, but because He is there, the pointer is accurate.

The scales tip every way. But there is a nail that fixes the centre. Therefore the register is true. The nail does not indicate any figure, but because of the nail the pointer marks accurately.

Upanishad: God is not what is manifested by the word, but that by which the word is manifested. He is that by which everything is manifested and which is not manifested by anything.

Not figures marked by a pointer, but that by which the pointer marks accurate figures.

That is why the perfect human being does not act for the sake of God, but by God and on behalf of God, and does not love human beings in God, but on behalf of God and through God.

God suffered in place of man—this does not mean that Christ's affliction diminished in the slightest degree the affliction of men, but that through the affliction of Christ (in the preceding centuries as much as in the following) the affliction of any afflicted man acquires the meaning and the value of expiation, if only he desires it. The affliction then acquires an infinite value, which can only come from God.

All expiation implies that it is God who is expiating.

The difficulties of the idea of redemption, and the absurdities that surround it, make it necessary to examine more closely the idea of punishment itself, and its relation to the idea of sacrifice.

All that St. Paul says about redemption is only acceptable if one regards humanity as a *single* living being—who sinned in the days of Adam, who was in tutelage to the law, who attains purity and freedom in death, and who rises again.

The expectation of the imminent end of the world is essential to early Christianity and explains many anomalies. No doubt it was the most popular part of the message.

The Last Judgement will be like this.—The soul which has just passed through what men call death becomes suddenly, irresistibly, convinced beyond all possibility of doubt that *all the ends* to which *all its actions* were directed during life were illusions, including God. Entirely penetrated in all its parts, including the sensibility, by this certainty, it re-lives in thought all the actions of its life.

After which, in most cases, it is seized with horror, desires to be annihilated, and disappears.

There are rare cases where nothing is regretted, or where at least the soul can fix on some actions which it does not regret, because they were unconditioned, they were pure obedience.

It is not seized with horror, but continues to be oriented, with love, towards the good.

However, it feels its personality as a barrier which hinders its perfect contact with the good, desires it to be dissolved, and disappears.

Perhaps one single act of pure obedience is enough. But if there has been one, there will have been many.

What is the connection between punishment and forgiveness? There is *reparation*—an offended man only forgives if the offender has undergone a penalty and humiliation, either by consenting to submit to it (as was frequent in the middle ages) or by being constrained to it until he says, like the whipped slaves at Rome: Forgive me, I have suffered enough.

Another connection is *cure*—it is hoped that the punishment will be a remedy to reform the criminal; once he has been reformed, this fact alone will secure his pardon.

These are two human relationships, but they can be transposed into the relationship between God and man, provided the rules of such a transposition are observed.

What are these rules?

The purpose of reparation is not to cure the criminal but the injured party, who cannot forget the offence or think of it without distress until he has seen the criminal suffer.

This corresponds with the need to pass suffering on. The captain who has been reprimanded by the colonel stomachs the reprimand until he can be relieved of it by reprimanding the lieutenant.

But if one has been offended by an inferior one passes the suffering back to the man who caused it, and with interest.

The broken china vase cannot be mended; but luckily the slave who broke it can be broken by the whip.

If the slave falls on his knees, it is enough, sometimes, simply to have him thus in one's power.

The slave who has been whipped—or even if he has only suffered the pain of begging for mercy—needs to find compensation in his turn.

Every evil stirred up in this world passes from one man to another (it is the Homeric myth of Atë) until it alights upon a perfectly pure being who suffers it in its completeness and destroys it.

The Father who is in heaven is not affected as a man is by our offences. But for that very reason, every offence committed directly against Him falls back upon the offender as a curse; and thenceforward he cannot help trying to free himself from this evil by doing evil to other creatures. He puts into circulation an evil which passes continually from one creature to another.

That is what happened to Cain—assuming that Cain sacrificed reluctantly.

The evil put in circulation in this way moves on and on until it falls upon a victim who is perfectly pure.

God who is in heaven cannot destroy evil; he can only send it back in the form of a curse. It is only God in this world, having become a victim, who can destroy evil by suffering it.

Thus the idea of evil as reparation leads to the idea of redemption, when correctly transposed.

The Father who is in heaven does not send the evil back, but because he cannot in any way be touched by it, the evil falls back.

The man who takes vengeance imitates God the Father. This is the wrong way to imitate God. Man is permitted only to imitate God the Son. That is why "No man comes to the Father save by me".

Nevertheless: "Be ye perfect as your heavenly Father is perfect." But here it is a question of imitating God the Father in his abdication, of which the complete fulfilment is the Incarnation.

Men have always felt the need to purify themselves by the sacrifice of innocent beings—animals, children, virgins. It is the highest degree of innocence when the sacrifice is voluntary.

The man who has suffered evil wants to be relieved of it by putting it elsewhere: that is what the desire for satisfaction is. He does not want to abolish the evil, but to abolish it out of his own life, and therefore to throw it out elsewhere.

But for God there is no elsewhere to which to throw the evil; the sphere of his existence is all-inclusive. God can desire only to abolish the evil. But it is only through contact with God that the evil falls into nothingness.

Thus the satisfaction which man gets by throwing the offence away from himself consists for God in submitting to it.

By eating the apple, Adam offended God, and this offence fell back again in the form of a curse because it didn't touch God. But the offence of those who drove nails into Christ's flesh did not fall back again as a curse; it touched God and disappeared.

Song of Orpheus: "Leges in superos datas—et qui tempora digerit—quatuor precipites deus—anni disposuit vices."— There are laws for the gods, even for the god who fixed the times and disposed the four swift turns of the year. (Seneca, Her Oet. 1093).

Id.: "jam jam legibus obrutis—mundo cum veniet dies— australis polus obruet—quidquid per Libyam jacet".[1]

The rapid spread of Christianity was due to the fact that all those unfortunate people so longed for the end of the world! And how easy that is to understand.

None of the cults or rival sects could offer so palpable a guarantee of the quite imminent end of the world as the life, death, and resurrection of Christ.

"omnes pariter deos—perdet mors aliqua et chaos—et mors fata novissima—in se constituet sibi".[2]

Cf. St. Paul. Death will be the last thing to be destroyed.

The Zodiac—"Leo flammiferis aestibus ardens iterum e caelo cadet Herculeus (a note says that he had fallen from the Moon), cadet in terras Virgo relictas, justaeque cadent pondera Librae."—Aquarius "... frangetque tuam, quisquis es, urnam".

"... in nos aetas ultima venit?" ... "O nos dura sorte creatos—seu perdidimus solem miseri—seu expellimus."[3]

Atreus, speaking of Thyestes "miserum videre nolo, sed dum fit miser".[4] The experimental cruelty of the Roman emperors.

"flendi miseris dira cupido est".[5]

Monologue of Seneca, as a character in the contemporary Roman tragedy *Octavia* (Nero died in 68). "qui si senescit, tantum in caecum chaos—casurus iterum, tunc adest mundo dies—supremus ille, qui premat genus impium—caeli ruina,

---

[1] In the end, when the laws are overthrown, the last day will come to the world; the Southern sky will fall upon Libya (*ibid.:* lines 1102-5).

[2] Death in some form, and chaos, will destroy the whole race of gods; and death will establish for itself new laws to follow. (Seneca: *Hercules Oetaeus*, 1114-17.)

[3] The Nemaean Lion will fall again, flaming, from the sky; the Virgin will fall again upon the lands she had left, and the weights of the just Balances will fall ... and will break thy urn, whoever thou art ... Has our last age arrived? What a hard fate we were born to—either we have lost the sun by misfortune, or we have driven him away. (Seneca: *Thyestes*, 855-8, 864-5, 878-81.)

[4] I don't want to see him unhappy, but while he is becoming unhappy. (*Ibid.*, 907.)

[5] For the afflicted there is a dreadful pleasure in weeping. (*Ibid.*, 953.)

rursus ut stirpem novam—generet renascens melior, ut quondam tulit—juvenis, tenente regna Saturno poli—tunc illa virgo, numinis magni dea—Justitia, caelo missa cum sancta Fide—terris regebat mitis humanum genus".[1]

The 4th race dares to hunt and fish "vomere immunem pruis—sulcare terram, laesa qua fruges suas—alterius alte condidit sacro sinu",[2] and, even more criminally, to extract iron and gold.

"neglecta terras fugit... Astraea virgo, siderum magnum decus".[3]

Sign of the Virgin, month of August (Libra, which follows autumnal equinox, 21 September).—15 August, feast of the Assumption of the Virgin. Feast of the Nativity of the Virgin, 8 September.

"non ursa pontum sicca caeruleum bibet". The she-bear is thirsty and wants to plunge into the sea, but cannot.

The 12 labours of Hercules are:

Nemean Lion	Cretan Bull
Lernaean Hydra	Diomedes' Mare
Arcadian Stag	Belt of Hippolytus
Boar of Erymanthus	Oxen of Geryon
Augean Stables	Apples of the Hesperides
Birds of lake Stymphalus	Descent to Hades (Cerberus)

He says, in Seneca, "Juno has removed the monsters" (to heaven).

He includes the Crab (assimilated to the Hydra?)—The Lion—But there is no other, except the bull.

Does this list correspond to an older Zodiac?

Description of the mysteries of Eleusis, H. fur. 842.[4]

---

[1] If [the world] lives to be older it will fall again into blind chaos, and the day of reckoning will come, when the crash of the fallen heavens will overwhelm impious mankind, so that for the second time there may arise a new race, reborn to be an improvement upon the present one, as there was indeed in the earlier time when Saturn held the dominion of the skies. Then it was the virgin Justitia, goddess of great sanctity, commissioned from heaven with the sacred trust, ruled the world with mildness. (Seneca: *Octavia*, 391–9.)

[2] ... to plough the hitherto unwounded earth, which was then found to hide its treasure much deeper in its sacred bosom. (*Ibid.*, 413–15.)

[3] The virgin Astraea, bright ornament of the starry sky, ... finding herself no longer honoured, fled the earth. (*Ibid.*, 422–4.)

[4] Seneca: *Hercules furens*.

If we put obedience to God above everything else, unreservedly, with the following thought: "Suppose God is real, then our gain is total—even though we fall into nothingness at the moment of death; suppose the word 'God' stands only for illusions, then we have still lost nothing because on this assumption there is absolutely nothing good, and consequently nothing to lose; we have even gained, through being in accord with truth, because we have left aside the illusory goods which exist but are not good for the sake of something which (on this assumption) does not exist but which, if it did exist, would be the only good . . . "

If one follows this rule of life, then no revelation at the moment of death can cause any regrets; because if chance or the devil govern all worlds we would still have no regrets for having lived in this way.

That is greatly preferable to Pascal's wager.

If God should be an illusion from the point of view of existence, He is the sole reality from the point of view of the good. I know that for certain, because it is a definition. "God is the good" is as certain as "I am". I am in accord with the truth if I wrench my desire away from everything which is not a good, so as to direct it solely towards the good, without knowing whether the good exists or not.

When once all my desire is directed towards the good, what other good have I to expect? I now possess all the good. That is what it is to possess all the good. How absurd to imagine any other happiness!

For the privilege of finding myself before I die in a state perfectly similar to Christ's when he said, on the cross: "My God, why hast thou forsaken me?"—for that privilege I would willingly renounce everything that is called Paradise.

Because all his desire was entirely directed towards God, and therefore he perfectly possessed God.

He was enduring almost infernal suffering, but what does that detail matter?

It is in respect of false goods that desire and possession are different things; for the true good, there is no difference.

Therefore, God exists because I desire Him; that is as certain as my existence.

I find myself in this world with my desire attached to things which are not real goods, things which are neither good nor bad. I must wrench it away from them, but that makes one bleed.

It is not surprising that desire should be different from possession so long as desire is attached to those things, because what it needs is something good, and they are not good.

So soon as it detaches itself and turns towards the good, desire is possession.

But this does not happen for all the soul's desire at the same time. At first only for an infinitesimal part.

Yet this grain of desire which is possession is stronger than all the rest of desire, which is empty.

If I desire only to desire the good, then in desiring the good my desire is fulfilled to overflowing.

It is no more difficult than that.

And I have no need to imagine something behind this word. On the contrary, the object of my desire must be nothing but the reality, completely unknown to me, which is behind the word.

I desire exclusively the good (I mean, that is what I ought to do), but I know that I know absolutely nothing about the good which I exclusively desire, except its name. And yet my desire is perfectly fulfilled, and I need absolutely nothing else.

The secret of salvation is so simple that it escapes the intelligence by its simplicity. It is like a play on words.

It is the same with some passages of the Upanishads on the Atman.

But merely possessing the secret is not everything. It is not easy to apply, because desire adheres to those things that are not goods.

What is the mechanism of this attachment?

What is it that constrains us to want to eat when we are hungry, drink when we are thirsty, get relief when we have a pain somewhere, enjoy consideration after being humiliated, change our posture after being too long in the same one, sleep when we feel drowsy, stop work when we are tired, see someone we love, shake his hand, talk with him, listen to him, have the use of our limbs and sense organs?

So long as we desire all these frivolous things, the centre of our soul is not fixed in the good.

How, why, do we desire them and find it impossible to avoid doing so? How can these desires be suppressed?

It is a question, not of making oneself insensible to pains and pleasures—that would be easier—but, while leaving intact all the soul's susceptibility to pains and pleasures, of not desiring to avoid the former and obtain the latter.

When the feeling of necessity takes very strong possession of the soul it often kills desire, and even the most natural desires.

That is the secret, then. Cut off all the desires by obedience, as with a sword.

Void
Those who have done a man harm are far away, out of his reach; those who are within reach have shown him kindness; so far from having any grievance against them, he owes them respect and smiles; and yet he is only able to smile at the cost of an effort which no one suspects, because such behaviour on his part seems merely natural.

If a man has to make a violent effort in order to behave as he would naturally be expected to—this is the void, a fathomless bitterness.

The void—an inner tension to which nothing in one's external situation corresponds.

Example of the void: concentration camp punishment of moving a stone from B to A, then from A to B, then from B to A, and so on all day. Very different from the same effort in real work.

R. "If I had to work simply to live, I couldn't do it. I can only work in order to better myself continually". (Void)

[R. What he said about the theft of potatoes. One has only to ask for what one needs. "Ah, but in order to beg for charity you have to have that sort of character". Referring to old J. "As for me, I couldn't humble myself like that and submit to picking grapes eight hours a day.—But suppose you *had* to?—Suppose I had to? Suppose I had to? . . . Well, I wouldn't do it! I'd find some other way out".]

The void serves for nothing except grace. Therefore it must be so far as possible eliminated from social life, because society is not composed of saints. There will always be enough of it for the elect.

The void is better than a psychological equilibrium achieved by the help of external things. But that kind of equilibrium is better than the kind that is invented by the imagination.

The imagination works incessantly to block up the tiniest cracks through which grace might enter.

There are also factors of equilibrium that are both real and imaginary at the same time. Smiles of Louis XIV. Money.

One could list in this way a hierarchy of factors of equilibrium other than grace, from the most real to the most imaginary (the latter being also those that include most of the unlimited).

[R. complaining about the compulsory levy of vinic alcohol from the big vineyard proprietors, which means that he makes no more profit than if he had three times fewer vines, 1200 acres.—"It means I'm working for nothing."]

Motives. Thoughts are fluid, they are swayed by fantasy, passion, fatigue. But work has to be carried on persistently, for many hours a day, every day. Therefore motives are required which are proof against the instability of thoughts, that is to say, against *relation*; in other words, what is required is absolutes, or idols.

The only alternative is the supernatural bread, every day.

Therefore, in the Cave the idolatrous passions are a necessity. What is needed is to find the least bad idols.

Christ experienced the total void, a moment before he was resurrected.

He suffered the whole of human misery, except sin; but he had everything that makes a man capable of sin. What makes man capable of sin is the void; all sins are attempts to fill voids. Thus my pitiful and soiled life is very close to his perfectly pure one, and so also are the basest lives. Whatever I do, however low I fall, I shall never be very far from him. But if I fell too low, I could no longer be aware of this truth. Only grace renewed every day allows one to know it every day.

To repent. To contemplate a past evil which one has perpetrated, and which is irreparable, knowing this and not seeking any excuse; to do this is to endure emptiness, the void.

Or if the evil is reparable, then the work of reparation is unrewarded effort, a labour in the void.

Everything is useful, etiam peccata. Do not believe this too much, because it is a thought that heals bitterness and fills a void, like the belief in immortality or in the providential ordering of events.

The void is supreme plenitude, but man has not the right to know this; and the proof is that Christ himself, for a moment, completely ignored it. One part of a man ought to know it, but not the other parts, because they would only know it in a base way, an imaginary way, and thus they would destroy it.

The base parts of myself ought to love God, but not too much, or it would not be the same God.

Negative virtue is work in the void. Not doing something. One makes an effort, and nothing external is changed. Not picking the fruit.

A representation of the world including a void, so that the world may have need of God. This presupposes some evil. "ὑπεναντίον ἀγαθῷ"[1]

And at the same time the world, as a manifestation of God, is full. "This is full, that is full".

The world manifests God and conceals God. "Thou art indeed the hidden God." And yet: "They were able to know God through the world which makes him manifest".

St. Peter's denial. To say to Christ "I will not deny thee" was already to deny him, since it was to suppose the source of loyalty to be in oneself, and not in grace. Since he was of the elect, this denial fortunately became clear. But in other cases, people's boasts may come true and be apparently confirmed, and they never understand.

How grateful I ought to be that I was born incapable even of picking grapes without the help of grace!

song of negro porters.

> Kilima muzuri mbali
> Karibu kinamayuto!

How beautiful the mountain is from far away! Why must it be so hard to climb?

The Almond Tree—
Woman in the snow under an almond tree is eating an apple, cuts herself, desires a child as red as blood and as white as

[1] opposite to the good.

snow, has a son, dies, is buried under the almond tree. The father marries again. Has a daughter. The son is ill-treated. The girl asks for an apple for herself and her brother. The step-mother offers the little boy an apple and slams the lid of the chest down on him, thus breaking his neck. Contrives that the little girl shall think that she herself killed him. Cooks him and serves him to the father, who has never tasted anything so delicious. The little girl weeps, put the bones in her prettiest handkerchief, and buries them under the almond tree. She feels better. A bird comes and sings

> mein' Mutter die mich schlacht,
> mein Vater der mich ass,
> mein' Schwester das Marlenichen
> sucht alle meine Benichen,
> bindt sie in ein seiden Tuch,
> legts unter den Machandelbaum.
> kywitt, kywitt, wat vör'n schön' Vogel bün ich![1]

wins by its singing a golden chain (for the father), a pair of red shoes (for the little girl), a mill-stone (for the woman). The father hears the bird sing and is overjoyed. The little girl weeps. The woman is in terror. The father receives his gift and is even more pleased; the little girl receives hers and is comforted; the woman is killed. The boy returns to life.

Cf. red indian stories about animals which have been eaten, and come to life again through their bones.

The Grail. A precious stone, made of combined water and fire.

[Ap., 1, 13; ποδήρη?[2]]

Isaiah "The earth shall be full of the knowledge of God, as the waters cover the sea". Cf. Plato.

Clement, v, 5—

"Pythagoras and his followers, with Plato also and most of the other philosophers, were best acquainted with the Lawgiver,

---

[1] My mother killed me,
My father ate me,
My sister little Marlene
collected all my bones,
put them in a handkerchief,
laid it under the almond tree.
tweet, tweet, what a fine bird am I!
[2] feet.

as may be concluded from their doctrine. And by a happy utterance of divination, not without divine help, concurring in certain prophetic declarations, and seizing the truth in portions and aspect—"
The symbol of the Bacchic orgies is a sacred serpent (Clem., Exh. heath.)—Hevia in Hebrew, female serpent)
Initiations—
Aphrodite—the offering consists of some salt and the phallus—
Zeus violates Demeter—Then as a punishment throws into her bosom a ram's genitals, as if they were his own
Sabazian mysteries—snake gliding over the initiate's breast (symbol of divinity)—
Core gives birth to a bull—
"the bull"
The dragon's father, and the father of the bull the dragon, On a hill the herdsman's hidden ox-goad
(reed of bacchanals)
swine of Euboileus swallowed up with the two goddesses—
In the Thesmophoria, they thrust out swines—
Cinderella—
The birds sing:

rucke di guck (bis)
Blut ist $\Big\}$ im Schuck
Kein Blut
Der Schuck ist [nicht] zu klein,
die rechte Braut $\begin{cases} \text{sitzt noch daheim} \\ \text{die führt er heim}^1 \end{cases}$

[The infinite desire in us for the good is the *symbolum*—what is smaller is not the good.
Inequality reversed in Cinderella That too large foot . . .]
Allerleirauh—A king, having promised his wife on her deathbed not to re-marry unless with someone as beautiful as herself, wants to marry his daughter.
The god-child of death—Human lives represented by lights (candles? torches?) which consume themselves.
A poor man seeks a godfather for his 13th child. God offers himself. The man refuses. "Du giebst dem reichen und lässest

---

[1] There is blood [no blood] in the shoe
The shoe is [is not] too small,
The true bride still sits at home [he leads her home]

den Armen hungern."[1] The devil offers himself. The man refuses—"Du betrügst und verführst die Menschen".[2] Death offers himself—"Ich bin der Tod, der alle gleich macht"[3]—"Du bist der Rechte, du holst den Reichen wie den Armen ohne Unterschied, du sollst mein Gevattersmann sein".[4]
λέων, lion, from λάω to see. Manetho says that the lion never sleeps. (In Egyptian, lion is m' and to see is m")—
Invasion of Egypt—ῥᾳδίως ἀμαχητὶ ταύτην κατὰ κράτος εἷλον[5]
Hyksos—some say that they were Arabs. The name means either "Shepherd-kings" or "Shepherd-captives".
Archaeology shows that the usurpation by the Hyksos lasted from about 1700 to 1580.
The ποιμένας[6] go to Judaea and build Jerusalem.
Josephus, quoting Manetho, assimilates them to the Hebrews. compare *Abel* and *Baal* and *Baldur*.

ὦ θεός, εἰς τὴν βοήθειάν μου πρόσχες,
Κύριε, εἰς τὸ βοηθῆσαί μοι σπεῦσον.[7]

Do not call God that which is seen and sees not, but that which sees and is not seen.
(we don't see God, we feel that we are seen by Him)

The grace of God as a trap
The words "I would be glad to wed the Black Bull o' Norroway"—
The rose of Beauty and the Beast—Das singende, springende—
Löweneckerchen—The jonquil of Proserpine—
The labyrinth—
The hunted stag who turns into a man and says: "It's well that I've got you! nu das is gut, dass ik dik hewe; ik hewe schon sess paar gleserne Schlitschau hivenen di caput jaget un hewe dik nig kriegen könnt".[8]

[1] You give to the rich and leave the poor hungry.
[2] You deceive and seduce men.
[3] I am Death, who make all things equal.
[4] You are the right one, you carry away the rich like the poor, without distinction. You shall be the godfather.
[5] Easily, without battle, I possessed it.
[6] Shepherds.
[7] O God, come to my help—O Lord, hasten to help me.
[8] It's well I've got you; I have worn out six pairs of crystal skates without being able to catch you. (Grimm, 'De beiden Künnigeskinner,' 'The Two King's Children').

(It had been foretold that this prince would be *killed* by a stag at the age of 16.)
Falada. The princess is thirsty. Her serving woman refuses to get her a drink. She dismounts from her horse and drinks from the stream. The third time, she drops the handkerchief which her mother had given her, marked with three drops of her blood, and she becomes unable to defend herself against the serving woman.
The first time, the drops of blood spoke and said:
"Ach Gott! wenn das deine Frau Mutter wüsst,
   das Herz im Leib ihr zerspringen müsst!
Dialogue with the horse:
O du Falada, dass du hangest.
—O du Jungfer Königin, dass du gangest;
  wenn das deine Frau Mutter wüsst das Herz im Leib ihr zerspringen müsst.[1]
Hangatyn, the God of Hanged Men.
ash (?) Yggdrasil—
   Die Lieder der Edda—Havamal.
"I know that I (Odin) hung on the windswept tree for three full nights, pierced with a spear and dedicated to Odin, I to myself, on the tree whereof no man can tell from the roots of what tree it springs"—
Odin had two ravens, Memory and Wisdom.
God of Hanged Men. Lord of the Gallows.
It was a custom to dedicate men to Odin by hanging them on a gallows and piercing them with spears—
Justin—I apol. LXI, baptism compared to natural generation.
Tertullian disapproves of infant baptism (*De Baptismo*).
Gregory of Nazianzen recommends baptism at 3 years. Read St. Augustine, *de baptismo. De peccati meritis et remissione*—
Joseph of Arimathea—Legend. *ZA

(1350)   EL 2 n = 44
                               Film reproduction
id. ed. by Rev. Skeat
Lachner Julius—The grail Romance and the Taret—
Occult review London 1921—v. 34 p. 278–84
Murray—Egyptian elements in Grail Romance
(Ancient Egypt—London 1916—p. 14, 54, 69—

---

[1] O Falada, how slowly you go—O princess, you've gone too far; if your mother knew, her heart would break.

La queste del saint Graal—9
Wolfram von Eschenbach
Waite—The hidden cherch of the Holy Graal
Formula antiqua receptionis Manichaeorum
Gerard, epist. Migne v. 142
Manichäische Handschriften der Sammlung Beatty Bd. I—(chapters?)
———————————————— der staatlichen Museen Berlin, Carl Schmidt, B.1.
Polotsky—Manichäische Homilien
Schmitt—Ein Mani-Fund in Aegypten—
Kephalaia—
Manichäische Handschriften der staatlichen Museen Berlin—Stuttgart 1933-7 Bd. I p. 1-144 (translated by Dr. Polotsky)
Jackson—The Manichaean fragment S.8 in Turfan Pahlavi—in oriental studies in honour of Cursetji Erachji Parry—London 1933—p. 163-71.
Henning Walter—Ein manichäisches Bet-und Beicht-buch—(Preussische Akad. der Wissenschaften zu Berlin Philosoph—historische Klasse—Abhandlungen—1936 Nr 10 p. 1-143.
Chavannes—Un traité manichéen retrouvé en Chine.
Bang W.—Manichäische Hymnen—Museen—1925 Tome 38—p. 155.
Allberry—A Manichaean psalm-book. Manichäische Handsschriften der Sammlung A Chester Beatty Bd 2.
Wieger—Taoism—Volume II.
The secret of the Golden Flower (taoist alchemy)
T'ai i chin hua Tsung chih.
Shing king.
Lao Tzu Tao te ching English Goddard.
Harlez—Taoist texts.
Balfour—Taoist texts (not interesting).
Chuang-Chou—
Reden und Gleichnisse des Tschung-Tse (German).
Senzaki—101 Zen stories.
Suzuki—Daisetz Teitare.
Zen Buddhism and its influence on Japanese culture.
Buddhist philosophy and its influence on Japanese culture.
Buddhist philosophy and its effects on the life and thought of the Japanese people v. 190.
Essays in Zen Buddhism—3 v.

An introduction to Zen Buddhism.
Japanese Buddhism.
Manual of Zen Bud.
Outlines of Mahâyâna B.
Studies in the Lankavatara Sutra.
Lankavatara sutra—edited by Buryie Nanjio.

Belhomme—Documents inédits sur l'hérésie des Albigeois.
Schmidt—Histoire et doctrine de la secte des Cathares ou Albigeois.
Broeckx Edmond—Le catharisme (Université).
Holmes—The Albigensian or Catharist heresy.
Warner, Henry James—The Albigensian heresy.

Lee—Folk Tales of all nations—1930.
Celtic sources—J. Jacobs: English Fairy Tales—Celtic
More celtic fairy tales
traditional sources (?)
Red Bull o' Norroway—
A king has three daughters. One night they talk about marriage—One of them wants a king—The 2nd wants a prince—The 3rd (the most beautiful) "I would be content with the Red Bull o' Norroway"—
Next day, the Red Bull comes to find her. She is hidden by her parents, but they are compelled to hand her over. The princess and the bull journey through many lands. One day she sees a pin in his hide. She pulls it out. A handsome prince appears and falls at her feet and thanks her. Then he immediately disappears. She searches for him.
Half dead with thirst and hunger, she meets an old woman who gives her 3 nuts which she must not crack "till her heart was like to break, and over again to break".
She comes to a land where everyone is talking about the "Duke o' Norroway's" wedding, which is to take place that very day—She sees him—Her heart was now like to break—She cracks the nut—Finds inside it "a wee wife carding". Offers it to the betrothed in exchange for one night with the duke—sings:
"Far hae I sought ye, near am I brought to ye—
Dear Duke o' Norroway, will ye no turn and speak to me?"

A wee wifie spinning
A wee wifie singing

The duke's servant, who has heard the singing and lamenting, advises him not to drink a sleeping potion—The duke recognizes the voice of his princess and tells her he has been in the power of an enchantress. They get married.

A nut not to be cracked "till her heart is like to break, and over again to break".

Far hae I sought ye, near am I brought to ye.

Dear Duke o' Norroway, will ye no turn and speak to me?

Firdausi—pr. E. M. Wilmot Buxton = The Book of Rustem—

"Come, sit beside me on this sand, and take
My head betwixt thy hands, and kiss my cheeks,
And wash them with thy tears, and say: My son!
Quick! Quick! for numbered are my sands of life,
And swift; for like the lightning to the field
I came, and like the wind I go away."

The little Feather of Fenist—The bright falcon, in R. Nisbet Bain's Russian Fairy Tales—

(Beauty and the beast) The youngest of the 3 daughters asks for "a scarlet flower"—An old man gives it, on condition that the father agrees to give his daughter to "Fenist the bright falcon". He agrees, but then regrets it.

The falcon gives her a flower by means of which she can call him at need. He gives her everything she wants.

The sisters wound the falcon. It goes away, saying: "Seek me in the land of Thrice-nine" ... "You must 'wear out slippers of iron, fret away reins of stone, break to pieces staff of steel, before thou findst me'."

She is given gifts on her journey.

She finds Fenist betrothed to a Tsarevna.

She says to him "I, thy lovely damsel, have come to thee from afar. I have worn out slippers of iron, I have ground down a staff of steel, I have fretted away reins of stone. Everywhere and all times have I been seeking thee, my love".

The second night, although he has drunk his potion, he is awoken by the maiden's hot tears falling on his face.

He asks his people which woman he should take as wife. "Her who sold me, or her who bought me back again?" They tell him the second.

In the course of her wanderings the maiden had met an old woman who sends her, with the help of a magic ball, to meet her sister. She gives her "a silver spinning board and a golden spindle, thou wilt spin a spindleful of flax and draw out threads of gold" (transmutation of flax into gold)—The second gives a golden apple on a silver plate—The 3rd. gives her information and advice (One present and one night must have got lost).[1]

Series of tales about the search for a country "where there is neither death nor old age".
Gypsy—The red king and the witch (Groom: Gypsy Folktales).
Japan—Urashima Taro—Marjory Bruce—A treasury of tales—Visu—Adland Davis—Myths and Legends of Japan.
Korean—The woodman and the Mountain fairies.
Holland—Rip Van Winkle.
Turkey—Youth without age, life without death.
Crow and daylight—Eskimo.
The crow goes in search of daylight, which is on a ball with which a baby is playing.
Story of the sister seeking her brothers—identically the same in Finland and among the Kabyles.
Albanian story—The princess who has married a snake. The Psyche type. Quest. "Serpent and redeemer"—Throwing a golden ball at some young men, in order to select a husband, the ball hit the snake.
Norwegian story.—The 12 wild ducks—A queen promises a witch that if she has a daughter she will give her whatever she shall meet on the bridge. She meets her twelve sons there. They have been transformed—
Pick thistledown, card it, spin it, weave it. Make 12 shirts. Do not speak or laugh or cry—
The king carries her away and weds her. "The king's guardian" accuses her of witchcraft—

East o' the sun and west o' the moon.—A poor man gives his

[1] See "The little feather of Fenist the Bright Falcon", in *Russian Fairy Tales*, from the Skazki of Polevoi, transl. R. Nisbet Bain (Harrap, 1915). By throwing the ball and following where it rolled, you reached your destination.

youngest daughter to a white bear, in exchange for wealth—(Psyche).
She spills three drops of hot candle grease on her husband. He tells her he must vanish into the castle of a witch, East of the sun and west o' the moon, and there marry a witch—"There is no way to that place"—She seeks. Inquires of all the winds. The North wind sends her to the place—She arrives on the day of the wedding.—
He must marry the one who can wash out 3 spots of candle grease. The more the witches scrub, the dirtier the shirt gets.— The "beggar lassie" has only to dip it in the water and it is white as snow. The warlocks and trolls are immediately paralysed. The two go off together.
(Thorre-Thomson, collection with this title)

Danish Tales (Ströbe)—The Deer Prince—Forbidden doors, but the princess breaks the spell by opening them.—
Griselda—the king consents to take a wife on condition he can choose as he likes—Chooses his gate-keeper's daughter.— Makes her promise to be unswervingly patient.—
The snake—Psyche—Childless couple adopt a snake. He sends them to ask the hand of the king's daughter for him. The king makes three conditions. To turn the fruit and leaves in his orchard into gold and silver. To encrust the paths and benches in his garden with jewels. To cover the palace with gold. The snake comes to the palace to take the princess. He coils himself round her until his mouth touches hers. Then he turns into a handsome prince. But because the king has burnt his snake's skin he turns into a dove and flies away.
The princess searches. A fox guides her. He makes her drink water from a brook to get strength.
She cures the sick prince with the blood of a bird and a fox.
"The pastor's wife"—As a penance she spends a night in church with a book; a number of people ask her for the book (some of them resemble the pastor, her husband, who gave her the book—but they are not him); she only gives it back to the pastor when he comes to ask for it again in the morning.
"The mill at the bottom of the sea."
English fairy tales retold by Steel—The black bull o' Norroway—

> To wilder measures now they turn,
> The black black bull of Norroway—
> Sudden the tapers cease to burn,
> The minstrels cease to play—

She eats of the bull when she is hungry—

> Eat out of my left ear
> Drink out of my right,
> And set by what you leave
> To serve the morrow's night—

He fights with the Old one and enjoins him not to move.
If he is
Edda Saemundar—1930
The British Edda
L. A. Waddell
Edda Saemundar—
Transl. Benjamin Thorpe
  Collection (1907)
Younger Edda—
  Rainbow, bridge between heaven and earth.
Elder Edda
  The High One's lay—(i.e. Odin)
Odin's Rune—Song
  (Saemund, born in Iceland about 1055, 50 years after the establishment of Christianity in Iceland. Went to Germany, France, Italy. Had a holy bishop for cousin. Became a priest himself. Died at 77. Wrote a history of Norway and Iceland. The Edda was discovered in 1643 and was then attributed to him.)
  I know that I hung, on a wind-rocked tree, nine whole nights, with a spear wounded, and to Odin offered, myself to myself; on that tree of which no one knows from what root it springs.
  Bread no one gave me, nor a horn of drink; downward I peered, to runes applied myself, wailing learnt them, then fell down thence.
  Potent songs nine from the famed son I learned of Bolthorn, Bestla's sire, and a draught obtained of the precious mead drawn from Odhr aerir—
  Then I began to bear fruit and to know many things, to grow

and well thrive: word by word I sought out words, fact by fact I sought out facts.

Runes thou wilt find, and explained characters, very potent characters, which the great speaker depicted, and the high powers formed, and the powers' prince graved.

(sequel, magic)

A son of Odin comes to plead with Hel (Hades) for the resurrection of Baldur. She replies: "If all things in the world, both living and lifeless, weep for him, then shall he return to the Aesir; but if any one thing speak against him or refuse to weep, he shall be kept in Hel—

Everything weeps, men, beasts, stones, trees, metals, except one witch, who is Loki, his murderer. The gods capture and torture Loki—

Baldur will not be resurrected until the end of the world.

"I saw of Balder, the blood-stained god, Odin's son, the hidden fate. There stood grown up, high on the plain, slender and passing fair, the mistletoe—

Odin

sons:

Thor, strongest of gods and men

Baldur

"It may truly be said of him that he is the best, and that all mankind are loud in his praise. So fair and dazzling is he in form and feature that rays of light seem to issue from him; and thou mayest have some idea of the beauty of his hair, when I tell thee that the whitest of all plants is called Baldur's brow. Baldur is the mildest, the wisest, and the most eloquent of all the Aesir, yet such is his nature that the judgement he has pronounced can never be altered."

Hermes Trismegistus—Pymander—1657

Transl. L. Ménard, 1867, publ. Didier

The Virgin of the World—in English

Dr. Anna Kingsford

Hermes Trismegistus—

Hermetica—Greek and Latin text and translation—Walter Scott—1924

Arm.

The book of quint essence 2 no. 16a

Jabir ibn Hayan al—Tartusi—

in hoc—alchemia (contains the Emerald Tables)

The public should be inundated with authentically beautiful medieval things.

We should relate and attach to the middle ages both the conservative idea and also what is authentic in the revolutionary idea—that is to say, the part of it which is neither fantasy of progress nor will to power but is simple desire for justice.

A life in which the supernatural truths would be read in every kind of work, in every act of labour, in all festivals, in all hierarchical social relations, in all art, in all science, in all philosophy.

Yes, but what about war? In war, one should read the supernatural truths concerning evil.

Religion and behaviourism.
The supernatural is the difference between human and animal behaviour.
This difference is something infinitely small.
The pomegranate seed or grain of mustard.
(Clement of Alexandria: the women of Athens believed the pomegranate came from the blood of Dionysus.)

Affliction.
When something which thought embraces in an instant has to be lived throughout a long period.
[9 Buddhist sins: killing—theft—sexual impurity—lies—laying up treasure—partiality—hate—stupidity—fear.]
The animal reflex of "playing dead"—which often holds out in face of torture and mutilation—is the reflex of a soul gripped by affliction. That is the mechanism of slavery.
Mixture of fire and water. Blood. Wine. Precious stones. Rainbow.
Noah. Discovers wine. God forbids him blood. Makes pact of rainbow with him. Redemptive sacrifice.
Zodiac in Pahlavi texts (Zoroaster).
Varak (Lamb)—Tora (Bull)—Do-patkar (Gemini)—Kalakan (Crab)—Ser (Lion)—Khusak (Virgo)—Tarazuk (Balance)

—Gazdum (Scorpion)—Nimasp (Centaur)—Vahik (Capricornus)—Dul (Waterpot)—Mahik (Fish).
Astronomers' 28 subdivisions.
Tir, 4th. month of the year, under Cancer. Month of the deluge.
Pahlavi. The male seed comes down from the brain. All that part of it that does not enter the womb circulates in the woman's veins, mixed with blood, and becomes milk. (Cf. Greeks.)
[Sky, metal, wind and fire are male. Water, earth, plants and fishes(?) female.]
[Generation according to the Thibetan Book of the Dead. The soul incarnates itself by participation in the desire of lovers; it incarnates itself into the sex corresponding to that one of the two desires with which it sympathizes.]

A sovereign good, that is to say a good which includes all possible goods. That is the hypothesis of the *Philebus*. So there is no incompatibility between goods.
This means that one does not really renounce a partial or secondary good for the sake of the supreme good.
But one ought to renounce the pursuit and desire of all those goods which are not the supreme good—that is to say, of all representable goods without any exception:
Not only does the supreme good include all goods, but they are only good as shadows of the supreme good.

Tropisms. The water scorpion (?), Ranatra, when taken out of the water, pretends to be dead. It is revived by waving a light in front of it. After a time it moves towards the light. If the light emits a great heat, it still moves closer until the heat overcomes it. Even when the heat of a lamp has almost killed them, Ranatras expend their last flicker of vital energy to drag themselves a little closer to it.
$\pi\acute{\alpha}\tau\epsilon\rho, \tau o\hat{v}\tau o\ \delta\grave{o}s\ \grave{\epsilon}\mu o\acute{\iota}\ \ldots$[1]

Transpositions. The Sirens do not offer Ulysses pleasure, but

[1] Father, grant me this.

knowledge. It is a pretty safe bet that this is also the lure in the coarsest seduction talk of any boy of 20 to any girl of 16 (Cf. the photographs, at Renault's). It is always good that is offered. No ·one is voluntarily wicked. This saying[1] indicates, not an identity, but an analogy between sin and error.

[Apocalypse—The bride of the Lamb is clothed in linen. Linen is the mark of the just.

The Lamb who has seven eyes, i.e. the seven spirits of God, opens the first seal. There comes a white horse, and the rider has a bow, and he is given a crown, and he goes forth conquering (6.2)—A red horse, and the rider is given power to take away peace from the earth, and a great sword—A black horse, and the rider has a pair of scales—A pale ($\chi\lambda\omega\rho\delta s$) horse, and the rider's name is Death and he kills with the sword, with hunger, with death, and with wild beasts.

Further on (19.13) the rider of the white horse is called πιστός, ἀληθινός and ὁ λόγος τοῦ θεοῦ[2]—and his garment is bloody. From his mouth there emerges a two-edged sword.

At last one of the 7 Angels carrying vials with the seven last plagues measures the new Jerusalem. He says to the kneeling John: Vide ne feceris... conservus tuus sum—Deum adora. But further on: Ego sum a et ω... Ego Jesus...

Ἐγὼ εἰμὶ ἡ ῥίζα καὶ τὸ γένος Δαυίδ, ὁ ἀστὴρ ὁ λαμπρὸς ὁ πρωϊνός[3]—]

Palms in their hands. φοίνικες ἐν ταῖς χέρσιν (cf. Odyssey).

Clement of Alexandria, Str. v 35... κιβωτοῦ...[4]

(Str vi 53, τῆς του Χαμ προφητείας...[5]) " Ἄτλας, ὁ μη πάσχων πόλος[6]—Schol. Arist.

Apoc. 1.20—μυστήριον translated as sacramentum—

Graal. Precious stones, union of the visible (luminous) and the tangible, symbols of the Incarnation. Other objects are not visible, what is visible is the light reflected on them. A precious stone is visible in itself.

Ezekiel "Thou wert the anointed Cherub... thou hast walked up and down in the midst of the stones of fire".

The stone of fire that purifies the lips (Isaiah).

[1] Of Plato.
[2] faithful, true, word of God.
[3] I am the root and the offspring of David, and the bright and morning star.
[4] of the coffer.
[5] the prophecies of Ham.
[6] Atlas, the impassive pole.

Don Quixote. Unreality of the aspiration for good in this world.

Human sexual energy is not seasonal. This is the best indication that it is not destined for a natural purpose, but for the love of God.

[Father and Son—First sins of a piously brought up child, in 1850—(puritanical parents). He doesn't confess that he made a hole in the pipe, and learns from this that his father is not omniscient (5 years old). This also reveals to him his own individuality, in the pleasure of sharing a secret with himself. He invents magic. Loses some of his belief in prayer after his father has forbidden him to pray for an expensive toy. At six years old, hates his father for several days after receiving corporal punishment.

Above all; having got his father to explain what idolatry is, and how it angers God, he puts a small chair on the table, when nobody is about, and kneels down and prays, saying "chair" instead of Lord; he then waits in vain for a sign of God's wrath.]

[Saint Th. of Lisieux: "I feel that a letter will produce no result unless I write it with a certain repugnance and for no other motive than obedience."]

Saint Th. of L. It would really be worth examining the absurdity of proposing as a model for the mass of people a destiny whose starting point was from absolutely exceptional circumstances. She herself had already committed this absurdity. The secret of her success is in having invented a "lift" for going up to heaven. It was this that pleased her contemporaries, and not her love for Christ.—Since 1914, and even more since 1940, her particular quality of saintliness is as inappropriate as it could possibly be.

"No one knows whether he deserves to be loved, or hated". But it is quite useless to ask oneself the question. The drama of salvation is played behind the curtain. If the love of God exists in oneself, it is impossible to verify its presence. It is not an object for consciousness. For it is God within us who loves God, and God is not an object. As for one's neighbour, when he thanks us Christ will make no mention of the charitable acts that we remember, for by the fact of remembering them we have "had our reward". And as for those that we don't remember, by definition we don't know if they occurred.

On the other hand, we have certain knowledge about the evil in us. When we do something we believe to be contrary to God's will, it is certain that we are guilty of disobedience, even if it is really something innocent. When we remember the afflicted whom we have not helped, we are certain of not having helped them.

So we ought to admit in principle that if there is judgement we shall undoubtedly be condemned. But we also ought not to attach any importance to this; we ought to be indifferent to it, and desire only to be perfectly obedient to God during all the time between the present moment and death. The rest does not concern us in any way.

The moment of death, intersection of time and eternity, where the two limbs of the cross meet. What Christ is to men, this moment is to the other moments of time. The mind's eye should be fixed on this moment, and not upon mortal life, nor upon eternity either, because our ignorance about eternity allows the imagination utter licence when we think about it.

Axiom: everything that belongs to me is of no value. Because true value and property are by essence incompatible.

Let the slave await the master until his physical strength is totally exhausted.

The waiting may take the form of some wearying activity. It is the soul that waits in immobility, which may subsist amid the greatest external agitation.

To fish all night and catch nothing. The patience of fishermen is a form, a beautiful image, of patience . . . (their specific form of spirituality ought to be based upon it. To each occupation its own spirituality.)

It is wrong to say that God gives gratuitously and that he owes nothing to men. Having created us, he owes us everything.

And in fact he gives us everything. But he does not compel us to receive. He asks us to consent to his paying his debt; and we refuse, or we only half consent. Since the creation is an act of love, it is the creation of a faculty of free consent.

What he owes us is to keep us in slavery. What we have to consent to is to be slaves.

If he offered us joy, power, and glory, it would not be in our power to refuse his gifts. He choses his gifts in such a way that we are free to refuse them.

It is within our power, it is easy, to refuse the cross.

We must not seek in the thought of the supernatural, either in this world or after death, for a loosening of the chains of necessity. The supernatural is more precise, more rigorous, than the crude mechanism of matter. It adds itself to this mechanism, but does not tamper with it. It is a chain upon a chain, a steel chain upon a brass one.

My existence is a diminution of God's glory. God gives me it so that I may desire to lose it.

Hymn of Cleanthes. The thunderbolt, that object of terror—is the Spirit, the Love by means of which the world is persuaded by God and consents to his domination. Marvellous—extraordinary. Identity of affliction and the divine love. When God seems to use compulsion—if one looks closely, it is persuasion.

A Roman slave, torn away from his own life, placed in the power of a master, ill-used, and finally crucified, must have died with his heart full of hatred—and consequently been damned—unless Christ descended into him. So if one thinks that Christ came only twenty centuries ago how is one to forgive God for the affliction of the Roman slaves?

Noted on the ship, in mid-ocean:
Waves and sea { Harmony (Pythagorean) music
Topology
Whole and parts—Invariant
Single thought of separated thinkers (thought, image of the thinker)

The Same and the Other of Plato
Image of the Trinity
(..)¹.

The idea of vertically superimposed levels in the life of the soul, the highest of them being above consciousness and the psychological—there is nothing more important. What is true on the highest level is false lower down, and reciprocally. Thus it is in the secrecy of the highest level that the love of God and the love of one's neighbour are one love. Below, in consciousness, the authentic love of God appears as treachery towards men (Hippolytus) and the authentic love of man as treachery towards God (Prometheus). Christ unites the two.
"hated by the gods for having loved mortals too much".
Russian legend of St. Nicholas missing a rendezvous with God through helping a peasant out of a bog.
[According to Philo, quoted by Eusebius, *Hist. Eccl.*, II, xvii, there was a sect in Egypt near Alexandria, in the 1st century, who lived ascetically, with a "sanctuary" in every house, and devoted their time to the *symbolic interpretation* of the Scriptures, with the help of ancient writings which contained interpretations of allegorical symbols, and which they used as models. Eusebius believes or *pretends* to believe that this was the New Testament; an absurdity.
(Compare with what Clement of Alexandria said, according to Isidore, about the "prophecy of Ham".)
They composed religious chants, lived chastely, ate only after sundown, or even only every three or six days.
($νομοθεσία$)² They regarded the law as no more than a body, the soul being the hidden meaning.
They relinquished property and lived outside the city walls, the men on one side, the women on the other. Called $θεραπευτάς$ and $θεραπευτρίδας$.³ They were to be found chiefly in Egypt, but also in Greece and elsewhere.
Philo's treatise entitled $περὶ\ βίου\ θεωρητικοῦ\ ἢ\ ἱκετῶν$.⁴
He says of them $ἀγαθοῦ\ τελείου$.⁵

¹ This line, in brackets in the French, reads as follows: *développés des essais de mécanicien d'aviation*. It may possibly refer to aero-engineering graphs, but I am unable to translate it.
² legislation.   ³ attendants.   ⁴ on the life of contemplation or of suppliants.
⁵ of good accomplishment.

Eusebius thinks they were Christians, converted by Mark himself, the founder of the Church of Alexandria, (but this seems very doubtful).]
(Eusebius, *Hist. Eccl.*, VI, xix, 7, quotes Porphyry on Origen:...
"He Hellenized in his opinions on creatures and divinity, and he injected Hellenic thought into the (non-Hellenic?) fables. For he read Plato continually, the writings of the best-known Pythagoreans were his constant companions, and he also used the works of Cheremon the Stoic. Having learnt from these books the method (analogical? interpretative? transpositive?) of the Greek mysteries, he applied them to the Jewish scriptures."
Origen (very early 3rd century) gets nothing but praise from Eusebius (contemporary of Constantine, died approx. 340).
N.B.—also, that Eusebius has nothing but superlative and unreserved praise for Christian women who kill themselves to avoid rape. He was a bishop.
(μεταλαμβάνω) to transpose—to change money.
Compare: μεταληπτικὸν τῶν παρ' Ἕλλησιν μυστηρίων τρόπον [1] and Christ's word to his closest disciples γένεσθε δόκιμοι τραπεζῖται Become good money-changers.[2]
Eusebius certainly has a motive for citing this passage of Porphyry. He treats Porphyry as a liar for having asserted that Origen derived from paganism. But he does not refute the rest.
Among other praise, Eusebius says of Origen (and of several others) ... φιλοσόφου βίου.[3] He says the same of the 1st century monks ... ἀρχομένους φιλοσοφεῖν ...[4]
[A mysterious passage—Eusebius, *Hist.*, IV, 26, quotes a letter from Melitho, a bishop, to Marcus Aurelius: "Our philosophy developed (ἤκμασεν) first among the barbarians, but it came to flower among your peoples (ἐπανθήσασα τοῖς σοῖς ἔθνεσιν) in the great reign of Augustus, your ancestor, and it was of good augury (αἴσιον) for your empire, because thenceforward the power of the Romans became great and brilliant... uphold the philosophy that thrived along with (σύντροφον) your empire, contemporary with Augustus, and

---

[1] the transpositive way of the Greek mysteries.
[2] A non-canonical saying. See under τραπεζίτης in Arndt and Gingrich: *A Greek–English Lexicon of the New Testament* (Cambridge University Press, 1957).
[3] of wisdom-loving life.   [4] having begun to love wisdom.

was honoured by your ancestors among (πρός, dat.) the other cults; and the best indication that our doctrine (λόγος) grew (συνακμάσαι?) auspiciously at the same time as the auspicious beginning of the empire is that it suffered no humiliation from the authority of Augustus (μηδὲν φαῦλον ἀπὸ τῆς Αὐγούστου ἀρχῆς ἀπαντῆσαι), but on the contrary every splendour and glory with the approbation of all.
(The year 0 of our era is the 43rd of the reign of Augustus, 14 years before his death.)]

Birds, the 3 delegates of the gods: Poseidon, Heracles and the "Triballian".
Poseidon: Τὸν ἄνδρα χαίρειν οἱ θεοὶ κελεύομεν τρεῖς ὄντες ἡμεῖς.[1]
βούλευμα[2] (v. 163)
Prometheus advises the man who has become king of the birds to demand from Zeus, as consort, βασίλεια, who hurls the thunderbolt.
Philo—*Legum allegoria* iii. 8a, on Melchizedek bringing the wine:
... so that they may be filled with the divine intoxication, which is more sober than sobriety itself. For he is the priest, the λόγος, possessing the one who is and conceiving him with sublimity.
Incarnation?
Assimilates bread to the word (bread of heaven, manna).

Peace, v. 1095; an interpreter of prophecies says of some verses which are quoted to him:
ὀυ μετέχω τούτων· οὐ γάρ ταῦτ' ἔιπε Σίβυλλα.[3]

Japanese No. It is Buddha who makes flowers grow from the branches of trees, to make men look upward. It is he who

---

[1] We three eternal beings salute the man.
[2] plan.
[3] I have no part in those. They were not spoken by the Sibyl.

makes the moon sink below the waves, so that the afflicted may know that God comes down.

Kabyle story. A noble white girl, with a negress for servant, goes to seek her seven brothers. She carries with her a bird (of the parrot type). The negress asks to be allowed to ride. The girl says "O my father and my mother, what ought I to do?". The bird replies "Carry on as you are." But one day she forgets the bird. Then she lets the negress mount the horse. The negress rides ahead and comes to a spring whose water turns negroes white. She washes in it. The noble girl washes at the neighbouring spring, which turns white people black. The seven brothers greet the negress as their sister, while the other feeds the camels. But, hearing her laments, the camels weep and grow thin, all except one, which is deaf; and because of this the truth comes to light.

Humility is not a bad opinion of one's own person in comparison to other people. It is a radically bad opinion of one's own person in relation to what is impersonal in oneself.

When once the impersonal has implanted itself in a soul and begins to grow there, it draws all the good to itself. The person retains as its own property only the evil. It follows from this that in comparing oneself with others one always finds oneself inferior, because one sees them as a mixture of good and evil.

An urgent, essential task: to make a logic of the absurd. To define so far as possible the criterion of truth and falsehood in the transcendent sphere, where contradiction is not out of place, the domain of mystery. In this domain greater rigour is required than in mathematics. A new rigour, of which people nowadays have no idea.

The criterion is that a true absurdity is a reflection, a transposition, a translation of one of the irreducible absurdities of the human condition.

So there is need for an investigation of these irreducible absurdities.

Theological use of the idea of limit.

The moment of Christ's death on the cross is the intersection of the created and the creating. Until then, the unity of the divine and the human in him must have been in a certain manner virtual, and tending towards the plenitude of reality which was reached only at that moment (a plenitude impossible to actually reach—a limit at one and the same time possible and impossible, like the paradoxes of Zeno, or like infinite series with a finite sum).

St. Paul says of Christ: ἔπρεπεν . . . τὸν ἀρχηγὸν τῆς σωτηρίας διὰ παθημάτων τελειῶσαι.[1] It was becoming that the captain of salvation be made perfect through sufferings.

Book on the "No", concerning a dance: in art, if something good is boring when it lasts 5 minutes, don't cut it down to 2½ m., but prolong it to 10 m., 20 m., an hour (Waley).

Something unbearable makes it possible to break through a ceiling.

Theatre—let the beginning and the end give the sense of time.

The contemplation of time is the key of human life. It is the irreducible mystery, upon which no science can get a hold. Humility is inevitable when one knows that one is not sure of oneself for the future. There is no stability unless one abandons the "I" which is subject to time and modifiable.

Two things irreducible to any rationalism: time and beauty. One must start from there.

Mabinogion. The impatient step-mother says "I lay this fate upon you. You shall never touch a bride until you have Olwen, the daughter of the Chief of the Giants". The youth blushes, and love runs through all his limbs. For a whole year Arthur searches in vain on his behalf to find if there is an Olwen somewhere. Then he himself sets off, accompanied by Arthur's knights. He arrives near her house, and sends to fetch her; and seeing her, he at once recognizes her. He says: "Ah, young maiden, I have loved thee!"

[1] *Hebrews* 2: 10.

There are no disappointments in fairy tales. One's wish is always fulfilled.

Pwyll who for a whole year, in the likeness of a friend, sleeps with that friend's wife without touching her, although he is authorized to do so.

Later he marries Rhiannon, of the birds.

("The birds of Rhiannon, they who awaken the dead and put the living to sleep.")

It was she who came to fetch him, on a horse which none, not even he, could overtake at a gallop until they said to her "for the love of him you love, wait for me".

Later, she is falsely accused of having killed her child, and cruelly punished.

The child is taken in by a noble and his wife and: "*They caused the boy to be baptized with the baptism they used then.*"

(written at end of 11th century or beginning of 12th)

The same in "Math":

"Yes, said Math, we will seek, I and you, by our charms and our illusion, to enchant a wife for him out of flowers." Now he had come to man's stature, and he was the handsomest youth that man ever beheld. And they took the flowers of the oak, and the flowers of the broom, and the flowers of the meadowsweet, and out of them invoked the fairest and most comely maiden that man ever saw. *And they baptized her with the baptism which was used there*".

Branwen. The seven survivors with the decapitated head of their lord, who live for eighty years, without a thought of sadness, in a palace by the sea where two doors are open and one is shut (they know that it must be kept shut). Finally one of them opens the door, which looks towards Cornwall.

"And when he looked, they were as fully conscious of the multitude of losses they had ever endured, and of the multitude of friends and companions they had lost, and of the multitude of evil that had come to them, as if it were there that they had met with them; and above all else of their lord." (splendid!)

Before these eighty years they had spent seven happy years at Harlech (above the sea). "Then they set forth to Harlech, and there they began to sit down. Meat and liquor was begun to be provided, and they began to eat and to drink. Three birds came and began singing a kind of song to them, and whatever of songs they had heard were all unpleasing compared thereto.

And a far sight it was for them to see them above the waters outside. And they were as clear to them as if they were with them; and at this feasting they were seven years."
(They were the birds of Rhiannon.)
The story begins with the king at Harlech, seeing some ships arrive.
Always the principle of prolongation.
Manawyddan, driven from town to town by the artisans because he works too well (13th.?)
[Geography: Pwyll, Carmarthen and Pembroke; Annwn, land of the dead || Branwen at Harlech (still exists)—Manawyddan, S-W. Wales, Hereford and Oxford ("centre" of the island). Math, Caernarvon (north).—Dream, id—Dream$_2$, (Arthur—, Montgomery)]
The "Mabinogion" was written by monks. In the 12th century they still *knew* that there was a pre-Christian baptism.
Snow and blood, in *Parceval* and
Indian story (p. 120)—"Dirty-Boy." The Sun and the Star become incarnated in human form for love of two daughters of a chief, who have rejected all suitors. The Star becomes an old woman in rags, and the Sun a dirty youth, with sore eyes, always bedridden; both of them in a most wretched tent.

The chief announces a contest: whoever shoots an eagle with an arrow shall have his daughters. The Sun says to the Star: "Grandmother, make me a bow and some arrows." She says: "What's the use? You cannot draw the bow." But, from pity, she makes them for him with a branch, some cord, and some twigs. Next day, shooting last of all, from his bed, he brings down the eagle.

The chief announces another contest. Whoever catches two "fishers", a very rare mountain animal, shall have his daughters.

The Sun says to the Star "Grandmother, make me two traps." She says "First get out of bed." But, from pity, she makes two traps from willow branches and sets them near the door. Two "fishers" are caught.

The chief sends his daughters to Dirty-Boy.
On the way, they pass the house of the Ravens and hear laughter.
The elder daughter enters the house and marries a Raven. She is cherished by the family.
The younger, in obedience to her father, goes to Dirty-Boy.

The old woman says to her: "Your husband is ill and will die. He smells too bad, you shouldn't sleep with him. Nurse him in the day-time and go back to your father's at night." She does so.

After three days, the old tent turns into the most luxurious of tents, the old woman becomes a magnificent lady with a dress covered in stars, and Dirty-Boy a splendid young man whose clothes shine like bronze. The Sun pours water over his wife, which covers her with flashing stars. He makes her pour away the water, which runs like a trail of gold dust from their tent to that of the chief.

It is a myth of the Incarnation and the Redemption. What is admirable is that the Sun and the Star, once they were incarnated, seem to have become partly unaware of their divine nature, as is proved by the old woman's replies: "You cannot draw the bow . . . First get out of bed . . . ", and her compliance out of pity.

Note that while the Sun is incarnated there is still a sun in the sky, because there are days and nights.

[*Okanagon*: Teit, Memoirs of the American Folklore Society, xi, 85, No. 6.]

Note, too, that a girl must have refused all suitors before the Sun comes down for love of her.

The beginning of newness (Zuni: Cushing, Report of the Bureau of American Ethnology, xiii, 379).

Before the beginning of the new-making, Awonawilona (The Maker and Container of All, the All-father Father) solely had being. There was nothing else whatsoever throughout the great space of the ages save everywhere black darkness in it, and everywhere void desolation.

In the beginning of the new-made, Awonawilona conceived within himself and thought outward in space, whereby mists of increase, steams potent of growth, were evolved and uplifted. Thus, by means of his innate knowledge, the All-container made himself in person and form of the Sun whom we hold to be our father and who thus came to exist and appear. With his appearance came the brightening of the spaces with light, and with the brightening of the spaces the great mist-clouds were thickened together and fell, whereby was evolved water in water; yea, and the world-holding sea.

With his substance of flesh outdrawn from the surface of his person, the Sun-father formed the seed-stuff of twain worlds, impregnating therewith the great waters, and lo! in the heat of his light these waters of the sea grew green and scum rose upon them, waxing wide and weighty until, behold! they became the "fourfold Containing Mother-earth" and the "All-covering Father-sky".

From the lying together of these twain upon the great world waters, so vitalizing, terrestrial life was conceived; whence began all beings of earth, men and the creatures, in the Fourfold womb of the World.

Thereupon the Earth-mother repulsed the Sky-father, growing big and sinking deep into the embrace of the waters below, thus separating from the Sky-father, in the embrace of the waters above."

The Crow and the Light
(Tsimshian: Boas, "Report of the Bureau of American Ethnology")
The world was without light. In the animals' town a chief and his wife lose their little boy. They weep so much for him every day that Heaven is importuned by their continual lament and sends him back. He eats nothing. But after two slaves have made him taste "scabs from their shin bones" (?) he becomes so voracious that he has to leave the country.

He flies away as a crow, but then lays aside his crow's skin. He thinks it will be difficult to find food in the darkness and, remembering the light of the sky from which he came, he resolves to bring it into the world. He puts on his crow's skin and flies back to heaven. He becomes the leaf of a cedar in the water which is drunk by the daughter of the chief of heaven. He emerges as a child born from her. He cries until he is given the box which contains the light of day, called ma. He flies back to earth with it.

(Infinitely less beautiful than the Eskimo story.)
To be swallowed in order to be given back to the world, method for stealing light, sun, or fire in a great many stories.
"Whoever is not born anew, or from on high . . . "

Tales from the Caucasus.
The youth who seeks for the country of eternal life and finds

it at last, and in it an immortal maiden named Beauty. After a little while he wants to see his family again. She tells him "You won't even find their bones"—"Why? I have only been here a short time"—"I told you from the first that you are unworthy of eternal life". He arrives at his home, learns that a thousand years have passed, and suddenly grows old and dies. The story is called "The earth will have its own".

A peasant and his son are thirsty, they see a fountain and drink, they say: "Ah! how good you are!" Immediately, the devil appears out of the fountain.

Fasting, vigils, etc.,—as acts of piety, it is good if they are easy. There is something marvellous in facility, something that is reflected in the quintets of Mozart and the songs of Monteverdi. I want to suffer violence from human beings, and to be obliged to do violence to myself on their behalf; but for God I would like to do only easy things. Except for the actual orientation of thought towards God, which is the supreme and intimate violence that the soul does to itself.

Revelation of Homer to Ennius in a dream. Varro: Haec duo caelum et terra quod anima et corpus. Humidum et frigidum terra, eaque corpus, caldor caeli et inde anima, sive:
"Ova parire solet genus pennis condecoratum
non animam",
ut ait Ennius
"et post inde venit divinitus pullis
ipsa anima"
sive, ut Zenon Citieus, animalium *semen ignis isque anima et mens*.[1]
(seed or sperm = fire = pneuma)
Epicharmus: καὶ γὰρ τὸ θῆλυ τῶν ἀλεκτορίδων γένος, ἁ λῇς καταμαθεῖν ἀτενές, οὐ τίκτει τέκνα ζῶντ' ἀλλ' ἐπῴζει καὶ ποιεῖ ψυχὰν ἔχειν.[2]

---

[1] These two, Sky and Earth, are a pair like life and body. Earth is a damp and cold thing, the body; heat is from the sky, and hence the soul—whether, as Ennius says, "Eggs is what the feathered tribe give birth to, and not life" and "Thereafter, by divine inspiration, comes life itself to the chicks"; or, as Zeno of Citium says, in animals the *seed is that fire which is life and mind*.

[2] And if you consider the matter strictly, the hen does not produce living creatures, but broods over them to make them come alive.

Varro—De Lingua Latina, v 60—Quibus junctis caelum et terra omnia ex se genuerunt, quod per hos natura
"Frigori miscet calorem atque humori aritudinem".
Principia mundi:
"aqua terra anima et sol.
"... quod gerit fruges, Ceres".
"Terris gentis omnis peperit et resumit denuo".
"Terra corpus est at mentis [mens] ignis est.
De mente humana
"Istic est de sole sumptus ignis"
idem de sole
"isque totus mentis est" (i.e. mens.)
Varro L.L., v 18 (de luna) ... hinc Epicharmus Enni Proserpinam quoque appellat quod solet esse sub terris; dicta Proserpina, quod haec ut serpens modo in dexteram modo in sinisteram partem late movetur.[1]
Enn. fr. 354-5 (de Nonius, 195, 10—)
"malo cruce uti des, Juppiter"
(give them a bad death, Jupiter!)
Frazer—At Pouilly (Burgundy), at the end of the harvest, an ox bedecked with ribbons, flowers and corn, was led round the field. The harvesters followed it dancing. A man dressed as a devil cut the last heads of corn and immediately killed the ox. Part of it was eaten at the evening meal the same day; part was kept for the spring sowing. At Pont-à-Mousson a calf born in the spring was chosen. At Lunéville the calf was killed by a Jew.

Pork. In Sweden and Denmark a pasty of pork (or boar?) is made at Christmas, sometimes with flour from the last sheaf of corn. (Cf. Herodotus). It is put on the table; but it is not eaten until the spring, at the time of sowing.

In Esthonia a piglet is killed at Christmas and roasted and then left on the table several days.

Corn Spirit known as "Poor man", "Poor woman".

Seuphonia (à propos of Dionysus)

[1] United with these, Sky and Earth produced everything from themselves, because by means of them nature "mixes heat with cold and dryness with wet".—Elements of the world: "water earth life and sun" ... "Ceres, since she brings the fruits" "The earth brought forth all peoples, and takes them back again." "The earth is body but the mind is fire". On the human mind: "That is fire taken from the sun", and likewise of the sun: "It is all composed of mind" ... Hence Ennius's *Epicharmus* calls her Proserpina, because she is wont to go underground and because she moves widely now to the right and now to the left, like a serpent.

Pig, sacred to Demeter? Some pigs fell into the chasm into which Proserpina was rapt? (source?) At the Thesmophoria pigs were thrown into the caves inhabited by snakes (?)

Black Demeter (?)

Indian stories illustrating the belief that the animals we eat are restored to life if their bones are dealt with in a certain way. The method is taught by a tribe which lives sometimes in human and sometimes in animal form (salmon, deer) and which eats its own children.

Edda (in prose), source of the Scandinavian story of Balder, son of Odin.

Frazer. When the god is a corngod, the corn is his proper body; when he is a vine god, the juice of the grape is his blood; and so by eating the bread and drinking the wine the worshipper partakes of the real body and blood of his god. (Homeopathic magic of a flesh diet.)

Aztecs eat the God Vitziliputzli in the form of a maize pasty modelled in the likeness of a God and consecrated by a ceremony which transforms it into the God's flesh.

Frazer's conjecture about the castrated priests of Cybele— that she required the power of their virility for the resurrection of Attis and of nature.

In order to work in us, God requires us to offer him our vital energy, to put it at his disposal.

Attis. Baptism in the blood of a bull, purification and new birth, at the spring equinox, date of the death and resurrection of Attis(?)

"He was addressed as the 'reaped green (or yellow) ear of corn', and the story of his sufferings, death and resurrection was interpreted as the ripe grain wounded by the reaper, buried in the granary, and coming to life again when it is sown in the ground."

Statue of Attis, in the Lateran museum in Rome, holding corn and flowers in his hand and crowned with pine-cones, pomegranates and other fruits.

Pomegranate, pine-cone—multiplying power of seed?

Adonis and Attis, tree-gods (myrrh and pine).

And the tree of the cross ... In ligno pependit ...

[A propos of Attis.]

Odin was called the "Lord of the Gallows, God of the Hanged". He says in the *Havamal*:

"I know that *I hung on the windy tree*
For nine whole nights,
Wounded with the spear, dedicated to Odin,
Myself to myself"
(thus he became a god)
(*extraordinary!*)
Arcadian Artemis, named the Hanged One?
  For the feast of Attis at Rome a forest pine was cut down and brought to the shrine of Cybele, it was decorated with garlands and violets and an image of Attis was fixed to the trunk. This was the 22nd March. On the 25th March Attis was resurrected.
  Coins of Troy representing an ox (or a cow) hung on a tree and struck with a knife.
  Find the reference for the anonymous 4th century work on the resemblance between Attis and Christ.
  The foundation of mythology is that the universe is a metaphor of the divine truths.
  There must have been a revelation connected with the discovery of corn and the vine. Was it Noah's revelation?
  And one, before that, connected with the invention of stock herding. Was it Abel's?
  And hunting? Nimrod? (Heracles?)
  "Eating the God". In India, Brahminic belief in the transubstantiation of rice cakes into human flesh? Reference?
  Cult of the oak, as being the tree most often struck by lightning. The tree rises towards heaven with all its strength. God sends it his flame.
  Oak wood was especially used for burning. (?)
  Procopius "The Slavs believe that one god, the maker of lightning, is alone lord of all things, and they sacrifice to him oxen and every victim."
  A Greek? "The Celts worship Zeus, and the image of Zeus is a tall oak."
  "The Maidu Indians of California believe that a Great Man created the world and all its inhabitants, and that lightning is nothing but the Great Man himself descending swiftly out of heaven and rending the trees with his flaming arms."
  Pliny. The Druids believed that mistletoe falls from heaven.
  Frazer conjectures that they thought it came down with the thunderbolt.
  Equivalent of the Eucharist?

In the legend of the Grail, the host that comes down to the grail on each Good Friday and renews its virtue.

Thompson: Indians of British Columbia. Words spoken by the young in the spring, when they eat the year's first berries and roots: "I inform thee that I intend to eat thee. Mayest thou always help me to ascend, so that I may always be able to reach the tops of mountains, and may I never be clumsy! I ask this from thee, Sunflower-Root. Thou art the greatest of all in mystery."

* * *

Australian legend of the bird married to a snake, which makes rain.

In Genesis, the snake crawls as a punishment. Therefore, it was formerly upright. Like the bronze serpent of Moses. It was upright like men and trees.

Animal sacrament. Dr. Pelkin on the Madi or Moru of Central Africa. Once a year the people seat themselves around a circle of stones. A young boy leads a chosen lamb all round the circle; each one takes a piece of its wool and places it on his body. A priest slaughters it on the stones and sprinkles the people with its blood, then marks each one individually with it. He then preaches a sermon. The flesh of the lamb is distributed among the poor; its carcass is hung on a tree near the stones. Before this ceremony, a great sadness is manifest among the people; after it, a great happiness.

This lamb must be connected with the Theban ram.

There are some shepherds in the Caucasus who take a sacramental repast with their loins girded and a staff in their hands.

At Abdera, once every year, a citizen was stoned, having been excommunicated six days before, "so that he alone might bear the sins of the people". (Find reference.)

It must be a pure being to bear the sins, because crime prevents expiation.

"At Babylon the criminal who played the god was scourged before he was crucified." (Find reference.)

The magic conception of a divinity subject to laws, so that it can be controlled by knowledge. The conception of a capricious divinity, like a royal personage who shows favour to whom he pleases. Look for the unity which is behind both of them.

The knowledge is not a technique, but depends entirely upon love. The favour is free, but not arbitrary, because it is just.

It was Hippolytus whom Aesculapius resuscitated when Zeus killed him (source?)

* * *

Not to break a single bone of the paschal lamb (Exodus xii, 46). Is that connected with the practice among peoples of herdsmen and hunters of not breaking the bones of the animals they eat, so that they may be able to be resurrected? Cf. the folklore of North American Indians.

"The youth who joined the deer", Thompson. "Two young deer, his brothers-in-law, ran ahead... The hunter killed both... The people ate and were glad. They saved all the bones and put them away in one place... When the deer were eaten, the bones were wrapped in bundles, and the chief sent a man to throw them into the water... The two brothers-in-law came to life when their bones were thrown into the water. Thus these Deer people lived by hunting and killing each other and then reviving." Later, the hunter returns to his tribe and teaches them to save the bones and throw them into water.

Water, agent of resurrection. Cf. baptism?

* * *

"And the Eternal saw that the wickedness of man was great in the earth, and that every imagination of the thoughts of his heart was only evil continually; and it repented the Eternal that he had made man on the earth, and it grieved him at his heart... I will not again curse the ground any more for man's sake; for the imagination of man's heart is evil from his youth".

"The Eternal—God said unto the serpent: Because thou hast done this, upon thy belly shalt thou go..."

"Make thee a serpent and set it on a pole; and everyone that is bitten, when he looketh upon it shall live!" And Moses made a serpent of brass and set it upon a pole; and it came to pass that if a serpent had bitten any man, when he beheld the serpent of brass he was saved."

Vertical serpent, apparently.

[What difference from the golden calf?]

Ataraxia is based on love. It is love that prevents one from being troubled. But when we are troubled, it is by love. Therefore it is simply a misdirected love.

Housman:

> To think that two and two are four
> And neither five nor three
> The heart of man has long been sore
> And long t'is like to be.

It is precisely because of this that number, as the Pythagoreans said, is divine.

Does not the custom of burial originate from the metaphor of the seed?

Perfectly pure beings in the *Iliad*; Patroclus and Polydamas?

Beauty and carnal love—Beauty is the face of the eternal 'yes'—Beauty is eternity in perceptible form.

Love of God is essentially an unconditional feeling. Independent not only of the misfortunes but also of the crimes into which the soul may fall. That is to say that crime ought not to prevent the love of God. But the love of God ought to prevent crime.

Penitent criminals would be too greatly privileged in comparison with the innocent, if the latter were not "made a curse" by affliction.

Justice is assured amid the hazard of events by the fact that those who are below the spiritual level where affliction does no harm are also below the spiritual level where one refrains from treating men cruelly when circumstances permit. Those to whom one can do harm are those who would do harm if they could. One can do no harm to those who would not in any case do harm to others; although it *is* possible to put them into a condition in which they are "made a curse".

The basis of the supernatural is asymmetry, non-reciprocal relations—"non-abelian" relations.[1]

The story of Christ is a symbol, a metaphor. But it used to be believed that metaphors produce themselves as events in the world. God is the supreme poet.

---

[1] In the mathematical theory of groups the term 'abelian' denotes any group of operations that are commutative, i.e. such that the order of operation is unimportant; the joint effect of two operators being the same irrespective of the order in which they are applied.

"The four idiots" (Folk-lore of Schoharie Hills)—The one who takes the oven to the bread for baking. The one who drags the cyder barrel into the kitchen to the jug. The one who takes some sunlight into the hay-loft instead of putting the hay out in the sun. The one who tries to jump into his trousers instead of pulling them on.

Certainly metaphors with a spiritual meaning. Sun and hay. Trying to bring God into this world instead of removing oneself out of the world.

Folklore theme of the *relative* character of force. The mouse looking for the strongest husband finally gets a virile mouse.

The whole problem of mysticism and kindred questions is that of the degree of value of sensations of presence.

Reginald Scot (?) [quoted by Hardwick] "the devil loveth no salt in his meat because salt is a sign of eternity and is used by God's commandment in all sacrifices."

Schoharie. "If, before cutting a loaf of bread, you pinch a piece off and throw it away, you will never want for bread."

"If you see the new moon and do not think of a red fox's tail, you will have good luck" (cf. white bear).

"... The very old tale of the Black Bull of Norroway mentioned in the complaynt of Scotland. 1549." Halliwell, Popular Rhymes and Nursery Tales (1849) p. 52–55, The Bull of Norroway. Beckwith, Bull of All-the-Land, Jamaica Anansi Stories, p. 1030. Carter: "Mountain White Folk-Lore, Tales from the Southern Blue Ridge, J A P L, 38 (1925) 357–59. Kittredge (?) p. 210. Aarne-Thompson, The types of the Folk-Tale. F.F. Communications, vol. 25, no. 74. (Type 425, "The search for the Lost Husband", form A "The Monster as Bridegroom".

Bolte—Polivka "Anmerkungen zu den Kinder-und-Hausmärchen der Brüder Grimm" 3 vol. Berlin 1913–18
(II, no 88—III, no 127—II, no 93)
Russian folk-lore—especially Ralston—Russian Folk-Tales, London 1873.
Clouston. Popular tales and fictions 2 vol. London 1887.
(I, 205–214)—Crans, Italian popular tales (1–7, 17–23).
Thorpe—Northern Mythology—3 vol. London 1857.
Yule-Tide Stories, London 1910.

Scarborough, Dorothy—On the trail of Negro folk-songs—1925.
Polson—Our Highland Folklore heritage—1926.
Parsons—Folklore of America.
Owen (Rev. Elias)—Welsh Folklore 1896.
Jacobs—English Fairy Tales.
Greenleaf and Mansfield—Ballads and sea-songs of Newfoundland.
Dasent—Popular tales from the Norse 1859.
Davies—Folklore of West and Mid-Wales 1911.
Burre—The handbook of Folklore 1914.
Burne and Jackson—Shropshire Folklore 1882.
Campbell—Popular tales of West Highlands—4 vol. 1890-93. I, 64-68—II, 208-213.
Cosquin—Contes populaires de Lorraine—2 vol. 1887.
[Professors of Folk-lore—Boas, Campbell, Columbia—Strauss, Bonner, Michigan—Thompson, Indiana University. Folklore Fellows Communications, vol. 25, no 74, "The Types of the Folk-Tale" vol. 29, no 106, "Motif-Index of Folk-Literature", celebrated collection of folk-lore at the Cleveland Public Library (White collection).]

Romany—Sun, kam or kạn (or guin?). Moon, chone.
"The people of Turkey", edited by M. St. L. Pool, London 1878.
Turkish tradition concerning the Gypsies. On arriving in Turkey they built a magnificent contraption with a wheel. But it didn't work. An evil spirit disguised as a sage told the Gypsy leader, Chen, that the wheel would not turn until he married his sister, Guin. He married her, and the wheel turned; and ever since then the Gypsies in Turkey have been called Chen guin. Ever since then, too, they have been condemned to wander, having been cursed by a Moslem saint.

Does Tzigane come from Chen-guin? And does Chen-guin mean moon-sun?

There is a myth common to the Eskimos and the Gypsies of Roumania about a young man who committed incest and was turned into a moon, his sister being turned into a sun. (The same myth existed, it seems, in ancient Ireland.)

Idea of original sin joined with that of creation.

An English Gypsy said his people regarded Christ as a Gypsy,

because he was poor, was a vagabond on a donkey, and was persecuted.
(Io and Prometheus, a pair. The punishment of vagabondage is also indicated in the story of Christ. And of Love in Plato.)
kekkavi, kettle—chinamangri, bill-hook or chopper—kam sun, a word sometimes passed as a secret, like chone or shule, moon, although they are very well-known.
The legend of the Moon and the Sun is in "A Winter in the City of Pleasure" by Florence K. Berger. But there the sun is male.
hokkani boro, great trick—pen dukkerin, fortune-telling—lel dudikabin, conveying away of property—chir o manzin apré lati, put under oath.
Shelta, secret Celtic language of the Tinkers—Soobli or Soobri, brother (Babylonian ubri?) Bewr, woman—Durra, bread—Pani, water (Romany)—Stall, go—Biyêg, to steal—odd, two—Thari, or bug, talk—Larkin, girl—thari, speak—Grannis, know—nyok, head,—riaglon, iron—krädyin, to stop—Oura, town (!)—[Ur]—Gyami, bad—Theddy, fire—blihunka, horse—Leicheen, girl—Soobli, man—binny, small—médthel, black—respun, steal—shoich, water—chimmes, wood—mailyas, arms—thari, word—bog, get—masheen, cat—cambra, dog—rawg, wagon—analt, to sweep—derri, bread—sunain, see—koris, feet—kradying, being, lying—okonneh, priest—turks, eyes—ainoch, thing—gut, black—gothni, child—crimum, sheep.
The ridias of the kiéna dont granny what we're a tharyin.
The people of the house don't know what we're saying.
Cosson kailyah corrum me morre sar,
Me gul ogalyach mir,
Rahet marent trasha moroch
Me tu sosti mo dièle.
(Talk of the Picts?)

Myth of the sun and moon. Relation of sin and time. Time is a punishment.
Wandering peoples. Descendants of Cain in the Bible (although Abel was the shepherd). In this case it is the murder of a brother.
The murder of Abel is another version of the original sin.

The myth of the Danaides and that of the sun and moon.

The Gypsies seem to see themselves as a people which has in a special sense witnessed and inherited the original sin.

Their word for diamond: o latcho bar, the true stone. (What is "Consuelo", book by a German Slav, and "Der letzte Taborit" by Herlossohn?)

In Russia the Gypsies were reputed to possess the secret of conserving heat.

Gypsy greeting: Sarishan!

The whole problem of mysticism and kindred questions is that of the degree of value of sensations of presence.

For the Greeks, infernal suffering—the Danaides, etc.—is purely and simply time, assigned as the punishment for sin.

Sanctity is the only way out from time.

In this world we live in a mixture of time and eternity. Hell would be pure time.

Gold, among the Hopi Indians, "seed of the sun".

Transmutation of metals into gold, symbol for the transmutation of matter into light.

In this mixture of time and eternity, joy corresponds to an increase of the factor eternity, and pain to a predominance of the factor time. So why is it that going through pain makes us more perceptive of beauty?

In this world we have to choose between time and eternity. In a sense this choice corresponds to choosing between joy and pain. And yet not ostensibly. How does this come to be so?

We have no need of belief in eternal life—because the only proof of such a life is the presentiments of eternity which we have in this world. And these presentiments are sufficient in themselves. It is true that they presuppose the plenitude of eternal life. But not necessarily for us.

Joy fixes us to eternity and pain fixes us to time. But desire and fear hold us in bondage to time, and detachment breaks the bonds.

The pursuit of joy attaches us to time. Joy is our escape out of time.

Pain keeps us nailed to time, but acceptance of pain carries us to the end of time, into eternity. We exhaust the indefinite length of time, we overleap it.

New birth. The seed, instead of engendering another being, serves to engender the same being a second time. Return upon oneself, closed circuit, circle.

Circular movement is also the symbol of apparent moving away, which is really an approach.

"He who is not born from on high will not enter the kingdom of heaven". It is necessary to come down from heaven in order to be able to return there.

"From water and the spirit." The first generating comes from blood.

Apocalypse—the kings of the earth and their armies make war against the Word of God, from whose mouth comes a two-edged sword, and its army of horsemen in white linen on white horses.

Unless one had the mark of the beast, one would find buying and selling impossible.

In heaven a woman clothed with the sun, and the moon under her feet and upon her head a crown of twelve stars, was crying in the pains of child-birth. A dragon with seven heads and ten horns stands before the woman to devour the new-born child, but the child is taken up to the throne of God; the woman flees into a wilderness for 1260 days (3 and a half years, which corresponds to Daniel's figure). Michael throws the dragon down ("ὁ δράκων ὁ μέγας, ὁ ὄφις, ὁ ἀρχαῖος, ὁ καλούμενος Διάβολος καὶ ὁ Σατανᾶς, ὁ πλανῶν τὴν οἰκουμένην ὅλην"[1]). A voice says in heaven: "Now is come salvation, and strength, and the kingdom of our God, and the power of the Christ; he hath been cast down who accused our brethren before God day and night. They over-

[1] Revelation 12: 9.

came him by the blood of the Lamb and by the word of their own testimony; they loved not their soul unto the death. Therefore rejoice ye heavens and ye that dwell in them; woe to the earth and to the sea, because the devil is come down to them, having great wrath, because he knoweth that he hath but a short time."

The dragon persecutes the woman, and she is given two eagle's wings to escape to the wilderness, where she is nourished for three and a half years, in safety from the serpent. The serpent casts out water like a river from his mouth, to overwhelm her. But the earth swallows up the river. The dragon goes to make war upon the remnant of her seed, those who give testimony for Jesus. And he stands upon the sand of the sea. And out of the sea there rises a beast with seven heads and seven[1] horns and ten crowns, to whom the dragon gives his powers, his throne and his authority. And the whole world admires the beast and adores the dragon and the beast. It is all-powerful for 42 months. (12 × 3 + 6, three and a half years.) It wars victoriously with the saints, all power is given to it, and it is worshipped by all except those whose names are written in the book of life. "εἰ τις εἰς αἰχμαλωσίαν, εἰς αἰχμαλωσίαν ὑπάγει, εἰ τις ἐν μαχαίρῃ ἀποκτενεῖ, δεῖ αὐτὸν ἐν μαχαίρῃ ἀποκτανθῆναι. Ὧδε ἐστιν ἡ ὑπομονὴ καὶ ἡ πίστις τῶν ἁγίων.[2]

Another beast rises up out of the earth, with two horns like a lamb, and speaking like the dragon; equal in power to the first beast. And the first beast having been mortally wounded in one of its heads and having recovered from its deadly wound, the second beast causes all men to worship the first. The second beast brings down fire to the earth in the sight of men and persuades them to make an image for the beast which was wounded with a sword and lived. And it is given power to put life into the image of the beast, and the image speaks, and those who do not worship it are put to death. And all have the mark of the beast on their forehead, its name or the number of its name.

The Lamb was with 144,000 virgins. (12^2 × 1000.) παρθένοι εἰσιν ... ἠγοράσθησαν ἀπὸ τῶν ἀνθρώπων ἀπαρχὴ τῷ θεῷ καὶ τῷ ἀρνίῳ ... ἄμωμοί εἰσιν.[3]

From the mouth of the dragon and the beast and the false prophet, three unclean spirits (diabolic trinity).

The Word of God and his army do battle against the kings of

---

[1] [sic] (for 'ten').   [2] Revelation 13: 10.   [3] Revelation 14: 4–5.

the earth and their armies, and the beast and the false prophet are cast into the lake of fire burning with brimstone. He is bound for a thousand years. After a thousand years, another battle.

The devil and the beast and the false prophet shall be tortured day and night for ever and ever. ξύλον ζωῆς ποιοῦν καρποὺς δώδεκα, κατὰ μῆνα ἕκαστον ἀποδιδοῦν τὸν καρπὸν αὐτοῦ.[1]
Evidently it is the axis of the poles.

πᾶν κατάθημα οὐκ ἔσται ἔτι. There shall be no more curse.

Begone, whosoever loveth and maketh a lie.

Names of Christ in the Apocalypse—

I am the first and the last and I am he that was dead and am alive for evermore and I have the keys of death and hell.

He who holds seven stars in his right hand, who walks among seven golden candlesticks.

The first and the last, who became a corpse and lived.

He who has the two-edged sword, sharpened on both sides.

The son of God, whose eyes are a flame of fire and his feet like the stone of Lebanon. (ivory? bronze?)

He who has the seven spirits of God and the seven stars.

He who is holy, he who is true, he who has the key of David, he who opens and no man shuts, and shuts and no man opens.

The Amen, the faithful and true witness, the beginning of the creation of God.

A lamb standing as if it had been slain, having seven horns and seven eyes, which are the seven spirits of God sent forth into all the earth.

The four animals: lion, bull, man, eagle—all of them winged, full of eyes, singing the glory of God.

A white horse, ridden by a crowned bowman (first seal).

A red horse, rider with a sword.

A black horse, rider with a pair of scales.

A pale horse, rider Death and hell.

5th seal: the martyrs arise and cry out.

6th seal: the stars fall—"mountains and rocks fall on us, hide us from the wrath of the Lamb".

Marked with the sign of God—144,000 of all the tribes of Israel, and then an innumerable multitude of all nations. All have washed their robes in the blood of the Lamb.

7th seal "there was silence in heaven, about the space of half an hour". The 7 angels blow their trumpets.

[1] Revelation 22: 2.

For forty-two months they shall tread under foot the holy city. My two witnesses shall prophesy 1260 days. Then the beast shall kill them. They shall lie three and a half days, then they shall come to life and go up to heaven in a cloud.

Number of 'Ιησοῦς: 888—, or 37 × 3 × 8. ‖ 666 = 37 × 3 × 6

(The mark of the Father would be 888?)

The only clear sign is that the mark of the Beast is necessary "for buying and selling".

Also, those who are with the Lamb are virgin.

Apart from that, symmetry of good and evil.

The Beast received a deadly wound and lived.

The kings and their armies are on the side of the Beast.

The locusts which will come up from the pit after the fifth trumpet will attack only those men who are not marked with the divine seal. They will not kill them but will torment them, as with scorpion bites, for five months, so that they vainly long for death. These locusts will be like horses harnessed for battle. They will have faces like men, and as it were golden crowns, and hair like women's, and teeth like lions', and a sound like chariots of war, and tails like scorpions, and stings in them, and the angel of the pit will be king over them.

Seals: 1st, archer ‖ 2nd, sword ‖ 3rd, scales ‖ 4th, death ‖ 5th, martyrs' cries ‖ 6th, the stars fall ‖ 7th, trumpets.

The angels blow their trumpets.

At the first, there is hail and fire mingled with blood, which falls on the earth and a third of it is burned up.

At the second, fire falls on the sea and a third of it is changed into blood. A third of all the ships are destroyed.

At the third, the star Wormwood falls and a third of the waters are changed into wormwood, which kills many men.

At the fourth, a third part of the sun, the moon, and the stars is extinguished, and there is darkness for a third part of the day and the night.

At the fifth, a star falls which opens the bottomless pit and the locusts come out.

At the sixth, the four angels of the Euphrates kill a third part of the human race, with their horses which have lion's heads and tails which sting like serpents and fire and smoke and brimstone ($\pi\hat{v}\rho$—$\kappa\alpha\pi\nu\acute{o}s$—$\theta\epsilon\hat{\iota}ov$) issuing from their mouths. The two prophets send forth fire which kills their enemies, they prophesy for $3\frac{1}{2}$ years, are killed by the Beast in the town where their lord was crucified, lie dead for $3\frac{1}{2}$ days, and then rise up and ascend into heaven. The temple of God opens in heaven. Seventh trumpet.

The woman clothed with the sun and crowned with twelve stars gives birth. The Beast comes out of the sea, the False Prophet out of the earth. The Son of Man and an angel send their sickles to reap lives on the earth. Then seven angels come forth with the seven last plagues, having received from the 4 beasts 7 vials filled with the wrath of God.

Plagues against those who bear the mark of the Beast.

1st vial poured on the earth—men afflicted with terrible sores.

2nd on the sea—it becomes like the blood of a corpse.

3rd on the rivers and fountains—they become blood.

4th on the sun—it scorches men.

5th on the throne of the Beast—Its kingdom grows dark and men gnaw their tongues for pain.

6th on the Euphrates—It dries up and the kings of the East assemble their peoples for the battle at the place called Armageddon.

7th on the air—There is lightning, thunder, earthquake, hail. The woman seated on the Beast is cursed.

The Word of God battles victoriously with the kings of the earth and their armies. The devil is bound for 1000 years. First resurrection.

Then he again seduces men, who battle against the celestial city and are destroyed.

Last judgement. The celestial Jerusalem comes down from heaven. Bride of the Lamb.

Thus, the plan is:

7 seals.

At the 7th the angels blow 7 trumpets.

At the 7th trumpet, the angels send 7 plagues.

7 seals: 1] archer || 2] sword || 3] scales || 4] death || 5] cries of martyrs || 6] fall of stars || 7] trumpets.

        (victory)   (hide us . . .)

7 trumpets—1] hail, fire, blood over ⅓ of the earth ‖ 2] fire turns ⅓ of the sea to blood ‖ 3] wormwood over ⅓ of the waters ‖ 4] extinction of ⅓ of the stars ‖ 5] locusts ‖ 6] horses and two prophets ‖ 7] war against heaven; Beast.

7 vials 1] sores on men—2] sea changed into corpse's blood ‖ 3] waters changed to blood ‖ 4] the sun scorches men ‖ 5] the kingdom of the Beast grows dark ‖ 6] Euphrates dries up, armies assemble for Armageddon ‖ 7] lightning, thunder, earthquake, hail. Destruction of Babylon. The Word of God triumphs over the kings. The devil is bound for 1000 years.

The fire falling on the sea turns it into blood.

He it is who came through water and blood, Jesus Christ. Not in water only, but in water and blood. And the Spirit is that which gives witness, for the Spirit is truth. For there are three witnesses, the spirit and water and blood, and the three are in one (εἰς τὸ ἕν εἰσιν).

He who believes in the son of God has the witness in him. He who does not believe in God makes it false, not having believed the testimony given by God concerning his son. And this is the testimony, that God has given us eternal life, and that this life is in his son. He who has the son has life. He who has not the son of God has not life. I write that for you so that you may know you have eternal life, you who believe in the name of the son of God.

ἐκ τοῦ θεοῦ ἐσμεν, καὶ ὁ κόσμος ὅλος ἐν τῷ πονηρῷ κεῖται.[1]

Whosoever has been born of God commits no offence, for the seed of God dwells in him, and he can commit no offence because he has been born of God. He who does not love dwells in death. He who hates his brother is a murderer, and no murderer has eternal life in him.

We shall be like him, for we shall see him as he is. And whoever has this hope in him, let him purify himself as he is pure. Whoever dwells in him does not commit offences. Whoever commits offences has not seen him or known him.

The spirit gives witness. The Spirit which changes water into blood. If Christ had come in water only, there would not be this witness of the Spirit.

---

[1] We are from God, and his whole world is given over to destruction.

Born from on high. The Spirit coming down to the man of flesh, to combine with water so as to make a new blood in him. What water? The seed?
"Kid, thou hast fallen into milk." The ancients believed that milk is the seed. To fall into milk, to return to infancy?
We have eternal life in us. There has been a real change, which is therefore bodily as well. This change is the new birth.
"I baptize with water, but he that comes after me shall baptize with the spirit and fire."
The "state of infancy" and "the death of the old man" are the same thing.
Not only in water, but also in blood; that must mean: he was not only man, but incarnate God. To be born from on high of water and the spirit is to become like him. Water and spirit is like earth (that part of it which is perfectly pure) and heaven. One has to be born from on high through a meeting of heaven and earth.
One should make a list of the things which have to be obtained by human means and not asked from God—and of the things which must be asked from God and which one must never try to obtain by human means.

"Mirror of simple souls". French mysticism of the 14th century.
Ruysbroek. *The sparkling stone,* ch. viii.
Sacrum commercium. Speculum perfectionis. Franciscan works.

>Jacopone da Todi:
>
>De lo 'nferno non temere
>e del ciel spem non avere;
>e de nullo ben gaudere
>e non doler d'aversitate.
>
>La virtú non è perchene
>ca'l perchene è for de téne,
>sempre encognito te tène
>a curar tua enfermitate.[1]

[1] Do not fear hell and do not hope for heaven; do not enjoy anything too much and do not grieve at misfortune. Virtue is not why and wherefore, her reason is beyond you. Ask no more, but apply yourself to healing your infirmity.

cf. Lauda xci "Spro' onne lengua amore"

—O alma nobilissima,
dinne que cosa vide!
—Veggo un tal non veggio
che onne cosa me ride.[1]

Those who have arrived at the absolute express themselves only by identities "the good is the good", "I is I" (atman)— because it is only an identity that expresses the unconditional.

To be detached from the fruits of action. For that, the soul needs an architecture in depth. Because the part of the soul that acts must strive passionately towards the fruits of action. Another part of it must be detached.

Havamal (in the *Edda*)—Words of Odin:
"I know that I hung on the wind-swept tree for three full nights, pierced with a spear and dedicated to Odin, I to myself, on the tree whereof no man can tell from the roots of what tree it springs."
God of Hanged Men, Lord of the Gallows.

Idea of sacrifice—Idea of giving something to God, to whom everything belongs . . . all one can give him is consent. This consent comes from God.
"Dedicated to Odin, I to myself."

The act of kneeling. Supplex et supplicium. To kneel is to offer oneself for whipping, beheading, or any punishment; it is to place oneself most conveniently for the sword. At the same time it is to put oneself near the thing that gives life, so that one is available for being engendered by pity. This gesture is related to the two symbols which in antiquity were the attributes of divinity and royalty, sword and phallus.

The baptismal water contains the two-fold symbol of death

---

[1] O most noble soul, what do you see?—I see such a non-seeing that everything smiles on me.

and life by analogy with the sea, which drowns and makes floods, and with seed. Rain is the seed of heaven falling on the earth. The seed of the maimed Ouranos, become sea-foam, made celestial Aphrodite rise out of the sea. The newly baptized person is drowned like humanity in the time of Noah, like the Egyptians in the Red Sea, and rises up like celestial Aphrodite. The same water kills and gives birth. But by itself it only kills; it gives birth in combination with the fiery spirit.

Trees grow by the water and light which come down from heaven. In the same way, the grain of mustard seed grows to a tree in our soul.

"We live the death of the Gods and the Gods live our death."

We must rediscover the idea of the metaphor which is real. Otherwise the story of Christ, for example, loses either its reality or else its meaning.

Doubt is a virtue of the intelligence, and consequently there is a doubt which is not incompatible with faith; and faith is not belief.

The unity of water and fire in the blood is the image of the unity of the Father and the Son in the Spirit.

The water is the Virgin, the fire is the Spirit, the blood is Christ.

God, the Virgin, and Christ in his humanity make a trinity which is the image of the other trinity.

The sea, the seed of Ouranos, and celestial Aphrodite.

The Creator, the creature, and the mediator.

The two harmonies of the Pythagoreans.—The common thought of separated thinkers.—The unity of contraries.

The Mother of Christ, that means the whole entire Creation.

Mary is the equivalent of the Creation. Hence the Immaculate Conception. The Creation as a totality is without a blemish. All the evil in it is only suffering.

Water is an image of the original purity and docility of the creation.

Definition of faith in the catechism of the Council of Trent.

"... for as the end proposed to man ... is far above the reach of human understanding, it was therefore necessary that it should be made known to him by Almighty God. This knowledge then is nothing else than faith, by which we yield our unhesitating assent to whatever the authority of our Holy Mother the Church teaches us to have been delivered by Almighty God; for the faithful cannot doubt those things of which God, who is truth itself, is the author." Bad.

"Symbol" of the apostles. Cf. the meaning of the word "symbol" in the *Symposium*.

Creation. Redemption. Sanctification.

"The bitter Withy". English ballad found in 1868. Jesus goes to play with a ball. Three noble children refuse to play with him. He makes a bridge out of sunbeams and goes across it; the children follow and are drowned. Mary puts him across her knee and gives him three strokes with a willow branch. He then says: "The bitter withy... shall be the very first tree that perishes at the heart."

Sir Gawain and the Green Knight—14th or 15th century text. The Pentagon (confused with Solomon's seal) is called "the endless knot". It is an endless figure, because one can draw it with a single stroke, like a circle ✿ "each line overlaps and locks in another".

"These (virtues: generosity, fellowship, purity, courtesy and pity that passes all qualities...) were established fivefold in this knight, and each one was established in another that had no end, and they were fastened on five points that never failed, nor met anywhere, nor sundered either, but finished always without an end at each corner, wherever the game began or concluded."

The purpose of human life is to construct an architecture in the soul.

Eternity is found at the end of an infinite time. Pain, fatigue, hunger give time the colour of the infinite.

The great obstacle to the loss of personality is the feeling of guilt. One must lose it.

The aim is to lose the personality. Since it is inseparably attached to the feeling of guilt, the true price of virtue is the abolition of this feeling. One can only fight against the feeling of guilt by practising virtue.

Human nature is so made that there is no other way to escape from the feeling of guilt, which is identical, at its centre, with the feeling of being *I*.

How can the point of reconciliation be found for the two contradictory obligations: on the one hand, to find that everything is good, and, on the other, to feel compassion and remorse?

To give purely, from pure love, implies that one would be willing also to receive. So long as one is prevented by pride from being willing to receive, one has no right to give.

Astraea, the Virgin—Justice, having fled from earth and taken refuge in heaven . . .

Within the universe there is no good, but the universe is good.

The collective soul is one-dimensional. It has no architecture.

Only through ceremony does it acquire depth, and ceremony reduces it to silence.

Propaganda is one-dimensional.

Compassion is the recognition of one's own misery in another. Recognition of one's own misery in the affliction of someone else. What makes it pure is the very mechanism in which La Rochefoucauld thought to discern its impurity.

A saint in affliction judges that his affliction is a good thing, but only with the part of his soul that does not feel it.

And remorse?

When our action is dominated by our sensibility, the illusion of "I" is still intact.

Or the other way round?

Ought I to call upon the will, or to rely for everything upon contemplation alone?

Choose contemplation alone, even though that way is longer and in appearance less effective.

Contemplation unmixed with will, purely obedient. We shall see what that gives.

Let virtuous actions be simply an incident of contemplation.
Compassion and humility are connected.
Humility is the root of all authentic virtues. Chastity, for example. Temperance. Patience.
Compassion is natural to man if the obstacle of the feeling of "I" is removed. It is not compassion that is supernatural, but the removal of that obstacle.
It is only humility that makes the virtues unlimited.
Act as the sun would do, if it knew. It is only without pity because it does not know.
Justice. To be as unconscious matter would be—if it was conscious.
Image of God.

"Forgive us our debts as we forgive . . ." The feeling of guilt is always connected with an accusing spirit. We lay the blame for our failures and shortcomings upon things and creatures other than us. In the end, we are accusing God.
If we forgive God for our sins, he forgives us for them.
All our debts are to God, and God is also our only debtor (how can we be angry with a man who offends us without being angry with God who has allowed him to succeed in offending us?). In offending God we incur an infinite debt, because he is infinitely good. In allowing people to offend us he incurs an infinite debt, because he is infinitely powerful. The debts cancel out.
The criminal blames God for his crimes. The innocent man feels guilty for his afflictions.

πᾶς γὰρ πυρὶ ἁλισθήσεται. Everyone shall be salted by the fire. Everything will be burned in the fire, but he who has already become fire will not suffer from it.
Everyone will be destroyed by contact with God, but he who has already become dead in spirit through love will be made perfect by this destruction.

If two of you are of one mind in all their demands . . .
apparently two men cannot be of one mind about everything

between themselves unless they are of one mind with God about everything.

The parable of the workers of the eleventh hour shows that there is only one single wage, and no differing degrees of glory.
The prodigal son asks his father for his portion, and begins by consuming it on the road to perdition. Then he knows hunger and works as a hireling, and is still hungry. And only then does he become himself again. εἰς ἑαυτὸν ἐλθών.
His portion was free will. One needs to have exhausted one's will in seeking the appearance of good in this world, and to have desired in vain for a long time, before one can come back to oneself and remember one's Father. It is to the prodigals—those who expend all their energy in pursuit of what seems to them good, and who still go on impotently desiring after their strength has failed—that the memory of the Father's house comes back. If the son had lived economically, he would never have thought of returning.
"Give me my portion", that is the original sin. Give me free will, the choice between good and evil.
Is not this gift of free will the creation itself?
What is creation from the point of view of God is sin from the point of view of the creature.
God asked us "do you want to be created?" and we answered yes. He still asks us at every moment, and at every moment we answer yes. Except for a few whose soul is split in two; while nearly their whole soul answers yes, there is one point in it which wears itself out in beseeching: no, no, no! This point grows larger as it cries, and becomes a patch which eventually spreads throughout the soul.

Habakkuk "O thou whose eyes are too pure to behold evil, who canst not look on iniquity . . . "
Every contact between God and man is pain on both sides. God cannot look upon evil, and man cannot look upon good. Prometheus and Hippolytus. Their torments are complementary. God loving man too much, man loving God too much.

[1] Habakkuk 1: 13.

Sacrifice is a gift to God, and giving to God is destroying. It is right, therefore, to think that God abdicated in order to create and that by destroying we are making restitution to him.

God's sacrifice is creation; man's sacrifice is destruction.

But man has the right to destroy only what belongs to him; that is to say, not even his body, but solely and exclusively his will.

Before drinking, one pours away a drop; that is giving it to God. One single drop from a cup, that is the proportion of his life that man can give to God. If he succeeds in giving that much, he is saved.

The drop one pours away is a gratuitous expense of energy. Every gratuitous expense of energy is a gift given to God and a destruction of part of the will.

When we pour away this drop, we throw it out of this world, beyond the horizon, beyond the sky.

Only a single drop, but we ask nothing in exchange for it.

Christ gave the whole of himself in the same way.

In what sense did Christ make expiation for humanity? To expiate is to restore what one has unjustly taken. Humanity stole free will, the choice between good and evil. Christ gave it back, by learning obedience. To be born is to participate in Adam's theft. To die is to participate in Christ's restitution. But we are only saved by this participation if we consent to it.

Salvation is consenting to die.

Abel was the first dead man. Is not Abel the first incarnation of the Word? The first-born of the dead? Is he the Pan of the Egyptians? And is it he (rather than Osiris) whose Passion was celebrated at Sais?

(Find the works of the Egyptian who assimilated the Hebrews with the Hyksos.)

Birth involves us in the original sin, death redeems us from it. The Cross of Christ, as the perfect model of death, death in itself in Plato's sense, has redeemed us all. But if we consent to being born and not to dying, we personally commit the sin of Adam, to our destruction.

Only God can be born without original sin. Because, for God, to be born is renunciation. The birth of Christ is already a sacrifice. Christmas ought to be as sad a day as Good Friday.

Every man, seeing himself from the point of view of God the creator, should regard his own existence as a sacrifice made by God. I am God's abdication. The more I exist, the more God abdicates. So if I take God's side rather than my own I ought to regard my existence as a diminution, a decrease.

When anyone succeeds in doing this, Christ comes to dwell in his soul.

As regards myself, I ought to repeat in the opposite sense the abdication of God, I ought to refuse the existence that has been given me, to refuse it because God is good. As regards other people, I ought to imitate God's abdication itself, to consent not to be in order that they may be; and this in spite of the fact that they are bad.

That is why we must serve the bodily needs of others, in so far as they are legitimate. For one must serve them as created beings. It is not for a created being to induce them to renounce their creaturely existence. Towards that end, the best one can do is to serve them gratuitously in their creaturely needs. Christ healed and gave food. Pure exchange of compassion and gratitude is the relationship between creatures that leads the soul into God's friendship.

Everything gratuitously given to a created thing is given to God, like a drop of wine poured on the ground from a cup.

If one thinks one has given something gratuitously, that very thought itself is a price, a reward.

Therefore one can never know whether or not one has given gratuitously.

A list should be made of those things which are true so long as we don't think them and become false as soon as we think them.

Like the Cretan—"I am a liar". At the moment when he is thinking it, he is not a liar. That sophism is very profound.

All the good and all the evil that one thinks of oneself is false at the moment of thinking it. That is why one should think only evil of oneself. And one must not know that it is false.

In certain negro tribes each man has his personal fetish; but they also believe in God. If one of them had the idea of proclaiming that his fetish was God himself, it would follow that it should reign over the whole universe. It was in this way that Israel gave to its national fetish—which was not represented by an image, but that makes no difference—the name of God.

That is why Moses prohibited images. So that Israel should continue to believe that its little national idol was God himself, the creator of the universe. They would not have believed it if the little idol had been a statue. Moses wanted them to believe it, for the sake of Israel's temporal greatness.

Christ, on the contrary, made God his only idol. That may appear to come to the same thing, but to make God one's idol and to make one's idol God are two contrary movements. Just as there are two contrary conceptions of royalty: to make one's desires the law, or to make the law one's desire.

The Arabs, who also aspired to temporal domination in the name of religion, continued the prohibition of images.

Images are a guarantee against a certain kind of idolatry. It is impossible to stand before a piece of carved wood and say to it: "Thou hast made the heavens and the earth." But the Hebrews, exalted by the presence of their own collective soul, could perfectly well address it in this way, because, not being a material object, it could not be obviously seen to be a created thing.

Rome wanted to suppress all thought of God and to allow men to adore only the power of the State. But it is impossible for men to forget God entirely.

The Hebrews called their own collective soul God; they pretended, and convinced themselves, that it was the creator and ruler of heaven and earth. This was not always easy to believe . . . Nevertheless, it seems that it must have given them an extra strength. As for the neighbouring peoples, they had to be conquered before they could be convinced of it.

Their neighbours were unwilling to associate with them except on terms which obliged them to practise idolatry, because their claim to possess God as a national fetish and to possess him exclusively implied a terrifyingly imperialist outlook.

With a people which was still weak and very unmilitary, and which had been broken by slavery, such an attitude could hardly succeed. With the Moslems it succeeded much better.

But the pretension which was fruitless for the Hebrews would have served the Romans excellently once they had established the Empire. And the Romans did want to adopt the Jewish religion. But a national religion cannot pass from one people to another like a suit of clothes. That is why the Romans chose the non-national form of the Jewish religion, the Christian form. The Jewish religion, with an addendum transferring the privilege of Israel to baptized Gentiles, made the perfectly appropriate religion for the Roman empire. The Old Testament, plus the passages of St. Paul on the transfer of the Covenant, and "go ye and teach all nations".

That is why the Old Testament was preserved.

Unfortunately for Rome, she left it rather too late. By the time of Constantine she was already collapsing. The business was delayed by prejudice and conservatism until it was too late to save the Empire.

St. Augustine's "City of God" marks a second transfer. The Empire had succeeded Israel, the Church succeeded the Empire.

If everyone who dies outside the Church is damned, the Church's power can be much more totalitarian than that of the Empire.

But the Church did not succeed because it did not dare openly and directly to assume temporal royalty. In view of the Gospel, this was difficult to do. Is that the meaning of "the gates of hell shall not prevail against it"? Very possibly.

The Jews were persecuted because, once the Church had annexed their privilege, their claim that they had still kept it made them too embarrassing.

Religion, in the true sense of the word, never entered into the question. On both sides, it was obstinacy inspired by purely temporal motives.

Hitler persecutes the Jews for the same reason. He would like to imitate them by calling the German collective soul Wotan and saying that Wotan created heaven and earth.

It is quite true that, under his Christian disguise, Jehovah the God of armies has conquered the whole world. Wotan is now trying to supplant Jehovah. He, at any rate, has no need to feel embarrassed by the Gospel.

This would be the time to make clear the difference between the collective soul and God.

In this world, God is a dissolvent. Friendship with Him

confers no power, but so long as He is present in his truth in the thoughts of men no earthly power can become quite stable.

Augustus' notion (if it was his?) of bringing the Eleusinian mysteries to Rome shows that in the Roman empire the spiritual problem was a problem.

No victory, absolutely no victory, of evil can alter the fact that evil is still evil.

On the other hand, a total defeat of the good may cause the good to cease to be good.

But so long as evil is judged to be evil, the good has not been totally vanquished.

A crucified thief turns towards Christ who is also crucified. That suffices; the good has not been totally vanquished.

A grain of good no larger than a pomegranate seed is enough.

Christianity should be purged of the Israelite heritage.

Because of the perfect spiritual purity of Christianity, too perfect for men, there was a hunger for the temporal among Christians. This hunger was at first assuaged by the expectation of the imminent Second Coming.

Then, when that expectation had worn out, it was assuaged by the Empire. And then, after the sack of Rome, by the Church.

For Protestants, who no longer have the Church, religion has become to a great extent national. Hence the revived importance of the Old Testament.

Dates. Decius killed in 251. Valerian (253–260) favours the Christians, and later persecutes them. Gallienus favours them. They are in favour for 40 years. Persecution in 303 under Diocletian. He abdicates in 306. Constantine declares himself a Christian in 312. Edict of Milan recognizing the Church, 312. Constantine sole emperor in 324. He dies in 337. Constantius (Arian) sole emperor in 350. Arian Council in 360. Julian. Valentinian (Catholic), in West, 364–375. Gratian (Cath.) 375–382. In 392, Theodosius (Cath.) sole emperor. (Humiliated by St. Ambrose.) He makes Catholicism the official religion of the Empire. Forbids both public and private pagan rites. (Gratian had already suppressed the privileges and confiscated the property of the pagan temples and clergy). Heretics, both

Arian and others, have neither bishoprics nor churches, and may not bequeath or inherit.

Cause of the conflict with St. Ambrose (according to St. Augustine). He had promised their bishops that he would pardon the Thessalonians, and had brutally punished them nevertheless. In penance for this, he prostrated himself in public.

[Saint Augustine; story of the Apollo of Cumae which wept before every victory of the Romans over the Greeks.]

[Laomedon making Apollo and Neptune work for him and not paying their wages.]

Sack of Rome, 410 (by Alaric).

The Apocalypse speaks of $3\frac{1}{2}$ years. 1260 days. $360 \times 3 = 1080$. $1080 + 180 = 1260$. [42 months are also $3\frac{1}{2}$ years: 36 months + 6 months.]

The woman, mother of the divine Child, has a place prepared in the wilderness for 1260 days.

Further on: καιρὸν καὶ καιροὺς καὶ ἥμισυ καιροῦ.

A time, times, and half a time.

Power is given to the beast after $3\frac{1}{2}$ years.

350 years.

$350 + 30 = 380$. This is practically the moment when the Catholic religion became the State religion. The Church was in fact nourished for $3\frac{1}{2}$ centuries in the desert, far from the serpent.

They shall tread my city under foot 42 months, and my two witnesses shall prophesy 1260 days. When their testimony ends, the Beast shall conquer them (but that is before Christ? ? ?)

A Greek oracle had foretold that the name of Christ would be adored for 365 years. Approximately the same period of time.

Anyone who, at the moment when he is thinking of God, has not renounced everything, without any exception, is giving the name of God to one of his idols.

Really to die, in the moral sense, means consenting to submit to everything whatsoever that chance may bring. Because chance can deprive me of everything that I call "I".

To consent to being a creature and nothing else. It is like consenting to lose one's whole existence.

We are nothing but creatures. But to consent to be nothing

but that is like consenting to be nothing. Without our knowing it, this being which God has given us is non-being. If we desire non-being, we have it, and all we have to do is to be aware of the fact.

Our sin consists in wanting to be, and our punishment is that we believe we possess being. Expiation consists in desiring to cease to be; and salvation consists for us in perceiving that we are not.

Adam made us believe that we had being; Christ showed us that we are non-beings.

To teach us that we are non-beings, God made himself non-being.

For God, sacrifice consists in letting a man believe that he has being. For a man, sacrifice consists in recognizing that he is non-being.

God entrusts to evil the work of teaching us that we are not.

The desire of creatures to be, and their illusion that they are, stirs up evil; and evil teaches them that they are not. God takes no part in this elementary stage of teaching.

Those who have fully recognized their own non-being have passed over to God's side. So far from teaching other creatures that they are non-being, they treat them on the fictitious assumption that they possess being.

Creation is a fiction of God's.

The quantity of evil in the world is precisely equal to the necessary amount of punishment. But it strikes haphazardly.

To suffer evil is the only way of destroying it.

No action destroys evil, but only the apparently useless and perfectly patient suffering of it.

The imaginary existence of thinking creatures who believe they exist is what rebounds in the form of evil. Evil is illusory, and whoever has escaped from the illusion is released from all evil. Moreover, evil is an illusion which can itself in certain conditions stimulate a man to escape from illusion.

Hell consists in perceiving that one does not exist and refusing to consent to this fact.

Purity attracts evil, which rushes to it like moths to a flame, to be destroyed.

Everything has to pass through the fire. But those who have become flame are at home in the fire. But in order to become fire it is necessary to have passed through hell.

The way to make use of physical pain. When suffering no matter what degree of pain, when almost the entire soul is inwardly crying "Make it stop, I can bear no more", a part of the soul, even though it be an infinitesimally small part, should say: "I consent that this should continue throughout the whole of time, if the divine wisdom so ordains." The soul is then split in two. For the physically sentient part of the soul is—at least sometimes—unable to consent to pain. This splitting in two of the soul is a second pain, a spiritual one, and even sharper than the physical pain that causes it. A similar use can be made of hunger, fatigue, fear, and of everything that imperatively constrains the sentient part of the soul to cry: I can bear no more! Make it stop! There should be something in us that answers: I consent that it should continue up to the moment of death, or that it should not even finish then, but continue for ever. Then it is that the soul is as if divided by a two-edged sword.

To make use in this way of the sufferings that chance inflicts upon us is better than inflicting discipline upon oneself.

Sufferings which it would be possible to avoid are in the same category, if there is a very clear obligation [not][1] to avoid them. Such as an obligation of behaving justly towards others. For example, a man obliged by lack of money to go without food all day is still under the obligation even if there is a chance of getting some by theft. Because theft is never possible for an honest man.

But, in view of the general and permanent condition of humanity it may well be that to eat one's fill is always a kind of theft.

(I have been guilty of many kinds.)

We should not regard privation as a spiritual exercise, or an offering to God, or the condition for acts of voluntary charity, but as a strict social obligation, that is to say, the equivalent of a necessity. And the higher part of the soul is in no way involved, except that, when the sensibility cries out that it can endure no more, it replies: "I consent that this should go on for ever."

The point which is the higher part of the soul has no function as regards life in the world except to contemplate each flying moment and, whatever its content may be, to say: "I consent

[1] The meaning of the passage appears to demand the addition of this word.

that this should stop immediately, and I consent that it should go on for ever."

When all its reserves of supplementary energy are exhausted and the vegetative energy which maintains life itself is engaged and begins to be used up, then the whole earthly soul cries out "Enough!" Because this is unbearable. The will that makes endurance possible has now vanished. The living flesh is attacked and is being devoured. (Prometheus, like Christ, is eaten.) It is then impossible for the entire earthly soul not to cry "Enough!" To whom does it address this command or supplication? It does not know, but it cannot help crying out. But if the eternal part of the soul replies, speaking to the true God: "For ever, if it is thy will", then the soul is cut in two pieces. The thing that one feels to be oneself is in the part that cries: "Enough!", and yet one supports the other voice. This is really to relinquish oneself.

One part of our energy is on the level of time. This is animal energy. It allows us to say: "This will not last more than an hour." It allows thought to travel through stretches of time. It is our supplementary energy, and it sustains desire and the will.

The vegetative energy, by which the chemico-biological mechanisms necessary for life are maintained, is below the level of time. When the former energy is exhausted and the vegetative energy has to be expended for something other than the biological functions for which it is destined, then a quarter of an hour seems like endless duration. Then it is that the cry: Enough! invades the soul, and the soul is split in two if it does not endorse that cry. It is then that the very sap of life flows away and the man becomes dead wood while still alive.

A quarter of an hour of this really is equivalent to an endless duration of voluntary efforts, so that after this quarter of an hour the part of the soul that has refused to cry "enough!" has travelled through the indefinite length of time and passed beyond time, into eternity.

This only happens to the man who has become rooted in love.

Mythology of women transformed into trees.

A tree's only movement is upward. Symbol of the state of pure contemplation.

The essential condition is that the supplementary energy shall have been exhausted. There are certain states of soul in which this energy supplies a man with the will-power to endure the most frightful tortures. Criminals in the middle ages who were tortured without confessing. But in such cases no amount of suffering or resistance to suffering is of the slightest avail for salvation.

The competitive sporting spirit enables a man to endure everything, without any real virtue. Among the Romans, Stoicism degenerated into being nothing more than this.

The supplementary energy which a man directs as he pleases towards what he thinks good for himself is the prodigal son's portion. It needs to have been totally expended before the soul can take a single step in the direction of eternity. If the energy then revives again, as often happens, it has to be expended once more. When the prodigal son was reconciled with his father, he was given more money and went off again; and returned again, and then again and again, and his father killed the fatted calf each time. But his absences grew shorter and shorter.—Is that perhaps the true account?

It makes little difference whether this energy is expended in seeking for worldly goods or for God; because, if we seek God before this energy has been completely exhausted, it will be a false God, even though he resembles the true one in every way. The son on the loose must inevitably waste his portion with prostitutes. It makes no difference whether or not one of them claims to come from his father. He will not take one step towards his father so long as he has a penny left.

What is essential is that he should spend and not make money. If instead of wasting his money with prostitutes he puts it out at interest, he will never return to his father's house.

The voluntary energy must be expended in such a way that it cannot be recouped, in such a way that it is exhausted. This means that the will must be directed towards things beyond its reach. It matters little what they are, so long as the will is stretched and strained without ever reaching them. It must be made to feel its limits and to keep on and on straining against them. Everything that it obtains must be felt to be valueless; it must seem that in exchange for an expense of energy one never receives anything good. There must either be failure or else success which is found to be valueless as soon as it is achieved.

If we value the goods of this world, we draw from them something which renews the energy expended in pursuing them.

But if one desires worldly things (for as yet one has no

conception at all of heaven) which are nevertheless impossible, then one's energy is expended without renewing itself.

A man who is capable of being satisfied by something possible, even if it be no less than to be emperor of the world, will not expend the portion given him when he left his father's house.

Once the voluntary energy is exhausted, desire—which has become impotent—is still directed towards the same earthly objects (it makes no difference that they sometimes bear heavenly labels) which were formerly aimed at by the will. The soul cries for the things it wants like an infant which has not yet learnt to walk. This is the first stage of becoming like a child again. But nobody attends. It cries and cries in an unheeding world. When it is too tired even to cry, it looks.

And then perhaps it remembers that there is another kind of good, in which even inanimate things have an abundant part.

How does this memory find entry into an earthly soul?

At this moment, when the voluntary energy is exhausted and the vegetative energy is exposed, the soul chooses between hell and heaven. And it does not know it is choosing.

Perhaps it is only re-making a choice decided since the foundation of the world.

Those who die without ever having exhausted their voluntary energy die without having made this choice—no matter whether they have lived a virtuous life or a criminal one. What happens to them once they are dead is a mystery.

Is this really how it is?

If at the moment when they are in imminent danger of finally exhausting their voluntary energy, they decide to invest it profitably instead of continuing to expend it—one may also say that they have chosen badly.

Impotent desire detaches itself from its objectives and turns back on itself. Then the idea of pure, unconditioned good, an inexpressible idea, enters the soul. And then the soul either cleaves to it or not.

This choice is a mystery.

If the soul cleaves to the idea of pure good, it begs never again to have to choose.

From then on its problem is to devote the whole of its energy to this good, of which it knows nothing except the name.

If circumstances happen to restore to the organism some of the energy which feeds the will, that energy must be expended without using the will. It must be expended in the way we spend a sum entrusted to us by someone else for a specific purpose; the obligation thus established being made use of to supplement necessity wherever the latter is not sufficiently compelling.

After the prodigal's reconciliation with his father, if he goes back to the town with money it is not as a son with his portion to spend, but as a slave who is charged by his master to make purchases from which he will get nothing and for which no one will thank him. To walk as far as the town and go from shop to shop making the prescribed purchases until the money is used up, to come back carrying parcels, or to go into the fields without money and spend the day labouring—it is all one for a slave. If he has spent the money honestly, for the prescribed purchases, he gets no thanks or reward. Perhaps he is blamed for not having gone to cheaper shops. If he has kept back a penny or spent it on himself, he is beaten.

That is how the supplementary, voluntary energy should be used up to the point of exhaustion in performing obligatory tasks.

Or else it should be burnt up in contemplation.

The important thing is that not one fraction of it should be left over, either for gratifying a whim or for the exercise of will. If a fraction of it remains, it is theft.

(I have never ceased to steal.)

When the vegetative energy is exposed to the attacks of circumstance and begins to be consumed, this energy itself must tear itself away from the biological functions which it sustains and must devote itself to God. This is spiritual death, which is also a physical operation. Man offers himself as food for God's creatures.

But this energy is not mobile; it is vegetative. It cannot give itself a direction. It is only a point of the soul at the opposite pole to it that can say: I consent that my flesh should be devoured until my death—or beyond that: throughout the whole duration of time.

Then there is as it were a transference of the pain from the earthly part of the soul, which has sinned, to the eternal part, which is innocent.

The soul divides in two, one part innocent and the other guilty, and the innocent part suffers for the guilty and justifies it.

The soul divides into an unlimited part and a part which limits. The compound which it was on the plane of the finite has ceased to exist. There is now a microcosm in which the original chaos, the original waters over which the Spirit moves, is reproduced. One part of the soul suffers on a level below the temporal, and every fraction of time seems to it to continue in perpetuity. The other part suffers on a level above the temporal, and it sees perpetuity as something finite. The soul is divided in two, and between the two parts is the whole of time. It is time that is the sword that cuts the soul in two. (In another sense, the sword is Love.) The sentient part of the soul is in hell, the part that is in heaven feels nothing, unless by contagion from the other part.

After that, there is a new creation, which the soul accepts—not for the sake of existing, since its desire is not to exist, but solely for the love of creatures, in the same way that God consents to create.

Consent to be created, as God consents to create—for the love of other creatures.

This new creation is like an incarnation. The second creation is not creation but generation. Christ comes into the soul and substitutes himself for it.

Those who have been born from on high are not the adopted but the true sons of God. But the Son is unique. So it is He who enters into souls.

But in that case the greatest of saints will not see the kingdom of heaven. For almost all of them have done or said things which, so it seems, Christ would not have said or done.

After all, there is perhaps only one man saved in a generation. For the others, those of them who are not definitely lost, one must imagine something equivalent to the ideas of purgatory, reincarnation, etc.

To be born from on high, of water and the spirit, of water and breath.

To be born from on high, to be born from water and breath —that is to say, after the dissolution of the soul—a microcosm within the primeval chaos—that is to be perfect.

Baptism is only the desire for new birth. When an infant is baptized, those who love it express their desire that one day it shall be born from on high. When an adult is baptized, himself expresses this desire. There is always an efficacious virtue in the desire for good. And all the more in the expression of such a desire, whatever form it may take. A ritual form is perhaps eminently efficacious. But in that case it needs to be unconditional, and not to imply submission to a social organization.

Ram	*Nemaean lion* ‖ Boar of Erymanthus (?) ‖ *Cretan Bull* ‖
Bull	*Hydra* ‖ *Three-headed Geryon* ‖ *Horses of Diomedes* ‖
Gemini	*Belt of Hippolytus* ‖ Birds of lake Stymphalus =
Cancer	Apples of the Hesperides ‖ Cerberus ‖ Arcadian
Leo	stag ‖ *Augean Stables* ‖
Virgo	All these stories must have a symbolic meaning.
Scorpio	In the case of the Stables it is only too clear. No
Sagittarius	effort of will can cleanse the soul of sin; it must be
Capricorn	opened to the waters of grace.
Aquarius	
Pisces	

Does this story correspond to the sign of Aquarius? [And the Nemaean Lion to Leo? The Hydra to Cancer? Hippolytus to Virgo?—The horses to Sagittarius, through Chiron ? ? ?—The Boar to Capricorn? (difficult to see how!)—Cerberus to Scorpio (difficult again!)—The Stag to Aries (!!!)? Taking the apples, he kills a dragon, which becomes a constellation.]

Aries and Libra. The slaughtered Lamb in one pan of the scales, the universe in the other. The pan with the Lamb at an infinite distance from the fulcrum, the other pan close to it. The vertical support as mean proportional between the two. The Cross is the balance.

Bull and Scorpio. The Bull is Osiris. The black Bull of Norway. Etc. The Minotaur. Europa's Bull. Why? Because of virile force and power of generation. Symbol of generation. The cow which gives milk is the symbol of Nature. India: "The cow of all desires". The water scorpion, when taken out of the water, pretends to be dead; but if a burning light is placed anywhere near it goes towards the flame, until it gets so near that the heat kills it.

Twins and Sagittarius. The Twins are Castor and Pollux. They are under Orion, who is Orus,[1] or Apollo. What can be said about these Twins?—The archer, Sagittarius, is said to be Chiron. A Centaur. So the horse is represented. It is said that

[1] The Egyptian Horus.

he took the place of Prometheus in Tartarus. He is a teacher and healer. Perhaps Sagittarius is also Apollo?

Cancer. Capricorn, goat's horn. What is to be said about Cancer? It is perhaps the same as the Hydra. It is Typhon, murderer of Osiris. The Sun at the summer solstice is harmful. It scorches. The horn is the cornucopia of the goat-nymph Amalthaea who fed Zeus with milk. Pan is assimilated to a young goat, as Zeus Ammon is to a ram.

Thor has some goats which he kills for food, taking care to leave intact the skin and the bones, from which he resuscitates them. One day one of them becomes lame, because a youth has pierced one of its bones to suck the marrow. Original sin.

1	2	3	4	5
Priam	Troan	Loridi	Einridi	Vingethor
6	7	8	9	10	11
Vingener	Mode	Magi	Seskef	Bedvig	Athra
12	13	14	15	16
Iterman	Heremed	Skjaldum	Bjaf	Jat
17	18	19	20	21
Gudolfr	Finn	Friallaf	Voden (Odin)	Sigi
22	23	24	25
Rerir	Volsung	Sigmund	Sigurd

— 25 generations in 1700 years? 5 in 340? 1 in 68? 20 in 1260?

Another genealogy. First there was the Father and Ymir with the other Rime-giants. [The drizzling rain that rose from the venom congealed to rime (?) and the rime increased, frost over frost, into the Yawning Void.] A cow emerges from the rime. It feeds Ymir. To nourish itself it licks a salty block of ice, which becomes a man, Buri. He has a son, Borr, who marries a giant's daughter. They have three children, Odin, Vili, and Vé, who rule heaven and earth. They kill Ymir and all the giants except two. They place Ymir in the middle of the Yawning Void, and make the world out of his body; his blood makes the sea and the rivers, his flesh makes the earth, his bones make the rocks, his skull makes the sky. They put lights in it. They give the circular confines of earth and sea for the giants to dwell in, and they give protection to men by a citadel called Midgard, which is Ymir's forehead. They make two trees into a man and a woman (Askr and Embla) and settle them near Midgard. Then they make for themselves a city, Asgard, which is Troy. The Father has a High Place there, from which he sees all things. He marries Frigg and begets the Aesir, who populate Elder Asgard. He is father of gods and men. The Earth is his daughter and his wife. She bears him Thor.

One of the roots of Yggdrasil[1] is among the Aesir; another is among the Rime Giants, where the Yawning Void used to be. There too is the Well in which wisdom lies. The Father had to give one of his eyes as the price for drinking at it. A third root is at Niflheim, the source of cold. The sky is the Aesirs' dwelling, and it is reached by climbing the rainbow.

There is the primal God. There are the three who fashioned the earth out of the giant's corpse. And there is a man, a descendant of Priam, whose date is close to the Christian era. For between Priam and Attila there are 25 generations, or 1700 years, counting 68 years for a generation ($68 \times 5 = 340$, $340 \times 5 = 1700$), and Voden is the 20th generation. Now, $68 \times 20 = 1260$, and if Priam is a little earlier than 1300 B.C. that brings us near the beginning of the Christian era.

The prose *Edda* (Skáldskaparmál) has a different reckoning, which makes Frodi, the grandson of Odin, reign in Denmark in the time of Augustus, when Christ was born. Men spoke of Frodi's Peace. There was a magic mill from which peace and prosperity flowed for him, until the slave girls who did the grinding became tired and began to grind his destruction.

The chronological difference is not very great.

Odin, descendant of Priam, has Frigg for wife and his second son, Baldr, is king of heaven and earth, like Odin. The other names do not coincide.

Is Odin the descendant of Priam an incarnation of Odin the God who made heaven and earth?

If so, it would be remarkable that the date should be so close to the date of Christ.

Odin came to the North from the Orient. Descended through twenty generations from Priam, and of a line which had reigned in Thrace until his day.

What does Herodotus say about it?

Leo and Aquarius. Lion of Nemea. Lion in the Apocalypse. What else? Water pot, water pourer. Water of grace.

[1] Mystical ash tree of Scandinavian mythology.

Virgo and Pisces. The Virgin is Justice, the virgin Astraea. She holds an ear of corn: she is Demeter and Proserpine. And Mary also? The Fish is the one which swims in the baptismal water. It is Christ. (Why two fish?)—Aquarius, Fish, Ram: natural sequence. Lion, Virgin, Scales?

The water of regeneration, the fish swimming in it—like Noah—the lamb sacrificed from the beginning, the bull who engenders everything and whose seed, becoming cow's milk, feeds us, the inseparable twins who are a single immortal (Trinity?)—the Crab, it seems, represents evil. The strength of the lion. Virginal justice. The scales by means of which the lamb's body raises creation as high as heaven. The scorpion which goes towards the light until the light kills it. The Archer who heals, teaches, and suffers for men (in the role of Prometheus). The cornucopia, the Grail, where there is always living bread and living water. The pourer of water who drowns the sinful soul in grace. The fish. The lamb. Etc.

The Virgin corresponds perfectly to the fish, the newly-born who grows up in the baptismal water. When grown up he is the Lamb, and when resurrected he is identical with the bull.

The Crab (the Hydra?), the Lion, and the Virgin are the three parts of the soul in Plato. The pair of scales is their harmony. The Scorpion is he who dies in order to approach the light. He is resurrected as the Archer (the Archer is the light itself) and the plenitude he receives is the Cornucopia.[1]

Crab. Lion. Virgin. Scales. Scorpion. Archer. Capricorn. || Water bearer. Fish. Ram. Bull. Twins. || From earth to heaven, then from heaven to earth and back.

June: Crab. July: Lion. August: Virgin. September: Scales. October: Scorpion. November: Archer. December: Capricorn. January: Water bearer. February: Fish. March: Ram. April: Bull. May: Twins.

The starting point is the inordinate; the Crab, the Hydra; the moment when it almost seems that the sun is going to break away from its course; the unlimited.

The lion is force; it is necessity.
The Virgin is justice and wisdom.
The scales. This is the Cross.

[1] Capricorn.

The scorpion which dies from love of the light.
The Archer who is the light.
The cornucopia which is the plenitude of God.
The water-pourer which lavishes torrents of water, torrents of grace.
The fish which swims in the water of grace.
The lamb sacrificed from the beginning.
The bull whose seed is our milk.
The two twin beings who are a single divinity.
The sacrificed lamb facing the cross.
lamb, scales—bull, scorpion—Twins, archer—crab, cornucopia—lion, water-pourer—virgin, fish—scales, lamb.
The sacrificed lamb is opposite the cross, the Fish is opposite the Virgin.

Pastoral peoples, milk drinkers, thought they were nourished by the seed of the bull. Is not "The living water" the seed? Orestes: ὦ γόναι, O most dear seed ... Had they imagined a pact by virtue of which the animals gave their seed, in the form of milk from their females, in place of their flesh? That would explain why any contact between meat and milk was forbidden.
A kid drowned in milk, that is a death which is like a return to the pre-natal state, to the state of seed. Baptism.
Similarly, bread—seed of the sun.

It is the world's beauty that compels the man who is worn out, the man who has used up all his inheritance and all his strength, to recollect that his father's slaves have a larger share of good than himself, who is the son. Beauty is the share of the good which is possessed by things in the world, it is the wages of the Father's slaves. When a man no longer desires to be himself, but simply a part of the world, like a stone, then it is that the Father kills the fatted calf.
At the decisive moment, it is by inert objects, by things, that man is saved.
In the same way, the body is a powerful instrument of salvation.
Place of the beauty of the world in the Old Testament.
The beauty of the world has almost disappeared from

Christianity, because the Roman Empire turned it into a political religion.

Matter, which was man's undoing, also procures salvation. It is the lance whose contact begins to heal the very wound which it has made. Cf. the story of the Grail.

The body is a lever by which the soul acts upon the soul. Through discipline imposed on the body the wandering energy of the soul automatically exhausts itself. If a goat is tethered, it pulls at the rope, turns round and round, and goes on pulling for hours and hours; but at last, when it is tired, it lies down. It is the same with the wandering part of the soul when the body is kept fixed. It fidgets and agitates, but in spite of itself it is always brought back to the body, and in the end it is exhausted and vanishes.

The soul needs to have been divided in two before one part of it can thus use the body against the other part.

Not only that, but the body must be obedient to the eternal part of the soul.

No violence need be used, because the body consents to this domination.

When the eternal part of the soul conceives an order, the body cannot do other than obey.

If it does not obey, then the order did not come from the eternal part of the soul, or else it was given without sufficient attention.

The body is a prison. The spiritual part of the soul should use it to shut in and imprison the carnal part. The body is a tomb. The spiritual part of the soul should use it to kill the carnal part.

May my body be an instrument of torture and death for all that is mediocre in my soul.

One should sometimes do violence to one's thought, one should sometimes nail the body down and leave thought to exhaust itself. But the body must be trained to listen only to the higher part of the soul. How?

Treat the lower part of the soul like a child which one leaves to cry until it is tired and stops. In the whole universe nothing pays any attention to it. Whereas God is attentive even to the silence which the eternal part of the soul addresses to Him.

"Don't listen to yourself."

Reduce to silence those animals within me whose cries prevent God from hearing or speaking to me. The best way to silence them is to pretend not to hear them. When any of them perceive that they are not being listened to they become tired in the end and stop. These animals within me will be heard by nobody unless I lend my voice. More than that, I must not hear them myself, or at least I must show no sign of hearing them.

They must always know, when they begin their cries, that they will be heard by nothing in the world—neither by things, nor by men, nor by God, nor by me.

These animals are the thing within me which incessantly, in diverse accents of sorrow, exultation, triumph, anxiety, fear, pain, and every other emotional nuance, keeps on crying "me, me, me, me, me".

It is a meaningless cry, and ought not to be listened to by anything or anybody.

These animals habitually keep on crying all day and all night, even during sleep, without a second's pause.

One must not lend them a voice to express themselves.

One must get them to be silent occasionally for a few moments. Then one must train them to be silent more and more often and for longer periods. And then, if possible, get them to be totally silent. If they can die before the body dies, that is the best.

So long as the body obeys them, they believe they are in communication with the universe. Because whenever the body moves ten paces the effect of perspective alters the aspect of the universe. But if the body does not obey them and if they are not translated into speech, they are compelled to recognize that nothing in the world is listening to them. When this has been impressed upon them many times a note of despair comes into their cries; they are weary before they begin their crying.

But as for the eternal part, whose every cry or murmur or silence is listened to, how could it ever become weary?

The animals are very cunning at getting the body's obedience by means of pretexts which do not seem to come from them. To make sure that the body disobeys them, one needs to impose something or other upon it unconditionally, either for a long time or at repeated intervals. Because one can be sure that these animals, being volatile and capricious, will sooner or later want something else. So that if one perseveres long enough one can be sure of thwarting them in the end.

But for this purpose it is essential not to keep records. The animals which say "me" are stimulated by the record-breaking ambition, and as soon as it comes into play no action and no abstention from acting is any longer of any avail. If one says to oneself "I did so-and-so for so long", it would be better not to have done it.

The prohibition of census-taking is perhaps the memory of a wise man's word based upon such an observation? There are some goods which are destroyed by being evaluated.

This really shows that only God can save by his grace.

What makes it perfectly clear that God's mercy is the only salvation is that the most essential rules for the good of the soul are rules which one cannot will to observe, because the very fact of thinking about them is a violation of them. We can only beseech God to remove such thoughts from our heart.

God has fashioned us in such a way that we are obliged to turn to him as suppliants.

And if we don't want to recognize God it is still exactly the same. One says "May I cease to have such thoughts!"; but as soon as one speaks in the optative mood it is a supplication.

To achieve less than others, knowingly, and without desiring to do as much as them, is a way of breaking the ambition to beat records. Or at least it is so if one is proud enough to feel that anything less than what others have is valueless... For there is a way of using pride in the service of humility.

Once the record-breaking ambition has been abolished, then one may adopt some daily practice in a steady way, or one may say "I will do such or such a thing so many times" and stick to it, and one can be sure that the animals in the soul will be irritated and will cry and howl and will realize their impotence to make themselves heard. For the body will not obey them if one's resolve comes from the centre of the soul. This is an effect of God's mercy.

If it is not against a resolution of one's own but against an external compulsion that the animals howl, it is even better. It is only necessary for the eternal part of the soul to consent that the compulsion should last indefinitely and without any reward, even a spiritual one. Because by counting on a spiritual advantage one is only giving that name to something which is food for the animals which shout "me!"

Everything that is conditional belongs to the sphere of these animals. Only the unconditional escapes them.

It is the supplementary energy that places the soul in the sphere of the conditional. One says "I'm prepared to go two kilometres if I can get an egg".[1] So one has the strength for two kilometres in spite of feeling tired. But total exhaustion is the feeling: "I couldn't go ten yards, even to save my life." This corresponds to a state in which the vegetative energy is all that is left, in which walking would use up an energy which is indispensable for the maintenance of the vital functions themselves.

In actual fact, since feeling is an unreliable indicator, the sense of exhaustion may be felt before or after the commencement of the state of exhaustion. But psychologically there is no doubt that it is the feeling that counts.

In the state of exhaustion wishes and intentions that allow of flexibility in their fulfilment are replaced by immediate and unconditional needs. It is then that the soul cries "I must . . . !"

I must see so-and-so! I must rest! I must eat! I must drink! This pain must abate for just a moment!

One should then reply coldly and cynically, like Talleyrand to the beggar: I don't see the necessity.

And add for the sake of love: I consent that this need, in its present or even greater intensity, should remain unsatisfied, uncompensated in any way, either for ever or until the disappearance of my soul and body.

The consent itself is the compensation. But one must not so appraise it, or it loses all its good.

There are some men who can invest an object outside themselves with so much of their supplementary energy that so long as this object exists they are never, even when at death's door, reduced to living upon their vegetative energy. Such are the giants who have hidden their life at the bottom of a lake.

These men cannot take one step towards eternity.

The soldiers of Napoleon were like this.

And perhaps also the martyrs, or those of them whose death was not like Christ's? In any case, the Polyeucte of Corneille was like this.

[1] This book was written in a time of shortages and rationing.

When the vegetative energy is laid bare and has to be drawn upon, then the universe disappears and need becomes the whole universe. The whole universe is concentrated in the soul's cry: "I am hungry!" "I am in pain!" "This must stop!" There is no longer anything good anywhere except in the immediate satisfaction of this need.

At this point, to reply: "I don't see the necessity" is to tear the eternal part of the soul violently away from the self and fix it to the not-self.

Since the need is unconditional, the consent to be deprived of it indefinitely is also unconditional. One's consent involves no concealed compensation, no tacit bargain, because there is nothing good in the whole universe for anybody, apart from the immediate satisfaction of one's own need.

Consent to the total and perpetual absence of all good is the only unconditional movement of the soul.

It is the only good.

It can only come at a moment when the whole soul is filled with such a cry of need that one believes that in the entire universe there is nothing good for anybody apart from the immediate satisfaction of one's own need. Then the consent to remain unsatisfied is unconditional.

At other times, consent to the absence of good is no more than a movement of fatigue; and behind the pretext of renunciation the good that one is really seeking is rest. In this case one's consent is only apparent, and is conditional.

True consent is related to the will in the same way that the contradiction in a mystery is related to the intelligence. It is absurd.

It is consent not to be.

To consent not to be is to consent to be deprived of all good, and this consent is the possession of total good. Only one does not know this. If one knows it, the good vanishes. Orpheus loses Eurydice when he looks at her. When Niobe has boasted of the number of her children, she sees them die.

But when we are reduced to the level of vegetative energy there is no danger of killing the good by being aware of it. The soul is entirely occupied with its cry of privation and pain.

When the whole soul is crying "I must have ... !", except for one point in it which replies "Why?" and "I consent to the contrary ... ", at that moment one is bearing one's cross. But

Christ has said that we must do it every day. How is that possible? Must we put ourselves in a position to suffer to that extent every day?

Perhaps.

When there is intense and pure joy one is equally empty of good, because then all good resides in the object.

There is as much sacrifice and renunication at the bottom of joy as there is at the bottom of pain.

[Seneca: Simul ista mundi conditor posuit deus—odium atque regnum.][1]

The passions—avarice, ambition, devotion to a person or a group, vices—accumulate a man's energy in some external object which acts as a stimulant, so that unless the object is destroyed he is never reduced even by the worst disasters to falling back upon the vegetative energy. That is why the passions are deadly. The man who delivers himself to them is not the son who wastes his inheritance with prostitutes, he is the one who puts it in a bank. He will not go hungry; he will not return to his Father.

The only thing that can save one from this danger is fastidiousness. If I think I see good in Napoleon, how can I not devote some of my energy to him? But if I then come to perceive that he is not good enough for me, the energy I have devoted to him will have been wasted.

At this point I have to make a choice. Either to face the loss; or else to disguise it by lying and persuading myself that he really is good enough for me.

The things of this world can serve as a bank for the portion of our energy at our disposal—it can be stored in them and even greatly increased by lucky speculations—but only at the price of lying to oneself.

When the portion is almost exhausted and one is on the brink of utter destitution the temptation to resort to such a bank, so as to save at least a few shillings, is almost irresistible. That is why a restricted and obscure life often degrades the soul worse than riches and power.

[1] The God who made the world made these two things together: hatred and domination.

The prodigal son spent his last pennies.

To return to the Father, one must have nothing left at all.

If one still has something left when one turns to the Father, then one is looking to someone else under his name.

May I be like one of thy hired labourers. That is to say, may I be entirely subject to thy will, in the way that inert objects are.

"You have never given me anything." "Because everything I have is yours." To be equal to God, one has only to be without free will.

If one is truthful one sees that every expenditure of energy is a loss of energy, so long as the energy is one's own possession. It is only by lying to oneself that one invests it for profit.

But with energy that is a loan from God it is different. That loan must be invested profitably.

"He placed in all things the seed of identity and unity which pervades everything."[1]

Unity, the seed of Zeus.

It is the Logos.

The Trinity is also there.

Zeus changes himself into Love in order to sow Unity. His seed (σπέρμα) is his Son. He becomes Love in order to generate.

Creation is the distance between the Father and the Son.

Isidorus (gnostic) said: Pherecydes composed an allegorical theology based upon the prophecy of Ham, to teach what are the winged oak and the embroidered cloth that hangs on it[2] (Clement of Alexandria vi. 6 (272)).

Fragment of Pherecydes:

Isidorus—so that it might be known what are the winged oak and the embroidered cloth on it, allegories in the theology of Pherecydes, who based them upon the prophecy of Ham.

Fragment of Pherecydes: They make many and great mansions for him. When they have completed everything, with goods and furniture and male and female servants and everything needed and when all is ready, they celebrate the marriage. And on the third nuptial day Zeus makes a large and beautiful

---

[1] H. Diels, *Fragmente der Vorsokratiker*, 5th edn., I, 48, fr. 3.
[2] Diels, op. cit., I, 47, fr. 2.

cloth and embroiders on it the Earth and the Ocean and the dwellings of the Ocean.

There were always Zeus and Kronos (or time?) and Chthonia; who took the name of Earth because Zeus gave her the earth as a present.

ORIGEN, *Contra Celsum*, vi, 42 (ii, 111, 13 k) Pherecydes, who was long before Heraclitus, said that there were two opposing armies, one led by Kronos, the other by Ophion (Ophis, snake). They agreed that those who fell into the ocean should be the losers and that the others should possess heaven. It is the same story as the gods and the titans, of Typhon with Horus and Osiris.

Fragment of Pherecydes: ... marriages to thee. Thus I honour thee. Be joyful and understand. It is said they were the first presents from the lifting of the veil. Thence the custom passed to gods and men. She ... rec ... (the cloth?)

Origen.[1] Celsus, commenting Homer, says that the speeches of Zeus to Hera are the speeches of God to matter, in the form of enigmas (i.e. symbols). At first she was bound by no rule, but God took and bound her and established her order according to certain proportions.[2] Those demons in her train who were insolent he punished by throwing them down towards this world. He says that Pherecydes interpreted Homer's words as follows: "Below this sphere is the sphere of Tartarus; it is guarded by the daughters of Boreas, and the Harpies, and the Tempest ($θύελλα$?). Thither Zeus hurls any god who is guilty of insolence."[3] He says that the peplos of Athena, seen in the Panathenaean procession, was also connected with these ideas. Because what it expresses is that a motherless and immaculate goddess dominates the unruly sons of Earth.

This Ophion who was thrown into the Ocean is the Serpent of Midgard, the son of Loki, which was thrown to the bottom of the Ocean by Odin and which, with its tail in its mouth, rings the world round. It is the Leviathan of the Bible. On the last day, Thor will kill the Serpent of Midgard but at the same time will die of its poisoned bite. It is the Serpent or Dragon of the Apocalypse. Etc.

If the Scandinavian mythology is of Trojan origin, all this is not surprising.

[1] *Ibid.*   [2] *Iliad*, XV, 18–24.
[3] H. Diels: *Fragmente der Vorsokratiker*, 5th edn. Vol. I, p. 49.

In the *Iliad* the Trojans bring a peplum to Athena.

The winged Oak is Yggdrasil.

According to Probus and Hermias—Zeus or the ether is what acts, the earth or Chthonia is what is acted upon, Kronos or time is the medium within which the things that happen happen.—The earth is the first principle of everything (?). Max. Tyr.: ... he examines the poetry of the Syrian—Zeus and Chthonia, and Love between them, and the birth of Ophion and the oak and the peplum.

Pherecydes died around 600 B.C. He is said to have had no master but to have educated himself, after acquiring the secret books of the Phoenicians (Suidas).

Therefore the "prophecies of Ham" would be one of those secret books of the Phoenicians, who are descended from Ham.

The river that Plato calls Oblivion and the Phoenicians the Styx is, in Pherecydes, the flow of the seed ($\sigma\pi\acute{\epsilon}\rho\mu\alpha$).

This river is the baptismal water.

The river in the Negro spirituals must come from an African tradition, because no river holds such a place in the Christian tradition.

The earth is an embroidered cloth on the axis of the world which joins the two poles.

The cloth is blown haphazard in all directions, but is held by the fixity of the tree.[1]

(Among the American Indians is it a religious or magical act to hang cloths on trees?)

Ham begat: 1st, Canaan who begat Sidon. 2nd, Cush, who begat Raamah and Nimrod, the founder of Babel and Nineveh. 3rd, Mizrain, from whom the Egyptians and Philistines are descended. So Cush must be the ancestor of the Ethiopians.

The Hebrews must have amalgamated, 1st, the story of the drunkenness and nakedness of Noah and of his sons' behaviour, and 2nd, a prophecy (after the event?) of the misfortunes of the sons of Canaan. If the conquest of Palestine took place at the same time as the Trojan war this double calamity must have impressed people's imagination.

The winged oak. Compare Yggdrasil, the wind-beaten tree.

[In the *Edda*, Sun and Moon are sister and brother.]

Read Diodorus Siculus, II, ch iii, on Druidism.

See Stonehenge, ruins of a celtic temple of the solar Deity.

[1] See pp. 276 ff.

Lucifer wanted to be God. What could be more natural? Love alone can make us consent not to be God. Love makes us consent to be no matter what, or nothing. Love is satisfied perfectly by the thought that God exists. One must love like this, or else be like Lucifer; anything else is servility.

If heaven were as it is pictured, one would be more unhappy there than on earth; because on earth one can hope to arrive sooner or later at any degree of perfection, whereas in heaven, as they describe it, some are worth less than others and consequently all are worth less than they might possibly have been, and yet one knows that there will be no progress any more.

How Christianity must have been poisoned by the Roman Empire for it to be possible for them to describe paradise like the court of a sovereign!

In a country village, there could be a theme for the Sunday sermon every week from seed-time to harvest in the parable of the Sower who scatters the seed and then leaves it, because it grows by itself and without anybody's working for it. This single thought is enough, if it is present every time one looks at the growing wheat.

St. Paul on Christ: "Who is the image of the invisible God, the first-born of all creation, for in him were all things created that are in heaven and earth, visible and invisible, whether thrones or dominions or principles or powers; all things were created through him and for him; and he was established before all things and all things in him, and he is the head of the body, the church. He who is the beginning, the first-born from the dead, that he might be pre-eminent in all things, for he chose that in him should all fullness dwell, and through himself to reconcile (also means exchange) all things unto himself, making peace through the blood of the cross, by himself, whether they be things in earth or things in heaven."[1]

Those last words are inexplicable within present-day Christianity.

[1] I Colossians 1: 15–20.

The thought here expressed is exactly the thought of Pherecydes: "sowing in all things the identity and unity which pervades everything".

This identity and this unity is Christ.

Christ is three-fold: 1st, The Son of God equal to the Father, being one God with him, begotten and not made. 2nd, The first-born of Creation, the Soul of the World, the unity spread abroad through everything, the harmony. 3rd, A human being (or several?).

The first-born of the dead; was it Abel?

God's first action towards exiled humanity was to allow an innocent man to be killed and to protect the guilty man from death.

If Christ has reconciled all things and established peace, it must be because all things are composed of contraries. It is a Pythagorean doctrine.

The harmony, the unity spread throughout all things is the seed of the Father. The seed of the Father is the children's milk. We live by drinking this unity from the things that are visible. The Father has a wife who transforms his seed into milk to feed us; she is nature. Shakti. The Virgin-Mother. It is only through her that we receive and drink this seed of the Father, which is the Son. χαῖρε κεχαριτωμένη.[1]

Christ has also a fourth being. He is a relation of God to himself; the Soul of the World, first-born of creatures; the man Jesus (and other men? and non-human creatures? angel, animal, tree, inanimate matter? cf. Origen). He is also the collective soul of the society composed of those who love him.

But this society is not really a society. It is a friendship. A collective soul can only be a false god.

For this I was born, for this I have come into the world, to witness to the truth. Whoever is of the truth hears my voice.

The supreme reason for which the Son of God was made man was not to save men, it was to bear witness for the truth.

To bear witness that the love between the Father and the Son is stronger than the distance between the Creator and the creature. That the thought of separated thinkers is one.

To bear witness for the truth. What truth? There is only one truth that is worth the trouble of witnessing to. It is that God is Love. The Son was separated from the Father in order to

[1] Hail, full of grace.

bear witness that they love one another. Bear witness to whom? To one another. God testifies before God that he loves God.

Trojan genealogy in the *Iliad* (xx, 215 ff.) Zeus begets Dardanus, who founds Dardania. Ilion does not yet exist on the plain; they live on Mount Ida. Dardanus begets Erichthonius, the richest man on earth. He has 3000 mares, beloved of Boreas. Erichthonius begets Tros, who has three sons: Ilus, Assaracus, and Ganymede, the most beautiful of boys, whom the gods kidnap. Ilus begets Laomedon, and he begets Tithonus, Priam, Lampus, Clytion, and Hicetaon. Assaracus begets Capys, who begets Anchises.

Dardanus. Erichthonius. Tros. Ilus, Assaracus, Ganymede. Laomedon. Priam.

Ammianus Marcellinus. Julian established freedom for the Christian sects "in order that licence should increase their dissensions, thus ensuring himself against the future danger of a unanimous people; for he had observed that the hostility of a wild beast towards man is less than the hostility of the greater part of the Christians against one another."

That is how the commandment "Love one another" was obeyed.

Ammianus [Pyramid, from πῦρ; shaped like a flame].

[At Syene (Aswan) when the sun is at a certain station in Cancer vertical objects cast no shadow at midday. And at Meroë, in Ethiopia, for more than 90 days the shadows fall on the opposite side to that in the northern hemisphere.]

Ammianus Marcellinus: "If anyone seeks attentively to unravel the numerous reproductions of knowledge of the divine and the origin of knowledge about the future, he will find that it was from Egypt that the knowledge of these things spread over the whole world. It was there first of all that men arrived, long before others, at the various origins of the religions, and the first beginnings of sacred things are carefully preserved there, enclosed in secret writings."

The wisdom of the Persian Magi (Zoroaster) would be of Indian origin. But the first origin would be Chaldaean. (?)

Apis is sacred to the Moon.

The festival of Adonis, according to the mystical cults it is an image of the ripe harvest.

Origin of the Gauls. Some say from the Dorians. The Druids say that some were indigenous and others came from distant lands and from beyond the Rhine. There is also a theory that these regions, which were then unpopulated, were occupied by fugitives from Troy. Geryon and Tauriseus, who were slain by Hercules, were tyrants of Spain and Gaul respectively. Marseilles was founded by an Asiatic people from Phocaea, refugees from the aggression of Cyrus.

"The Druids, of more elevated mind and, as the authority of Pythagoras decreed, united in fraternities (sodaliciis consortiis), raised themselves by the study of hidden and profound matters and, in contempt of the human, declared that souls are immortal." (The Euhages tried to unveil the secrets of nature, the Bards celebrated warlike exploits.)

[When Julian took over the administration of Gaul there was a personal tax of 25 gold pieces a head.]

"Ut auctoritas Pythagorae decrevit" may mean (in the bizarre language of this writer) not under the influence of Pythagoras, but in conformity with his doctrine.

Invocation to Bacchus in Seneca (Oedipus). Lucidum caeli decus—adverte virgineum caput[1] . . . [to hide himself from Hera, simulata virgo] Ganges—Araxes—Cithaeron was polluted "Ophonia caede".

Dionysus has a special connection with the story of Oedipus. The Sphinx is an indication that this story came from Egypt.

Cadmus, "Sidonio hospiti".

The absence of good, or rather the feeling of its absence, is affliction. The sun in Plato being the good, darkness represents affliction in the myth of the cave. The first darkness, when the captive freed from his chains is still within the cave, is the frightful sense of its own wretchedness that the soul has when it begins to withdraw into itself and to recognize the falsity of the things it formerly thought good. The second darkness, result of

---

[1] Bright ornament of the sky, turn your virginal head. (Seneca: *Oedipus*, 403, 408).

the dizziness on emerging from the cave, is the sense of affliction in the soul of the man who possesses the good without knowing that he possesses it. It is the dark night of the spirit of St. John of the Cross. In time the eyes grow accustomed and the sensation of light appears; but then the eyes are raised towards a new and more luminous object and once again are dazzled. This is the alternation which St. John of the Cross notes between the sense of damnation and the sense of salvation. The alternation recurs at each upward step, and therefore lasts longer the higher a man raises himself in the scale of increasingly luminous objects; and longest for him who ends by looking at the sun itself, as it is in itself. Similarly St. John of the Cross says that the state of the dark night of the spirit, with its alternations, lasts longer the further the soul is destined to progress on the way to perfection.

When the captive is in darkness, he has the feeling that he possesses sight but is surrounded by darkness; which is true. But when he emerges into the light, he has the impression of being blind. This is what St. John of the Cross calls the feeling of damnation.

The Sun being the Good, sight is the faculty of loving in the soul, and the light can be nothing except Love. If Plato calls it truth, it is in the same way that the Holy Spirit, which is Love, was called by Christ the Spirit of truth. Lighted objects are beauty. The last of them is the moon, which is pure beauty in God, the Word.

This close analogy between Plato and St. John of the Cross, which is certainly not due to immediate derivation and probably not to indirect derivation either, shows that mystical truth is one, like arithmetical or geometrical truth.

Example of prayer.
Say to God:
Father, in the name of Christ grant me this.
That I may be unable to will any bodily movement, or even any attempt at movement, like a total paralytic. That I may be incapable of receiving any sensation, like someone who is completely blind, deaf and deprived of all the senses. That I may be unable to make the slightest connection between two thoughts, even the simplest, like one of those total idiots who not only

cannot count or read but have never even learnt to speak. That I may be insensible to every kind of grief and joy, and incapable of any love for any being or thing, and not even for myself, like old people in the last stage of decrepitude.

Father, in the name of Christ grant me all this in reality.

May this body move or be still, with perfect suppleness or rigidity, in continuous conformity to thy will. May my faculties of hearing, sight, taste, smell and touch register the perfectly accurate impress of thy creation. May this mind, in fullest lucidity, connect all ideas in perfect conformity with thy truth. May this sensibility experience, in their greatest possible intensity and in all their purity, all the nuances of grief and joy. May this love be an absolutely devouring flame of love of God for God. May all this be stripped away from me, devoured by God, transformed into Christ's substance, and given for food to afflicted men whose body and soul lack every kind of nourishment. And let me be a paralytic—blind, deaf, witless and utterly decrepit.

Father, effect this transformation now, in the name of Christ; and although I ask it with imperfect faith, grant this request as if it were made with perfect faith.

Father, since thou art the Good and I am mediocrity, rend this body and soul away from me to make them into things for your use, and let nothing remain of me, for ever, except this rending itself, or else nothingness.

Words like this are not efficacious unless they are dictated by the Spirit. One does not voluntarily ask for such things. One comes to it in spite of oneself. In spite of oneself, yet one comes to it. One does not consent to it with abandon, but with a violence exerted upon the entire soul by the entire soul. But the consent is total and unreserved, and given by a single movement of the whole being.

Is it from this that the metaphor of marriage is taken? This relation between God and the soul resembles the relation between a bridegroom and a still virgin bride on their wedding night. Marriage is a consented rape. And so is the soul's union with God. The soul feels cold and is not aware of loving God. It does not know, of itself, that unless it loved it would not consent. But the conjugal union is being prepared, and by means of it a man's person will become simply an intermediary between his flesh and God.

Some souls love God as a woman loves her lover. But loves of this kind are not lasting. It is only married couples who are one flesh for ever.

(But all these spiritual phenomena are absolutely beyond my competence. I know nothing about it. They are reserved for those who possess, to begin with, the elementary moral virtues. I can only speak of them haphazard. And I cannot even sincerely tell myself that I am speaking haphazard.)

Beginning of an Italian story: A young man helps an old woman in distress. She thanks him. "May you marry the princess Belle of the World!" He goes home and says to his father: "I am off to find the princess Belle of the World. She alone shall be my wife, and none other." He inquires of the Great Wind, which says: "I have never heard tell of her, but I will send my breezes to search."

One is sure that he will find her, and that she will be much more beautiful even than he hoped.

This is an image of the Good.

A cobbler is to marry a princess—who promised him her hand because he had saved her—. She has fixed a meeting-place and the date, which covers three days. He goes there, but he has spoken of the affair at his lodgings and they have given him a sleeping draught. So when he reaches the place he falls asleep. The princess, who has arrived in a magic coach, weeps and calls to him but cannot wake him. She goes away, leaving an embroidered handkerchief, but a little shepherd steals it. The same thing happens on the two following days. She gives the little shepherd a message for him, that she will await him at her father's castle for seven years. He asks a wise man the way to the castle. The wise man says: "You must go across this forest, the castle is on the other side. But you probably won't get there in seven times seven years. All who have attempted it have died or given up." The cobbler goes to the forest with an axe and begins to cut, because there is no path. But the thickets grow again faster than he can cut. He tries here, there, and everywhere, but it is always the same. Pursued by a lion, he climbs a tree, and from the top of it he sees the vast extent of the forest. He is in despair. But he remembers the wise man's words "Go across this forest". He has the idea of going across the tops of the trees. It takes him seven years. At last he finds himself before a castle, where there are festivities because the princess is to be married the next day. He enters, in rags and unrecognizable. He marries the princess.

The mystical meaning is plain.

God visits the soul, but it is asleep. If it were awake, the spiritual marriage would take place effortlessly, without any ordeal. Perhaps it was like this for some of the saints?

He goes away, leaving some trace of his passage, letting us feel that he awaits us. We have to pass through evil, to the extreme limit, in order to reach him again. We attack our sin, we hack and cut; but it grows even faster. There is no hope in this method.

The only way is to pass above our sin. It is a painful and slow method, but possible. One makes a real advance and one reaches the end.

What is meant by this method of advance above the level of evil, like a man going from tree-top to tree-top?

It means not trying to abolish the evil in oneself, but advancing to the end.

Through all sins, keep the good in mind. Don't think about the evil to be destroyed, but about the good.

Meditate further on this image of the forest.

The king who sees a raven's blood on a marble floor (badly transposed, it is really snow) and falls ill with longing for a woman all white and scarlet and black.

The piece of stuff torn from a cloak to be a sign of recognition (σύμβολον).

The bull who gives food to a starving child (the child hits the bull's back and the food appears); it has itself buried, saying it must be exhumed after a year and a cup of blood, a cup of milk, and a cup of water be brought to the ceremony.

"Jesus Christ who came through water and blood. Not in water only but in water and blood."[1]

I John 5: 6.

The boy who climbs the mountain of glass three times, dressed first in black, then in yellow, then in white.

The cobbler (the one who crossed the forest) spends three nights in three chambers of a magic castle. One yellow, one red, and one black. In order to deliver the princess, he has to lie down but not go to sleep, and to stay calm and fearless whatever may happen. Some witches come and hurl insults at him; finding him impassive, they take him to a well and are about to throw him in, but at that precise moment the clock strikes one. Exclaiming "Our fatal hour!" they let go of the cobbler and disappear. The second night, exactly the same, but a pyre instead of a well. The third also, except that he was to be thrown down from a tower. The princess is saved.

Evil seems to be without limit. But there is a limit, so that he who is brave and patient (ἐν ὑπομονῇ) is saved at the very last moment, when he thinks he is already lost.

[The race known as Iberian, Mediterranean, Berber, Basque, Silurian, Euskarian—of "Hamitic" speech (Gallas, Berbers)—of African origin?—first inhabitants of the Nile valley—the Pelasgians of Greece, the Etruscans of Italy, the Hittites of Palestine—the culture in England before the arrival of the Celts, resembling that in the mountains of southern India. Would this be the race, this social matrix, which is everywhere described by the term "autochthonous"? Still the dominant type in the west of England and of Ireland.]

[Professor Rhys conjectured that the people whom Caesar called "Aquitani" were not celtic and not aryan but were Iberians of Hamitic speech. He also believes that Druidism is Iberian, and that the polytheism of Gaul is celtic.]

Welsh poem *Book of Taliesin*. To be read.

Stonehenge, called by Diodorus a temple of Apollo. According to the British tradition (Geoffrey of Monmouth?) these stones of miraculous virtue were brought from the farthest coast of Africa by the giants who first colonized Ireland. They were placed on Salisbury plain by Merlin.

The "Thirteen Treasures of Brittany". Sword, basket, drinking horn, chariot, cord, knife, cauldron, whetstone, vestment, checkerboard [pan? platter?].

Is this a zodiac?

[The word Hamitic refers to Cham, who is called Ham in German and English.]

Egypt, Chaldaea, India, Crete, Troy—centres of wisdom.—And Phoenicia.—And England (druidic centre).

Thales was half-Phoenician. Pherecydes knew the secret books of the Phoenicians.

The prophecy of Ham. Those are the "men of old, nearer to the Gods than we are", of whom Plato speaks.[1]

If the Trojans went to Thrace, it is not surprising that the cult of Dionysus and Orphism should come from Thrace. It is evident in the *Iliad* that the Trojans are dearer to God than the Achaeans.

Herodotus "The Getae think there is no other God than theirs". Why should this people not also be the chosen one?

The idea of resurrection from bones implies that the blood is fabricated in the bones. (The Scythians burned the bones of sacrificial animals.)

Plato "The generation of the marrow is the basis of the bones, the flesh, etc; for when the soul is attached to the body the threads of life are knotted together in the marrow, implanting the mortal species there. And the marrow is born from elsewhere ... God, having mingled [the pure elements] in proportion and composed from them a universal seed for all mortal life, created the marrow from it ... And to the soil which was to harbour the divine seed he gave a round shape and he called that part of the marrow the brain."

Therefore, if the marrow was intact, it should be possible to reconstitute life from the bones.

Burning, for solid things, must have been like libation for liquids. The cup represented the universe, so the drop poured from it was offered to the super-celestial world. In the same way, fire makes a thing disappear from this world and transports it to the other. To burn the bones, which contained the life, was to transport the life into the other world.

As the result, certainly, of a decadence of thought, this ceremony came to be taken as the condition of the thing for which it was the symbol; exactly as baptism became, for narrow Catholics like Augustine. Thus Hector begs Achilles to respect his corpse in the way that a medieval knight begged for time to

---

[1] *Philebus*, 16 c.

make his last confession. But Achilles wanted not only to kill Hector but to damn him.

Whereas interment is a preparation for resurrection.

Atlantis. Why should it not be, purely and simply, America? And when, for some reason or other, people had lost the art of navigation which made it possible to go there, they thought it had sunk into the sea.

Hephaestus and Athena are a doublet. The Holy Spirit. (This Hephaestus is surely not the son of Hera?)

The sun's rays are stored in the tree—which rises towards the sky under their impulse—and they flash out from the dead wood if it is rubbed. Wood is a reservoir of light. Prometheus is surely connected with wood. And this explains the emphasis on wood in the Book of Wisdom,[1] in relation to Noah, and in the first Christian writings, in relation to Christ.

The living wood stores the solar flame. But it is the dead, dry wood that gives it to men.

Thus the tree is the hero of a sacrifice analogous to the Incarnation.

"I am come to throw fire upon the earth."

Both Aeschylus, concerning Prometheus, and Plato, concerning Love, use adjectives meaning "dried-up" which would be more appropriate to wood or to a tree than to a man.

The tree of life gives fire. The tree of sin gives fruits. (But is this antithesis correct?)

Wood that is burnt suffers a passion.

Menhirs must have been stone imitations of a flame.

And when we speak of "burning" with love, the word must come from the tradition of seeing the wood burning for love of us, to give us warmth and light.

The Sun, the Father. The wood, Christ. The light, the Spirit. The sun gives the light to the tree and the tree gives it to men.

[1] Apocrypha.

The kings of Atlantis led the bull to the column, and at the summit they cut its throat.

"The son of man must be lifted up."

If the bull was related to the sea, as it was to the moon, the phenomenon of the tides must have been known.

Salt is the symbol of eternity. "Everything shall be salted in the fire." The fire transports into eternity what it obliterates from this world.

All other kinds of destruction are transformations. Only fire annihilates.

Fire is the light that destroys. It transforms things into light.

By growing, the tree receives and stores a light which makes it rise upwards and produce fruit, and which will end by transforming it entirely into light.

Relation between Noah and Poseidon—Osiris—Dionysus—Celestial Aphrodite born from the sea.

Pythagoreans. Number is the specific relation of each thing to God, who is unity. The universal ratio is the Logos, the divine Wisdom, the divine Word, with which the universe is in conformity through love.

American Indian story of the hunter who goes to live with the deer, marries one of them, and learns the method of killing the young deer for food, with their consent, and of resuscitating them afterwards by throwing their bones in a river—this must refer to the origins of stock farming, which would have begun through a pact with the animals.

This water that resuscitates is like the baptismal water.

There is an analogy between this operation and the planting of seed. That is why Plato described the marrow as seed.

The spirit of the first part of Genesis is opposed to that of the rest of the Pentateuch. He whom God loves dies prematurely by a violent death, without issue. He whom God hates has a long life and a numerous posterity, and builds a town. God did not prevent the man he loved from being killed.

This shows that the source of the narrative is Egyptian.

Genesis is not presented as a deliverance of God to Moses, like Numbers, Leviticus, etc.—therefore Moses got it from human sources. The history of the Hebrews after Abraham surely comes from their more or less confused memory of real events. But the first part of Genesis, before the genealogy of Abraham, can only be a transposition of Egyptian material, more or less well understood and adapted. For Moses was initiated into the secret wisdom of the Egyptian priests, though doubtless only to a lower grade, and not fully. It was only in magic that he was their superior. Nevertheless, we may regard the first 10 chapters of Genesis as a fragment of an Egyptian sacred book. And perhaps also the story of the tower of Babel. (Yet there is no trace there of the Egyptians' belief that they were the[1]

[The Egyptian priests said that for 11,340 years, that is to say, since 11,800 B.C., there had not been a god in human form.]

Pan is the most ancient god; the first of the eight gods. Heracles is the first of the second series, of twelve gods. Osiris is the first of the third series. Then comes his son Horus. After that there is not another human god.

Heracles is 17,000 years before Amasis (whose date is about 569 B.C.). Osiris is 15,000 years before Amasis. So there were 12 gods from Pan to Osiris, in 2000 years, or one god every $\frac{2000}{12} = \frac{1000}{6} = 166\frac{2}{3}$ years.

If the rhythm is constant, Pan precedes Heracles by $\frac{2000}{12} \times 8 = 2000 \times \frac{2}{3} = \frac{4000}{3} = 1,333\frac{1}{3}$ years. The most ancient of the gods would be about 19,000 B.C. But there is no guarantee that the rhythm is constant.

The son of Semele was 1600 years before Herodotus, the son of Alcmene 900 years before him, and Pan the son of Penelope, who comes after Troy, was 800 years before him. Herodotus wrote about 450 B.C. Therefore the date of Semele would be 2050 B.C., of Alcmene and Amphitryon 1350 B.C., of the second Pan 1250 B.C. The Trojan war was therefore between 1350 and

[1] Sentence unfinished in MS.

1250 B.C. Hercules while still young spared Priam as a child. So the Trojan war would be nearer 1250, in the 2nd quarter of the 13th century B.C. According to modern calculations, Pharaoh died in 1224 B.C.: Proteus, who succeeded him, received Helen. There must be a slight error somewhere.

The first command of the Eternal to Abraham is to depart. When he reaches Canaan the Eternal promises this land to his posterity. He goes on to Egypt, where there is already a Pharaoh. (They treat him with marvellous humanity.) It is long afterwards that the Eternal enjoins circumcision. Abraham must have learned in Egypt that the Egyptians practised it.

Herodotus says: "Only the men of Colchis, the Egyptians, and the Ethiopians practised circumcision originally. The Phoenicians and the Syrians of Palestine themselves admit that they learnt it from the Egyptians" [he believes that Colchis was peopled by colonists from Egypt—it is the country of Medea—dragon as at Thebes . . .]

The fact that the covenant with Abraham was circumcision and not something original shows that the Hebrews were no more elect than the Egyptians.

The three persons who come to Abraham have nothing to do with the Trinity. They are the Lord and two envoys. The Lord does seem to be an incarnation of God. Would it not be Melchizedek? The epoch of Melchizedek corresponds in a singular manner to that of Dionysus, who went to India.

Lot's daughters. The only explanation of this passage is that there must have been a tradition in which Lot was the only surviving man; a universal deluge, replica of the Flood (referred to in the *Timaeus* and in Nonnos) from which only one just man escapes. Moreover, Lot gets drunk with wine, like Noah. One of the two peoples descended from Lot's union with his daughters is the Ammonites, worshippers of Zeus Ammon, whom Herodotus regards as a mixture of Egyptian and Ethiopian.

Circumcision is like libation. God is given a drop from each cup of wine, and a piece of each man's flesh.

Herodotus begins his history with the war of Cyrus against Solon. It was Cyrus who restored the temple of Jerusalem.

Herodotus went as far as Tyre in his travels. How is it that he heard nothing about Jerusalem?

"Making your children pass through the fire." It cannot be a sacrifice, because it would amount to a massacre. It must refer to a form of baptism.

Ezekiel: "Wherefore I gave them statutes that were not good and judgements by which they could not live" (xx, 25). It is St. Paul's idea.

Words of God, through Ezekiel, at Tyre:
"Because thou hast said 'I am a God . . . ', because thou hast set thine heart as the heart of a God (behold, thou art wiser than Daniel, there is no secret that they can hide from thee!) because thou hast set thine heart as the heart of a God, therefore I will bring strangers upon thee, the terrible of the nations . . . They shall bring thee down to the pit, and thou shalt die a violent death . . . Wilt thou yet dare to say before them that slay thee 'I am a God'? but thou art a man, and no God, in the hands of them that slay thee."[1]

These words might very well be addressed to Christ.

"Thou art a man, and no God, in the hands of them that slay thee."

When Nimrod, grandson of Ham, the first who was powerful on earth, founds Babel, all men are together. So therefore the descendants of Japhet and Shem obey him.

Abel = Pan? Nimrod = Heracles? (But Heracles was 2000 years before Osiris; if Noah is Osiris . . .) Enoch = Hermes? Ham = Horus?

Job was prosperous at first, so that his justice might be seen. For he might have been oppressive, and he was not.

Similarly Christ had exceptional powers, so that it might be seen that he did only good.

God gives Satan all power over Job, except over his person. "He imputed no injustice to God."[2]

God gives Satan all power over Job, including his person, but excepting his life.

---

[1] Ezekiel 28: 2–9.
[2] Job i: 22. S.W. used the translation of the Bible by the French Rabbinate (ed. M. Zadoc Kahn) in which the complete verse reads: "En dépit de tout, Job ne faillit point et n'imputa pas d'injustice à Dieu."

There must have been a third part which was lost and in which God gives Satan power also over Job's life. And when Job was dying without having cursed God, then God revived him.

This third part was replaced by the speech of Elihu and the speech of God.

Is not Job the righteous man of Isaiah? "A man of sorrows and acquainted with grief." Perhaps in the 3rd part he was killed, and without saying anything more. Perhaps his self-styled friends stirred up the people to kill him.

Seneca, of Bacchus, "Cornigerum caput".[1]

Does not the conquest of India by Bacchus signify that Orphism was of Indian origin? But Herodotus says nothing about that conquest.

Job, by his prayers, saves his persecutors from God's wrath. That does not really make sense unless they have really done him harm. The dramatic movement requires that they should do him real harm.

Seneca's *Medea*. The central verses are: "Sola est quies—mecum ruina cuncta si video obruta;—mecum omnia abeant. Trahere, cum pereas, libet."[2] That is why she does not want to know that Jason's desertion of her was forced and unwilling. She wants to destroy everything she loves.

In Greece, the depiction of the most atrocious misery is suffused with a light of spirituality and poetry. Roman works are unsurpassable for cold and frightful horror. Seneca, Ovid's *Tristes*, Plautus, Tacitus. Rome's only message is the horror of affliction void of spiritual life. Similarly in the works called "elegiac", Catullus, Tibullus, Propertius. That is what remains of the greatest of Empires.

But the Roman Empire was never really destroyed. It is what

---

[1] Horned head.

[2] There is no rest for me except in seeing everything fall to ruin along with myself. It is pleasant, when perishing, to drag other things down as well. (Seneca: *Medea*, 426–8.)

still afflicts the world. Its contamination of Christianity was so profound that Christianity became its means of survival.

The Trojan Women. Tolle felices, miserum, licet sit—nemo se credet. Removete multo—divites auro, removete centum—rura qui scindunt opulenta bubus—pauperi surgent animi jacentes—est miser nemo nisi comparatus.[1]

The hunter pursues his victims. But the shepherd feeds his and cares for them, and he is not a successful shepherd unless there is affection between him and his flock. There is a contradiction in the shepherd's craft (cf. that Shropshire novel). This contradiction must have been one of the earliest and most intense subjects of men's reflection.

There is an echo of it in the beginning of the *Republic*. Apollo was a shepherd. Was he the first? Abel was a shepherd. Pan is the god of shepherds. It was shepherds who received the tidings of Christ's birth.

He is the Shepherd, and at the same time the Lamb.

Shepherds were accursed or sacred in Egypt. Astronomy revealed to Babylonian shepherds.

There could not be affection unless there was a pact and free consent. The animal consents to its own slaughter. But, for such generosity, it must be God.

Zeus puts on the skin of a slaughtered ram when he appears to Heracles.

Abel's sacrifice, which is so pleasing to God, is his death.

Were there ritual sacrifices of shepherds?

Among the Thebans, one half of the people slaughtered sheep and the other half slaughtered goats. No doubt this was an elementary division of labour, to avoid breaking a pact with the animals. Those who raised sheep ate goat's flesh, and those who raised goats ate mutton. The Egyptians sprinkled the sacrificial burnt meat liberally with oil; the oil quickened the flame. The inflammability of oil explains the affinity between the olive and

---

[1] No one need think himself miserable, unless he compares himself with the fortunate. Leaving aside the very rich, in gold or in land or in flocks, the minds of the poor buoy one another up; and no man is wretched except by comparison. (Seneca: *Trojan Women*, 1021–6.)

the Holy Spirit. They must have regarded oil as potential fire in a liquid form.

But water extinguishes fire; it is the opposite of fire. The union of water and fire is a Pythagorean harmony. It is realized in wine.

Water, oil, wine—thesis, antithesis, synthesis.

Yellow, white, and red in folk tales should represent oil, water, and wine.—But are there examples of yellow, white, and red? I don't know.

What are black, white, and red? Ashes, water, blood? Fire blackens.

"Salted by the fire." Cooking preserves things. Originally, meat must have been put in the fire to consecrate it. Then it was discovered that this turned it into a different kind of food. Roasted meat appears in religious regulations.

Water and oil will not mix. Hostile elements. It is only as wine that water and fire will mix.

God separated the waters below and the waters above. And this is the first separation we have to make in our microcosm.

The Egyptians thought that their fertilizing water came to them from the world below. Was it from this that they got the idea of making it the abode of the eternally living dead?

It is because of the analogy between respiration and combustion that the Spirit, which is fire, is also breath. Hence a combined representation of energy as a fiery breath.

Milk being the liquid which contains the father's seed, the vital flame, oil must have been regarded as milk coming from God.

Job. It must be a story of God—incarnated, suffering, dead, resurrected and redeeming—which was translated into Hebrew, and to some extent secularized, by a Jew. Job is the suffering just man of Plato, so just that he appears unjust.

What is called the "second Isaiah" is also perhaps partly non-Jewish. In any case, it is a compilation with a confused basis.

The theme of a great part of the Psalms is the suffering Just Man.

Christ is at the same time the shepherd, the lamb, and the door of the sheepfold. Trinity.

The shepherd cares for the lamb and feeds it, then sells it to the butcher, who kills it.

The lamb's silence is taken as consent.

The oil burns the animal offered for sacrifice. Like Hephaestus nailing Prometheus to his cross—$ἄκοντα\ ἄκων$.[1]

Prometheus is loved even by his executioner. He is Love. It is impossible for him not to be loved.

To pour the blood of slain animals on the earth (as God ordered Noah) is surely a hunter's ritual, to prevent the species that feeds him from dying out. He thinks that the dead animal is resurrected from the blood.

The blood of Abel, too, flowed on the earth.

And the blood of Christ.

Two physiological doctrines.—One of them situates life in the blood, the other, like Plato, in the marrow. The second is the doctrine of American Indians and Scandinavians. The first is held by the Hebrews. But for the paschal lamb they observe also the second. So the first goes back to a hunter's civilization, the second to a herdsman's. Hunters could believe in a resurrection from the blood. Shepherds could not.

Nor could they believe in resurrection from the bones. Both must be hunters' traditions.

Herding must have been established upon this idea of the resurrection of animals. When it was seen not to correspond to the facts, the doctrine of voluntary sacrifice was adopted, both to banish the feeling of guilt and to explain why the animals didn't run away.

God takes the form of a lamb, to be slaughtered, and of an ox, to be a slave.

The castration of the ox should be a theme of myth.

Is the castration of Ouranos by Cronos connected with it?

(Pherecydes. There is Ouranos, Chthonia, and Cronos. God, matter, and becoming. Plato retained that. Becoming is on the side of evil. And yet, Saturnia regna? There must be a confusion of two separate themes.)

[1] both of them unwilling.

Zeus in the *Gorgias* "Let Prometheus be told".[1] So Prometheus was charged by Zeus to watch over men.

The three "Persons" of the Trinity. Persona. The three masks of God. Is the castration of Osiris—since Isis recovers all his body except the genitals—related to the bull and the ox?

The bull consents to lose his creative power in order to become man's slave.

God possesses power of life and death, but he voids himself of both and is made a slave.

Artemis sends a boar and, in the person of Atlanta, kills it. Was the boar regarded as an incarnation of the moon in anger? Was this the reason that it was forbidden?

The stick of Meleager. Breath is within man, like fire within wood. When it comes out, the man dies.

Hanging. Man is killed by gravity. Is that the symbol? His invincible tendency to fall causes his death. Was there the idea of an ordeal? If the man can stay up in the air he need not die. Let everyone come and witness that he fails.

Why was it more unreasonable for the Egyptians to worship a calf than for Catholics to worship a piece of bread?

The Hebrews did not mean to betray the Eternal when Moses stayed on the mountain; but since they no longer had the man whose words were the words of God they desired a visible image of Jehovah. Aaron considered this very natural.

If it is idolatrous to believe that God dwells in a particular metal image of a calf, why is it less idolatrous to believe that he dwells in a particular temple?

"Our fathers worshipped on the mountain." No heresy has ever been more strongly condemned than worship in high places is condemned in the Old Testament.

Nevertheless, the good Samaritan is the neighbour. The Samaritan woman of loose life believes in Christ. Of the ten lepers it is only the Samaritan who comes back to thank Christ. Christ refuses to curse a Samaritan village. It was a sufficiently clear disavowal of the Old Testament and also, by anticipation, of the Church.

The Samaritan woman bore witness for Christ, and the Samaritans said "We know he is the saviour of the world".

The Canaanite woman. "I am not sent but unto the lost

---

[1] *Gorgias*, 523 d.

sheep of the house of Israel." He was not permitted to heal simply for the sake of healing.

This woman's humility was the sign of her faith. For she might have said his behaviour was due to his inability to help her.

Even if God does no good for us, believe that he desires it and can do it. That is contradictory. It is faith. Humility brings about this marvel.

Through the monopoly of the temple the Hebrew priests tried to make religion a purely social thing. It was Israel, and not this or that individual Israelite, who had dealings with God.

This is why it was only through exile, which completely destroyed the people, that they were able to find God, the God of the solitary soul, the Father who is in secret. Daniel prayed alone in his room. The cult had become a secret one.

Hence the tone of the book of Isaiah, and of some of the psalms, etc.

The book of Job must be both ancient and recent. A Hebrew converted to so-called idolatry could have translated it integrally in the 10th or 9th century. But it must have been found and adapted by a Hebrew of the exilic period, and of a generation born in exile. It was only on them that the thought of the affliction of the innocent could have made an impression.

At that time, too, those elegies must have been composed which were ostensibly spoken by David and later confused with his authentic poems. Perhaps they were largely inspired by Chaldaean and Persian texts (and perhaps they even took care to imitate David's language?).

There is no more reason to believe in the authenticity of the texts attributed to David than of those attributed to Solomon.

The Pharisees tried to re-establish the old religion, the social Jehovah.

It was good that Israel should be a slave, even to Rome. That is why Christ paid the tribute money.

One could say that Jeremiah was in a sense inspired when he counselled submission to Nebuchadnezzar. But in that case Moses was not . . .

It was good that the temple should be destroyed.

Only the universal is true, and man can fix his attention only upon the particular. This difficulty is the source of idolatry.

The Song of Songs is also perhaps—no, probably—a translation.

We should try to establish at what point the question emerges of a marriage between God and Israel.

But the bride in the Song of Songs is not Israel. It is a soul.

Just as the monopoly of Shiloh, and then of Jerusalem, made religion a social thing, so does the monopoly of the Church.

Osiris was not only killed but tortured. He was enclosed in a coffer, where he died by suffocation, slowly and in terror. Antigone's death was of the same kind.

The coffer is like the mirror of Zagreus.[1] Osiris let himself be measured.

It is the symbol of the Creation. The Passion is the punishment for the Creation. The devil traps God by the lure of Creation, which seduces God through love. But for this very reason he is not really trapped, because he himself is nothing but love.

Faith consists in believing that God is love and nothing else.

But that is still not the right way to put it.

Faith consists in believing that reality is love and nothing else.

Like a child in play, hiding from its mother behind a chair, so God plays at separating himself from God behind the creation.

This joke of God's is what we are.

Believe that reality is love, while still seeing it exactly as it is. Love what is intolerable. Embrace what is made of iron, press one's flesh against the metallic harshness and chill.

This is not any kind of masochism. What excites masochists is only the semblance of cruelty, because they don't know what cruelty is. In any case, what one has to embrace is not cruelty, it is blind indifference and brutality. Only in this way does love become impersonal.

If love finds no object, the lover must love his love itself, perceived as something external. Then one has found God.

---

[1] Cf. the myth of Dionysus entering into a mirror, and the myth of Narcissus. See also p. 329.

"Amare amabam."[1] If he had stuck to that, he had found the way.

As the Hindus perceived, the great difficulty in seeking for God is that we have him within us, at the centre of ourselves. How can I approach myself? Every step I take leads me away from myself. That is why we cannot search for God.

The only way is to come out of oneself and contemplate oneself from outside. Then, from outside, one sees at the centre of oneself God as he is.

But coming out of oneself means total renunciation of being anybody and complete consent to being merely a thing.

Many human beings, worn down by affliction, have come to be no more than a thing in their own eyes, but without their consent. In such cases there is perhaps nothing more to be done, because one cannot consent to becoming what one has already become in spite of oneself.

Under the influence of real love—but they can only be loved by a miracle—they may become someone again, if only for a few moments, and thus have a chance, however slight, of winning eternity by consenting to fall back into the state of being a thing.

Thus the man who gives a piece of bread without saying a word, if his way of giving it is right, sometimes gives eternal life at the same time. A gesture of this kind may possess a redemptive value far higher than many sermons.

Christ has done that for us. By becoming food for us he persuades us that we are somebody, and thus makes it possible for us to wish, as he did, to become simply a thing.

To give a piece of bread is more than preaching a sermon, as Christ's Cross is more than his parables.

To ask for a piece of bread is also a great deal.

Charity to a hungry poor man is to give him bread. Charity to a well-fed rich man is to ask him for bread.

Best of all is to be a hungry mendicant, and to beg, and to give away some of what one receives.

Perhaps St. Francis ought to have founded a secret order, with no vow except of secrecy.

---

[1] St. Augustine, *Confessions*, III, 1: "I loved to love... I sought what I might love, in love with loving..."

It is too easy to talk about these things without doing them.

One cannot come out of oneself by willing to do so. The harder one wills, the more one is oneself. One can only desire and supplicate.

As regards the vertical, in the sense of upward movement, we are the same as a child is, before it can walk, as regards the horizontal.

To understand this is to become humble again like a child.

One is nearer the sky at the top of a mountain than in the plain. But one is no nearer to flying. One is exactly as far away as before.

That is why pride is a mistake.

When we fly, if we are really flying, we have come out of our self, and there is no more pride.

The good begins at a point beyond the reach of will, as truth begins at a point beyond the reach of intelligence.

Beyond the intelligence, and therefore beyond the law.

The true law is an unwritten law, as Sophocles knew. For the letter kills. So Moses did not come from God.

Israel was that society of brigands, described by Plato, which tries to establish an internal justice of its own.

Rome, with its Roman law, was of the same species.

Although evil is the opposite of good, it is obliged to contain an image of it. For everything bears witness to the good. Cain bears witness like Abel, Judas like Christ. But the one desires to bear witness, the other does it as if by mistake.

All of us have been put into this world, like Christ, in order to witness to the truth; and whatever we may do, we shall be bearing witness to it.

Once we have understood this, we can no longer be afraid of disobeying God.

And yet the anxiety does continue in one part of the soul.

What joy to be certain that one will obey God in any case, unconditionally, and even in spite of oneself, since everything obeys him. If our soul does not consent to obey him, our flesh will consent; and our obedience will then conform to mechanical law.

When a man consents to obey God, the spirit in him obeys,

that is to say, it becomes subject to the laws of spiritual phenomena; and by a mechanism of which we know nothing the rest of his being adapts itself to the spirit sufficiently for those laws to operate. When a man does not consent to obey God, then there is no spirit in him. But the carnal soul and the flesh which compose his whole being are obedient; that is to say, they are subject to mechanical law.

The devil himself wanted to disobey, but could not.

Two unconditional truths which neither my sins nor my afflictions have altered, do alter, or can ever alter in any way:

The Good is real.

The entire universe and all its parts, including myself, are perfectly and exclusively obedient to the Good.

God is our only debtor; for no created thing can harm us or deprive us of any good except with his permission. To forgive him his debt is to recognize that he always and unceasingly gives us as much good as we consent to receive.

God's great crime against us is to have created us, is the fact of our existence. And our existence is our great crime against God. When we forgive God for our existence, he forgives us for existing.

We have to know that we are nothing, that the impression of being somebody is an illusion, and we have to carry submission to the point of consenting, not only to be nothing, but at the same time to be under the illusion of being something. Then the wheel of obedience has turned full circle; we have returned, in appearance, to the place where we began, the place of those who do not love God. And then God pardons us for existing.

God pardons us for existing so soon as we are willing to consent to exist only in so far as God wills our existence.

We can exist only as criminals.

When crime has impregnated the soul to the point where it is totally poisoned, repentance implies a total rending away from oneself; and there cannot be such repentance without sanctity. But this only happens to criminals who are in affliction. The prosperous ones do not have their crime deeply enough embedded in their souls.

A theory of human punishment needs to be worked out.

Why has there never been, throughout the Christian era, a

legislator inspired by God? Why has no saint ever framed any legislation?

Christian inspiration has never been able to relate itself to the things of this world. So the Incarnation comes to seem like a crowning event, a completion, instead of a commencement.

When everyone regarded seed as an image of the kingdom of God, the whole life of a peasant could be a prayer and his patience could be the patience which is a supernatural virtue, ὑπομονῇ.

There ought to be a spiritual almanac for peasants, with a theme for meditation all the year round.

Seed-time—when the sower's seed falls on stones, or on barren ground, or on good ground.

That is to say, God gives the totality of good to everyone at every moment, but we only receive what we choose.

Plough the soul as one ploughs the earth to prepare it for the seed. Labour the soil of oneself.

This theme should continue throughout the period of tillage and conclude at the sowing.

And then "Except a corn of wheat fall into the ground and die". It is a theme that can last from the harvest, when the wheat is cut down and killed, until the next seed-time. Ploughing the fields is the preparation for a burial.

Ask God to kill and bury us spiritually while we are in this world. Burial in total renunciation and silence.

Especially Mark iv, 26.

"So is the kingdom of God, as if a man should cast seed into the ground; and should sleep and rise night and day, and the seed should spring and grow up, he knoweth not how. The earth bringeth forth fruit of herself; first the blade, then the ear, and then the full corn in the ear. And when the fruit is brought forth, immediately he putteth in the sickle, for the harvest is come." (Immediately after this comes the parable of the grain of mustard seed.)

Once the ground is well prepared, if only the seed is received by it and is protected from interference, it grows all by itself. The light and water that fall from the sky make it grow.

A theme for meditation between sowing and harvest. By day, whatever one may be doing; in the evening, before going to bed; at night, if one wakes up; say to oneself now and then: all this time the seed is growing. And although the peasant doesn't think of it all the time, there is always somewhere inside him the happy certainty that the crops are growing.

When the soul has once received an atom of the love of God, there is nothing to do but wait and let it grow.

It is only necessary to keep watch, as the peasant watches over his field.

Ask God to plant a seed in the soul and send it light and rain.

The harvest is spiritual death. When the seed has increased and the ear of wheat is formed, to its full size, then God intervenes to transform finite good into infinite good. He sends spiritual death, the death after which a man no longer lives but God lives in him.

Theme for the harvest.

Ask God for spiritual death.

Ask, while cutting the corn, to be cut off in the same way from our selves and from everything dear to us and from everything we think we possess.

At harvest-time, compare the scythe (or the blade of the mower) to a sword, and take for a theme the words "I come not to send peace, but a sword". And add St. Paul's words: "The Holy Spirit divides asunder."

At the threshing—unfortunately there is no comparison for the flail or the thresher; but one can meditate upon the wheat's destiny, which is to make bread.

At this point there is one special theme, though it should also be recalled throughout the year: "I am the bread of life ... And the bread which I will give is my flesh which I will give for the salvation of the world."[1]

Peasants should keep a little grain to grind and make eucharistic bread for themselves all the year through.

Explain to them that work does literally consume and burn up the flesh, and therefore in a sense their own flesh has been transformed into this bread. To consecrate this bread makes it Christ's flesh. By eating and digesting it Christ's flesh becomes their flesh. The cycle is completed.

Ask that we may transform ourselves into Christ and Christ into us.

Ask that God may transform our flesh into Christ's flesh, so that we may be food for all the afflicted.

Placed one after the other, the parables round out the year.

[1] Simone Weil has here used the word 'Salut' for the Greek ζωή.

Man's soul is ploughed up by his work on himself and by the harassments of chance. It is made ready for the sowing. An infinitely small seed of good falls on it, without the man himself being aware; he only perceives it later. It grows by itself. When it is ripe, God sends it spiritual death. Then the ear of corn is thrust into the ground, buried, and brings forth fruit in due season. Or else it is ground and turned into bread. The man no longer lives in himself, but Christ lives in him; his flesh has become Christ's flesh and is eaten by the afflicted. So the cycle of a human life is like that of the year. It is all labour up to the time of sowing.

At every blow of fate, every pain, whether small or great, say to oneself "I am being worked on".

Along with these themes of spiritual meditation, there should be presented in correlation the current scientific ideas of transformation of energy in the growth of plants, in nourishment, and in work. Add to this a conspectus of the elementary and essential knowledge of astronomy, mechanics, physics, chemistry and biology, and relate the whole to the sequence of the parables.

This presupposes a study circle.

There should be special masses, on Sunday or in the week, for the members of such a group, with texts from the agricultural parables corresponding to the season, so as to punctuate the sequence of studies.

There ought to be an order whose members would live as farm hands and would initiate and conduct these study circles. They would be laymen, but they would preach at the special masses.

They would need to be men of very wide culture.

While it is true in a sense that the flesh, which is consumed in work, passes into the product, it is also true that the wheat is not the product of the work. What the work does is only to provide some of the necessary conditions. It is the sky itself which gives of its own substance, in the form of light and water, and thus comes down to be transformed into an ear of wheat.

Another theme for meditation during the tillage and sowing is: "Behold the birds of the air, for they neither labour nor sow."

They neither labour nor sow, and yet they have food.

One may labour and sow, and still die of hunger.

There is no guarantee.

One must labour and sow, not in order to reap, but from pure obedience. Act, while renouncing the fruits of action.

All these themes are appropriate for any culture of cereals.

For fruit trees, "you shall know the tree by its fruit". Christ's essential word (along with: if you ask for bread, you will not receive stones).

Also the grain of mustard seed.

For the vineyard, during the whole dressing period, that is to say the whole winter, the theme is: "I am the vine, ye are the branches; the branch that abides in the vine bears much fruit; the branch severed from the vine shall be burnt."

Ask to be re-grafted on the vine; for we are severed from it.

That is appropriate all the year round.

At the wine-press, recall the miracle of Cana and the Last Supper.

Ask that our wine may be changed into that wine, into the blood of Christ.

Whenever extra hands are engaged, recall the parable of the workers of the eleventh hour.

For all those who have been hired, all who have been summoned and have said yes and have come to the vineyard and started to work, even though they had only two days to live, the payment is the same. The payment is God. He is without degree.

For stock farming, there are all the passages about the lamb, the sheep, the gate of the sheep-fold, the good shepherd.

Also Isaiah "As a sheep ... he was oppressed and he was afflicted, yet he opened not his mouth".

(Whence comes the opposition between goats and sheep? Christ follows the Theban tradition. Zeus Ammon.)

There is nothing applicable, I think, to the ox and the cow.

For women, there are some sayings which refer particularly to them.

For mothers of families "a woman when she is in travail hath sorrow ... but as soon as ... "

Compare all pains and afflictions to birth pangs.

For young girls, the parable of the wise virgins. Every young girl lives provisionally, in a state of expectancy, ready for a time when she will leave the paternal roof to begin a new and unknown life.

So it is with every human soul. The arrival of the betrothed corresponds either to grace, or to death. But more to grace.

Housewives often search feverishly for something which seems to be deliberately hiding itself. At such times, recall the metaphor of the lost piece of silver. Just as my search for it is feverish and desperate, so is God's search for me, and I hide myself to avoid being found.

In mythology and folklore there are a great many parables similar to those in the Gospel; they only need to be picked out.

And one could invent new ones. (With inspiration from the Holy Spirit.)

There ought to be an appropriate and specific parable to link with God every activity of life in every social condition; so that the whole of a human life could be simply a parable.

Every perfect life is a parable invented by God.

For every kind of human life there ought to be a possibility of living it in perfect sanctity. If there is any social condition in which this is impossible, that condition ought to be abolished.

To judge a social condition from this point of view it is necessary to have a concrete conception of every possible modality of progress towards perfection.

This conception, too, is a monopoly of the Holy Spirit.

Every action implying the relation of one human being with other human beings, or with things, truly involves an original and specific relation with God, which has to be discovered.

It is this that the Pythagoreans called "number".

As a stage on the way, it is a good thing that in any activity there should be a part of the soul that remains withdrawn and concentrated in God, but it is not the end of the way. A very different relation is needed between worldly activity and the spiritual part of the soul. Every worldly activity should be so performed that there appears in it the meaning with which God created it.

That part of the soul which is made for God should at first withdraw from the universe, even while the rest of the soul is taken by worldly things, in order to try to see God; but it should then turn to look upon the upper surface of the things of this world, the surface that they present to God. Only in this way is the entire soul restored to God.

In relation to God, we are like a thief who has burgled the house of a kindly householder and been allowed to keep some gold. From the point of view of the lawful owner this gold is a gift; from the point of view of the burglar it is a theft. He must go and give it back. It is the same with our existence. We have stolen a little of God's being to make it ours. God has made us a gift of it. But we have stolen it. We must return it.

The soul which has attained to seeing the light must lend its vision to God and turn it on the world.

The self, as it disappears, must become an empty space through which God and the creation contemplate one another.

Then the part of the soul that has seen God must transform every relation with a created being or thing into a relation between that being or thing and God.

Every relation between two or several created things— whether thinking beings or matter—is one of God's thoughts. We ought to desire a revelation of the thought of God corresponding to each relation with our fellowmen or with the material objects with which we are involved.

To refrain from conceiving those relations for ourselves is only a step on the way. The end is to conceive each of them, specifically, as a thought of God's.

And that is a miracle; because it is a contradiction to speak of God thinking a particular thought. A contradiction can only become fact by a miracle.

"With God all things are possible" is, in itself, a meaningless phrase; it means simply that "all things are possible", which is a thought absolutely void of content. The real meaning is: in the domain of the transcendent contradictories are possible.

A particular thought of God's. This is one of those contradictions which are not fallacies, but openings into the transcendent; they are like doors on which one must knock again and again, because in the end they will open.

This contradiction can be recognized as one of those doors because it is unavoidable. We know by experience that truth is always and only universal and that reality is always and only particular, and yet the two are inseparable; they are indeed one and the same. There is no escape from this.

When a contradiction is impossible to resolve except by a lie, then we know that it is really a door. One must pause and knock, and keep on indefatigably knocking, in a spirit of insistent, humble expectancy. Humility is the most essential virtue in the search for truth.

The creation is a tissue of God's particular thoughts. Each of us is a knot of those thoughts. When we have understood that by ourselves we are nothing, we have still not taken the first step. We have to become such that every one of our thoughts—that is to say every relation of our soul with everything connected with it by any relation in the past, present, or future—shall coincide with a particular thought of God's.

In the course of 2000 years the Old Testament has rendered its readers so suggestible that they see everything in it from the point of view of Israel. The Latin historians did the same for Rome, and so on.

A man can be persuaded to make the most absurd judgement if he is placed, by suggestion, at a point from which this judgement appears true. Having once adopted it he will maintain it, if he stays where he has been put instead of walking round the object in question. This power of suggestion is eloquence. All of us nearly always direct a powerful flow of eloquence upon ourselves. And in favourable circumstances eloquence is also very effective with other people.

The fixed point of view is the root of injustice.

Plane geometry is an exercise in thought without a point of view. Everything is on one plane.

In every sphere, it is an indispensable purification of thought to set out the subject on one plane, thus eliminating any point of view about it, by the use of deductive intelligence.

But several cross-sections have to be taken, as in a mechanical drawing. A single cross-section leads to error.

Story of the cobbler. Someone's attempt to translate a spiritual experience.

The impression of hanging from a rope and passing, hand over hand, across the abyss of hell (the rope is the daily recital of the Lord's Prayer in Greek); this is very much like the image of the cobbler crossing a forest from tree-top to tree-top.

It is the evil in us that hides the absolute Good from us. But so long as we are thinking about the struggle against evil, each bit of evil we destroy grows up again as before. Our thought must be oriented, with longing, through evil towards the infinitely distant good.

But it remains true that the negative conception of virtue is the right one.

Through the treachery of his landlady, the cobbler fell asleep at the appointed meeting-place. He ought not to have told the landlady that the princess had given him a rendezvous.

One must not let the lower part of one's soul know that one has such a rendezvous. It must be kept secret even from oneself. Or rather, above all from oneself. The devil has no hold over things that are kept completely secret from oneself. The devil does not enter into what is secret. That is where the heavenly Father dwells.

That is why it is perhaps better that the supernatural virtues, faith, charity, should be implicit rather than explicit.

To break secrecy is legitimate only when there is a strict obligation to bear witness.

Before the rendezvous there should be complete secrecy. Afterwards, it is not so rigorously necessary. But there should still be secrecy unless there is an obligation to break it.

The supernatural virtues should always be implicit for a certain time; and those people, if there are any, in whom they remain implicit until death are perhaps the most privileged.

Albanian story of the princess married to a snake. Variant of the Psyche story. There are two varieties of stories of this kind. In one, the princess is God and the animal-man is the soul; in the other it is the reverse. The two varieties are often fused in the same story. This one is of the second variety. The snake is the son of a king of the Underworld. He wants to come upon earth and have the form of a marvellously handsome prince. But he is only allowed to have this form at night. The stepsisters burn his snake's skin and he must vanish. To find him again the princess goes down to the Underworld. She obtains permission to bring him back to earth.

But first she must go to a witch and ask her for water; and whatever loathsome drink the witch gives her she must drink it and say it is delicious.

This is the amor fati.

She is only able to find her bridegroom again because one scale has remained intact among the ashes of his skin.

This is the σύμβολον of the *Symposium*, the glass slipper of Cinderella, the princess's ribbon in the story of the cobbler. When God has come to find us and gone away again, he leaves some token of himself. Without that, we should seek him in vain.

The prince can only have his princely form at night, and for his bride. At other times he is a snake. Compare the story of Heracles in Herodotus. God can appear only in disguise.

When one race was replacing another at the dawn of history (for example, when the palaeontologists' "homo sapiens" replaced the earlier types) the conquered may have seemed to the conquerors to be more animal than human. [Even today, many Americans feel this way about the Japanese, and perhaps it is reciprocal.] But one of the defeated may have been God incarnate. Perhaps this is one of the origins of the image of God disguised as an animal.

The Albanian story is based upon a mythology in which the snake is God; the snake is what the Lamb is for Christians.

In other similar stories there is a bull instead of the snake. Both snake and bull are lunar animals.

A dragon is the same thing as a snake.

The serpent of bronze, too, is God.

Problem: why was it good to make a serpent of bronze and criminal to make a golden calf?

This serpent of bronze continued to be the object of a cult until a very late period.

Moses had felt that the Jews could not do without an animal made of metal.

I Kings, xix. "Behold, the Lord passed by, and a great and strong wind . . . before the Lord; but the Lord was not in the wind: and after the wind an earthquake; but the Lord was not in the earthquake: and after the earthquake a fire; but the Lord was not in the fire: and after the fire a still small voice."

An electrifying touch. A touch of mysticism isolated among these hideous stories.

Strong wind; earthquake; fire; still small voice.

Elijah anoints a king of Syria.[1]

In Samaria, "the Sepharvites burnt their children in

---

[1] I Kings 19: 15.

fire... "[1] "He will baptize in fire" must certainly be an allusion to these practices.

Perhaps it was then that Job, etc., was translated into Hebrew?

It was only Hezekiah—100 years before the capture of Jerusalem by Nebuchadnezzar and 230 after the death of Solomon—who destroyed Moses' serpent of bronze. Until then they had continued to burn incense to it.

The sole aim of Moses appears to have been to establish a strong power.

Albanian story. A prince builds a temple which the whole world admires. An old man looks at it and says nothing. On being questioned he says: "It lacks one thing to make it perfect.—What?—The nightingale called Ghizari.—Where is it to be found?—That I cannot tell you. I only know that its song is the most beautiful ever heard." The prince goes off to find the nightingale.

Splendid.

The nightingale is the Holy Spirit. There is indeed something lacking to a temple that is without it.

In fairy and folk tales we know at once which characters are on the side of good and we are certain they will be completely successful in the end, through every trial. This exactly expresses the truth in the spiritual domain to which the stories refer. When it is applied to the affairs of this world it is just silly.

The third son in the stories, who is an idiot and who has marvellous adventures, is the philosopher of the *Theaetetus*, who is an idiot in the affairs of this world; like the νήπιοι, the naive, in the Gospel.

Folk tales contain a spiritual treasure of incalculable antiquity. Doubtless older than the mythologies.

The story of the giant who hides his life is older than Samson.

Fugitives from Troy may have diffused many folk tales.

The story of the almond tree in Grimm is certainly much older than that of Atreus and Thyestes, which is probably a much deformed and mutilated version of the same myth.

In the tales, when someone sets off to win a princess, or any treasure, though without even knowing where to seek, then,

[1] II Kings 17: 31.

provided he abandons all else for the sake of his quest and has no thought of return, and is untiring, and is dauntless before any danger, we are absolutely sure he will succeed.

Which proves that in these quests it is always God who is seeking, or being sought.

The wedding with which the stories end is the spiritual marriage between God and the soul. That is why there is nothing more to say except "they lived happily and had a large family".

In the microcosm as in the macrocosm, in the soul as in the universe, pure and authentic good is completely hidden. So one is always right to condemn oneself absolutely. If there is some true good in a man, it can only be unknown to himself.

If I have done some good to a human being, and if I remember it afterwards—even for a moment and when I am alone—that is enough to reverse the debt, so that he now becomes in truth the creditor and I the debtor.

Similarly, no doubt, if someone has done me harm.

If I have any debtors, it can only be without my knowing it. So how can I find any debtor to forgive?

As for me, I have no debts, I am myself a debt. My very being is a debt. God can only forgive that debt by causing me to cease to exist—to cease while I am still alive in this world—and then by selling what remains, after my person has been annihilated, so as to provide food for his creatures.

Sell all thou hast; that includes one's own person. You have not sold everything until you have sold yourself as a slave. But one doesn't sell oneself; one is sold.

To love means loving created beings and things as the divine Word loved them at the moment when it emptied itself in order to become a slave; and it means loving God as Christ did at the moment when he cried on the cross "My God, why has thou forsaken me?" Love this world as the divine Word loved it when for the sake of this world it parted from God. Have these two loves at the same time. This double love, of which each part is impossible and their combination impossible to the second degree, is the love of Christ which passeth knowledge.

This love consists of a certain attitude towards the things of this world.

God is always absent from our love, as he is from the world; but he is secretly present in pure love.

When the presence of God is visible in love, then it is the presence of something other than God. The heavenly Father dwells only in secret.

The meaning of all those princely marriages in the folk tales is contained in the Spanish copla: "Possible loves—are for fools—Wise men feel—impossible loves".

The thought of death gives a colour of eternity to the events of life. If we were granted everlasting life in this world, our earthly life, by gaining perpetuity, would lose that eternity whose light shines through it.

"Through detachment, feed upon this totality." It is detachment that makes all things become eternal.

In the *Poetic Edda* the use of prose narrative to link the lyrical verse fragments suggests a primitive state of the *Iliad* as a mixture of prose and verse. The prose would later have been versified in more or less successful imitation of the poetic parts, with new episodes added, also more or less successfully imitating the original. Whoever did this must no doubt have been responsible also for nearly all the part concerning the gods. By nearly all I mean all except (1) the intervention of the gods in the action; and (2) the passages with a profound meaning. That is to say: first, Zeus setting up his golden scales; second, the words of Zeus to Hera (the golden chain by which she was held); third, perhaps, the shield of Achilles. The two latter passages were commented by Pherecydes.

Passage in Justin Martyr (2nd century) about the old man he met once and never saw again, who urged him to leave Plato for Christ. This man must have been a gnostic. From the way he speaks about the prophets he cannot be referring to the canonical books of the Old Testament. Much more likely the "prophecies of Ham" (cf. Clement of Alexandria, quoting Isidore). And, again, the ancient books used by the Jewish monks of Egypt, according to Philo (quoted by Eusebius), in interpreting the scriptures must have been those same "prophecies of Ham". What else could have been more ancient than the Scriptures?

How thoroughly all that was destroyed! How successfully it has been kept dark!

If the "tree of the world" (the winged oak) comes from Ham, it is quite easy to believe that a religious tradition was introduced into Scandinavia by Trojans or Phoenicians.

Odin "hung on the tree, dedicated to himself"—if this is of Hamitic origin (Egyptian, Phoenician, Trojan...) it is comprehensible that there should be such mysterious affinities with Christ.

[Which tree is the ash?]

The embroidered cloth on the winged oak would have spread perpendicular to the trunk. It represents the earth, seen as flat.

Or obliquely, rather than perpendicularly.

If you are in the middle of the sea, the sea is spread around you like a circular cloth, ruffled by a wavy movement. (Hence in the *Edda* "the wind-beaten tree".) From the centre—the point where you are—to the pole there is a straight line, motionless or turning on itself. [Problem: one can think of a straight line and of a straight line turning on itself. What is the difference between the two thoughts? Very strange. A point turning on itself is motionless. And why should not its movement move the world? Unmoved mover.] To this oblique straight line turning on itself the heavenly bodies, sun, moon, planets, stars, are attached like fruits to a tree. The tree's root is below the cloth, below the world. "The tree whose root none knows" (*Poetic Edda*, runes of Odin). Aïdes, the Invisible, the Receiver of all, is beside the root. There too is the fount of wisdom, of which Odin drank in exchange for one of his eyes.

This representation of the world, like that of the round cup, and the "egg of the world", must go back to the earliest navigation. It seems to me it is only the sea's undulations that could suggest a cloth that floats.

And how long ago was the earliest navigation? mystery. Neolithic? Or earlier?

The cloth is swayed and ruffled by the changing winds, but it is attached to the polar axis. Its movements are limited by this attachment and by its own size.

Image of the combination of limit and the unlimited. The

wind that makes the cloth seem to flow is unlimited. It is the dynamic principle of becoming.

Very, very beautiful image.

Zeus made this ample and beautiful cloth, and embroidered it, in honour of his wedding. With Chthonia, no doubt? (who must be Plato's primal matter, virgin and mother?)

This cloth is a lover's gift, a betrothal gift. It was embroidered by love. It was woven by love.

Zeus as weaver. Web of limit and the unlimited.

This universe has the beauty of a lover's gift.

[Cronos, in Pherecydes, is on the side of good. Enemy of Ophion. The passages in the Apocalypse about the serpent thrown down from the height of heaven must come from Pherecydes.]

According to Philo, quoted by Eusebius (*Praeparatio Evangelica* I, 10, 50), Pherecydes got these stories from the Phoenicians.

The almond tree in the Grimm story, under which the little brother's bones are buried—after the mother herself has been buried there—and on whose branch is the bird which sings so sweetly; would it be the tree of the world?

Very probably.

The bird drops down a gold chain and a pair of slippers. Two gifts which seem to have equal value. This version of the story must go back to a time when shoes were as precious as golden chains. Very, very remote.

And the story of the seven swans with shirts made of anemones, must it not be earlier than the weaving of materials?

Seven swans, just as there are seven dwarfs in *Snow White*. Seven here stands for humanity as a whole. The heavenly bodies around the pole?

The name 'Ιησοῦς makes 888. 8 is 7 + 1. Humanity and God. Symmetrically, the name of the Beast makes 666. 6 is 7 — 1. Humanity without God. Perhaps it was never anything else except this symmetry that St. John had in mind.

As far as Christ is beyond ordinary humanity in the sense of good, so far is the Beast in the sense of evil. The distance is infinite. The infinite can only be expressed as 1.

St. John perhaps thought that something would really come some day whose number was equivalent to 666, by symmetry.

He must also have thought, because of Daniel, that the interval between Christ's Passion and his return in glory would be 3½ centuries.

888. Three eights. Was no doubt regarded as an image of the Trinity.

The Dragon, the Beast, the False Prophet, a sort of trinity of evil.

The black bull of Norway. "As for me, I would be glad to marry the black bull of Norway." It is the story of Europa. But in the case of Europa it was a bull of Crete. Is it always a maritime people, since the bull comes out of the sea? In the story of Psyche too, unless I am mistaken, it is a monster who comes from the sea. Celestial Aphrodite, too, comes from the sea. Perhaps the stories always choose a country from which sea raiders come? Possibly because the symbolic story is mixed, as Herodotus says in the case of Europa, with a real story of a young girl carried off by pirates? There could have been a Viking chief called the black Bull of Norway. I think it is only in Great Britain that this particular story has the bull in it (and certainly it is only there that it is a bull of Norway).

For whoever is on the sea, immersion means passing over to the other side, to the side where the root of the tree of the world is. One passes to the other side of the veil. It is the same thing as piercing the egg-shell of the world. Baptism. Baptism, like Easter eggs, is an Easter rite.

Was the mast originally oblique, pointing to the pole? Perhaps.

And was the axis of the pole, prolonged downwards, regarded as a balance? Perhaps with the sun as counterweight to the weight on the other side, the weight below.

Was not the sailor's punishment of being lashed to the mast the first form of crucifixion?

And was not the hanging of a sailor on the mast—preferably a willing victim—a process of sympathetic magic, the sailor's relation to the mast being that of the sun to the polar axis?

(Blessed tree, on whose branches—hung the ransom of the world!—Thou wert made a balance for that body—and bore away the prey of hell.)[1]

Perhaps in the beginning human sacrifice was the only form

---

[1] From *Beata, cujus bracchiis* ... (Fortunatus of Ravenna).

of execution. The death penalty for murder does not seem to be primitive, since Cain's life is protected and it is only to Noah that God says "whoso sheddeth man's blood, by man shall his blood be shed". Perhaps human sacrifice required only voluntary and pure victims. The forms it took (hanging, crucifixion, the stake) are perhaps the origins of those punishments.

They must have thought of the sun as being attached. At the summer solstice it is on the point of getting free from its bonds—but only on the point.

Or again, is hanging not an attempt to graft oneself on to the tree of the world—the true vine—from which one is a cut-off branch? To graft oneself by death.

In any case, it is certainly a sacred symbol.

Is the hanged man the fruit whose flesh men eat and whose juice they drink?

The sun is hung on the tree of the world. Solar energy comes down to the trees and hangs there in the form of fruit, which men eat.

The pomegranate for example. Its juice is the blood of Dionysus.

The juice of the grape is the blood of Christ.

Even if the Trojan descent of Odin is false, a Thracian origin could very well be true; in which case there would be an Orphic element in the *Eddas*. Balder is undoubtedly Dionysus.

He is the only god who dies before the end of the world, but also the only god who is resurrected after the end of the world.

The mistletoe kills him. No doubt the mistletoe is sacred; and doubtless, too, because the mistletoe is identified with him. In one sense, he is killed; in another sense, he gives his life. Only the plant that represents him can kill him. It is the only one that is not bound by oath. Since it was sacred to the god it was not asked to swear not to kill him (that, no doubt, is the reason).

Why is the mistletoe sacred? Image of the ball of fire falling on oak trees? Or image of the earth suspended on the tree of the world? Or as a plant with its roots in the sky? Or as the celestial root of the oak?

To get an idea, one would need to see mistletoe on an oak—which I have never done.

Athena's embroidered cloth. Gift from this world to the Holy Spirit.

Impalement. An imitation of the tree of the world rising from the sexual zone up to the head along the vertebral column—the route of the duct along which the seed ought to rise, according to the Hindus.

The shield of Achilles is the world. A round shield, like the ocean around a ship. He who is behind the shield is on the other side of the veil.

The tree of life is the polar axis, whose fruits are the stars. Whoever eats of the sun will live.

Whoever eats the light will live.

If we had chlorophyll we should feed on light, like the trees.

Christ is our chlorophyll.

Thor fishing for the Serpent which lies in the ocean. In Job there is talk of fishing for Leviathan. "Canst thou draw out leviathan with an hook . . . ?"

"He maketh the deep to boil like a pot . . . he is made without fear."

"Will he make a covenant with thee? Wilt thou take him for a servant?"

So he has made a covenant with God.

"Deck thyself with majesty . . . then will I praise thee thyself . . ." (Allusion to Christ?)

May not Daniel be a mythical character of the Chaldaeans? (It's difficult.) Or was there confusion between a mythical and a historical person?

Why "Noah, Job and Daniel" in Ezekiel?

Abel. Enoch. Noah. Ham. Nimrod. Melchizedek. Job. Daniel. 8 persons who were perfect in all things (all of them men).

Job must be a revealed text of some other religion. (Origen says the book of Job dates from before Moses.) Perhaps also the Song of Songs. But what religion? Phoenician? Canaanite?

A list should be made of passages in the Bible referring to Leviathan.

The Protestants say that the woman of heaven in the Apocalypse is the Church. According to the passage of the Gospel of the Hebrews, quoted by Origen, about "my mother the Holy Spirit", she might be the Holy Spirit.

Words of Christ: "Even so did my mother, the Holy Spirit, take me by one of my hairs and carry me away to the great mountain Tabor."[1]

....

[Abel—Pan ‖ Enoch... ‖ Noah—Dionysus—Osiris ‖ Ham—Hermes ‖ Nimrod—Heracles ‖

A woman in the heavens, clothed with the sun, and the moon under her feet, and crowned with twelve stars, was crying out and labouring with child. A dragon stood before her to devour her child. The child is carried up to the throne of God and the woman flies to a wilderness prepared for her. That is to say, she falls down to earth.

The dragon too is thrown down to earth; the old serpent, the devil, who deceived the whole world. And then a voice in heaven said "now is come salvation, and strength, and the kingdom of our God and the power of his Christ".

This happened in heaven and not on earth because, on the contrary, "woe to the earth and to the sea, for the devil is come down unto you, having great wrath".

So it was only after this that God and his Christ were masters in heaven. Evil, having been driven out of heaven, came down here.

Until then, it was before the face of God accusing day and night the brethren of the angels. But they overcame it by the blood of the Lamb and the "logos"[2] of their testimony and they loved not their souls[2] unto the death. That is why it is said: Rejoice ye heavens and ye that dwell in them, but woe to the earth and the sea...

This must apply also to the angels. In the preceding account it is the angels who conquered the dragon. The angels overcame by the blood of the Lamb.

The dragon, thrown down on earth, persecutes the woman, who has also fallen down to earth. She flies, on eagle's wings, to the wilderness. The dragon makes a flood of water to carry her away. But the earth opens and swallows up the flood.

[1] Apocryphal gospel of the Hebrews, quoted by Origen and Jerome.
[2] Revelation 12:11. SW has translated literally the Greek λόγος and ψυχή.

Is this a version of the story of the flood?

The woman is nourished in the wilderness, far from the face of the serpent, "for a time and times and half a time".

The dragon goes to make war with the remnant of her seed, and comes to the sea shore. A beast comes out of the sea; a leopard with bear's feet, the mouth of a lion, and seven heads and ten horns. The dragon gives him his power. After this, there is no more about the dragon; except when an angel having the key of the bottomless pit, and a chain, casts him into the pit and binds him for a thousand years. The martyrs of Christ live with Christ a thousand years. Then Satan is unbound and seduces the nations and gathers them together for a battle against the holy city. Then the fire of heaven consumes them, and the devil, the beast, and the false prophet are cast into a lake of fire. That is the end.

Earlier: the people tread the holy city under foot for $3\frac{1}{2}$ years. Two prophets prophesy for $3\frac{1}{2}$ years, two olive trees, two candlesticks; a fire devours their enemies, and whoever hurts them is killed. When they have finished their testimony, the beast from the pit shall kill them; their bodies will be seen for $3\frac{1}{2}$ days, to general rejoicing; then the spirit of life from God shall revive them and they shall ascend up to heaven, and the seventh angel shall sound his trumpet. The temple of God in heaven is opened and a great wonder appears in heaven (the woman with child).

The woman is the mother of Christ. If she is the Spirit, her fall to earth corresponds to Prometheus' gift of fire.

It is natural that the Holy Spirit and the devil should fall down to earth at the same time.

3,500 years before Christ corresponds approximately to the birth of Enoch—which must be the name of some Egyptian god.

It is not said whether the two prophets are together or not.

All that is too difficult. But the Apocalypse is surely full of the traces of now vanished mythologies.

Matthew 23, 35. How did Zacharias, the prophet of the reconstruction of the temple, come to be killed in the temple? The Bible is silent about this. In general, who were all these murdered prophets?

Divine love is unconditional love. To love a human being in God is to love him unconditionally. One can only love a being unconditionally if one loves an attribute of him which is indestructible.

In an ordinary human being there is only one indestructible attribute—the fact that he is a created thing.

In those who have been born twice, who have been born from on high by the spirit, who have passed through the death and resurrection of Christ, there is a second indestructible attribute —that of being a child of God.

Therefore there are two unconditional loves toward human beings. One is expressed in the precept "love your neighbour as yourself", the other in the precept "love one another".

What we ask from human love is an impossibility, a vicious contradiction. We do not wish to be loved conditionally. We should angrily repulse anyone who said: "I will love you as long as you are in good health. If you are ill, I won't love you any more." But at the same time we don't want a love which lumps us in with a mass of other people. We should repulse anyone who said "I love all blondes, and you neither more nor less than the others" or "I love all Parisiennes". What we want is an unconditional preference. But all the attributes which distinguish us from other people are conditional and may disappear. We deserve unconditionally only the amount of attention due to the most destitute of creatures; in other words, to something infinitely small.

And nevertheless it is true that we deserve not only to be preferred but to be loved uniquely, exclusively. But the thing in us which deserves that is the uncreated part of the soul, which is identical with the Son of God. When the self which is a composite of attributes has been destroyed and the uncreated part emerges, then "I no longer live in myself, but Christ lives in me"; whoever loves a man in that state and because he is in that state is loving Christ in the form of that man. It is an impersonal love.

To love in God is to love a person impersonally.

"Love your neighbour as yourself"—that means love him unconditionally; for love of self is unconditional. One may find oneself horrifying, but one still loves oneself.

Love's object is the good. To love an ordinary human being unconditionally one needs to have perceived in him an unconditional good.

There is no unconditional good in any man who has not

reached the state of mystical union, except the possibility of reaching it.

To love men unconditionally one must perceive in them thoughts which are subject to material mechanisms but whose vocation is towards the absolute good.

The aspiration for good exists in all men—for every man desires, and all desire is desire for good—and this aspiration for good, which is the very being of every man, is the one good which is always unconditionally present in every man.

One must love in all men either their desire or their possession of good, as the case may be.

Or, using a different vocabulary, one must love in all men either their desire or their possession of God.

That is what it is to love unconditionally. That is what it is to love human beings in God.

In hell, by definition, there is no longer the desire for good. Therefore it is impossible that one should suffer there.

What we love in other human beings is the hoped-for satisfaction of our desire. We do not love their desire. If what we loved in them was their desire, then we should love them as ourself. Because we do not love a good within ourself, but we adhere to a desire there.

Desire is always suffering, because it is unsatisfied. Reciprocally, all suffering is caused by unsatisfied desire. Love which adheres to the desire of another is compassion.

It is impossible to feel compassion for all desire unless one has contemplated the pure universal ideas of desire and of good; in other words, unless one has contemplated God.

If we contemplate the Good, we see every desire, even the most horrible, as an aspiration towards good, even though erroneous.

Instead of loving a human being for his hunger, we love him as food for ourselves. We love like cannibals. To love purely is to love the hunger in a human being. Then, since all men are always hungry, one always loves all men. The hunger of a few men is partly satisfied; in them one ought to love both their hunger and its satisfaction.

But the way we actually do love is very different. Thanks to their companionship, their words, or their letters, we get comfort, energy, and stimulation from the people we love. They affect us in the same way as a good meal after a hard day's work. So we love them like food. It is indeed an anthropophagous love.

And our hatred, our indifference, are anthropophagous too. You were hungry and you have eaten me.

And indeed we ought to eat him.

Is this kind of affection legitimate towards those who are no longer themselves, those in whom Christ lives?

Surely, towards them and towards them only.

Because in them desire and satisfaction and the nourishment they provide for others are all one and the same thing.

But when love is directed towards them it cannot be a possessive love. Just as a man who buys a Greek statue cannot feel he is its proprietor—unless he is a brute—although he has paid money for it. Pure good eludes all particular relationships.

Apart from this kind of love, all human relationships are ghoulish. To love someone means to love drinking his blood.

Whenever affection is at all violent it means that life is a stake. One can only love purely if one has renounced life.

He who loves his life loves his kindred and friends in the way Ugolino loved his children. Nothing is real for the man who loves in this way.

Reality only becomes perceptible for the man who accepts death.

That is the meaning of "By renunciation feed upon this universe".

What greater gift could have been offered to created beings than the gift of death?

It is death alone that teaches us we have no existence except as a thing among a lot of other things.

[How can the resemblance be explained between the Apocalypse and the poem of Nonnus? Did Nonnus copy the Apocalypse? But if so, why? Or is the Apocalypse of Orphic or Egyptian inspiration?]

Both our love and our reason are subject to this paradox: that they are universal faculties which can only respond to particular objects.

Conceive this observation as a theorem.

It is only God who combines in unity the universal and the particular. God is a universal person. Someone who is everything.

We do not love humanity, we love a particular man. This is not a legitimate love; it is only legitimate to love humanity.

But to love divinity and God in particular is all one love.

In God the universal and the particular are identical. In this world they are locked together by a harmony. That harmony is the Incarnation. We ourselves should live by this harmony. It is the true life.

To be able to love in our neighbour the hunger that consumes him and not the food he offers for the appeasement of our own hunger—this implies a total detachment.

It implies that one renounces feeding on man and wants in future to feed only on God.

But God's substance only feeds, at the beginning anyway, a point in our soul that is so deeply embedded in the centre that we are unaware of its existence.

The rest of the soul is hungry and wants to feed on man.

Only those can be saved who are held back by something against the impulse to approach what they love; they are those in whom the feeling for beauty has given rise to contemplation.

Perhaps that is why Plato says that beauty alone has come down from heaven to earth to save us.

Here below, to look and to eat are two different things. We have to choose one or the other. They are both called loving. The only people who have any hope of salvation are those who occasionally stop and look for a time, instead of eating.

"One eats the fruit, the other looks at it."

The eternal part of the soul feeds on hunger.

When we do not eat, our organism consumes its own flesh and transforms it into energy. It is the same with the soul. The soul which does not eat consumes itself. The eternal part consumes the mortal part of the soul and transforms it.

The hunger of the soul is hard to bear, but there is no other remedy for our disease.

To make the perishable part of the soul die of hunger while the body is still alive. In this way a body of flesh passes directly into God's service.

Plato, *Laws*: Ἀγύμναστον ὅτι μάλιστα ποιεῖν τὴν τῶν ἡδονῶν

ῥώμην τὴν ἐπίχυσιν καὶ τροφὴν αὐτῆς διὰ πόνων ἄλλοσε τρέποντα τοῦ σώματος.

"So far as possible, cause the power of the sensual pleasures to atrophy by diverting their flow, and what feeds it, towards other parts of the body, by means of work."

Extremely accurate. The energy in the seed is nourishment for the sexual organs and their activity, but also for other organs and their activity. If other organs consume that energy, sexuality dies of inanition.

One can project sexuality upon any kind of object: collector's hobby, money, power, group membership, cat, canary, God (but in this case it won't be the true God).

Or one can kill sexuality and effect a transmutation of the energy it contained.

This operation is what detachment is.

Every attachment is of the same nature as sexuality. In that, Freud is right (but only in that).

God has deposited in us a supplementary energy. It is the talent in the parable. Some exploit it themselves automatically, to the accompaniment of sensual pleasure. Others give it as food to the better part of their soul.

Mark: "The earth bringeth forth fruit of herself", "automatē".[1] Hence automatism. This passage shows, as clearly and precisely as possible, that there is a spiritual mechanics with laws as rigorous as our mechanics, only different.

σπείρων, the sower; the same word is used for the male who impregnates the female. There is certainly this double meaning in the Gospel parables about the seed. "The seed is the word of God".[2] The seed is breath of fire, pneuma. The seed which entered the Virgin was the Holy Spirit, pneuma hagion. The Holy Spirit is also the seed which falls on every soul. To receive it, the soul must become simply a matrix, a vessel; something plastic and passive, like water. Then the seed becomes an embryo, and at last a child; Christ is born in the soul. What used to be called "I" and "me" is destroyed, liquefied; and in place of it there is a new being, grown from the seed that fell from God into the soul. That is what it is to be born anew; to be born from on high; to be born of water and the spirit; to be born of God and not of the will of man or the will of the flesh. After this operation, "I no longer live, but Christ lives in me". It is a

[1] Mark 4: 28: αὐτομάτη ἡ γῆ καρποφορεῖ   [2] Luke 8: 11.

different being that has been engendered by God, a different "I", which is hardly "I", because it is the Son of God. There are no "adopted children". There is no adoption except in the sense that, as a parasite lays its eggs in an animal's flesh, God places a sperm in our soul which, when it has grown, will be his Son. It is thus that celestial Aphrodite, who is Wisdom, emerges from the sea. Our soul ought to be nothing except a place of welcome and nourishment for this divine germ. We ought not to give food to our soul. We ought to give our soul as food for this germ. After which it will itself obtain direct nourishment from everything that formerly nourished our soul. Our soul is the egg within which this divine germ grows to a bird. As an embryo, the bird feeds on the egg; once it has grown it breaks the shell and emerges and pecks for grain. Our soul is shut off from all reality by an enclosing skin of egoism, subjectivity, and illusion; the germ of Christ, placed in our soul by God, feeds on this; when it has grown enough it breaks the soul, explodes it, and makes contact with reality. That is Love in the microcosm. Love in the macrocosm, when once its golden wings have grown, breaks the egg of the world and passes to the place beyond the sky.

Farmers' wives who keep chickens ought to be told about these symbols and their meaning.

Baptism is an act of sympathetic magic. Just as water is sprinkled in order to bring rain, so baptism is an act representing a new birth with a view to bringing about a real new birth.

To go through baptism in the belief that it will lead to a new birth is to testify that one really desires it; and therefore one should receive it.

To have a child baptized is to testify that one desires a new birth for him. Therefore one ought to help him to achieve it.

These results will only happen if one is really thinking of new birth and if one really believes in the efficacy of the sacrament.

It is only an external form, whatever it may be, whose efficacity in itself, as a form, one believes in, that enables the soul to exert an equally real action upon itself on the spiritual plane as on the plane of obligations. The body is the indispensable intermediary through which the soul brings real action to bear upon itself. Suppose a large sum of money is entrusted to me on deposit. I would like to have it for myself. Its return is called for. I would still like to have it for myself; but my body goes with the money to the appointed place, leaves it there, and returns without it. After a time I forget it. My soul has become detached from it.

I can push my body further towards the good than the point my soul is at; so the body pulls the soul after it.

This operation is carried out continually on the plane of obligations, and any other way of proceeding is imaginary.

But on the spiritual plane the same operation is only possible if one is sure that a certain physical form of behaviour possesses spiritual efficacity. It may have any form whatsoever, but it must be a definite form. Whatever is physically sensible must necessarily have a particular existence. The choice of the form is arbitrary; but a choice must have been made; and it must not seem to have been arbitrary, or even that there was any choice.

Always the same paradox in the relation between universal and particular.

The selected form is a convention between man and man, but entered into for the sake of good and consequently ratified by God.

In order that the form may be an object of certainty, one must believe it to have been established by a God-inspired man or, preferably, by God himself incarnate in the world.

Is it a good thing, or a bad, that the sacraments should be subject to social conditions?

It seems to me that it is altogether bad, and that priests ought not to have the power to withhold a sacrament. They should simply warn the faithful that the sacrament is an ordeal and involves a risk.

It seems to me that a sacrament which is subject to social conditions is no longer a sacrament.

The devil, who is the master of everything social in this world, interposes himself between man and God.

Zeno the Stoic: animal seed is a fire—The sperm is emitted and received by the effect of love, and so is the lightning, which is the flash of love that links Heaven and Earth. The fiery animal seed is also breath of life, and in the same way the lightning is identified with the Holy Spirit.

The moon evokes a serpent; does not the lightning also evoke a serpent?

Justin's interpretation of baptism. Birth proceeds from the mixed male and female fluids. To cleanse the defilement of such a birth one must vanish and re-emerge from a water which is pure.

In the seminal fluid water and fire are mingled. Their separation is death. One merges into a pure water and the fire of heaven comes down to it and creates from it a new living being.

"Born anew from water and spirit",[1] that is to say, from the primordial elements; the man has undergone a new creation. More than new birth. New creation.

One part of the soul wishes to fulfil an obligation, such as returning a deposit; another part does not wish it. They struggle. The body is the arbiter. It is only the body that can be the balance upon which the soul is weighed against itself. In a sense the body is the judge, just as the balance judges between weight and weight. As the Cross is the balance between heaven and earth, so is the body between the soul and the soul.

It is this that is the body's eminent dignity.

It is the body that eats, but it is also the body that fasts. It is the flesh that sleeps, but it is also the flesh that keeps watch.

Obligations imply action, and the body is the appropriate arbiter of the soul's conflicts about action.

But there is a more profound conflict—the conflict about the soul's regeneration. One part of the soul desires the light that regenerates, another part does not desire it. Spiritual regeneration is not an act, it is not a series of movements, it is nothing upon which the will can get a hold. But nevertheless the body is the only balance that weighs the soul against the soul.

Therefore the conflict will remain undecided, the choice will not be made, unless there is some bodily act which is linked, by convention, with the regeneration of the soul in the same way that the bodily act of taking the deposited money back to its owner is linked, by nature, with honesty. It must be a convention with God, between God and the man. This is what is called a sacrament.

Since spiritual regeneration is a change which is undergone by anyone who desires it, and is not a willed action, it is appro-

---

[1] *Souffle* (breath, πνεῦμα).

priate that the bodily rite which is conventionally linked with it should be something which is conferred by someone else when it has been asked for.

That also is part of the definition of a sacrament.

But there should be no conditions attached, beyond the fact of asking for it. Spiritual regeneration is subject to no condition except a true desire. Asking, which is the sensible image of desire, ought to be the sole condition for receiving the sensible image of regeneration.

If a man truly believes that the rite will really bring about his regeneration, the fact of asking for it implies doing such violence to the evil within him that all the other circumstances accompanying his request are insignificant by comparison. To kneel in the snow for three days and nights would add nothing to the difficulty. To condemn to death the evil within oneself is so difficult as to be at the extreme limit of possibility. Nothing can be more difficult.

But to make a request of this kind only reaches the extreme limit of difficulty if one is certain that the rite one is asking for will involve the death of the evil within oneself.

That is why faith is an indispensable intermediary for making the body an arbiter in the spiritual conflict of the soul with itself.

Faith creates the truth to which it adheres. The certainty that a rite or ceremony gives spiritual regeneration confers that efficacy on it; and this is not the effect of a phenomenon of suggestion, which would imply illusion and falsehood, but of the mechanism here analysed.

The domain of faith is the domain of truths created by certainty. It is in this domain that faith is legitimate and is a virtue. A virtue creative of truth.

It is necessary to discriminate this domain.

If one does something with the certainty that one is obeying God and with no other motive or intention than this obedience, it is certain that one is obeying God.

But does it follow that, with this intention, one may do anything whatsoever?

This is the great problem; it is the problem of the *Gita*.

I still do not properly understand it.

There are three mysteries, three incomprehensible things, in this world. Beauty, justice, and truth.

They are the three things recognized by all men as standards for everything in the world. The incomprehensible is the standard for the known.

What wonder if terrestrial life is impossible!

We are like flies caught inside a bottle, attracted to the light and unable to go towards it.

Nevertheless, it is better to remain stuck inside the bottle throughout the whole of time than to turn away from the light for a single moment.

Will you have pity, O Light, and break the glass, at the end of this perpetual duration?

Even if not—one must stay pressed against the glass.

One needs to have traversed the perpetual duration of time within a finite period of time. In order that this contradiction may be possible it is necessary that the part of the soul which is on the level of time—the part that reasons discursively and measures—should be destroyed.

It can only be destroyed by an affliction which it accepts or by a joy so intense as to plunge it in pure meditation. Or are there still other ways?

The Zen Buddhist technique of the koan is a method for effecting this destruction.

And perhaps Plato possessed a method of this kind, in what he called dialectics?

For the part of the soul below the level of time, a finite duration is infinite. In the same way that there is an infinity of points in the length of a yard.

If the lower layer of the soul is laid bare and exposed through the destruction of the discursive part,[1] and if in this way perpetual duration is traversed within a finite lapse of time, and if throughout that perpetuity the soul remains turned towards the eternal light, then perhaps in the end the eternal light will have pity and will envelop the entire soul within its eternity.

That part of mathematics which concerns diverse orders of infinities (theory of wholes, topology) contains a treasury of infinitely precious images which can be applied to supernatural truths.

When the lower layer of the soul is laid bare and turned

[1] i.e. the part of the soul that is on the level of time.

toward the eternal light, that is the separation and reunion of water and the fiery spirit; it is the transformation of which baptism is the symbol.

The union of pure water and the eternal light is the miracle of Cana, the transmutation of water into wine.

Trees and plants grow from the perfectly pure water which falls from the sky (the dew that feeds them) and from the light which falls from the sky. Vegetable sap and wine are mixtures of this heavenly water and fire. The chlorophyll of the sap has the property of fixing and crystallising the heavenly fire. Was it because they grow from this mixture of heavenly and pure elements that trees were worshipped? Is the metaphor of the tree of the world related to this?

On the other hand the water and the fiery spirit from which man is born are fleshly, earthly, and impure.

Was it the original purpose of hanging to transform the man into fruit on a tree, annulling his carnal birth in exchange for a new birth from the heavenly water and fire? If so, it would be the same symbol as baptism, which would explain the link between Christ's baptism and his death on the Cross.

Just as baptism by immersion is a simulated drowning, so there may have been an initiation ceremony which was a simulated hanging. That would explain the epithets applied to Odin, to Arcadian Artemis (according to Frazer), etc.

It may be that all these punishments were originally initiation ceremonies which symbolized regeneration.

[N.B. When it is supposed that ritual simulated killings are a survival of primitive human sacrifice, the opposite is no less possible. It could quite equally legitimately be supposed that human sacrifices were a corruption of ceremonies in which originally the killing was only simulated.]

In the middle ages it was attempted to bring the guilty to the virtue of repentance before execution, and it may be that in primitive times it was thought that punishment inflicted by the law should be at the same time a sacrament leading to the guilty man's regeneration.

It is a sublime thought.

The sword of the law should be like the sword of Rama, whose contact, when it cut a man's head off, sent the man to heaven.

But naturally the Hebrews, who had divested religion of all spirituality, regarded hanging as a malediction.

For this reason, the crucifixion can have a double meaning.

The intermediate part of the soul, which disorders every soul which is a bad compound of water and the spirit, must be destroyed so as to leave the vegetative part directly exposed to the fiery spirit which comes from beyond the heavens.

Denude oneself of everything that is above the vegetative life. Lay bare the vegetative level and forcibly turn it towards the heavenly light.

Destroy everything in the soul that is not closely allied to matter. Expose naked to the heavenly light that part of the soul which is little more than inert matter.

The perfection proposed to us is the direct union of the divine spirit with inert matter. A perfect image of perfection is inert matter regarded as thinking matter.

This is the justification for what the Hebrews called idolatry.

But better than a carven idol is something without a human face: such as a stone, or bread, or a star.

If we imagine a spirit combined with the sun, that is a perfect image of perfection.

That is why this universe made of inert matter is beautiful. More beautiful than the most beautiful human beings.

The inertia of matter corresponds to the justice of divine thought.

A human thought can dwell in the flesh. But if a thought dwells in inert matter, it can only be divine.

Therefore, if a man is changed into a perfect being and his thought is replaced by divine thought, his flesh, beneath its aspect of living flesh, has become in a sense a dead body.

A man has to die and his corpse be reanimated by a living breath which comes directly from above the heavens.

If God can incarnate himself in an ordinary man at a certain moment of his life, why not in a seed within a woman's body?

Ideas based upon God's incarnation imply that spiritual rebirth is God's taking possession of a man. This implies a breach of continuity. Other ideas do not rise above the level of obligation and law.

To place divinity on the level of obligation is to transform society into an idol. That is why Protestantism, which puts morals in the foreground, declines irresistibly into a national religion. It places morality first because the idea of sacrament has become weakened.

The Reformation weakened the idea of sacrament because the sacraments had been usurped. When a society obtains the monopoly of the sacraments and grants them only upon conditions, there is usurpation.

When the devil offered Christ the kingdom of this world, he resisted the temptation. But his bride, the Church, yielded to it. And have not the gates of hell prevailed against her?

But the text of the Gospel, the Lord's Prayer, and the sacraments still retain their redemptive power. It is only in this sense that hell has not prevailed.

The word of Christ guarantees nothing more than this, and in particular it in no way guarantees perpetuity for Christianity.

(If Christianity disappeared, would it be followed in a few centuries' time by another religion, and would that religion arise from a new incarnation?)

Today, if a son of Jewish or atheist parents is baptized, this means that he is joining a social group, namely the Church, in the same way that by holding a political party's card he becomes a member of the party.

This is usurpation. The bride of Christ has behaved like Clytemnestra. A usurping and adulterous wife.

[A propos of Clytemnestra, and of Orestes being saved from the massacre and hidden in a foreign land, this same theme recurs everywhere; the theme of the infant God as a fugitive, in exile, kept hidden and brought up in secret. Zeus, Dionysus, Christ... This signifies, among other things, that the growth of the seed of supernatural love deposited in the soul must be kept profoundly secret even from the soul itself.]

The parable of the sower indicates that God continually sheds his grace with absolute impartiality upon all men; the parable of the workers of the eleventh hour indicates that God awards an absolutely equal recompense to all those who answer his call by devoting their bodies in obedience to him. After that, how can people dare to conceive of inequality in spiritual things? True, we find it in this world; but the reason for it must lie with men, and God effaces it in those whom he hides within himself.

God is conceived as the indirect cause of everything, but as the direct cause only of what is purely spiritual. Therefore, as regards indirect causality He is all-powerful; but this omnipotence defines itself as an abdication in favour of necessity. As regards direct causality, God's power in this world is something infinitely small.

Everything that is pure good is ordained by God. Everything that occurs, without any distinction, is permitted, that is to say consented to, by God. But this consent is an abdication. So it is not the exercise of a kingly power.

"Thy kingdom" is the pure good. "Thy kingdom come" means let evil disappear. What is asked for by this petition is the end of the world.

"Thy will be done"; but God's will is to abdicate in favour of necessity. So this petition implies consent to the existence of the world.

May thy kingdom come; and yet, since it is not thy will to reign here below, thy will be done.

One asks for the disappearance of the universe, and one consents to its presence.

Further on, one asks God's forgiveness for our existence and one forgives him for causing us to exist.

One consents to exist, but at the same time one asks to be delivered from evil, and consequently from existence.

Hallowed be thy name.

God has placed the skies between himself and us, in order to hide himself; he lets us have only one thing of his, which is his name. This name is really given to us. We can do what we want with it. We can attach it like a label to any created thing. But in doing so we profane it and it loses its virtue. It is only when it is spoken without imagining any representation of it that it has its virtue.

The creation is the word God speaks to us; and it is also God's name. Relation, which is divine Wisdom, is God's name.

A perfect man is God's name. (Microcosm.) His way of being hallowed is to be made a curse by being hung on the cross.

The very conception of Microcosm implies Incarnation. A human being whose soul is the Soul of the World.

In the material order, things between which there is no difference can be different. For example, one can conceive abstractly two identical pebbles.

But in the order of the good, what is identical is one; and two things are only two if they differ from one another.

Therefore a perfect man is God.

But in the order of the good there is only descent and no ascent. So God descended to dwell in this man.

The only way we can play a part in this operation is by a method resembling sympathetic magic. Australian sorcerers pour water on the ground in order to bring rain. In the same way we can descend in order to induce God to descend to us. That is what the virtue of humility is.

Descending movements are the only ones within our power. Ascending movements are imaginary.

The distinction between the order of the good and the order of existence throws light on all the mysteries about God.

We possess a little power. By abdicating from it and consenting to everything, we become all-powerful. For nothing can then happen without our assent.

Is that the hidden meaning of the words "All things are possible for the man who has faith"?

The connection expounded in the Gospel between faith and particular powers (healing, blighting a fig tree) is such a coarse idea as to be intolerable if taken literally. Or so it seems to me.

God abdicated from his divine omnipotence, and emptied himself. By abdicating from our small human power we become, as regards emptiness, equal to God.

The divine Word was equal to God in divinity. It emptied itself and became a slave. We can become equal to the divine Word in emptiness and slavery.

"None goes to the Father save by me", that is to say that humility is the only way.

The Incarnation is simply a figure of the Creation. God abdicated by giving us existence. By refusing it we abdicate and become, in that way, similar to God.

God created us in his image, that is to say he gave us the power to abdicate in his favour, just as he abdicated for us.

The virtue of humility is incompatible with the sense of belonging to a social group chosen by God, whether a nation (Hebrews, Romans, Germans, etc.) or a Church.

How can the sacraments be rescued from a usurping social organization? By killing the dragon who guards the treasure?

The idea of the unconditional virtue of the sacraments has

perfect beauty. But it ought never to be possible to withhold a sacrament.

Administer the sacraments in such a way that nobody can have any cause for drawing back from them, except through hatred and fear of the good. That is far from being the case now. It is possible to have legitimate reasons for holding back. Which is a scandal.

If the heavenly Father bestows sunlight and rain on the just as well as the unjust, certain sacraments ought to be bestowed without any discrimination of any kind.

Discrimination is called for only in the sacrament of ordination, because to be ordained a priest involves responsibility.

The Church tries to use Paradise for blackmail and to damn anyone who rejects her infallibility.

She will only become holy if she abdicates by renouncing her power to withhold the sacraments.

Even absolution ought to be granted to whoever asks for it, though he should be warned that if he receives it without true repentance it will make for his condemnation, and he should be encouraged to solicit such a penance as will drive repentance like a nail into his soul. But after this warning he should be given what he wants.

Give whatever is asked. This facility is precisely the thing that could inspire in people's souls a sacred awe.

Exercise spiritual authority only when a spiritual directive has been asked for; but exercise it then with severity. Encourage people to seek spiritual direction.

But there should never be any element of social constraint. All obedience should be freely consented.

Christ expressly forbade his followers to seek authority and power. Therefore his Congregation (the Church) ought not to be a society.

If one is alone, shut up in one's room, one is heard by the Father who is in secret. If two or three are gathered together in the name of Christ, he is there. Apparently there ought not to be more than three.

A child who is naughty and disobedient and does silly things under the eyes of his mother—because he feels that while she is there he is safe from consequences—becomes alarmed at his freedom when he is far away from her.

In the same way, if the faithful were always granted whatever they asked, in spiritual matters, they would begin to be frightened and to seek refuge in God.

By attaching conditions to communion, the terror and majesty which ought to accompany this mystery are eliminated. Moses lifted up the serpent of bronze and whoever had been bitten could look on it.

It is through lack of faith that the sacraments have been hedged round with conditions.

Either this will be changed, or Christianity will perish.

In any case, a new religion is needed. Either a Christianity so modified as to have become a different thing; or something else.

Poetic Edda. Gold = water's flame. Guarded by a fish (? pike).

Plato classifies metals as being of water. Gold is water combined with fire.

Symbol of new creation of the soul.

Was not alchemy a method for decomposing impure matter, separating out its water and fire, and combining them in gold? And did not the method imply that each chemical operation must be accompanied by the corresponding spiritual operation?

The flame of water. That is why gold had curative virtue.

China. "Vegetable gold."

Analogy between gold and vegetable sap. The alchemists regarded the production of gold as a sort of spiritual marriage.

There is a passage in some book of alchemy about the nakedness of the bridegroom and bride when, after the preliminary betrothal and wedding ceremonies, they come to the nuptial union.

Union of pure water and fire.

Precious stones too are a union of water and fire.

The stone that provides food, the Provençal Grail, equivalent of the Eucharist. Christ also is both stone and bread.

There must have been some cults in which a precious stone was worshipped.

A power comes to reside in any object which has been approached with intense feeling by large numbers of men. To adore this power is idolatry. True adoration consists in contemplating such an object with the thought that it has become divine through a convention ratified by God.

But the Jews who prayed in the Temple and nowhere else were as "idolatrous" as the pagans.

Just as any collection of syllables may be by convention the name of God, so any piece of matter may by convention contain the presence of God. Thus one may by convention speak, hear, see, touch and eat God.

It is only in this way that the body can arbitrate, like a balance, in the conflict between that part of the soul which desires God's presence and the part which feels horror at it.

The revolt of all the mediocre part of the soul is a sign that the presence of God is real.

God's presence cuts the soul in two; the good on one side, the evil on the other. It is a sword. There is nothing else that produces this effect. So God's presence can be proved.

God is the Good. He is neither a thing nor a person nor a thought. But in order to grasp him we have to conceive him as a thing, a person, and a thought.

Love consents to all things and commands only those who are willing to obey. Love is abdication. God is abdication.

The good is never a product of evil, but evil is in a sense produced by good.

Evil is between God and us; love has to pass across it.

Love consents to be an object of hatred.

God allows evil to exist. We ought to do the same for any evil that we have no means of destroying. We ought to allow evil to exist outside ourselves. But only outside ourselves. That is to say, beyond our power of control.

Storm. Lightning strikes at the sea. Then the rainbow appears, the pact between God and the world. Is not this celestial Aphrodite? Is not the rainbow, a mixture of divine water and fire, the girdle of Aphrodite?

Apocalypse. If the sacrificed Christ is the universal redeemer, he must be the redeemer of the blessed angels. Consequently, Christ must have been sacrificed for the first time at the separation of the good and the bad angels—what theology calls the "second moment" of the Creation. There is here a singular conception of an original chaos in which good and evil were everywhere mixed—the devil being before the face of God—and which was followed by a violent separation which left the heavens to the exclusive rule of God, and the earth to the devil.

What are the resemblances and what are the differences between this idea and the Manichaean doctrine?

The good angels triumph in the blood of the Lamb. The Lamb is, in a sense, slaughtered in heaven before being slaughtered on earth. Who slays it?

The devil comes down to earth. At this moment original sin appears. The serpent was in heaven; it falls to earth and climbs into the tree.

The woman must be the Holy Spirit.[1]

A time, times, and half a time. Half seven times.

[Hammer, a Nordic sacred symbol? Why?]

[The wolf son of Loki is chained by a chain made of six things which *do not exist*: (sound of cat's footfall—woman's beard—mountain's root—nerve (?) of bear—breath of fish—bird's saliva). There is a limit, agreed by pact, to the possible transformations of matter.]

[The pact which led to the wolf being chained by something impossible cost a God his right hand.

Necessity, compromise between God and matter.]

Snorri: "The third root of the ash (Yggdrasil) stands in heaven, and beneath this root is a spring which is very holy and is called Urth's well. There the gods have their judgement seat, and thither they ride each day over Bifrost, which is called also the God's Bridge (the rainbow)". Confirmed by the *Poetic Edda*.

There are three Parcae: Past, Present, Future. Urth is the Past. Therefore her well is the same as "the cold water which gushes from the lake of Memory" in the Orphic poem.[2] This confirms what Snorri says about the Thracian origin of the Scandinavian divinities.

---

[1] The woman of Revelation 12: 1.
[2] H. Diels: *Fragmente der Vorsokratiker*, 5th edn., I, p. 415.

It is this water from the well of the Past that keeps the tree of the world always green.

If the Jewish people had really been a chosen people, Christ would not have chosen to be born among them when he was made a curse.[1] His birth was in the territory of the two accursed peoples, Rome and Israel.

If Christ had recognized Israel as being elect, the difference between his attitude towards the Pharisees and towards the Samaritans would be unintelligible.

Christ was made a curse. And so was his Bride, the Church. But in quite a different way.

Hell shall not prevail. This means only that so long as the sacraments are administered they will possess all their virtue for whoever receives them with a pure heart.

"Salted with fire." An obvious allusion to the baptismal rite of passing through fire, which is referred to with so much horror in the Old Testament. Demeter[2] salted Neoptolemus[3] with fire. Or at least she began to do so.

It is strange that he who said "Another shall come, who will baptize with the Holy Ghost and with fire" should be the patron of the festival at which people jump across bonfires.[4]

"Everyone shall be salted with fire"[5] could be taken to be as imperative as "whoever is not born of water and the spirit". Why is there no sacrament whose material is fire?

It is impossible that the whole truth should not be present at every time and every place, available for anyone who desires it. "Whoever asks for bread." Truth is bread. It is absurd to suppose that for centuries nobody, or hardly anybody, desired the truth, and then that in the following centuries it was desired by whole peoples.

When peoples lacked the truth, like the Jews before Nebuchadnezzar, the Romans, and others, it was because they refused it.

The Jews and the Romans together crucified Christ. But they

---

[1] Galatians 3: 13: κατάρα. [2] Thetis? [3] Achilles?
[4] Les feux de St. Jean (see p. 332). [5] Mark 9: 49.

did even worse to him when Christianity became the religion of the Empire with the Old Testament as a sacred book.

Would it not be the Church established in this way that is the false prophet with horns like a lamb and the tongue of a serpent?[1]

Whatever has not been available at all times and places to whoever desires the truth is itself something other than truth.

It is because of insufficiency of faith that it is felt necessary to add social belief to it. That is why the Church's social usurpation has been accepted. The Inquisition protects everyone against the temptation of doubt. Knowing that to doubt will mean death, one knows one ought not to doubt.

Except for rebellious natures, on whom it has the opposite effect. But what is it that has made them so rebellious?

Social constraint produces such a good imitation of all the effects of faith—and with the advantage of not saving the soul!

Perhaps the forbidden fruit, for unborn souls, is the spectacle of carnal love. They are forbidden to descend to it—they do descend—they become incarnate. Perhaps that is what the transcendantal choice is.

Perhaps the state of soul of two lovers at the moment of union is the instantaneous form of a destiny which will unwind itself throughout a whole life.

Perhaps that state of soul depends partly upon the configuration of the stars at that moment (cosmic rays).

(If God is between the couple, like a two-edged sword, at the actual moment of union, the child is holy from birth. Is it possible?)

If we are born in sin, it is evident that birth constitutes a sin.

The soul comes down and incarnates itself in order to know good and evil. On high, it knows only good (Cathar tradition).

Is this the meaning of the forbidden door in so many folk tales?

The parable of the good seed and the tares is absolutely Manichaean. God sowed good seed only. It is the devil who sows tares. God lets them both grow together until the good is fully ripe, because they are so intertwined that it would be impossible to destroy one without the other. The harvest is the end of the world.

[1] A reference to Revelation 13: 11?

God having produced pure good, the devil mixed evil with it in such a way that God can no longer separate them without destroying both.

Stories of testing and weeding out in the folk tales.

The devil is really very strong.

God cannot make this world better. He could only destroy it. He chooses to let it be, so that the good may mature.

And why not? Evil can do no harm to what is good. It hurts only the mediocre.

The cross hurts the impenitent thief, but not the good thief, nor Christ.

Biology. A product that inhibits a reaction is a product resembling the catalytic agent of that reaction.

Exactly like the serpents of the desert and the serpent of bronze, etc.

Admirable.

I think science ought to consist entirely of such images.

Science ought to be as stimulating to explore as folklore.

This symbolic language of God's is as valuable as any sacred Scriptures.

God can become a piece of bread, a stone, a tree, a lamb, a man. But He cannot become a people. No people can become an incarnation of God.

The Devil is the collective. (Which in Durkheim is the divinity.) This is clearly indicated in the Apocalypse by that beast which is so obviously the Great Beast of Plato.

Pride is the devil's characteristic attribute. And pride is a social thing. πλεονεξία.—Pride is the instinct of social conservation. Humility is the acceptance of social death.

I am more and more afraid that in the Apocalypse the False Prophet represents, in the author's mind, the Church.

(N.B. what is the date of the earliest mention of the Apocalypse?)

The mortal blow that the Beast received, was it not the crucifixion of Christ? And when the Beast revived, was it not through the adoption of Christianity as the official religion? Perhaps the author of the Apocalypse simply foresaw that event. Christians must have hoped for it and thought about it long before Constantine. They could have hoped for it from Piso;

and the Apocalypse seems to have been written at just about that time, in the reign of Galba.

Would not the book's essential purpose be a warning against that corruption of Christianity?

No people has ever been assimilated to God.

The Devil is the father of all prestige, and prestige is social. "Opinion, queen of the world." Therefore opinion is the devil. Prince of this world.

If two or three of you are gathered together in my name, I shall be there with you.

But suppose there are four? Would it be the devil who was among them?

Perhaps.

Then what about the Councils?

Perhaps . . .

Luckily, "the gates of hell shall not prevail". There remains an incorruptible nucleus of truth.

God as stone, tree, animal, man, etc. Grail, Yggdrasil, Lamb, Christ.

Assuming it ever existed, the philosopher's stone, which enabled entropy to be reversed, must on this account have contained a requalifying energy.

That is why there is so much in the alchemists about the generative power.

[Did they try to compound their own into a chemical preparation?

Cf. folklore stories about placing one's life outside oneself.

Cf. what V.D. said to me about Christ at the Last Supper.]

"Out of their belly shall flow rivers of living water." This might have a very precise meaning in Plato's physiology. See the *Timaeus*.

Why does not the reunion of two or three Christians in the name of Christ count as a sacrament?

In the Bible it is always: You shall put your enemies to flight, you shall massacre them, etc., so that your God shall be manifest. It is never: You shall send corn to relieve famines, etc., so that your God . . .

The devil who came to Christ, offering to accomplish for him the centuries-old promises to the Messiah, who else could it be but Jehovah? (One aspect of Jehovah—because there is another aspect of Jehovah which is the true God.)

Mei Ti—end of 6th or beginning of 5th century B.C.
"If men loved the bodies of others as they love their own, who would wound or kill? If they loved the goods of others as their own, who would steal? If the prince of the State loved other States as his own, who would commit aggression?"
But "He who loves others will be loved in his turn; he who benefits others will reap benefit in his turn".
"All these injustices [theft, killing] are disapproved by decent people everywhere, but if injustice expands to the point of attacking another State, then they no longer disapprove of these things, but call them justice . . . They are like a man who sees one black spot and calls it black, but when he sees a mass of black spots he calls it white . . . "

Tantalus—surrounded by food and drink which he can never grasp, for all his desperate straining.
It is the same with men and the good. We are surrounded on all sides and continually solicited by the good, and yet the strongest will and the most violent efforts cannot procure us a tiny part of it.
Make no effort, remain motionless, beseech in silence.
If Tantalus had stayed quite motionless among the fruits and living springs, Zeus would have had pity in the end and given him food and drink.
By patience, exhaust God's patience.
To anyone who stays motionless, waiting with equal docility for good or evil or the absence of both of them, God can only do good.
Tantalus is too stupid to learn, even after endless time, that

since his efforts are certainly useless immobility would be more becoming.

A strong will can obtain many things. For example, Napoleon. Many things, but not the good. Not even an atom of good.

Humanity as a whole is Tantalus.

The story of Tantalus, son of Zeus, the first murderer (cf. Cain), represents in the Greek mythology a version of the story of original sin. The story of Niobe is another version. In some of the accounts she is the daughter of the first man. Her fault was in believing that her children belonged to her.

Tamed by experience, Tantalus averts his eyes and keeps his mouth shut, biting his lips, when the fruit-laden branches bend towards him. But when the fruit is actually brushing his lips he cannot resist trying to seize it. Then the branch swings away, far into the sky; and Tantalus, in a frenzy of raging thirst, drinks from the nearest stream, which fills his mouth with dust.

I am often like that.

In what sense is Tantalus' punishment eternal? It is so because Tantalus is incapable of a motion of love. But if through love of the will of Zeus he gave up trying to assuage his thirst and hunger, his torment would come to an end some day.

That God is the good is a certainty. It is a definition. And it is even certain that God—in some way that I do not know—is reality. This is certain, and not a matter of faith. But it is an object of faith that every thought of mine which is a desire for good brings me nearer to the good. It is only by experience that I can test this. And even after the experience it is still not an object of proof but only of faith.

To possess the good consists in desiring the good; therefore the relevant article of faith—which is the sole article of true faith—is concerned with fecundity, with the self-multiplying faculty of every desire for good.

From the mere fact that a part of the soul truly and purely and exclusively desires the good, it follows that at a later point in time a larger part of it will desire the good—unless it refuses to consent to this development.

To believe that is to possess faith.

Is there really, as the Gospel seems to indicate, a connection between this and healing the possessed, walking on water, and moving mountains? The symbolic connection is clear. But is there a literal connection? At present this problem is beyond me.

x

Even materialists place somewhere outside themselves a good which far surpasses them, which helps them from outside, and towards which their thought turns in a movement of desire and prayer. For Napoleon it was his star. For Marxists it is History. But they place it in this world, like the giants of folklore who place their heart (or their life) inside an egg inside a fish in a lake guarded by a dragon; and who die in the end. And although their prayers are often granted, one fears they must be regarded as prayers addressed to the devil.

No human being escapes the necessity of conceiving some good outside himself towards which his thought turns in a movement of desire, supplication, and hope. Consequently, the only choice is between worshipping the true God or an idol. Every atheist is an idolater—unless he is worshipping the true God in his impersonal aspect. The majority of the pious are idolaters.

For every creative mind (poet, composer, mathematician, physicist, etc....) the unknown source of inspiration is this good to which a beseeching desire is directed. It is the continual experience of each of them that he is receiving inspiration.

But some of these minds conceive the source of inspiration as being above the sky, and others conceive it as below. Not that they express it in this way to themselves; or if some of them do, their way of explaining it to themselves or to others does not always correspond to their thought. But whatever words they use, or if they use none, they are in fact looking with expectation, desire, and supplication towards a source which is either above or below the sky. If it is above, there is authentic genius. If it is below, there is a more or less brilliant imitation of genius, sometimes much more brilliant than genius itself. Whether the source of inspiration is above or below the sky depends upon the nature of the good which is conceived to be contained within the inspiration. Inspiration from a source above the sky is conceived as nothing but obedience. In this case, inspiration is not desired for the sake of producing beautiful things, but there is a desire to produce beautiful things because inspiration is the source of the things that are truly beautiful. Seek first the kingdom and the justice of the heavenly Father, and then receive whatever is given.

Thus it is the place occupied in his soul by the desire for inspiration, totally irrespective of the opinions he may profess, that decides whether the attitude of an artist or a scientist is religious or idolatrous.

In the same way a picture can be said to be of pious or of idolatrous inspiration, totally irrespective of its subject.

To know that God is the good or, more simply, that the absolute good is the good, and to have faith that the desire for good is self-multiplying in the soul, provided that the soul does not withhold its consent from the operation—these two simple things are enough. Nothing else is needed.

Only, it is necessary to keep constant watch to prevent oneself from refusing to consent to the internal increase of the good—to prevent oneself unconditionally, no matter what may happen.

This certainty, this faith, and this watchfulness—they are all that is necessary for perfection.

It is infinitely simple.

But it is in this simplicity that the greatest difficulty lies. Our carnal thought has need of variety. Who could endure an hour's conversation with a friend, if the friend kept on repeating nothing but: God, God, God ... But variety means difference, and everything that differs from the good is evil.

The carnal part of the soul, which needs a variety of things, should occupy itself with the varied affairs of this world. But through all these various things, the fixed part of the soul should keep its gaze upon the fixed point where God dwells.

If a hollow sphere revolves there are only two immobile points and everything else, absolutely everything, moves. The intermediaries between the two points revolve, and yet the relation between them is immobile.

One of the two poles should be God, and the other the fixed point in the soul, that is to say, God's presence in the soul.

Because our lives are falsehood, the thing I call 'me' is not at the centre of my soul. That is why everything that directly concerns the centre of my soul is external to what I call 'me'.

And that is why all who are inspired, by no matter what sort of inspiration—it may be purely mundane, such as a mechanical invention—feel the inspiration as something external to themselves.

Or, again, one could argue in this way: How could there proceed from me more good than there is in me? If I make progress in the good it must be through the influence of some external good.

If the desire for good equals the possession of good, the desire for good is the producer of good, that is to say it produces the desire for good.

Outside me there is a good which is superior to me and which influences me for good every time that I desire the good.

Since there is no possible limit to this operation, this external good is infinite; it is God.

And even here it is not a question of belief but of certainty. The thought of the good inevitably involves all these thoughts, and it is impossible not to think of the good.

Since there is no limit to this operation, the soul must finally cease to be, through total assimilation to God.

At every stage of the transformation the soul may refuse a further stage. In this case, perhaps it remains for a time at the stage it has reached. But only for a time. It then falls back—and progressively, in the same way that it has climbed. But so long as the pure desire for good has not completely faded, so long as even a particle of it remains, the soul can recover itself and rise again. It will rise higher than the first time. But if, having risen higher, it again refuses, then the whole process is repeated.

A soul may attain by this oscillating progress to any height whatsoever; but it is a wretched way of progressing.

Is it possible to attain, in this world, to a point from which one cannot fall back again?

I have no idea.

I would like to believe it.

To lose, in this world, the capacity to choose between good and evil which we acquired through original sin—what could be more desirable.

τοῦτο....[1]

The soul's only choice is between travelling towards nothingness through more and more good or through more and more evil. The limit of both good and evil is nothingness. But it is not a matter of indifference whether one arrives at nothingness through good or through evil.

On the contrary, it is the only thing that matters and everything else is indifferent.

And why does it matter?

For no reason. It is important in itself. It is the only thing of unconditional importance.

[1] τοῦτο δός ἐμοί: grant me this.

But on an even higher level, absolutely nothing matters. For if I fall to the lowest depth of evil, that does no harm to the good.

Because we live in falsehood, we are under the illusion that happiness is what is unconditionally important.

If someone says: "How I would like to be rich!", his friend may answer: "Why? would it make you any happier?", but if someone says "I want to be happy", no one will answer "Why?"

Tell me your reasons for wanting to be happy.

Or if someone is hurt and wants help. Tell me your reasons for wanting help.

Frivolous questions. Who would dare ask them?

But we ought to put them to ourselves and to reflect that, in the first place, one has no reason for wanting to be happy, and then that happiness is not a thing to be desired without reason, unconditionally; for it is only the good that is to be desired in this way.

That is the foundation of Plato's thought.

It is a thought so contrary to nature that it can only arise in a soul which is entirely consumed by the fire of the Holy Spirit, as no doubt the Pythagoreans were.

So it has not been understood, or even perceived, in Plato's works.

The same criticism applies to happiness when it is glorified as eternal felicity, eternal life, Paradise, etc. Happiness of every kind should be criticized in this way, and satisfaction of every kind.

St. John does not say: we shall be happy because we see God; but: we shall be like God, because we shall see Him as he is.

We shall be pure good.

We shall no longer exist. But in that nothingness which is at the limit of good we shall be more real than at any moment of our earthly life. Whereas the nothingness which is at the limit of evil is without reality.

Reality and existence are two things, not one.

That too is a central thought of Plato's; and equally little understood.

> (Justin, St. Augustine, etc., said that Plato had learned from Moses that God is Being. But from whom did he learn that God is the Good, and that the Good is higher than Being? Not from Moses.)

Whenever we find ourselves thinking this kind of thing: "I must find happiness", "I must eat", "I must get rid of this pain", "I must avoid this danger", "I must get news of such-and-such a friend", and all the other thoughts involving "I must", we should reply coldly to ourselves "I don't see the necessity".

And all the more when the thought is "Nevertheless, I must..."

It is easy to make that reply, but to be as completely convinced of it as Talleyrand was when he made it to the beggar is not so easy.

Yet why should I not succeed, through love of God, in loving myself as little as Talleyrand, through hardness of heart, loved the beggar?

Can love of God have less power than egoism over our sensibility?

Praise to God and compassion to creatures. There is no contradiction when we reflect that, in creating, God abdicated. One must approve God's creative abdication and be glad to be oneself a creature, a secondary cause, with the right to perform actions in this world.

A victim of misfortune is lying in the road, half dead of hunger. God pities him but cannot send him bread. But I am here and luckily I am not God; I can give him a piece of bread. It is my one point of superiority over God.

"I was hungry and you fed me." God can beg for bread for the afflicted, but he cannot give it to them.

In the Roman Empire people were so desperate, deracinated, submerged in boredom and disgust, that there was only one thought that could appeal to them: the imminence of the end of the world. This thought, this expectation, which was encouraged by various prophecies, must have existed throughout the whole Empire. But the Christians alone, it seemed, had a palpable proof. After the destruction of Jerusalem the certainty seemed even greater.

Both their success and their reputation as criminals must surely have been due to their message about the end of the world.

People committed suicide with extraordinary facility at that time; but the foundations of social life were so rotted that suicide was not enough; it left too much horror intact. The expectation of the end of the world was a collective, a cosmic equivalent of suicide.

They really believed the end of the world was coming, and they called it "the good news".

"My Lord, what a morning—when the stars begin to fall!" They were just about as happy as American Negro slaves.

It is not surprising that this good news had such a success among the slaves.

Apocalypse. If the heavenly birth referred to is that of Jesus Christ (and not of the lamb before the foundation of the world) (but it is a question), then it was when Jesus was born that St. Michael threw Satan down to earth from heaven. Until then he was in heaven, before the face of God, accusing men.

It is very strange.

"Woe to the inhabiters of the earth and of the sea! for the devil is come down unto you, having great wrath, because he knoweth that he hath but a short time."

"And I saw the dragon... persecuting the woman... and he stood upon the sand by the sea.

And I saw a beast rise up out of the sea... and the dragon gave him his power, and his throne, and great authority..."

This accords with the feeling that on the whole there is—perhaps—less good upon earth since Christ than before.

The reign of Augustus was fairly established only a short time before the birth of Christ. With only a slight disparity of dates one could say that the domination of the world (as the world was then conceived) fell to Rome at about the same time that Christ was born.

The Beast must surely be Rome.

But the reign of the Beast is still continuing today.

What is the other Beast, with horns like a lamb and speaking like a serpent, who received the power from the first beast and caused it to be worshipped?[1]

There must be some Protestants who say it is the Church.

Atreus, in Seneca: "Laus vera et humili saepe contingit

[1] Revelation 13: 11 ff.

viro—non nisi potenti falsa."[1] So falsehood is the advantage enjoyed by power. That is why it is a gift of the devil.

Seneca:
"Jam tempus illi fecit aerumnas leves.
—Erras; malorum sensus accrescit die;
leve est miserias ferre, perferre est grave."[2]

id.:
.... nec ventrem improbum
alimus tributo gentium, nullus mihi
ultra Getas metatur et Parthos ager,
non ture colimur nec meae excluso Jove
ornantur arae.[3]

And behold, a woman in the city, which was a sinner, when she knew that he sat at meat in the Pharisee's house, brought an alabaster box of ointment, and stood at his feet behind him weeping, and began to wet his feet with tears and did wipe them with the hairs of her head, and kissed his feet and anointed them with the ointment...

... Since I came in she hath not ceased to kiss my feet...

... Wherefore I say unto thee: her sins which are many, are forgiven. But to whom little is forgiven, the same loveth little...

... Thy faith hath saved thee. Go in peace.

God forgives us what we ask him to forgive.

He who thinks his sins are few asks little from God and loves little.

But a cheap prostitute cannot help knowing that her sins are many, because society won't allow her to forget it.

A man who has lived blamelessly, if he feels within himself the roots of every possible crime and asks God's pardon, although he has not committed crimes, may have the privilege of loving God as much as a prostitute.

[1] Genuine praise often goes to a humble man; only the powerful get false flattery. (Seneca: *Thyestes*, 211–12.)

[2] "Surely time has brought him resignation." "You are wrong. He feels his troubles more every day. Bearing misery is easy; going on bearing it is hard." (*Ibid.*, 305–7.)

[3] I do not fill my wanton stomach at the people's expense. I have no land except what the Getae and Parthians hold. I am not worshipped with incense, nor are my altars adorned, to the neglect of Jupiter. (*Ibid.*, 460–4.)

Nothing could be purer than her action, which involved complete self-forgetfulness. She had even forgotten that her contact was a pollution.

To turn towards the good in this way, without any regard for oneself, one must feel in one's very bones the wretchedness of the human condition and the degradation to which the flesh is subjected or exposed.

The soul must have been pierced through by the bitterness of human misery, to the point where life holds no more hope at all.

Then the tears which spring from the depth of shame are a pure tribute to the good.

When the whole of my thought is shame, then the whole of my thought goes towards the good which is outside myself. My soul and body follow my thought, and I am not even aware of it. I am no longer even aware that I insult the good by approaching it.

In the unhesitating impulse which leads her to touch Christ, there is perfect humility.

The love is proportional to the forgiveness of the debt, but whoever understands is aware that there is an infinite debt to be forgiven.

If I avert my desire from the things of this world, as being false goods, I have the absolute, unconditional certainty of being in accord with truth. I know they are not goods and that nothing in this world can be regarded as a good except by dint of lying; I know that all objectives in this world are self-annulling.

To turn away from them—that is all. Nothing else is necessary. That is the virtue of charity in its plenitude.

My reason for turning away from them is that I judge them to be false by comparison with the idea of the good. So I relinquish the totality of worldly things for the sake of the good. I wrench away the whole of my desire and my love from worldly things in order to direct them towards the good.

But—it will be asked—does this good exist? What does it matter? the things of this world exist, but they are not the good. Whether the good exists or not, there is no other good than the good.

And what is this good? I have no idea—but what does it

matter? It is that whose name alone, if I attach my thought to it, gives me the certainty that the things of this world are not goods. If I know nothing more than that name I have no need to know any more, provided only that I know how to use it in this way.

But is it not ridiculous to abandon what exists for something which perhaps does not exist? By no means, if what exists is not good and if what perhaps does not exist is the good.

But why say 'what perhaps does not exist'? The good certainly does not possess a reality to which the attribute 'good' is added. It has no being other than this attribute. Its only being consists in being the good. But it possesses in fullness the reality of that being. It makes no sense to say the good exists or the good does not exist; one can only say: the good.

The things of this world exist. Therefore I do not detach from them those of my faculties that are related to existence. But since the things of this world contain no good, I simply detach from them the faculty which is related to the good, that is to say, the faculty of love.

Sexuality. There is in our bodies a mechanism which, when it is set in motion, makes us see good in the things of this world. It must be left to rust until it perishes.

Although I know that the things of this world are unworthy of my desire, I find nevertheless that my desire is attached to them, and I lack the energy to wrench it away.

Efforts of will are illusory.

If I make them, my soul disbelieves me.

All I can do is to desire the good. But whereas all other desires are sometimes effective and sometimes not, according to circumstances, this one desire is always effective. The reason is that, whereas the desire for gold is not the same thing as gold, the desire for good is itself a good.

If the day comes when all the desire in my soul is detached from the things of this world and directed wholly and exclusively towards the good, then on that day I shall possess the sovereign good.

Will it be said that I shall be left without an object of desire? No, because desiring in itself will be my good. Then will it be said that I shall still have something left to desire? No, because I shall possess the object of my desire. Desire itself will be my treasure.

That is why the Scriptures make use of two images: "He that drinketh of this water shall thirst again" and "He that drinketh of this water shall never thirst again". This water is the good.

It is because everything in our world is the wrong way round that the attributes of God appear to us as negations (he is without limits, etc.) and that possession appears to us disguised as desire. What we call desires are what in reality constitutes possession. Possession wears the mask of desire, like the princess in the stories dressed as a servant girl.

To recognize this fact is to discover, in the words of the Upanishad, the place of the desires which are reality, the place that is hidden behind the veil of falsehood. When desire is reality it is possession.

When I desire to see a friend, it is not the meeting with him that I desire, but the good that I suppose to inhere in it. If I detach this desire, if I wrench it away from its object and direct it towards the pure good, it becomes a much greater good than the one I hoped for in seeing my friend.

That is why "whatsoever you abandon for my sake, you shall receive it a hundred-fold in this world".

The abandonment itself is the hundred-fold.

In abandoning a father for Christ there is a hundred times more good than in the father; and so on.

But it by no means follows that one receives a hundred times, or even the smallest fraction of, the satisfaction, pleasure, etc., that are associated with the things one abandons.

Possession is not satisfaction. The two things are quite unrelated.

Satisfaction, pleasure, joy, happiness, felicity, are all of them part of the things of this world, which are not goods.

If the word joy or felicity is used in speaking of the other world, it is only as a metaphor, in place of saying the good.

In the same way that 'exists' and 'does not exist' have no meaning in relation to the good, so privation and satisfaction have no meaning in relation to the desire for good. This desire is not fulfilled, since it is itself the good. It is not unfulfilled, since it is itself the good.

It is our desire for things of this world, which are not goods, that is either unfulfilled or fulfilled. We feel deprivation and satisfaction in the same way that we feel physical pain or well-being. They are animal sensations. But we must wrench our desire away from them.

Since satisfaction contains no good, deprivation contains no evil. The good has no contrary. But one may call it an evil to have one's desire attached to the things of this world, because so long as desire is attached in this way one has the illusion of a pair of contraries: good—evil.

Desire is in itself the good. Even when it is wrongly directed it is still the potentiality of good.

That is why hell can only be nothingness. Where there is no possibility of good there is no desire, and there is no thinking creature.

When once the whole of one's desire is turned towards God one has no desire to eat when one is hungry. Nevertheless, apart from exercises in asceticism, one does all one can to procure food.

Why? No motive is necessary. The body's energy happens to be so directed.

If one sees a starving man, one has no desire that he should get food, yet one does all one can to procure it for him, even if it means depriving oneself of necessities.

Why? This is the great mystery.

One's physical sensibility itself, when once desire has been uprooted from it, has acquired a universal quality.

Is it possible to understand this mystery? The physical sensibility, consumed in the fire of the divine love, the Holy Spirit, becomes universal.

Compassion alone makes it possible to contemplate affliction. Being pulverized by one's own affliction, one is unable to contemplate it; and someone else's affliction is only seen as affliction if one feels compassion for it.

Our sensibility is by nature universal, but it becomes selfish because our desire is involved with it.

When desire is entirely directed towards the infinite Good outside oneself there can be no regard for oneself and consequently no egoism.

It is because one thinks of affliction as an evil that one stifles one's natural compassion.

Compassion is natural, but it is stifled by the instinct of self-preservation. It is only the possession of the entire soul by supernatural love that revives the activity of compassion.

But I still do not really understand this mystery.
It is a mystery analogous to the mystery of beauty.

There is no man, however hard-hearted, who does not feel compassion about the afflictions presented in the theatre. This is because he can be disinterested; he has nothing to gain and no fear of danger or contamination. So he can lose himself in the characters of the play. He gives free rein to his compassion, because he knows the situation is unreal. If it was real he would turn as frigid as ice.

Many of the Christians throughout the centuries who have wept over Christ's crucifixion would have been unmoved if they had seen him on the cross. Their tears have done them no good.

The man who has devoted all his desire to the good is as freely compassionate at all times as the spectator is in the theatre.

His thought does not run away from the sight of affliction, because he knows that affliction is not an evil. But he suffers at it, because he knows that affliction is painful. And suffering impels him to try to remedy it.

That is all it is. That and nothing else. It is so simple that even in the act his right hand is unaware what his left hand is doing.

Saga of the Volsungs. Odin is appealed to by one of his descendants, a king who is childless—Odin sends him an apple, which he shares with his wife.

Birth of Sigurd "He was sprinkled with water and given the name of Sigurd".

Prose Edda—Thor, grandson of Priam, is brought up in Thrace, where he becomes a tyrant, and marries a sybil. Odin is his descendant in the 18th generation.

20 generations, therefore, between Priam and Odin.—This is 600 years, if we adopt Herodotus' scale. So Odin would be approximately—700.[1] Odin went from Thrace to Saxony. And his son Balder was ruler of Westphalia.

They were called the Aesir because they came from Asia. They disseminated their language in the North.

---

[1] i.e. 700 B.C.

Odin, the Hanged God. That is his description in the poets of the 10th century. (?)

Gold was called 'Freya's tears'.

A great-grandson of Odin (Frodi) was king of Denmark in the time of Christ and Augustus. 21 generations for about 1200 years; 60 years for a generation. Odin would have been a king of Thrace later than Alexander.

"Peace of Frodi", proverbial expression like pax Romana. "Flour of Frodi", gold. Story of the mill which made the sea salt.

The Aesir exact from all things an oath to do no harm to Balder; therefore things could be thrown at him, for fun, without hurting him. But the mistletoe was forgotten, and the mistletoe killed him.

He could return from the underworld on condition that he was wept for by all things and everyone without a single exception—Odin sent to request all and everyone to weep.—But one giantess refused.

Noah's rainbow (it occurs also in the prose Edda) is a mediation between heaven and earth, a way of salvation. The Tower of Babel was intended to be the same thing; but it started from the earth instead of the sky, and therefore it was wrong.

The rainbow is a limit to God's wrath.

"Whoso sheddeth man's blood, by man shall his blood be shed: for in the image of God made he man."

The death penalty for murder is a witness to man's divine destination.

In order that the law itself may not be polluted by murders, it must be divine.

In antiquity, laws were regarded as divine.

God said to the devil: "He is in thine hand; but save his life."

But that is not the whole story. To complete it we must know whether in the pangs of death Job will still respect God. It would be a drama in three acts instead of two. And that does indeed seem to be the general plan of the poem. It is then seen to be the story of a god who dies and is resurrected. For Job is a god, since he is able to claim legitimately that he is perfect.

But in that case God's speech to Job, which is of similar inspiration to several of the psalms, must have been added by the Jews. Except for the final words against Job's friends.

"Here shall the proud waves be stayed."[1]

Or was God's speech spoken to the resurrected Job?
And in the original poem the devil cannot have ascended to meet God face to face.

2 Kings, xviii. Up to the time of Hezekiah, son of Ahaz King of Judah, who was as pious as his forefather David, the Israelites were still burning incense to Moses' brazen serpent. Hezekiah caused it to be broken up. (It was called Nehushtan.)

Lists of images of Christ.
Prometheus.
The mean proportional in Greek geometry.
Proserpine.
Osiris.
Dionysus.
Attis.
Adonis.

Grimm's fairy tales
{
Snow White.
The sister of the Seven Swans.
The killed, eaten, and resurrected child in "The Almond Tree", related to the paschal lamb and to the animals in American Indian stories, killed, eaten, and resurrected through their bones.
}

"Dirty boy", incarnation of the Sun in an American Indian story.
Orestes.
Hippolytus.
The just man in the *Republic*.

[1] Cf. Job 38: 11.

Wisdom in the *Phaedrus* (if Wisdom became visible . . .)[1]
Job (dead and resurrected in an original version?)
The brazen serpent.
Zagreus (identical with the moon?)
The slaughtered ram under whose appearance Zeus manifests himself to the Egyptian Heracles.
Odin ("I know that I hung . . .")
Melchizedek ("made like unto the Son of God")
Noah.
Krishna and Rama (especially Krishna).
The bride in "The bull o'Norroway"
   (Far hae I sought ye, near am I brought to ye;
   Dear Duke o'Norroway, will ye not turn and speak to me?)
Antigone.
Tao ("I am the Way").

Any being whose "I" (aham) is the atman is a man-God.

The ancients recognized a supreme God and also a mediator God who was worshipped by the mystics. In addition they had household and national deities to protect them in mundane affairs.

Israel had the idea that by making God himself one's national deity one could make sure of triumphing.

They made God the object of their idolatry.

The Midgard Serpent of the *Edda*, who is at the bottom of the sea, is the same animal as Leviathan in the Bible.

"The white God . . . nine maids, all sisters, bore him for a son."

In the prose *Edda* humanity proceeds from the principle of evil.

Edda. God made the world out of the corpse of evil.

" . . . Much dearer to the vultures than to their wives."[2] Such is human love. One loves only what one can eat. When a

---
[1] Plato, *Phaedrus*, 250. If wisdom became visible to the eye of sense she would inspire "terrible passions".
[2] The corpses of the slain, in the *Iliad*.

thing is no longer edible one leaves it to anyone else who can still find nourishment in it. Human love operates only within limits. Some change could happen to me, such that none of those who love me would pay any more attention to me. It is not I who am a good for those who love me; I merely provide the occasion for their enjoying something that is not me.

Whether that something is mud or God depends solely upon my desire.

Human love is not unconditional. I love a fruit, but I no longer love it when it is rotten.

I can become much dearer to the vultures than to any human being, and any human being, even the most beloved, can become much dearer to the vultures than to me.

There are two lines in the *Iliad* that express with incomparable power the wretched limitation of human love. This is one:

" . . . on the ground
they lay, much dearer to the vultures than to their wives."
And this is the other:

"After she[1] was worn out with tears, she began to think of eating."

It is not true that human love is stronger than death. Death is much stronger. Love is subdued to death.

It is easy to love what is alive. It is difficult to love what is dead. Love for a dead man is not subdued to death, because its object cannot die. But such a love, if it really is love and not day-dreaming, is supernatural. Niobe's love is human, Electra's is supernatural. And yet Electra too must have remembered to eat . . . ?

The death of someone we love is horrible because it exposes the truth about the sort of love we felt for him. Because it reveals that our love for him was not stronger than death.

The love for what does not exist is stronger than death.

But, to love what does not exist—how absurd! It is madness. And it is the soul's salvation. It can be proved that there is no baseness to which circumstances may not, in certain cases, reduce a soul that is incapable of loving what does not exist.

To love what does not exist, while knowing it does not exist, is torment for the soul.

To love what is threatened with extinction, while knowing it is exposed to this threat.

[1] Niobe, weeping for her children.

It is the order of the world, it is this necessity, which is their sovereign master and which reduces them to conditional existence, that makes the things we love unworthy to be loved. Necessity makes all our love objectless. It is our one and only enemy. And for this reason it is necessity itself that we must love.

There are two objects for us to love. First, that which is worthy of love but which, in our sense of the word existence, does not exist. That is God. And second, that which exists, but in which there is nothing it is possible to love. That is necessity. We must love both.

Love requires its object to exist (in this world) and to be lovable. But there is no such object for our love. Yet on the other hand our love is our very being, which nothing can eradicate from us.

We can pretend that some terrestrial things are lovable. Or we can pretend that what is really lovable is in this world. Or we can wear out and exhaust a part of our love, while the other part turns sour and becomes hatred.

But if we refuse to do any of those things we undergo a marvellous change, which reveals the secret. We love the two things which it is impossible to love: that which does not exist and that which is not lovable.

Existence and amiability (the quality of being able to be loved) are conditions for love. If one loves something that lacks the first quality and also something that lacks the second—but it is essential to love both of these two things—then one is loving unconditionally.

Love is a divine thing. If it enters a human heart it breaks it.

The human heart was created in order to be broken in this way. It is the saddest waste if it is broken by anything else. But it prefers to be broken by anything rather than by the divine love. Because the divine love breaks only those hearts which consent to be broken; and this consent is difficult to give.

The Gospel parable of the king who issues invitations to a feast and is met with refusals disguised under all sorts of pretexts is a proof that the reasons for our alienation from God are not causes but pretexts for our alienation. At least this is true of those who have listened, even if only for half a second and with half an ear, to the invitation. An official does not neglect God because he is absorbed in schemes for advancing his career, but he absorbs himself in the schemes in order to avoid thinking about God. And there may even be members of monastic orders, some of them canonized and seeming to deserve their reputation as saints, who have found a pious pretext to refuse the invitation.

At the first moment, when the invitation is heard almost unconsciously, the entire soul is mediocre, because the infinitesimal trace of purity is only just beginning to appear in it. And the mediocre shuns and flees from the light. When one is mediocre, how can one bear to expose oneself entirely to the light? One would rather turn one's desire and one's energy to the most abject affairs.

And yet those who are mad enough to expose themselves will become light. For whatever is manifested is light. But no one knows this beforehand.

So it is impossible to go into the light unless one is attracted by its brilliancy to the point of completely forgetting that one is mediocre. Like the prostitute at the feet of Christ.

But if we turn towards God with the thought that we are not mediocre, and if this thought is not speedily and crushingly corrected, then it is not really towards God that we have turned. For God is a touchstone which shows all human gold to be false gold; but at the same time it transforms false gold into the real, divine gold, which shines only in secret. This touchstone is also a philosopher's stone.

A little child who sees something bright is so totally absorbed in his love for the shiny object that his whole body leans towards it and he quite forgets it is beyond his reach. Then his mother picks it up and puts it near him. That is the way in which we ought to become as little children.

It is in the power and fixity of our desire that we should become like children. A child stretches his hands and his whole body towards a bright object, even if it is the moon. If a child is hungry he cries with his voice and his whole body, tirelessly, to be given milk or bread; and the grown-ups are touched and smile, but he is in deadly earnest. His whole body and soul are concentrated on the single fact of desire. Nothing is less puerile than a little child. It is the adults who play with him who are puerile.

(I greatly fear the little Thérèse of Lisieux was more often like those adults than like a little child.)

A child does not will to obtain the bright object or the milk, he makes no plans for getting them; he simply desires, and cries.

The will and the discursive intelligence which makes plans are adult faculties. We must use them up. We must destroy them by wearing them out. It is of little importance whether we possess a large or small share of those faculties. What matters is that we should persevere to the end and use them up completely.

The discursive intelligence can be destroyed by the contemplation of clear and inescapable contradictions. Koan. The Mysteries.

The will can be destroyed in the accomplishment of impossible tasks. Superhuman trials in folk tales.

It makes little difference what task I choose, so long as it is just beyond the strength of my will. Suppose my will is so weak (and in my case it is very weak) that it is more than I can do to sweep out my room every day. Then in that case all I have to do is to will to sweep my room every day. There will be days when I shall succumb and leave it unswept. The next day I shall continue, with a renewed effort of will. Then I shall succumb again. And so on.

The important thing is that if one perseveres without pride and in spite of failures, the will is gradually worn out and finally disappears. Once it has gone, one has passed beyond will into obedience.

It is also possible, of course, to let both the will and discursive intelligence atrophy through lack of exercise. But in that case one is still on this side of the barrier. Tamas. And sometimes they are exercised so as to develop them. But this is pride. Raja. The right way is to exercise them so as to use them up. Sattva. Once they have been completely destroyed, one has passed beyond the gunas.

Nevertheless, when constrained by obedience, one will still be able, by means of it, to be as effective as other men are by means of will and discursive intelligence.

We dislike to see affliction because it compels us to see what it is we love when we love ourselves. It is against nature to love someone who is afflicted. But affliction compels us to do so; because when one is in affliction one is obliged to love an afflicted person or else to stop loving oneself.

True compassion is a voluntary, consented equivalent of affliction.

Natural pity consists in helping someone in misfortune so as not to be obliged to think about him any more, or for the pleasure of feeling the distance between him and oneself. It is a form of cruelty which is contrary only in its outward effects to cruelty in the ordinary sense. Such, no doubt, was the clemency of Caesar.

Compassion consists in paying attention to an afflicted man and identifying oneself with him in thought. It then follows that one feeds him automatically if he is hungry, just as one feeds oneself. Bread given in this way is the effect and the sign of compassion. This is what Christ thanks us for.

Because, just as the gift of bread is simply the effect and sign of compassion, so compassion itself is the effect and sign of being united to God by love. The sight of an afflicted man frightens away every kind of attention except that which has made contact with God.

It is only God who can pay attention to an afflicted man.

The book of Job is a miracle because it expresses in a perfect form things which a human mind can only think and conceive under the torment of intolerable suffering, but which are formless at the time and which fade away and are irrecoverable when the suffering abates.

The composition of the book of Job is a particular instance of the miracle of attention being paid to affliction.

The same is true of the *Iliad*.

The attention runs away from affliction as it runs away from the true God, and by the same instinct of self-preservation; because both the one and the other oblige the soul to feel its nothingness and to die while the body is still alive.

The only soul that can fix its attention upon affliction is one that has been killed by a true contact with the true God (it makes no difference if, through an error of language, it believes itself to be atheist).

Nor can an afflicted man pay attention to affliction; if his condition prevents him from attending to anything else, he pays attention to nothing at all. In cases of extreme social degradation (prostitutes, recidivists) there is a total incapacity for concentration and perseverance. This incapacity is both a cause and an effect of their degradation.

The same incapacity for paying attention to affliction that inhibits compassion in someone who sees an afflicted man also inhibits gratitude in an afflicted man who is helped. Gratitude presupposes the ability to get outside oneself and contemplate one's own affliction, from outside, in all its hideousness. This is too horrible.

It is only unconditional love that can compel the soul to expose itself to moral death, and unconditional love has no other object than unconditioned good, which is God. Therefore it is quite certain that only a soul which has been killed, knowingly or not, by the love of God can really pay attention to the affliction of the afflicted.

Affliction is the criterion. Is that its providential function?

Christ on the cross, abandoned body and soul. In that condition he alone could love the Father. The Father alone could love him in that condition.

It is time that tortures us. Man's whole effort is to escape from it, that is to say, to escape from past and future by embedding himself in the present, or else by inventing a past and a future to suit himself.

One escapes from time by remaining below it—the flesh provides the method—or by passing above it into eternity. But in order to pass above we have to traverse the whole of time, in its infinite extent, although our lives are but a moment. For those who love him, God provides the method.

The only man who feels all the bitterness of affliction, completely and at the centre of his soul, is the man who tries, like Job, to continue to love God in the depth of affliction. If he ceased to love God he would not suffer so much. Prometheus was the same. In this state the soul is lacerated, nailed to the two poles of creation: inert matter and God. This laceration is a copy, within a finite soul, of God's creative act. Perhaps it is necessary to pass through that in order to emerge from creation and return to the origin.

Whoever is gripped by affliction before he has even begun to love God is destroyed.

Perhaps one can regard this disaster as equivalent to a premature death. Its results are unknown.

It may be that even our greatest cruelty cannot really do

harm to another soul, but if this is so we don't know it and we have no right to know it.

Zagreus. Narcissus.

Zagreus went into the mirror like a trap. Narcissus too. Zagreus and Narcissus are the same being. The divine Word.

This mirror is the creation. God is trapped by evil when he contemplates what he has created. He is caught and subjected to the Passion.

By creating, through a superabundance of goodness, God gave the opportunity for evil to exist.

The sole reason for thinking that the universe is good is that God, though eternally aware that evil would arise in it, willed eternally to create it.

God is not proved by the goodness of the universe, but the goodness of the universe by God; or rather, it is a matter of faith.

But the universe is beautiful, even including evil, which, as part of the order of the world, has a sort of terrible beauty. We feel it.

To put oneself in somebody else's place means wishing material solace for him, if that is his own preference, rather than spiritual progress.

Nevertheless, one ought not to put oneself in somebody else's place when he wants to harm his neighbour.

But to desire spiritual progress for somebody when he himself has no desire for it is something other than compassion.

And perhaps, in the long run, compassion can do more to help his progress.

Rufinus, history of the monks of Egypt, P.L.,[1] vol. 21, pages 387 ff. A saintly hermit asks to be told which saint he resembles. He is told: a village singer. Until recently this singer had been a thief. When asked if he has ever performed a good action he recalls after much searching of memory that once, when his band had captured a nun, he prevented the others from raping her and brought her safely home. And another time he gave a woman money to pay tax arrears for which her husband and son were in prison and under torture (such was the Christian Empire!). She was pretty and she offered herself as his slave;

[1] *Patrologia Latina* (J. P. Migne).

she had not eaten for 3 days. After hearing this, the saint made the man a monk.

Another time the answer to the same question is: a certain headman of a village. Except for begetting three sons his chastity had been complete.

He had practised hospitality and justice; had tried always to ensure that no one suffered on his account (cf. *Book of the Dead*).

Most of the Egyptian monks worked in the harvest; they were paid in flour, of which they gave the greater part to the needy. *Vitae Patrum*, Migne, P.L.[1] vols. 73, 74.

May the hazard of events deprive me, without any action on my part, of everything that others have renounced from love of God; and at the moment when this happens may I have forgotten that I ever wished it to happen.

Verba Seniorum,[2] Pelagius et Johannes iv, 49— v, 31. vii, 27–32 (place where a temptation occurs), 37 (body and soul).

Pledge your body to the walls of the cell, and let your thoughts stray where they will.

The body is a lever for salvation. But in what way? What is the right way to use it?

id. viii, 19. x, 34–44.

93.—This monastic life was a material advance for those who came from the poorer classes. Shepherds used to sleep on the bare ground, eat dry bread, or salt fish when they could, and drink water; they washed in the river.

x, 111—To go to heaven by one's own will is wrong.

xi, 1—5—6, xii, 2 (difficulty of prayer), xv, 18, xii,[3] 8, 13, 14.

In affliction the divine love is the only help.

A hermit who had not seen a man for ten months meets a shepherd who had not seen a man for 11 months.

It is impossible for men who deprive themselves voluntarily to reach the degree of destitution to which some men are reduced by affliction.

---

[1] *Patrologia Latina.*   [2] In Migne, *Patrologia Latina*, Vol. 73, book 5.
[3] Conjectural (obscure in MS.).

One must give one's life for those one loves, but one must not kill oneself.
[Another collection, anonymous translator, Book 3 of "Vitae patrum".[1]]
Cassian, P.L., 49,[2] de Coenobiorum Institutis [Spiritual necessity of manual labour in solitude] [Spiritual necessity of the walls of the cell].
Collection translated by Paschasius for Martin de Dumes. *Vitae Patrum*, Book VII. Martin, 2 (utility of fasting and vigils: humility). 19 (I am not there).—23.

Leave it to God to avenge the offences we receive, offer our hatred to God; if our God is the true God the hatred in us will be burnt up by contact with the Good. Otherwise, we are making our hatred an object of idolatry.

When contact has once been made, through total renunciation, with the true God it is then desirable to turn all one's desires without exception towards God in prayer; for this contact burns up all the evil in them and transmutes the energy which sustained them into sustenance for the love of God.

It was in this way that Christ, in the night of Gethsemane, turned his physical fear towards God.

124 "only your humility conquers me".
find what Rufinus says (History of the Monks of Egypt, Migne, P.L. vol. 21, 387 ff.) concerning Ammon (vol. 21).
Desert Fathers:
An. Stay where you are at the moment of temptation.
Ar. Keep the body fixed and let your thought wander.
Macarius. If the thought dwells upon the offences received from men it forfeits the power to fix itself upon God.
Pastor. Better to stint oneself a little every day than to keep a total fast for two or three days.
An. Not to climb up to heaven by one's own will.
Allois. Say "In the world there is only myself and God" (Even so, it is too many).
"It is possible to attain to perfection in one day."
Agatho. Nothing is more difficult than prayer. In all other

---

[1] In *Patrologia Latina*, Vol. 73. [2] i.e. *Patrologia Latina*, Vol. 49.

tasks of the religious life, however exacting, one can sometimes rest; but there is no rest in prayer, up to the end of one's life.

Zacharias. Silence.

Find the Greek collection, *Apophthegmata Patrum*, Migne, P.G.,[1] vol. 65, 102.

Punishment of criminals.

They should be cured by a hard and laborious but healthy and happy open-air life in unpopulated country, where they would be employed in work like road-making, etc. And only when cured, and if they feel the need of it, should they be made to suffer.

Demeter, Isis, children "passed through the fire", as in the Old Testament; St. John the Baptist "I indeed baptize you with water, but he shall baptize you with the Holy Ghost and with fire". Was there in antiquity a rite of baptism by fire, of which the ceremony of jumping over "St. John's fires" is a survival? Was there a ceremony of pretending to pass new-born children through a flame?

Sons by adoption, adoptive children of God—what does that mean? Nothing, or else this: that no human being is a child of God, except when the Word, God's only Son, enters into him and speaks the word "Father" to God through his mouth.

To ask for something in the name of Christ means to ask it on his behalf; this means that Christ uses a man's mouth to ask something from his Father; and then indeed it is always granted. For this belongs to the sphere of the wise persuasion exerted upon necessity by Love (*Timaeus*).

The Just Man of Isaiah "So disfigured did he look that he seemed no longer human."[2]

Isaiah: "The Eternal saw with great indignation that there was no more judgement. And he saw that there was no man, and wondered that there was no intercessor; therefore his arm brought salvation unto him; and his righteousness it sustained him."[3] Gîta "For the re-establishment of order I assume an ego..."

---

[1] *Patrologia Graeca*. [2] Isaiah 53: 2 (Jerusalem Bible).

[3] Isaiah 59: 15–16. Simone Weil is here quoting from the Bible as translated by the French Rabbinate (ed. M. Zadoc-Kahn, Paris, Durlacher).

IV

LONDON NOTEBOOK
(1943)

The proper method of philosophy consists in clearly conceiving the insoluble problems in all their insolubility and then in simply contemplating them, fixedly and tirelessly, year after year, without any hope, patiently waiting.

By this standard, there are few philosophers. And one can hardly even say a few.

There is no entry into the transcendent until the human faculties—intelligence, will, human love—have come up against a limit, and the human being waits at this threshold, which he can make no move to cross, without turning away and without knowing what he wants, in fixed, unwavering attention.

It is a state of extreme humiliation, and it is impossible for anyone who cannot accept humiliation.

Genius is the supernatural virtue of humility in the domain of thought. That is demonstrable.

So long as a man's thought still moves in the sphere inhabited by the most refined and subtle human minds it is susceptible to human control and limited by human judgements.

When once it passes above this sphere it can no longer look to any human control or limit.

At this moment the temptation of pride is stronger than it was before.

Whoever finds himself in this situation can only avoid aberration, illusion, or falsehood, by the grace of God, if he implores God with all his heart and with total faith and humility.

Failing that, he must either go down again a little, into the realm where his friends' thoughts can meet his, or else let himself be caught by the devil.

In either case he may produce the illusion of genius, so that his name will be glorious for centuries.

Nevertheless it is blasphemy to give the name of genius to what is incapable of truth.

The connection between humility and true philosophy was known in antiquity. Among the Socratic, Cynic, and Stoic philosophers it was considered part of their professional duty to put up with insults, blows, and even slaps in the face without the slightest instinctive reaction of offended dignity.

Since Christian apostleship was a similar or identical

profession, Christ's precept to his disciples "turn the other cheek" should be seen in this way, as an obligation pertaining to a particular function, and not as an obligation of Christian life.

The pure and simple accomplishment of prescribed actions and neither more nor less, in other words obedience, is the same thing for the soul as immobility is for the body. That is the meaning of the *Gita*.

How does one know that an action is prescribed?

We should carry out our human obligations within the social context in which we are set, unless God specifically orders us to withdraw from it.

Arjuna's fault was in having said that he would not fight, instead of having implored Krishna—not at that moment but long before—to prescribe what he ought to do.

Who knows what the answer would then have been?

The *Gita* and the *Antigone* have apparently opposite meanings, but in reality the same spirit. They are complementaries.

By a providential arrangement, both truth and affliction are mute.

By this voicelessness, truth suffers affliction. For only eloquence is happy in this world.

By this voicelessness, affliction possesses truth. It has no way to lie.

There is another providential arrangement, by which both truth and affliction possess beauty.

Consequently, although they are mute, the attention can dwell on them.

It is truly and literally true, as Plato makes Socrates say in the *Phaedo*, that Providence and not necessity is the sole explanation of the universe. Necessity is one of the eternal dispensations of Providence.

In the true portrayal of affliction, what creates beauty is the light of justice in the attention of the man who portrays it; this attention becomes contagious through beauty.

Only a just man made perfect could have written the *Iliad*.

When humanity fell away from a civilization illumined by faith, probably the first thing it lost was the spirituality of labour.

Today, what is seething in our society is precisely the aborted conception of a spirituality of labour.

Would this be a sign that a cycle is completing itself?

Before slavery began there was a civilization with spirituality of labour. There are infallible signs of it. The traditions of the gods establishing the human crafts; Dionysus and Eleusis; the echo of the traditions reflected in Archimedes' "give me a stance"; the "statera facta corporis"; and the balance and plumb-line, etc. in the Egyptian story.

These symbols were given us with their meanings attached.

"Through the dharma the weak gives orders to the strong." In the same way that the gram outweighs the kilogram on a balance with one arm longer than the other.

By reading this symbolism the soul ceases to be overwhelmed by continually reading force in matter.

God has inscribed his signature in necessity.

Postulate:
This universe is a machine for making the salvation of those who consent to it.

(That is what St. Paul says: All things work together for him who loves God.)

Desire and accomplishment.

The desire to become less imperfect does not make us less imperfect.

The desire to become perfect does make us less imperfect.

It is therefore a fact of experience that perfection is real.

Plato, no doubt, knew it.

It is St. John's proof in his epistle, the proof by eternal life.

Christ on the cross had compassion for his own suffering, as being the suffering of humanity in him.

His cry: "My God, why hast thou forsaken me?" was the cry of all men in him.

When that cry rises in a man's heart, pain has awoken in the depths of his soul the part where there dwells, buried under sins, an innocence equal to Christ's own.

Lear "Is there any cause in nature that makes these hard hearts?"
It is the substance of Christ's cry.
Théophile.[1] "Ah! que les cris d'un innocent..."

The perfectly pure creature (the Virgin) is creation *in its character as* the creative will of God.
It is an intersection of God and the Creation.
The divine Incarnation suffering death is another intersection.
In the Zodiac, if the Balance has the same signification as Justice (or the Virgin, Astraea) alongside it, just as the bull, facing it, has the same signification as the ram (Osiris, Zeus Ammon, Agnus Dei), then the autumnal equinox represents the Virgin just as the spring equinox represents Christ crucified. The two intersections of the equator and the ecliptic represent the two intersections of God and the creation. Cf. the *Timaeus*. The whole changing existence of the universe, enclosed within the year, unfolds between these two intersections—between water and blood (Epistle of St. John).
It should be the same with the human soul. Microcosm.

Thales "Everything is water", i.e. everything is obedience.
Even God's power is also obedience. The Virgin is the creature's obedience, Christ crucified is God's obedience.

Concerning hell:
Christ said "There is nothing hid which must not be manifested."
Or rather—

---

[1] Théophile de Viau: "Ah! with what difficulty the cries of an innocent man... learn the right accent to touch those hearts of steel!"

"There is nothing hid, but that it should be manifested."
And St. Paul said:
"All things that are manifested become light".[1]
Therefore, on the day of the Last Judgement, when creation is seen naked in the light of God, which makes it totally manifest, it becomes nothing but light. There is no more evil.
(This is also a Manichaean idea.)
The devil and the damned suffer throughout the whole of time, but the coming of eternity puts an end to time.

But in these matters everything is impenetrable and unthinkable; it is better to have no opinion at all.

One thing seems certain, however. When the divine seed which has been placed in the created being becomes ripe, all the evil in him is abolished and all the good vanishes by becoming merged with God.

How dare people pretend that the souls of the blessed are other than God or are separate from him, when Christ has commanded us "Be ye perfect as your heavenly Father is perfect".

But theologians have had to pretend it because if people were told that the choice is between annihilation on the one hand and disappearance by merging with God on the other hand, they would not see enough difference between the two to make it worth while to choose the good.

Whereas, by showing them an endless whipping on the one hand and an inexhaustible supply of sugar on the other, one gets docile children of the Church.

The educational methods of the Roman slavemasters—promises and threats—projected beyond death.

The Polyeucte of Corneille is a good example. "But already in heaven the palm is prepared." A dog jumping for a lump of sugar.

"Who is the slave whom his lord made ruler over his household?"

God has entrusted to every human being the function of treating all creatures in the same way as God.

"He shall make him ruler over all his goods."

The reward is certainly a total identification with God.

---

[1] Cf. Ephesians 5: 13: τὰ δὲ πάντα ἐλεγχόμενα ὑπὸ τοῦ φωτὸς φανεροῦται.

It seems clear from Matthew 12, 32–33, that [Saint] Augustine committed the sin against the Holy Ghost.

It appears that this blasphemy consists in asserting that evil can produce pure good, or that pure good can produce evil.

"Have we not performed many miracles in thy name?" "Far from me, ye whose acts are unlawful."[1]

So the only criterion is justice. It is because Christ was just, not because he performed miracles, that we must recognize him as God.

"Love your enemies", etc., has nothing to do with pacifism and the problem of war.

"Your enemies" can have two different meanings.

It may mean those who do harm to your person and to what you personally hold dear.

In so far as I have suffered in my personal life because of the Germans, in so far as things and people to whom I am personally attached have been destroyed or hurt by them, I have a special obligation to love them.

Or "your enemies" may mean enemies of the faith.

If I am prepared to kill Germans in case of military necessity it is not because I have suffered from their acts. It is not because they hate God and Christ. It is because they are the enemies of every country in the world, including my own, and because, to my acute pain, to my extreme regret, it is impossible to prevent them from doing harm without killing a certain number of them.

There is very profound truth in the Greek sophisms proving that it is impossible to learn.

We understand little and badly. We need to be taught by those who understand more and better than ourselves.

For example, by Christ.

But since we do not understand anything, we do not understand them either. How could we know that they are right? How could we pay them the proper amount of attention, to begin with, which is necessary before they can begin to teach us?

That is why miracles are needed.

---

[1] Cf. Matthew 7: 22–3.

That is why, thanks to a providential dispensation, supernatural wisdom is sometimes accompanied by certain powers which are rare among men, but which are also found in mediocre and bad men.

Curing physical maladies, reading thoughts, etc.

But the chief of all the miracles of this kind is beauty.

Whenever one reflects upon the beautiful one is brought up against a blank wall. Everything that has been written upon the subject is miserably and obviously inadequate, because it is a study which must take God as its starting point.

Beauty is a providential dispensation by which truth and justice, while still unrecognized, call silently for our attention.

Beauty is really, as Plato says, an incarnation of God.

The world's beauty is indistinguishable from the world's reality.

Zeus, being angry with men because of their crimes, wished to destroy them. Prometheus interceded on their behalf and was not listened to, so he gave them fire. The fire of divine love, the Holy Spirit. After that, there was no longer any question of their being punished. It was Prometheus who was punished.

Silence of the little girl in the Grimm story who saved the seven swans, her brothers. Silence of the Just Man of Isaiah. "He was oppressed, and he was afflicted, yet he opened not his mouth." Silence of Christ.

There is a sort of divine convention, a pact between God and himself, which condemns truth in this world to silence.

The silence of Christ under blows and mockery is the twofold silence of truth and affliction in this world.

"All this power and the glory thereof is delivered unto me", said the Father of Lies.

The devil also manufactures an imitation of beauty, so that this criterion too is only distinguishable through extreme attention.

But there is one thing which I think the devil cannot do.

He cannot inspire an artist to paint a picture which, if placed in the cell of a man confined to strict solitary confinement, would still comfort him after twenty years.

Duration discriminates between the diabolic and the divine. That is the meaning of the parable of the wheat and the tares.

Essential point of Christianity—(and of Platonism)—:
It is only the thought of perfection that produces any good—and this good is imperfect. If one aims at imperfect good, one does evil.

One cannot really aim at perfection unless it is really possible; so this is the proof that the possibility of perfection exists in this world.

Respiratory yoga—perhaps it is not so much a technique as a way to make breathing itself a sacrament?

There is absolutely no possible solution of problems of origin (the origin of language, of tools, etc.) except that of their institution by God. This is obvious. Language does not arise from non-language. A child learns to speak, but that is because he is taught. And he has to learn to work, etc.

Does the divine instruction imply an original incarnation?
It seems probable. It corresponds to the traditions.
The tradition concerning Osiris is of an Incarnation both for instruction and for redemption.
And was the second function also a historical memory of the past, or was it a presentiment of the future?
Perhaps we do not possess the necessary data for forming even a supposition about this.
The Virgin is like a replica of the infancy of Christ; pure innocence.
Christ was perfectly obedient from infancy; and yet, on the Cross, "what he suffered taught him obedience".

Truth which becomes life; this is the evidence of the Spirit. Truth transformed into life.

To understand the symbolic value, in St. John's eyes, of the water and blood that issued from Christ's body we would need to know more about the meaning of those Tibetan beliefs concerning the effects of perfect virginity, which sets flowing in the veins a colourless liquid (the divine "ichor"?)

Does it follow from this belief that normal blood in a perfectly virgin being is the sign of the union with God in love? And does the presence of water with the blood bear witness to perfect virginity?

It is certainly not by chance that the biographical part of the Gospel of St. John begins with water changed into wine and ends with that issue of water and blood.

It is necessary to be changed back into water, so that the Spirit may turn that water into blood.

Become nothing but complete passivity, corpse-like inertia, and let the Spirit of God create life out of this energy.[1]

In the terminology they used, how much was simple imagery and how much was mystical-biological theory? It is difficult now to conjecture.

Where Dickens rings most false is in the passages in which he has described the humble people of England just as they are. Why is it that reality, when set down untransposed in a book, sounds false?

In nature there is heat energy, mechanical energy, vital energy, life-giving energy in seed, radiant energy in light.

Our science knows only the first two.

Are the last two identical? They seem to have been so regarded in antiquity.

The Spirit—or fiery breath, $\pi\nu\epsilon\hat{\upsilon}\mu\alpha$—gives life. The ancients (Pythagoreans, Stoics) defined the male seed, in the function of generation, as a $\pi\nu\epsilon\hat{\upsilon}\mu\alpha$.

The allocation laid down at the beginning of Genesis,[2] by which the green herb, stalk and leaf, is the animals' portion and the grain and fruit—that is to say, germs and seeds—are for man, is an image of the two contrary destinies: the carnal destiny of animals and the spiritual destiny of man.

[1] i.e. the unused energy? Or perhaps the word 'energy' here is a *lapsus calami* for 'inertia'.
[2] Genesis I: 29–30.

Perhaps this symbolism is at the origin of agriculture, and especially of the culture, by selection, of wheat and the vine.

There must have been something of this kind, if one thinks of the ear of corn of Eleusis, and of Astraea, the Virgin, in the sky, and also of Dionysus, and of the bread and wine of Melchizedek.

Bread consists entirely of seed; not of life itself, but of the life-giving principle. Similarly wine and grapes. (There is in fact a chemical analogy between alcohol and the sex hormones.)

The flesh of Christ and his blood were composed not of living but of life-giving substance.

"It is the πνεῦμα that quickeneth; the flesh profiteth nothing."

"The words I have spoken to you, they are spirit and they are life."

"I am the living bread which came down from heaven: if any man eat of this bread, he shall live for ever: and the bread that I will give is my flesh, which I will give for the life of the world."

The flesh becomes bread through sacrifice.

In the Australian tribes, the women collect the seed of seed-bearing grasses. From this one can imagine the progressive creation of wheat, which, if the seed-gathering is a rite and a sacrament, represents a collaboration between God and man. One can then understand that a religion should have been established upon it.

Aeschylus says, evidently quoting a sacred formula of the Mysteries, τῷ πάθει μάθος. Through suffering, learning (imparted by God to man). But he does not say of what the imparted wisdom consists. We discover this when we read the same formula completed in St. Paul—with the same play on words, characteristic of a sacred formula, between πάθος and μάθος—ἔμαθεν ἀφ' ὧν ἔπαθεν τὴν ὑπακοήν, he learned obedience from what he suffered.

This wisdom is obedience.

But then had he disobeyed?

Is there a secret version in which, corresponding to human disobedience through lack of love, there is divine disobedience through excess of love?—God disobeying himself out of pity for men? This would be exactly the myth of Prometheus.

And indeed both the story of Prometheus and his name seem like an illustration of the saying τῷ πάθει μάθος.

God disobeying God and brought back to obedience through expiation.

Apart from death, man's punishment in Genesis consists solely of imposed submission. Work and death; passivity of woman in love and child-birth.

Work is something resembling death. It is submission to matter.

But beauty is a snare of God's to obtain our consent to the obedience to which he constrains us.

Human punishment ought to imitate God's method.

Reduce the criminal to obedience by constraint, while offering him enticements which will one day win his consent.

It is always a failure if a guilty man dies without ever having once felt that his condemnation was his greatest good fortune.

Physical and moral pain are things which overwhelm the soul; surely we ought not to refrain from making use of them? Why let such precious gifts of God run to waste? But to pervert their use is appalling.

If one judges a criminal to be incurable, one has no right to punish him; one ought only to prevent him from doing harm. The infliction of a punishment is a declaration of faith that in the depths of the guilty there is a grain of pure good.

To punish without that faith is to do evil for evil's sake.

Indirect mechanism of a crime.

My criminal error, before 1939, concerning pacifist circles and their activity, was due to incapacity caused by the devastation of physical pain for so many years. Being in no state to observe their action at close quarters by meeting and talking with them, I failed to detect their propensity for treason. But I could easily have reflected that the state I was in disqualified me from serious responsibilities and made it obligatory to refrain from them. What prevented me from seeing this was the sin of laziness, the temptation of inertia. I desired so intensely to refrain from that sort of responsibility that I dared not consider impartially the legitimate reasons for refraining; like a seminary pupil tortured by violent carnal desires who dare not so much as look at a woman.

I had so often succumbed to laziness and inertia in small things that when I was faced with something important I felt I must blindly resist the temptation of inertia—instead of coolly examining the possible advantages and disadvantages of action or inaction.

Thus the weakness of not writing a letter, or not making my bed one day when I felt tired, by accumulating in the course of many days, finally led me to the sin of criminal negligence towards my country.

This is an example of a universal mechanism.

Once we have understood how it develops minute personal failings into public crimes, then nothing is a minute personal failing. One's little faults can only be crimes.

Which is appalling, because one commits faults.

We ought never to cease feeling criminal so long as we lack perfection, and we ought to beseech silently with our whole soul to obtain it, until death puts an end to this torment or until God's patience is exhausted and he grants us perfection.

Once this degree of understanding has been reached, one really is the most criminal of men—except for those who have the same understanding. For all our little faults are really crimes when reason has clearly obliged us to see them as such. Great criminals commit few crimes. We commit many little faults; but that means, when once one has learnt to see them as they are, that one commits many crimes every day.

The sole remedy is to suffer this in misery until God takes pity. Because the human will, however one strains it, gets one no nearer to perfection.

---

money, markets, soldiers
before 18th century—Wallenstein

Today, if a man sold himself as slave to another, the contract would be juridically invalid, because liberty, being sacred, is inalienable.

If the words have meaning, when the men of 1789 declared property sacred, along with liberty, they defined it as inalienable and withdrew it from the sphere of trade.

But facts have demonstrated that the words have no meaning.

When science is conceived as it is today, what can its motives be? And from this point of view is it a good or a bad thing, or mixed, and in what proportions?
Analysis of good and evil by motives.
Apply this method *in every sphere.*
A universal method of discrimination for educating oneself, and others, and a whole people.
Do not try actually to discern the motives by observation or introspection—which are always more or less deceitful—but first establish theoretically the list of possible motives for a particular action, in the light of its originating idea.

Christ has defined the virtue of obedience: "I seek not my own will, but the will of him who sent me".

The difficulty about science (cf. manuscript)[1] can only be solved by the idea of an impersonal God.
The object studied by science is God's impersonal Providence.

Parable of the Sower (Luke 8, 5). The first category are those who refuse their consent. The fourth are the elect.
The soil contains a certain amount of nourishment for plants. If a large part of it goes to the thorns, the wheat cannot grow for lack of nourishment. Similarly, when a great part of the soul's energy is given to worldly things the eternal part cannot receive the energy indispensable for its growth.
But the way to pass from the third category into the fourth is immediately obvious. It is done by weeding, by pulling up the thorns. In other words, it is detachment, and the method has been extensively studied by the mystics. All that is clear and familiar.
But what about the second category?
Stone. Thorns do not grow from stones. There are souls which are not interested in the things of this world, but neither have they any energy to put at God's service; and so they remain sterile.

[1] Perhaps a reference to her essay, 'Classical Science and after' (in *On Science, Necessity, and the Love of God*, Oxford University Press, 1968).

That is exactly my case.

One might conclude that there are some souls with a natural deficiency which irremediably unfits them for the service of God. And I am one of them.

Is there any remedy?

Is there some way of making wheat grow out of stones?

The only way is, if a seed has fallen into a hollow place in a stone, to water it and keep on doing so whenever the water evaporates.

One ought therefore to expose oneself to earthly stimulants, as much as is possible without violating any of one's obligations, and offer the energy thus acquired as food for the divine seed lodged secretly in the heart.

That is more or less what I have instinctively done up to now.

It implies an immense debt of gratitude to any human beings who have acted as stimulants.

It is a method which ought perhaps to be communicated to others whose affliction is similar to my own?

Fortunately, there are other souls which are like the good ground. Or rather, one must hope so. For it is painful that the seed's growth should have to be precariously maintained, in constant danger, in the face of almost impossible difficulty, and with an anxiety which continues to the very end. Up to the very end the stalk will wither if it is left a few hours without water.

And in this case detachment is even more rigorously necessary than for the souls which are good ground. For if thorn and weed absorb a few drops of the water which has to be renewed continually, the wheat will inevitably shrivel.

One must acquire energy from worldly things, but not allow one atom of it to be used for worldly things.

Literally, it is total purity or death.

For a soul of this kind it would seem that the state of perfection is precluded except at the very moment of death.

What a joy it is to know that these are not the universal conditions of spiritual good for all men! If it always had to be purchased at such a painful price it would be a difficult effort to wish it for those one loves.

One must remember that a plant lives by light and water, not by light alone. So it would be a mistake to count upon grace alone. Energy from this world is also needed.

But when one is entirely deprived of this world's energy one dies. So long as my heart, my lungs, and my limbs can function at all this is experimental proof that there is still a drop of water on the stone to nourish the heavenly wheat.

Make sure it gets the water, even if this means the death of the flesh from inanition.

If only my flesh and blood are dried up before the divine stalk, nothing else matters.

To have had no fruition and no right to any wages does not matter. There are marvellous fruits and marvellous rewards for others.

But where to find the courage to deprive one's flesh and blood of the last drop of water and give it to the divine stalk? It is only under compulsion that one can do such a thing. It is the sort of thing that can be done by slaves, who have been trained under the whip.

So the only hope is that the divine mercy will plunge one into slavery and training by the whip.

I have had a little training, but not nearly enough. I could have more if I desired it. The difficulty is to make the desire real.

Heraclitus, fr. 90— πυρός τε ἀνταμοιβὴ τὰ πάντα καὶ πῦρ ἁπάντων ὅκωσπερ χρυσοῦ χρήματα καὶ χρημάτων χρυσός.

All things can be changed into fire, and fire into all things, as merchandise can be changed into gold and gold into merchandise.

God is the sole good. All the goods contained in things have their equivalent in God. God is the sole measure of value.

This universe is a snare for capturing souls, in order to deliver them, with their consent, to God.

It is the eternal model for punishment.

Real love wants to have a real object, and to know the truth of it, and to love it in its truth as it really is.

To talk about love of truth is an error; it should be a spirit of truth in love. This spirit is always present in real and pure love.

The Spirit of truth—the fiery breath of truth, the energy of truth—is at the same time Love.

There is another love, which is false.

Here below one can only love men and the universe, that is to say, justice and beauty. Therefore truth is something that qualifies the just and the beautiful.

Πνεῦμα, the fiery breath. It is the energy evoked by love. How marvellously, therefore, this word applies both to the genital semen in carnal love and to the engendering of good by the love between God and a human soul!

Authentic respiratory yoga is undoubtedly based upon the idea of the πνεῦμα. It is what is called the breath of life. But what exactly is the relation between this idea and respiration? Πνεῦμα is also connected with respiration. And respiration is a form of combustion. A candle is the image of human life. This has always been known.

Heraclitus talked only about fire. πνεῦμα makes its appearance only with the Stoics. Is this perhaps because Yoga penetrated into Greece from India after Alexander? Yet on the other hand did not the Pythagoreans, according to Diogenes Laertius, believe that the genital semen is a πνεῦμα?

A candle is the image of a human being who at every moment offers up to God the continuous internal consumption by burning which constitutes the vegetative life.

That is what it is to offer time to God.

It is salvation itself.

The breathing exercises of authentic respiratory yoga are probably no more than a pedagogic, mnemotechnic method for impressing upon the soul its vow to make this offering. Similarly the practice of "repeating the Lord's name" and many other such practices.

To partake of a sacrament in a state of unworthiness harms both the soul and the body.

The presence of Christ on earth in the flesh is like a communion officiated by humanity itself.

It was an unworthy sacrament because Christ was murdered.[1]

[1] Cf. I Corinthians 11: 27.

The human race fell into the same state as an individual who has partaken of communion in a state of unworthiness.

The criterion for those things which come from God is that they show all the characteristics of madness except for the loss of capacity to discern truth and love justice.

Humility is above all one of the qualities of attention.

The first of all political problems is the manner in which the men entrusted with power spend their days. If they spend them in conditions which make impossible a prolonged effort of attention at a high level, it is not possible that justice should be maintained.

Attempts have been made to find mechanisms for the maintenance of justice which would dispense with the need for human attention. It cannot be done. God's Providence is opposed to it.

Human attention alone can legitimately exercise the judicial function.

Niobe's crime was that she counted her children. In the Buddhist story about the repetition of the Lord's name, the old man is saved as soon as he stops counting his repetitions.

St. John of the Cross is describing the same transformation when he says: "I knew no more . . . I lost my flock . . . "

We should derive from this an idea of the role of money in a perfect society.

There are idiots who speak of syncretism in connection with Plato. But there is no need to syncretize what is all one thing. In Thales, Anaximander, Heraclitus, Socrates, Pythagoras, there is the same doctrine, the single Greek doctrine, expressed through different temperaments.

Perfect illustration of the different powers of the soul, in Mark 13, 34:

"As a man taking a far journey, who left his house and gave

authority to his slaves, to every man his own work; and commanded the porter to watch."

The soul is that house, its various faculties are the slaves, and the porter is love.

Matthew 11, 27. "No man knoweth the Son but the Father; neither knoweth any man the Father, save the Son, and he to whom the Son will reveal him."

Therefore men know God, through Christ; but they do not know Christ.

There is a great difference between a truth which is recognized as such and introduced and received into the mind as such, and a truth which is active in the soul and endowed with the power to destroy within the soul those errors that are clearly incompatible with it.

One might think there was no difference between the two. But in fact it is not so. By observing mankind we find the difference confirmed every day.

The active power in truth is the πνεῦμα ἅγιον, the divine energy.

To have a great deal of inert truth in the mind is of little use.

But by degrees an infinitesimal grain of active truth destroys all error.

"A grain of mustard-seed is the smallest of all seeds . . ."

The same distinction applies to falsehood. There is inert error, and there is active error, which destroys truth. It is the devil.

There cannot be active truth and active falsehood at the same time in a soul. But the activity of truth awakens falsehood from its inertia and evokes defensive reactions; that is how the temptations of saints arise.

In some souls there is only inert truth and inert falsehood. They are the majority.

But there are some in which falsehood and others in which truth exists in an active state. The latter are on the direct road to sanctity.

The exchange of love between God and the creature is a vertical jet of fire like a lightning flash. It strikes in a straight line from the highest point of heaven to the lowest depth of the abyss ("by the lightning thou guidest the universal Mediation ... ")[1]

"to comprehend what is the breadth, and length, and depth, and height".[2]

Total humility means consent to death, which turns us into inert nothingness.

The saints are those who have really consented to death while they were still alive.

τοῦτο δὸς ἐμόι, κύριε.[3]

The Gospel of St. John indicates a theory of evil other than that of sin and expiation. This implies another theory of the Passion and the Redemption; there is an indication of that other theory in St. Paul (" ... that he might be the first-born among many brethren").[4]

John 9: "Rabbi, who did sin, this man, or his parents, that he was born blind?" Jesus answered "Neither hath this man sinned nor his parents: but that the works of God should be made manifest in him."

Compare "That which he suffered taught him obedience".

The mechanism of royalty can be seen in the story of the man who asked Christ to adjudicate a divided inheritance with his brother. By refusing to act as judge, Christ refused to be king of the Jews, which obliged the Pharisees to refuse to recognize him as Messiah; and since he was influential enough to bring the wrath of the Romans upon Judaea, and yet refused the position which would have enabled him to protect the country, they thought it their duty to bring about his death. If we look at the matter through the eyes of Hebrew patriotism, this was entirely legitimate.

Whenever, in any unorganized society, a man showed signs of inspiration he was made a judge and by degrees he became king.

[1] ᾧ σὺ κατευθύνεις κοινὸν λόγον ... (Cleanthes: *Hymn to Zeus*).
[2] Ephesians 3: 18.   [3] Grant me this, Lord.   [4] Romans 8: 9.

"Father, give me my portion." (parable of the prodigal son). My portion consists in autonomy. I waste it with prostitutes.

"The slaves in my Father's house have bread." Bread is the good. The slaves are inert matter. One desires to become inert matter in order to cease at last from being disobedient.

One only reaches that point after a process of exhaustion which takes time. The prodigal son first spends all his money and it is only after it is all gone and when he begins to be hungry that he wishes he was one of his father's slaves.

In the same way, it is only after we have exhausted all the natural faculties in us (will, intelligence, natural tendency towards loving) in the effort to produce good, and have recognized that we are incapable of any good, that we fall prostrate before God.

"We are worthless slaves." That is the highest point a human creature can attain to. For glass, there is nothing better than absolute transparency. For a human being there is nothing more than to be nothingness. Every value in a human being is really a negative value. It is like an opaque stain on glass. If a piece of glass is covered with such blemishes it may easily believe it amounts to something and is much superior to some perfectly transparent glass through which the light passes as if there was nothing there. That is why "Whosoever exalteth himself shall be abased; and he that humbleth himself shall be exalted." There is no need to see this as a compensatory process. It is simply that we are born with a congenital deformation of the sense of direction, which gives us the impression of a descent when we are rising and of an ascent when we are descending.

It is like the case of minus numbers. It one proceeds from, -20 to -10 there is a diminution from the point of view of absolute quantity, and anyone who is aware only of modifications of that quantity will believe in this diminution. But in the total series of numbers the passage from -20 to -10 is an increase.

We are born far below zero. Zero is our maximum, the limit we can only reach after having passed through a series which has an unlimited number of terms (for example $-\frac{1}{2^n}$). And zero is the state in which one is a worthless slave.

$$\kappa\acute{\upsilon}\rho\iota\epsilon, \tau o\hat{\upsilon}\tau o \ \delta\grave{o}\varsigma \ \dot{\epsilon}\mu o\acute{\iota}.[1]$$

[1] Lord, grant me this.

St. Thomas Aquinas, commentaries on Aristotle's *Ethics*, viii, 7, quoted by Maritain:

"Friendship . . . cannot exist between beings too far removed from one another. Friendship presupposes that they are close to one another and have attained to equality with one another. It is the part of friendship to make an equal use of the equality already existing between men. And it is the part of justice to bring to equality those who are unequal: once this equality has been attained, the task of justice is accomplished. And in that way equality is at the term of justice and is at the beginning and origin of friendship."

This is absolutely contrary to Christianity. How can these people think themselves Christians? One might ask them if justice has brought man and God to equality before there can be a union of love between them. And if the Samaritan was not moved by friendship for the man set upon by thieves.

Aristotle is the corrupt tree which bears only rotten fruit. How is it that people cannot see this?

The Pythagoreans said: "Friendship is an equality composed of harmony" and "there is harmony between things which are not similar, nor of the same nature, nor of the same rank . . ." Friendship is the equality that results from mediation.

"Love . . . makes equalities and does not search for them" (Rotrou).

If Maritain, St. Thomas, and Aristotle were right, how could Christ ever have called his disciples his friends?

"God so loved the world that he gave it his only-begotten Son."

The whole of Christianity is absolutely contrary to this thought.[1]

There is something mysterious in the universe which is in complicity with those who love nothing but the good.

The elder son in the parable of the prodigal son—suppose he represents matter, which has never been disobedient?

After all, are there not passages in the New Testament—about angels, powers, dominions—which seem to suggest this?

---

[1] [*sic*] The thought referred to must be the quotation from St. Thomas Aquinas, above.

They could be the physical forces which operate in the world. Which would confirm their resemblance to the gods of the Greek mythology. Similarly the Hindu gods.

Kneeling at mass and saying "Sanctus, sanctus, sanctus..." one joins the chorus of all the voices of the universe.

(In the Old Testament too—in the Psalms—there are passages where God's messengers appear to be the forces of nature.)

Zodiac:

Capricorn, horn of abundance. God's plenitude. Water carrier, creation in its purity. Fish, incarnation. Ram, passion. Bull, the same as the Ram.

Twins; division?

Crab, excess, revolt of creation, evil.

Lion, brute force. Virgin, justice. (That is certain, Astraea, Dikē.) Scales, brute force subdued to justice. Scorpion, love turned towards God. Sagittarius, divine light. Capricorn, God's plenitude. And then over again from the beginning...

Must find out about Christmas in Egypt. And at what season the Nile is in flood.

This is all clear, except for the relation between ram and bull.

Twins, division of God, Trinity? The Devil appears at the same time (cf. the beginning of Genesis and of Revelation), and therefore the Crab immediately afterwards. The Trinity very often appears as a duality, because the Spirit is taken for granted (Revelation, Gloria).

In any case I see two quite clear sequences—from Capricorn to the Ram and from the Crab to the Scales.

Plenitude of God, Creation, Incarnation, Passion.

Evil (excess of the creature), brute force, Justice, equilibrium.

Scorpio: the creature which immolates itself to God by fire.

Sagittarius (love as the archer), God who pierces the heart of his creature with an arrow.

Then the plenitude of God.

Twins—was it because of sin that the original human creature was cut in two? (Aristophanes' myth in the *Symposium*).

History must begin with the Bull. God's sacrifice. Sin and fall of the creature. Evil. Brute force. Justice. Equilibrium. The creature goes to immolate itself in God. God wounding his creature with love, by an arrow in its heart. Plenitude of God. Creation (new?). Incarnation. God's sacrifice. And it begins over again. God's sacrifice is the beginning and the end of history.

April	May	June
Christ's Cross (in Eternity).	Sin.	Evil.
July	August	September	October
Brute force.	Justice.	Equilibrium.	Aspiration for God.
November		December	
Wound of love inflicted by God.		Plenitude of God.	
January		February	
New Creation.		Appearance of Christ in the saint's soul.	

March
Christ crucified again in the person of the saint.

In any case the Zodiac was certainly the symbolic expression of a liturgy of the seasons, or even of several liturgies at once (corresponding to several degrees of initiation).
It was related to the seasons and not at all to the constellations.

When God wants to give us any particular thing, he tells us to ask him for it and even to be importunate. If we obey, he gives us the thing. By our supplications we constrain him to do what he wants with us; and he only does what he wants with us [manuscript: add the necessity of *truth*] if we ask him to.

Rosary—method for releasing the soul from thraldom to number. Money ought to perform the same function.

Gospel—the devils entering the herd of swine as it rushes to drown itself. Conservation of matter in the spiritual order, in the sphere of good and evil. In order to get rid of evil it must be transferred. Only God can really destroy it. To destroy evil we have to transfer it to God. For example, we do this when we contemplate the Holy Sacrament.

Note that in Egypt the pig was sacred to the redeemer, Osiris. According to Meleager's account there was an affinity between the boar and Artemis.

A society in which the two poles are obedience and attention—labour and study.

In Plato's myth of the Cave, the fire is physical force, or energy in the sense in which modern physics uses the word.

Christ on the Cross suffered with compassion the suffering of all humanity concentrated in himself.

He uttered his cry (My God, why hast thou . . .) in the name of humanity as a whole.

Labour is consent to the order of the universe.

Pleasure is the illusion that there is some good attached to one's own existence.

It is a permanent illusion, and even sorrow is mixed with some pleasure.

But at certain moments, brought on by an excess of physical suffering, the illusion disappears completely. One then sees one's existence naked, as a mere fact in which there is no good whatsoever. That is frightful. And that is the truth.

(Therefore, may I experience many such moments and never forget the lesson they teach.)

A carnal motive on a low level, but honourable in its way, such as the military comradeship which makes a man want to share the danger of death with his comrades, makes it easy to sacrifice one's life. Because the fact that it is carnal disguises the reality. Under its influence one can face what one knows is certain death, but without seeing it.

On the other hand, to go to one's death from pure obedience to God is to go naked to death. Obedience disguises nothing. It is perfectly transparent.

That is why Christ feared death more than other men.

Folk tale: "... the nightingale called Gizar:—where is it to be found?—That I cannot tell thee. I only know that its song is the most beautiful that man's ear has ever heard."

Marvellous. A being of which one knows only its name and its perfection, and absolutely nothing else; and that is enough to enable one to find it. It is God.

Origen says that the Book of Job is earlier than Moses himself.

Origen—quotation of a saying of Christ in the Gospel of the Hebrews: ἄρτι ἐλαθέ με ἡ μήτηρ μου τὸ ἅγιον πνεῦμα ἐν μία τῶν τριχῶν μου, καὶ ἀπήνεγκέ με εἰς τὸ ὄρος τὸ μέγα Θάβωρ.[1]

Albanian story of the girl married to a snake, who at night becomes a marvellous young man; one night her sisters burn the snake's skin, and he disappears. She will only find him again if she can find one scale intact among the ashes. He is the son of the king of the underworld. In order to come to him she must spend some time in the service of a horrible old woman— "whatever she gives you to drink, drink it and say it is delicious". (Avoid the sin of the murmurator.)

[Blood-stained closet of Bluebeard: certainly it means the evil in the world.]

Teaching of Milarepa:

"The idea of nothingness gives rise to pity.

Pity abolishes the difference between oneself and others.

By losing the distinction between oneself and others one becomes identified with their interests."

---

[1] Even so did my mother, the Holy Spirit, take me by one of my hairs and carry me away to the great mountain Tabor. See page 281 above.

Milarepa:
"Having meditated upon gentleness and pity,
I forgot the difference between myself and others."

Milarepa:
"If you ask yourself whether your sins will be forgiven, your desire for virtue obliterates your sins."

"This is the way for you to follow after my death: Reject everything that egoism makes seem desirable, if it is harmful for other creatures. And on the other hand do what seems sinful, if it benefits other creatures, for it will be a work of religion. If anyone who knows these things forgets them and knowingly commits sins, he will be hurled to the depths of hell."

First half of the Lord's Prayer.

"Hallowed by the name."

By using the name of God we can orient our attention towards the true God, who is beyond our reach and is inconceivable by us.—Without the gift of this name we should have only a false earthly God, conceivable by us. This name alone makes it possible for us to have a Father in the Heavens, about which we know nothing.

"Thy kingdom come"

May thy creation disappear absolutely, beginning with myself and everything to which I am attached in any way whatsoever.

"Thy will be done"

Having absolutely relinquished every kind of existence, I accept existence, of no matter what kind, solely through conformity to God's will.

"On earth as it is in heaven"

I accept the eternal decree of the divine Wisdom and its entire unfolding in the order of time.

It is not easy to think all those things with all one's soul. To do so, we have great need of the supersubstantial bread,[1] of forgiveness for our past trespasses, and of deliverance from evil.

Very probably Lucifer is a star which disrupted the order of the celestial phenomena.

Blind man's stick. To perceive one's own existence not as itself but as a part of God's will.
Blind man's stick and cube—the two keys for the ascent of thought.

Mirror of Simple Souls, v, 12—image of iron and fire.

exhaust the human faculties (will, intelligence, etc.) so as to pass over to the transcendent.
Cf. *Mirror of Simple Souls*, ix, 18.

xiii, 1
"Who believeth a thing which is not? Soothly none, for the truth of believing is in the being of him who believeth."

For anyone who possesses artistic and poetic culture and a keen sense of beauty the least deceptive analogies for illustrating spiritual truths are aesthetic analogies.

Take Christ as one's model. But not by saying: He did so-and-so, and therefore I . . .
It is a bad painter who looks at the model and says "she has a high forehead and arched eyebrows; so I must put a high forehead and arched eyebrows on the canvas", and so on.
A true painter, through paying attention, becomes what he

---

[1] Following St. Jerome and other authorities, Simone Weil always translated τὸν ἄρτον ἡμῶν τὸν ἐπιούσιον ('our daily bread' in the familiar translation) as 'our supersubstantial—or supernatural—bread'.

looks at. And while he is in this state his hand moves, with the brush attached.

This is even more clearly seen in Rembrandt's drawings. He thinks Tobias and the angel, and his hand moves.

It is in this way that Christ should be our model.

We must think Christ—Christ himself and not our image of Christ.

Think Christ with one's whole soul.—And while one is in this state the intelligence, the will, etc., and the body, perform acts.

Evil is not eliminated immediately in this way. But progressively it is.

To do this one must think Christ both as man AND as God.

Perhaps any thought is equally effective, so long as it really wrenches us away from ourselves towards God? (Any thought that contains the perfect?)

Philosophy (including problems of cognition, etc) is *exclusively* an affair of action and practice. That is why it is so difficult to write about it. Difficult in the same way as a treatise on tennis or running, but much more so.

Subjectivist theories of cognition are a perfectly correct description of the condition of those who lack the faculty, which is extremely rare, of coming out of themselves.

A supernatural faculty.

Charity.

It is not, alas, conferred by baptism.

[Every theory of cognition accurately describes some mental state or other (?)]

The supersubstantial bread.—God bestows it upon the universe continually, so as to maintain the order of the world there.—Why not upon us also, if we desire it, so as to nourish and maintain our own order? It is daily bread, because its witness is the daily revolution of the stars.

[Chinese fairy-tales, tr. Martens.]

Little boy from a poor family becomes a cowherd at the age of 12. Has to look after a cow. After a few years the cow has become splendidly beautiful, and golden all over. One day (7th day) it offers to take the boy up among the stars to marry the Weaving Maiden (the daughter of the king of the heavens, who weaves the stuff of the clouds). He agrees. They ascend to the sky. The wedding takes place. But the couple are separated by a river and can see each other only once a year. (Herd Boy, Weaving Maiden, constellations on opposite sides of the Milky Way.)[1]

R.—referring to W.
"—But why is he so determined to see me?—Oh, from kindness, pure kindness! If you only knew how kind he is! He thinks of you here, all alone, and very ill ..."
People say this sort of thing because their attention is fixed at the point where they are uttering the words, instead of being transferred automatically to the point where the words are being listened to.
What makes this transference possible?
Tools. Sculptor's implements. Musical instruments; e.g. violin.
Anyone who talks to someone else without making this transference has not really learned to talk, just as anyone who moves his lips when reading has not really learnt to read.
Cf. Maine de Biran. In a general way=

> Idea of transferences of attention.

Sumerian flood.—The gods have been hungry ever since the flood began, from lack of sacrifices. As soon as Uta-Napishtim offered a sacrifice:
"the gods smelt the sweet savour—and they gathered like flies around the sacrifice",
then they resolved never again to destroy humanity—

Irish story—strawberry jam
The Irish story ("A flock of birds"?) in which the sister of a youth who has been executed returns home and, in an upsurge of vitality, to throw off the effect of his death, devours a whole

[1] *The Chinese Fairy Book*, ed. R. Wilhelm, transl. F. H. Martens (Fisher Unwin, 1922). The Herd Boy is a constellation in Aquila, the Weaving Maiden one in Lyra. They are separated by the Milky Way.

pot of strawberry jam—and for the rest of her life she cannot bear even to hear strawberry jam mentioned.

If a romantic adolescent fabricated a tragedy out of some imaginary great love, it could not modify his or her attitude to strawberry jam.

<u>transference</u> ‖ It is only real feelings that possess this power of transferring themselves into inert matter.

For living man here below, in this world, sensible matter—that is to say, inert matter and flesh—is like a filter or sieve; it is the universal test of what is real in thought, and this applies to the entire domain of thought without exception. Matter is our infallible judge.

From this alliance between matter and real feelings comes the significance of meals on solemn occasions, at festivals and family or friendly reunions, even between two friends, and so on (also sweets, delicacies, drinking together . . .) And the significance of special dishes: Christmas turkey and marrons glacés [plum pudding]—Candlemas cakes[1] at Marseilles—Easter eggs—and a thousand local and regional customs (now almost vanished).

The joy and the spiritual significance of the feast is situated *within* the special delicacy associated with the feast.

The most important part of teaching = to teach what it is to *know* (in the scientific sense). Nurses.

---

[1] The 'naveto de Sant Vitou', associated with the church of St. Victor at Marseilles, according to Mistral.

INDEX

Abelard, 78, 134
Abraham, 116, 118, 251; and circumcision, 252
Aeschylus, 47, 48, 49, 249, 344; *Choëphoroe*, 48; *Prometheus Bound*, 249
Affliction, 33, 69, 82, 91, 102, 139, 173, 178, 263, 326-7; and compassion, 94, 95, 97, 209, 318, 328; in Plato and St. John of the Cross, 242-3; and the theatre, 319
Algebra, 6, 25, 29, 30, 39, 40, 46; history of, 52-4
The Almond Tree. *See* Grimm
Analogy, 11, 98; educational method, 3; method of work, 9
Antigone. *See* Sophocles
Aphrodite, 77, 163, 207, 250, 288, 300
Apocalypse, 86, 99, 116, 175, 199-204, 217, 237, 280, 281-2, 285, 300, 304; date of, 313
Archimedes, quoted, 25, 337
Aristotle, 81, 84, 85, 335
Atë, 69, 153
Atheism, 84, 308; S.W.'s in adolescence, 137
Athena, 74, 119, 238, 249, 280
Augustine, St., 86, 117, 130, 139, 215, 248, 311; definition of evil, 121; sin against the Spirit, 120, 340
Augustus, Roman Emperor, 180-1, 216, 227, 313
Awonawilona, 186

Bacchus, 89; and India, 254
Bach, 36, 44, 47
Baptism, 224, 278, 288, 290, 293
Beauty and the Beast, 164, 168
Behaviourism, 173
Bhagavad-Gita, 291, 332, 336
The Bitter Withy, 208
Bluebeard, 359
Book of the Dead (Egyptian). *See* Egypt
Book of the Dead (Tibetan), 174
Buddha, 121, 181
The Bull o' Norroway, 164, 167, 170-1, 195, 225, 278, 322

Capital, Rotation of, 56-7
Cathar tradition, 303
Catholicism, modern, 50, 138
Chemistry, 36, 40
Christianity, 30, 80, 81, 216, 230, 295, 299, 303, 304, 305, 355; before Christ, 79; and St. Francis, 83; under the Antonines, 91; and end of the world, 152, 155; poisoned by Roman Empire, 239, 255
Cinderella, 163, 272
Circumcision, 252
Cleanthes. *See Hymn to Zeus*
Cobbler, Story of the, 245-6, 247, 270, 271
Corneille, 33, 233, 339
Cratylus. *See* Plato
Crow and the Light, The, 187
Cube, Perception of, 71, 72, 88, 91, 361

Descartes, 3, 25, 28, 31, 39, 40, 45, 48, 62; *Regulae*, 24
Dickens, 343
Dickmann, 23, 57, 81
Diderot, *Neveu de Rameau*, 41
Dionysus, 91, 110, 173, 242, 250, 279, 295, 321, 337, 344; and Thrace, 248; and India, 252
Diophantus, 52-3, 62
Dirty Boy, 185-6, 321
Druids, 121, 191, 238, 242
Durkheim, 304

East o' the Sun and West o' the Moon, 169-70
Easter, 69, 278
The Eddas, 165, 171, 190, 206, 226, 227, 238, 275, 276, 299, 301, 319, 320, 322
Education, A scheme of, 46
Egypt, Egyptians, 7, 54, 93, 116, 121, 142, 164, 179, 207, 212, 142, 164, 179, 207, 212, 255, 256, 258, 276; and education of Moses, 117; *Book of the Dead*, 126, 330; Ammianus Marcellinus on, 241; and *Genesis*, 251; and circumcision, 252; and inspiration of *Apocalypse*, 285

Electra, *See* Sophocles
Eleusinian Mysteries, 216, 337, 344
Embroidered Cloth: of Zeus, 236–7, 238, 276, 277; of Athena, 280
Energy, Supplementary, 73, 220, 222, 223, 233
Energy, Vegetative, 73, 220, 222, 223, 233, 295
Energy, Voluntary. *See* Energy, Supplementary
Epinomis. See Plato
Eskimoes, 71, 196
Euripides, 47

Falada, 165
Faust (Goethe), 44, 50, 55–6; quoted, 22, 24
Father and Son (E. Gosse), 176
Fenist, The Little Feather of, 168
Firdausi, quoted, 168
Flood, the, 252, 363
Folklore: African, 192; Albanian, 169, 271, 272, 359; American Indian, 99, 104, 162, 185–7, 190, 191, 193, 250, 257, 321; Australian, 192; Burgundian, 189; Caucasian, 187–8, 192; Chilian, 72; Chinese, 362–3; Danish, 170, 189, Eskimo, 71, 169, 187; Esthonian, 189; Finnish, 169; Gypsy, 169, 196; Irish, 110; Italian, 245; Kabyle, 169, 182; Norwegian, 169; Russian, 168; Scandinavian, 257, 301; Swedish, 189; Welsh, 183–5
Francis of Assisi, St., 83, 150, 261
Frazer, Sir J. G., 189, 190, 191, 293
Freud, 25, 287

Geometry, 36, 87, 98; non-Euclidean, 93
Ghizari (Gizar), the nightingale, 273, 359
Goethe. *See Faust*
Gorgias. See Plato
Grail, the Holy, 70, 162, 175, 192, 230, 299, 305
Gregorian Chant, 69, 75, 87
Grimm, the Brothers: *The Almond Tree*, 161–2, 273, 277, 321; *The Seven Swans*, 321, 341; *Snow White*, 277, 321; *The Two King's Children* 164; *The Valiant Little Tailor*, 93
Gypsies, 98, 169, 196, 198; language, 197

Ham, 253, 280; Prophecies of, 179, 236, 238, 275, 276
'Hamitic' speech, 247
Hanging. *See* Punishment
Hebrews, 70, 103, 120, 134, 212, 238, 257, 297, 300, 302; in Egypt, 117, 251; and image worship, 214, 258, 272, 294
Hebrews, Gospel of the, 280–1, 359
Hegel, 16, 17, 18, 33, 37, 42
Hephaestus, 74, 249, 257
Heraclitus, 83, 237, 351; quoted, 349
Herodotus, 75, 189, 227, 248, 253, 272, 319; on circumcision, 252
Hesiod, 74, 78
Hindus, 261, 280, 356
Hippolytus, 179, 193, 321; and Prometheus, 211
Hitler: and Wotan, 215
Homer, 4, 47, 48, 188, 237
Hopi Indians, 198
Housman, A. E., quoted, 194
Hymn to Zeus (Cleanthes), 178; quoted, 353

Iliad, 10, 14, 35, 69, 145, 148, 194, 238, 275, 322, 327, 336; and Book of Joshua, 144; Trojan genealogy in, 241
Image worship, 214–15
India, 248, 350; and Persia, 242; and Orphism, 254
Inquisition, the 303
Israel, 100, 120, 214, 215, 259, 270, 302, 322

Jacopone da Todi, quoted, 205–6
James William, 26
Jehovah, 100, 115, 215, 258, 259; not worshipped by Jews in Egypt, 116; and temptation of Christ, 306
Jerusalem, 164, 253, 260; and Cyrus, 252; destruction by Romans, 312
Jews. *See* Hebrews
Job, 75, 91, 116, 121, 139, 253–4, 256, 259, 273, 280, 320, 322, 327, 328, 359
John, St. (Evangelist), 86, 93, 129, 144, 151, 277, 337, 338, 343, 353; summary of Fourth Gospel, 104–9
John of the Cross, St., 110, 132, 351; and Plato, 131, 243
Julian, Roman Emperor, 241, 242

INDEX 367

Krishna, 322, 336

Last Judgement, the, 152
Laws. See Plato
Lear. See Shakespeare
Leibniz, 25
Lenin, 109
Lord's Prayer, the, 140, 210, 270, 295, 296, 360
Love, physical, 9, 10; anthropophagous, 284–6

Mabinogion, 183–5
Mallarmé, 93
Manichaeism, 70, 301, 303, 339
Marcion, 70, 109
Marcus Aurelius, Roman Emperor, 20, 180
Maritain, Jacques, 355
Marx, Marxism, 21, 23, 109, 308
Mathematics, 5, 6, 27, 31, 36, 39, 56, 72, 86, 90, 92, 109, 126, 142; Arab, 62; Greek, 80, 85; Hindu, 62
Mauriac, François, 15
Mei Ti, quoted, 306
Melchizedek, 115, 116, 118, 181, 252, 280, 322, 344
Milarepa, quoted, 359–60
Moses, 115, 116, 142, 251, 258, 262, 272, 280, 299, 311, 321, 359; and image worship, 214; and Jeremiah, 259
Moslems, 214

Napoleon, 42, 48, 72–3, 233, 235, 307, 308
New Testament: Matthew, 77, 98, 282, 340, 352; *Mark*, 264, 287, 302, 351; *Luke*, 287, 347; *Romans*, 353; *I Corinthians*, 350; *Galatians*, 302; *Ephesians*, 353. *See also* St. John, St. Paul
Newton, 25, 28
Niobe, 234, 323, 351
No plays, 181, 183
Noah 110, 116, 118, 119, 173, 207, 238, 249, 250, 253, 257, 279, 280, 320, 322

Odin, 110, 165, 171, 172, 190, 191, 206, 226, 227, 237, 276, 293, 320; Trojan descent, 279; and Thrace, 279, 319; image of Christ, 322
Oedipus. *See* Sophocles
Old Testament: Genesis, 118, 127, 251; *Exodus*, 99, 193; *Leviticus*, 99, 100, 251; *Numbers*, 251; *Deuteronomy*, 99, 100; *Joshua*, 144, 145; *I Kings*, 272; *II Kings*, 273; *Isaiah*, 162, 254, 256, 267, 332, 341; *Ezekiel*, 253. *See also* Job, Psalms
Osiris, 110, 212, 250, 251, 253, 258, 321, 342, 358; and Antigone, 260
Othello. See Shakespeare

Pacifism, 345
Pan, the god, 93, 212, 251, 255
Pantheism, 111
Pascal, 157
The Pastor's Wife, 170
Patrologia Latina (Migne), 329–32
Paul, St., 116, 131, 155, 215, 239, 253, 337, 339, 344, 353; on redemption, 152
Peasant life: symbolism of, 96; parable of the Sower, 239; parables applicable to, 264–7
Pentagon (symbol), 208
Pericles, Age of, 8
Persia, 54; Pahlavi zodiac, 173–4; Indian origin of Magian lore, 242; and elegies of David, 259
Peter, St., 161
Phaedo. See Plato
Phaedrus. See Plato
Pharisees, 117, 259, 302, 353
Pherecydes, 236, 237, 238, 240, 248, 257, 275, 277
Philebus. See Plato
Philoctetes. See Sophocles
Philolaus, 85, 88, 90, 98
Physics, 134; teaching of, 3; non-reciprocal relations, 138, 194
Plato, 8, 11, 17, 18, 47, 75, 104, 109, 129, 132, 134, 139, 162, 174, 242, 249, 250, 299, 311, 341, 351, 358; the great animal, 120, 304; and St. John of the Cross, 131, 243
Cratylus, 77; *Epinomis*, 85, 86; *Gorgias*, 16, 86, 258; *Laws*, 286–7; *Phaedo*, 336; *Phaedrus*, 52, 83, 322; *Philebus*, 16, 86, 90, 93, 174, 248; *Republic*, 52, 71, 131, 255, 321; *Symposium*, 74, 86, 93, 272; *Theaetetus*, 273; *Timaeus*, 70, 85, 86, 88, 252, 305, 332
Platonic love, 5, 50, 52
Prodigal Son, the, 223, 354
Progress: 'the idea of is poison', 79

368　INDEX

Prometheus, 17, 69, 73, 74, 75, 109, 110, 179, 197, 257, 258, 328, 341, 344, 345; and Hippolytus, 211; and Christ, 220, 321
Protestants Protestantism, 41, 216, 280, 295, 313
Psalms, 256, 259, 356. *See also Song of Songs*
Punishment, 153, 263; hanging, 258, 278, 279, 294; as sacrament, 293
Pythagoras, Pythagoreans, 56, 92, 109 121, 162, 194, 207, 250, 268, 311, 343, 350, 351, 355

Racine, 4, 32, 47, 48; quoted, 125
Rama, 293, 322
'Reading '(technical term employed by S. W.), 11, 73
Record-breaking, psychology of, 232
Republic. See Plato
Revelation, Book of. See Apocalypse
Romains, Jules, 9, 46
Rome, Roman Empire, 82, 103, 120, 214, 215, 216, 221, 230, 239, 254, 262, 270, 297, 302, 303, 312, 353; Beast of the *Apocalypse*, 313
Rousseau, 19, 42, 43

Sailing ships, 33-4
Samaria, Samaritans, 258, 272-3, 302
Scandinavia: and Trojans, 276; Thracian origin of Scandinavian divinities, 301
Schoharie Hills, Folklore of, 195
Scholasticism and modern science, 6
Seneca, quoted, 155, 156, 235, 242, 254, 255, 313, 314
Sexuality, 10, 287, 316
Shakespeare, 47; *Othello*, 49; *Lear*, 338
Sir Gawain and the Green Knight, 208
Slaves, American Negro, 313
Snow White. See Grimm
Socrates, 18, 43, 45, 48, 336, 351
Song of Songs, quoted, 105; 'probably a translation', 260
Sophocles, 4, 32, 47, 49, 262; *Antigone*, 32, 33, 49, 71, 322, 336; *Electra*, 32, 33, 49, 323; *Oedipus Rex* and *Oedipus Coloneus*, 32, 33, 49; *Philoctetes*, 26, 32, 49; *Trachiniae*, 31
Sower, Parable of the, 239, 295, 347-9
Spinoza, Spinozism, 7, 10, 24, 42, 90

Stoics, Stoicism, 75, 84, 221, 343, 350
Stonehenge, 238, 247
Surrealism, 29, 80
Symposium. See Plato

Taboo, supernatural property of, 126-7
Talleyrand, 233, 312
Tao, Taoism, 84, 121, 322
Temptations, list of S. W.'s, 4-5, 35
Thales, 56, 248, 338, 351
Theaetetus. See Plato
Théophile de Viau, quoted, 338
Thérèse de Lisieux, St., 176, 325
'Thirteen Treasures of Brittany', 247
Thomas Aquinas, St., 130, 355; 'not faith but social idolatry', 133
Thucydides, 81, 87
Timaeus. See Plato
Trachiniae. See Sophocles
Trent, Council of, 130; definition of faith, 207-8
Trojan war, date of, 238, 251-2
The Two King's Children. See Grimm

Upanishads, 158; quoted, 151, 286

Valéry, Paul, 9; *Monsieur Teste*, 54
The Valiant Little Tailor. See Grimm
Varro, M. Terentius, quoted, 85, 188-9
Venise Sauvée (unfinished tragedy by S. W.), 72, 93
Vieta, 52, 54, 62
Vinci, Leonardo da, 44, 47
Virgin, the, 139, 207, 240; in Zodiac, 99
Void, the (technical term employed by S. W.), 72, 102, 139, 159-61
Volpone, 148

Water Scorpion, the 174, 225

Xenophon, 116

Yggdrasil, 165, 227, 301, 305; and the Winged Oak 238

Zamiatin, E. (author of *We*), 8
Zeus, 73, 74, 89, 163, 191, 255, 258, 295, 341; in the *Iliad*, 275; as weaver, 277; and Tantalus 306-7
Zodiac, the, 75-7, 99, 155, 173-4, 225, 226, 227-9, 247, 338; not related to the constellations, 356-7. *See also* Persia

www.ingramcontent.com/pod-product-compliance
Lightning Source LLC
Chambersburg PA
CBHW071144300426
44113CB00009B/1074